The Arms of the Howland Family

PLYMOUTH ROCK
The place of landing, December 21, 1620
By permission of A. S. Burbank, Plymouth

MAYFLOWER PILGRIM DESCENDANTS

IN

CAPE MAY COUNTY
NEW JERSEY

Memorial of the Three Hundredth Anniversary of the
Landing of the Pilgrims at Plymouth

1620 —— 1920

A Record of the Pilgrim Descendants who early in its History
settled in Cape May County, and some of their
children throughout the several States of
the Union at the present time

BY

Rev. Paul Sturtevant Howe, LL. B., Ph. D.

CLEARFIELD

Originally published
Cape May, New Jersey
1921

Reprinted by
Genealogical Publishing Co., Inc.
Baltimore, Maryland
1977

Reprinted from a volume in the library
of the Maryland Historical Society

Library of Congress Catalog Card Number 76-46706

Reprinted for Clearfield Company by
Genealogical Publishing Company
Baltimore, Maryland
2014

ISBN 978-0-8063-0747-3

Foreword

These Cape May County descendants of the Mayflower band have been, until Dr. Howe arrived, a "lost tribe," many of them uninformed of their illustrious origin, others informed but indifferent to the interest of the subject.

In common with the people in many other sections, the people of our County have never been sufficiently interested in perpetuating the record of the doings of their period, and much of local history that would be valuable to present and future generations has been lost; for there have been stirring events and great deeds done in our section as in others and by our citizens in all of the great war crises which have visited the colonies and the nation since the first settlements.

It is fortunate for history, and equally fortunate for our "old families" that Dr. Howe has come among us and applied his enthusiasm, his ripe knowledge and trained skill to the unravelling of the tangled skein of descents, and establishing for all time the ancestry of the numerous families, the records of which he has investigated.

It has taken him many months and upon many journeys, for wherever there have been records apt to shed light upon his subject, there he has gone, and indefatigably probed, questioned and examined.

This book is the result of these arduous labors and is a lasting monument to his sincerity and interest in a subject of greatest importance. It is also a permanent and absolutely reliable record of incalculable value to this and all succeeding generations of the families discussed and a contribution to the general history of the nation, whose worth is beyond computation.

Dr. Howe, author of this volume, is the son of the Rev. Elbridge Gerry Howe, who was the former pastor of one of the first off-shoots of the Pilgrim Church, at Plymouth. His mother, Mary Soule Sturtevant, was descendant of fourteen of the Mayflower passengers, including Captain Myles Standish, whose son, Alexander, married Sarah, daughter of John Alden and Priscilla Mullins, and had Sarah Standish, who married Benjamin Soule, through which marriage the name Soule has been continued in Dr. Howe's family.

The author's early days were spent in Plymouth County, the successive generations of the family having remained within a few miles of the first landing place until the last generation. Early in life the author and afterward Trinity Academy at Cheshire, Connecticut, attended the Episcopal College and the University of New York—his education being completed by five years foreign travel in Europe, including two winters in Russia a year in the Holy Land, the Orient and Northern Africa. The degree of Doctor of Philosophy was conferred upon him in 1919 in recognition of credits obtained in special post graduate work and an extended thesis upon the Early History of the Colony of Plymouth, including the Laws of the Colony, and the Polity and Theology of the Pilgrim Church.

Upon his call to the rectorate of the Church of the Advent at Cape May, Dr. Howe found the descendants of the Pilgrims had long lived here, and that the older families and himself had a common ancestor in John Howland, the Pilgrim. This volume, the contribution of the author to the community, is the result of some three years investigation of the early history of the settlement of the county, and the history of the families to the present time. It is the most complete genealogical record, aside from its special investigation of the various lines of Mayflower descent, ever published upon the subject of Cape May ancestry, and corrects misleading statements of former writers. The genealogical tables are in the most condensed form, and no distinction has been made by Dr. Howe between the successful and the unsuccessful, the rich and the poor. No one has been denied a place in this book whose Pilgrim ancestry is clearly proved, and no consideration could bring into these lists the names of those who have not a proved claim to that much-envied ancestry.

For those who wish to know in brief of the early history of the Pilgrims, the Introduction includes the most condensed statement upon the subject, and the interesting period of the migration of the early whalers is outlined, with an account of the first years at Cape May. It is the wish of the publisher and author that the volume may be a permanent contribution to the history of our County and the people who have gone out from it.

AARON W. HAND,
County Superintendent of Public Schools

August 1, 1920

CONTENTS

ERRATA—On page 68 for Thomas Cushman read Robert Cushman. On page 90 for first date of will of John Howland, 1763, read 1673 New Style. On page 192 for Nicholas Leaming read Nicholas Lennig.

Mayflower Descendants in Cape May County

REV. PAUL STURTEVANT HOWE, Ph.D.
Rector of the Church of the Advent,
Cape May, N. J.

Pilgrim Descendants

"The Lost Colony of Mayflower Descendants in Cape May County" would be a fitting title for this reverent attempt to show the genealogical connection between the Old Colony of Plymouth, where the author was reared, and the County of Cape May, where the author is now a resident pastor. And in truth for many years the Pilgrim ancestry of our County of Cape May was unknown to the outside world, and long forgotten by the descendants within the County itself. Doubtless, in the early days, letters passed from Hannah Gorham Whilldin of Cape May to her brothers and sisters, of whom there were ten, in the Old Colony, and it is even possible that such letters could be found, as Goodwin says in his Pilgrim Republic of like letters in Plymouth County, in old garrets and out of the way places where they are not looked for. How long the memory of the early home remained, we cannot say, but we can be certain Barnstable, the home of the Gorhams, and Yarmouth, the home of the Whilldins and Eldredges, were not immediately forgotten. As far as the older documents relate, no mention is made of the Plymouth ancestry of the settlement, and by the third generation it is probable no memory of it was left—the settlers were too busy, and perhaps too practical, to think of ancestry.

The several writers upon the subject of the history of Cape May have all overlooked and seemed to have no knowledge of the most interesting fact in our history—a fact of the greatest interest to the student of peoples and their migrations, namely, that the early settlers of the County brought with them the stock of the Pilgrim Fathers of Plymouth and that the majority of the older families are, by intermarriage, of Pilgrim descent. Here in Cape May a grand daughter of

3

the Pilgrim John Howland was buried—the grave unknown, probably ¡washed away by the encroaching sea—here
she lived and reared her family, and her descendants are
many, both here, as well as among the many hundreds who
have gone out into other parts of our country—some in distant States, who do not suspect their Pilgrim ancestry.

The most complete published genealogical record of the
county is the work of the Rev. Daniel Lawrence Hughes, D. D.,
entitled "The Divine Covenant Fulfilled in Pious Households, from 1711-1891." It contains an account of the
author's ancestors on both sides, the several collateral lines
of descent, and his family and descendants to the year 1891,
yet Dr. Hughes does not show the slightest knowledge of his
own Pilgrim ancestry, or that of his wife, who family history he writes out in detail. Descended from the Pilgrim
John Howland in two lines, and his wife in still another, he
was utterly unconscious that he was providing for the student
and investigator one of the most important contributions to
the subject of Pilgrim ancestry ever written. In attempting
this work, I acknowledge my great indebtedness to Dr.
Hughes' valuable record. Necessarily all the genealogical
material of "The Divine Covenant Fulfilled in Pious Households" is included in this book, the connection with the Pilgrim ancestor being indicated and traced out and, as far as
possible, the several lines being brought down to date, making
double the material of the original work. In the additional
notes at the end of the volume, other names and dates are
given, including the notice of the Lawrence Family, as given
by Dr. Hughes, although not, as far as known, of Mayflower
ancestry. Thus all the genealogical material of Dr. Hughes'
work, now out of print, is included in the records following.

Miss Eleanor Harris, of Philadelphia, has given me valuable
assistance in the history of the Whilldin-Edmunds line, and
Mrs. Joseph C. Eldredge, of Cold Spring, and Mr. Joseph
Linerd Eldredge, of Philadelphia, have given valuable aid.
The unpublished work of the late Charles Welsh Edmunds

4

has been at my disposal, through my membership in the
Pennsylvania Historical Society, where Mr. Edmunds' price-
less work is deposited.

Stillwell's "Leamings of Cape May" shows the same
lack of information as to the intermarriages of the family
the author is describing, and there is no hint that the first
Thomas Leaming married into the Pilgrim stock, Hannah,
his wife being fourth in descent from John Howland. On
this three hundredth anniversary of the Landing of the Pilgrims at Plymouth, when all things pertaining to the Pilgrims and their descendants are in the thought of the whole
nation, I express this belief, that there are more descendants
of the Mayflower in Cape May County, New Jersey, than in
Plymouth County, Massachusetts, the landing place.

The connecting link between the settlement in the Old
Colony of Plymouth and the settlement at Cape May is the
manuscript known as the "Wast Book" of Colonel John
Gorham, written during the Louisburg expedition, 1745, a
part of which document first appeared in the January, 1898,
number of the New York Genealogical and Biographical
Record, that publication having printed notes of it with other
interesting records relating to the Gorham family in the
April and October numbers of 1897. In April 1898, the New
England Historical and Genealogical Register printed a fac-
simile of the complete document, which is given in this volume in so far as it pertains to the subject of Mayflower ancestry in Cape May County.

By the Peace of Utrecht in 1713, Cape Breton Island was
given to the French, who at great expense had erected a
powerful fortress, enclosing and commanding the ample harbor, furnishing a rendezvous for French fleets and privateers
—an increasing danger to the New England fishermen on the
Banks. The overthrow of the stronghold was proposed in
1745, Governor Shirley of Massachusetts having induced the
legislative body of that Colony to undertake the reduction of
the threatening fortress.

A force of some three thousand six hundred men, mostly from Massachusetts under Colonel William Pepperell, accompanied by a fleet of one hundred New England vessels and a British squadron under Commodore Warren, carried the undertaking through to a triumphant conclusion. The investment began April 30, 1745, and the garrison of sixteen hundred men surrendered forty-nine days later. The part of Colonel John Gorham, the author of the ''Wast Book,'' in the capture of Louisburg is related by himself in a letter to Sir William Pepperell, Parson's Life of Pepperell, page 240 (quoted in New England Historical and Genealogical Register, April, 1898).

Letter of Colonel John Gorham to Sir William Pepperell, and the "Wast Book"

Halifax, July 5, 1751.

"I did your message to our Governor, who since tells me he has wrote your honor. I take the freedom to remind your honor how I came to be in that glorious expedition against Louisburg. I was sent up to recruit from Annapolis Royal, by Governor Mascarene, as that fort was then in great danger of falling into the hands of the enemy, and this expedition being then in embryo, I was importuned by Governor Shirley, and desired by your honor and many more of the council, to raise a number of men, and purchase whale boats and proceed in the expedition, as I did, upon condition of my having the liberty of going home (to England) with your honor's packet in my sloop, as soon as the English flag should be hoisted at Louisburg. But I was disappointed in this, and received no commission in his royal regiment. My father died, and most of his regiment at Louisburg. But I thank you for giving me the Commission of Colonel of my father's regiment and now I solicit a letter of recommendation abroad, and assistance to carry through my memorial to the Legislature of Massachusetts."

In 1752 Colonel Gorham's widow wrote a letter to Governor Cornwallis, dated Boston, June 8, in which she says: "My dearly beloved husband in his loyal service to the King has expended his entire fortune." (Bourne Papers, Harvard College Library.)

While still at Louisburg, in the leisure moments following the victory, Colonel Gorham wrote out the history of his family, beginning with the ancestor who first came from Eng-

7

land, and continuing the line down to the marriage of Hannah Gorham and Joseph Whilldin, and their removal to Cape May. The manuscript is entitled :—

The Rise of the Family of Gorhams (Louisburg February 7, 1745-6) taken from Captain George Gorham.

My Great Great Grand Father and family came out of some part of England and lived at Marshfield and had one Son Nam'd aftr him John Gorum, alias Gorham—Which Son aftr Having Marryed With an Howland and had Severall Children Went home to England and Returnd Soone again to his family—

His Father Lived & Died att Marshfield and whats Remarkable He was a Joiner and Made his Coffin himself for Severall Years before he Died and Used to Keep apples in It as a Chest Untill He died & used it.

The Son John that marrid Desire Howland and Went to England Moved from marshfield to Barnstable and Settled there In order to begin a Township afterward Called Barnstable. Built mills—tan fatts etc.

Children—Namly—Sons James—John—Joseph—jabez and Shubell now Living.

Daughters—Elzebeth—maryd a Hallet att Sandwich. Temperance maryd Thomas Baxter an old England man. Lived at Yarmouth—— Desire Gorham—maryd Capt. Haws Yarmouth—having his Leg Cut off Died with it.

Lydia-Gorham Maryd Coll John Thacher.

Hannah—maryd a Wheelding boath movd to Cape-may.

The last line in this extract from Colonel Gorham's "Wast Book" is the connecting link between the Old Colony of Plymouth and Cape May.

WAST BOOK BELONGING TO JNO GORHAM
Began in Louisburg August 28th, 1745

The Rise of ye Family of Gorhams Louisburg Feb y 1745/6
Capt George Gorham, taken from

my Great Great Grand father & family Came out
of Some part of England and Lived att Marshfield
and Had one Son Named after him John Gorum
John Gorum, alias Gorham --- Which Son after Gear

Having Marryed With an Howland and Severall Children
Went home to England and Returnd so one again to
hir family ---

His Fathers Lived & Dyed att Marshfield and whats
Remarkable He was a Joyner and Made his Coffin
himself Severall years before he Dyed and Used to
keep apples In It as a Chest Untill He died & used

the Son John that marrid Howland and went to England
Moved from Marshfield to Barnstable and Settled
there Inordr to begin a Township Built Mills Tan fatts &c
Childen Names --- Jos Jamy --- John --- Joseph
Jaber and Shubell now Living
Daughters --- Elizbth --- mery a Hallet att Sandwich
Temperance married Thomas Baxter an old England man
Lived att Yarmouth ---
Desire Gorham married Capt Haws Yarmouth
Having his Leg Cut of Dyed with It
Sydia Gorham Marryed Cole John Thacher
Hanah --- marryed a Wheelding boate to moode h.
Cape may

The "Wast Book" of Colonel Gorham

The "Wast Book" was for many years among the papers of Eben Parsons of Byfield, Massachusetts, who married in May, 1767, Mary Gorham, and became the possession of his son, Gorham Parsons, upon whose death in 1844, the book was handed down through several generations of the family, until it came into the possession of Mr. John Gorham of Cleveland, Ohio. (See New England Historical and Genealogical Register for April, 1898).

The "Wast Book" contains one error—Captain John Gorham was the son of Ralph, not of John, as Colonel John states. This is proved by the record of Plymouth Colony.

The three facts upon which the Pilgrim ancestry of Cape May County rests are stated in this record.

(I.) Captain John Gorham married Desire Howland, daughter of John Howland of the Mayflower. From the records of Plymouth Colony and other sources we find that Desire Howland, daughter of the Pilgrim, was born at Plymouth in 1624, died at Barnstable, Plymouth Colony, 13 October, 1683; married at Plymouth in 1643 to John Gorham. Desire came of a large family, the children of her parents, John and Elizabeth (Tilley) Howland, being ten in number. There are four John Gorhams named in the "Wast Book," which of course must be distinguished. (1) The Colonel John Gorham of the Louisburg expedition of 1745, the author of the "Wast Book." (2) His great-great-grandfather, whose son was named for him. (3) The son, Captain John Gorham; but here we find a mistake, Captain John Gorham was as has been said the son of Ralph, not of John. (4) John Gorham, the son of Captain Gorham, brother of Hannah Whilldin, of Cape May.

9

Colonel Gorham's mistake is not surprising. It is what we find everywhere when an attempt is made to record a family history from memory, or hearsay, which means relying upon the memory of some one else. The Rev. Dr. Daniel Lawrence Hughes makes a similar error when he says his great-grandfather was Jeremiah Eldredge instead of the actual ancestor, Aaron Eldredge, an error which has confused many, and will be referrel to later in this introduction. Through a similar error it was formerly supposed that John Howland married Elizabeth, daughter of Governor Carver. The venerable John Howland (descendant of John Howland the Pilgrim) president of the Rhode Island Historical Society, contributed to Thacher's History of Plymouth, published in 1835, an account of his family, beginning in the formal style of the time :— "Unaccountable as it may appear, it is unhappily true that very few of those men who first arrived from England, and commenced the settlement of the New England Colonies, left any memorials for the information of their descendants respecting the place of their birth or residence in the country they left, or any account of those branches of their respective families which they left behind." (Thacher's History of Plymouth, page 129.) The venerable head of the Rhode Island Historical Society then gives for the benefit of posterity the genealogy of his family, stating that his ancestor, the Pilgrim, married Elizabeth, daughter of Governor Carver. When Governor Bradford's manuscript was recovered in 1855, after its disappearance for eighty years and discovery in the Library of the Bishop of London, it was found that John Howland the Pilgrim married Elizabeth, daughter of John Tilley, and not Elizabeth, daughter of the first Pilgrim governor, and we have the interesting illustration of a president of a historical society who did not know his own ancestry. Furthermore, the supposed descendant of the first governor of Plymouth Colony placed a stone at the grave of the Pilgrim with the inscription :—"Here ended the Pilgrimage of John Howland. He married Elizabeth, daughter of Governor Carver," and for a generation the stone stood, a monument to John Howland the Pilgrim, and also a monument to the fact that tombstones do not always tell the truth. President Howland died a year before Bradford's manuscript was recovered, believing himself to be a descendant of Governor John Carver.

Captain John Gorham was baptized at Benefield, Northamtonshire, England, 28 January, 1621, and died of a fever after taking part in King Philip's War, 5 February, 1675-6. A part of the "Wast Book," not included in the fac-simile given, states that, "Captain John Gorham was a Captain of a Company of English and Indians and Went to the Fight of King Philip—or Swamp Narraganset fight and there Was Wounded by having his powder Horn Hit and Split against his Side and Wounded—and Dyed att Swansey."

He married, as has been said, Desire Howland, daughter of John of the Mayflower, in 1643, and had eleven children:—

(1) Desire Gorham, born at Plymouth 20 May, 1644, married, as the "Wast Book" shows, Captain John Haws of Yarmouth, who "having his Leg Cut off Dyed with it;" she was an ancestor of the writer of this volume.

(2) Temperance Gorham, born at Marshfield 5 May, 1646, married Thomas Baxter, "an old England man."

(3) Elizabeth Gorham, born at Marshfield 2 April, 1648, "maryd a Hallett att Sandwich."

(4) James Gorham, born at Marshfield 28 April, 1650.

(5) John Gorham, born at Marshfield 20 February, 1651.

(6) Joseph Gorham, born at Yarmouth 16 February, 1653.

(7) Jabez Gorham, born at Barnstable 16 August, 1656.

(8) Mercy Gorham, born at Barnstable, 20 June, 1658, (name omitted in Wast Book).

(9) Lydia Gorham, born at Barnstable, 11 November, 1661, "maryd Coll John Thacher."

11

(10) Hannah Gorham, born at Barnstable 28 November, 1663, "maryd a Wheelding boath movd to Cape-may"— Wast Book. (11. Shubell also mentioned in Wast Book.)

(II.) The marriage of Hannah Gorham and Joseph Whilldin, "Wheelding," in the Wast Book, and so spelled in some of the early Cape May records, was before 1683, and was in Plymouth Colony before the migration to Cape May. The Yarmouth Whilldins were numerous—the name appearing repeatedly in the early history of the town. The "yarmouth Regester for marriages & burialls," preserved in the Plymouth Colony Records, gives under the date of 1647 the name of "henery Wilden maried to Eed—the twentyfift of Janu—," and in 1650 in "yarmouth Regester of ye beirthes of children," there is recorded the birth of "Sara Whilden born the twenty one of June." In the same register the next entry is the record of the birth of Nicolas Eldred (Eldredge), August 18, followed by "Sara Eldred (Eldredge) born october the tenth." Undoubtedly the Eldredges of Cape May County as well as the Whilldins are of the same Yarmouth origin. The record of the birth of a daughter to William Eldred is in the Yarmouth Register of Births of the date 1648, "about the sixteenth" of January.

(III) The third fact established by the "Wast Book" makes that manuscript the most important record in the genealogical history of Cape May County. "Hannah (Gorham) maryd a Wheelding boath movd to Cape-may.". The exact date of their arrival at Cape and the mode of transportation are unknown, and cannot be determined with certainty— whether they made the journey directly from Yarmouth in the Old Colony of Plymouth, sailing with other families and children, a distance of some three hundred miles, requiring three to five days in the sailing boats of the time; whether they were a part of the preceding migration to Long Island and Connecticut—all this is uncertain. It is certain, however, that the whaling industry brought the New England emigrants here. Dr. Maurice Beesley in his ''Sketch of the Early History of the County of Cape May'' says: ''The original settlers or those who were here previous to the year 1700 were principally attracted (as authors heretofore quoted sufficiently corroborate) by the inducements held out by the whale fishery; and Long Island supplied the principal proportion of those who came prior to that time. The names of those who were known to be whalers (collected from the secretary's office, Trenton and Cape May records, given in note) were: Christopher Leamyeng (Leaming) and his son Thomas, Caesar Hopkins, Samuel Matthews, Jonathan Osborne, Nathaniel Short, Cornelius Skellinks, (Schellenger), Henry Stites, Thomas Hand, and his sons John and George, John and Caleb Carman, John Shaw, Thomas Miller, William Stillwell, Humphery Hewes (Hughes), William Mason, John Richardson, Ebenezer Swain, Henry Young; and no doubt many others.'' The following act was passed by the Assembly of 1639: ''Whereas the whaling in Delaware Bay has been in so great a measure invaded by strangers and foreigners, that the greatest part of oyl and bone received and got by that employ, hath been exported out of the Province to the great detriment thereof: Be it enacted, that any one killing a whale or whales in Delaware Bay, or on its shores, to pay the value of one tenth of the oyl to the governor of the Province.'' This was perhaps the first game law of the County.

In his history of West Jersey, 1698, Gabriel Thomas tells us of the whaling and other industries of the County: ''The commodities of Cape May County are oyl and whale bone, of which they make prodigious quatities every year having mightily advanced that great fishery, taking great numbers of whales yearly. This County, for the general part of it, is extraordinary good and proper for the raising of all sorts of cattell, very plentiful here, as cows, horses, sheep and hogs, &c. Likewise, it is well stored with fruits which make very pleasant liquors,'' (quoted by Dr. Beesley).

The manuscript of Thomas Leaming, born 9 July, 1674, died 31 December, 1728, married 18 June,1702, Hannah Whilldin[4] (Hannah Gorham[3], Desire Howland[2], John Howland[1]), gives us a still further account of the whaling fishery of the early days:— "In July, 1674, I was born at South Hampton on Long Island. When I was eighteen years of age (1692) I came to Cape May and that winter had a sore fit of the fever and flux. The next summer I went to Philadelphia with my father Christopher who was lame with a withered hand, which held him till his death. The winter following, I went whaling, and we got eight whales, and five of them we drove to the Hoarskills (near Cape Henlopen), and we went there to cut them up, and stayed a month. The first day of May we came home to Cape May, and my father was very sick, and the third day, 1695, departed this life at the house of Shamgar Hand, Then I went to Long Island, stayed that summer and in the winter went whaling again, and got an old cow and a calf. In 1697, I went whaling again and made a great voyage; and in 1697, I worked for John Reeves all summer, and in the winter went whaling again."

David Pieterson De Vries entered Delaware Bay in 1631, evidently for the purpose of engaging in the occupation of whaling, and left a small colony near Cape Henlopen, on Lewes Creek, naming the settlement Swaanendale. Within a few months the infant colony was destroyed by the Indians, and De Vries, who had been chosen governor or director, found on his return the following year, "only the ruins of the house and its pailsades, half consumed by fire, and here and there the bones of the colonists." (Bancroft.) He left a portion of his party there while he himself spent some time in Virginia; but concluding that the undertaking would not be a financial success, he carried the latter party back to Holland in 1634. Nevertheless, De Vries found some whales and in his diary makes mention of them: "March 29th, 1633, found that our people had caught seven whales; we could have done more if we had good harpoons, for they had struck seventeen fish and only saved seven."

But a more skillful race of followers of the sea were being trained in the difficult and hazardous calling of whale fishing, and to them and their descendants, some of the old stock of the Colony of Plymouth, we owe the discovery of the possibility of a successful prosecution of the occupation in these waters, and the permanent settlement of the County.

As early as the 9th century the Norwegians sailed as far as Greenland in pursuit of whales, and between the 14th and Fifteenth centuries whaling was an important industry of the Bay of Biscay and adjoining waters. We read that whales' tongues were a considerable article of commerce, and in 1261 were subjected to a special tax. Upon the decline of the industry in the Bay of Biscay, the activities of the whalemen were transferred to the northern waters—the coast of Spitzbergen becoming the center of an extensive fishery, conducted mainly by the Dutch, who, it is said, supplied all Europe with oil during the latter half of the Seventeenth century, employing in 1680 as many as 260 ships and about 14,000 men in the occupation. From this date the Dutch undertaking began to decline, and the business was then taken up in the Eighteenth century by Great Britian, and encouraged by a generous bounty. In time New England became the center of the occupation.

On April 2nd, 1668, an agreement was entered upon the records of Easthampton binding certain Indians of Montauket in the sum of 10 pounds sterling to accompany a whaling expedition on account of Jacobus Skallenger and others of Easthampton. The Indians engaged "to attend dilligently with all opportunitie for ye killing of whales or other fish, for ye sum of three shillings a day for every Indian: Ye sayd Jacobus Skallenger and partners to furnish all necessarie craft and tackling convenient for ye designe."

15

The town of Southampton, Long Island, was settled in 1640, by colonists who came from Lynn, in Massachusetts Bay. Here the ancestors of many of the Cape May County families first came—the name of Jacobus Skallenger mentioned above, Stephen Hand, James Loper and John Foster appearing on the records of the vicinity.

We see, then, that the early history of Cape May is associated with the whaling occupation, and the first settlers came here in pursuit of that calling.

By 1690, Joseph Whilldin and Hannah Gorham his wife with their children were settled here. In 1705, and for three years following, Joseph was sheriff of the County, and repeatedly held the office of justice of the peace—evidently he became a man of prominence from the first.

Unlike the early history of the Pilgrim settlement at Massachusetts, the beginnings of history in Cape May County are involved in obscurity. No chronicler, like Governor Bradford, gives a complete history of the times, and the facts we are able to gather from diaries and records are fragmentary and disconnected. Until 1857 no attempt was made to write a history of the early days of the County, and to Dr. Maurice Beesley we owe the first outline—his careful work is still our authority for the period. Hudson visited Delaware Bay August 28, 1609, "but finding the water shoal, and the channel impeded by bars of sand he did not venture to explore it." Captain Cornelius Jacobese Mey visited our shores and explored Delaware Bay in 1623, and to him the County of Cape May is indebted for a name. He built Fort Nassau, at Timber Creek, the site of which is now unknown, Dr. Beesley says, but we now know it was near Gloucester. The first record of a transfer of lands from the Indians is of the date 5th of May, 1630, when on behalf of the Dutch West India Company, Samuel Godyn and Samuel Bloemart purchased through agents a tract of land sixteen miles square. The purchase was made of nine resident chiefs. Early settlements of Swedes were made along the shore of the Delaware Bay, and Campanius, the Swedish pastor, paid a visit to the scattered members of the flock as early as 1648, making the following entry in his diary: "On the 16 May, 1648 having obtained a proper passport from the Governor and Council, I sailed in the Lord's name, with my family from Elfsborg, in New Sweden on board the ship Swan, and on the 18th came into the bay. The distance between Elfsborg and the bay is nine miles; and on account of the numerous banks in the river, we were three days descending into the bay. On the 19th we came to Cape May."

In 1665, the Dutch under the command of Peter Stuyvesant sailed from New York in seven vessels with six to seven hundred men. Entering the Delaware Bay, they captured all the Swedes, took possession of their forts, and carried the officers and principal men as prisoners to New York. Some afterwards were taken to Holland. The remaining Swedish settlers escaped dsiturbance because of their obscure condition, and submitted to their conquerors. Dr. Beesley's conjecture that upon the downfall of New Sweden, some of the Swedes, chagrined and mortified at a defeat so bloodless and unexpected, fled from the arbitrary sway of their conquerors, and sought an asylum where they could be free to act for themselves, without restraint or coercion, as the provincial power of New Sweden had perished forever, is hardly sustained by the facts, and the presence of scattered Swedish settlers on these shores antedates Stuyvesant's expedition, as the pastoral visit of Campanius, eight years before, shows.

Early Titles to Land

By the theory of the English law of the 17th century, the discoveries of the Cabots gave to the British Crown the title to all the lands on the eastern coast of North America, the Dutch claims upon the Hudson and the Delaware never being expressly recognized by the British government. In 1606 the London Plymouth Companies acquired a patent to the territory now included in New Jersey, in which zone either company might claim land, although neither affected or attempted to erect permanent colonization. In 1634, King Charles I granted New Albion, including the territory of New Jersey, to Sir Edmund Ployden, but no permanent settlement was accomplished. The first separation of the land of New Jersey from the English crown was on March 12, 1664, when Charles II granted to his brother James, Duke of York, certain territories in New England and Long Island "lying and being toward the west of Cape Cod," and all the mainland from the west bank of the Connecticut to the east side Delaware Bay. All this territory was to be held in free and common socage as of the manor of East Greenwich, subject to the annual rent of 40 beaver skins should they be demanded. The Duke never came into actual possession of his lands, and while the Dutch were still in possession, executed, on June 23 and 24, 1664, deeds of lease and release to Lord John Berkeley and Sir George Carteret by which they acquired "all that tract of land lying and being to the westward of Long Island and Manhitas Island, and bounded on the east part by the main sea and part by Hudson's river, and hath upon the West Delaware Bay or River and to the northward as far as the northermost branch of the said Bay or River of Delaware, which is 41 degrees 40 minutes of latitude, and crosseth over thence in a straight line to Hudson's River in 41 degrees of latitude, which said tract of land is hereafter to be called by the name or names of Nova Cesarea or New Jersey. (Columbia University Studies in History, Economics and Public Law, Vol. XXX, The Province of New Jersey, Edwin P. Tanner, Ph. D.)

Through the reconquest of the Dutch and the subsequent return of the territory to the British crown, the title again fell into the hands of the king and was again granted to his brother, the Duke of York, including the land of New Jersey. (Leaming and Spicer—Grants and Concessions). In the meantime Berkeley had sold his interest in New Jersey to two members of the Society of Friends, John Fenwick and Edward Byllenge, for the sum of 1,000 pounds. Carteret received a new conveyance to a portion of the former province of New Jersey, including all the land north of a line drawn from Barnegat to a certain creek on the Delaware next below Rankokas Creek, giving Carteret more than one half of the territory which was again called New Jersey. Both Fenwick and Byllenge lost control, through debt, of the land acquired by them, the interest of the Society of Friends being cared for by William Penn and other friends associated with him.

Carteret then consented to a new division of the province, a line beginning at Little Egg Harbor and running to a point on the Delaware in 41 degrees north latitude having been settled upon as a boundary between the two portions, now called East and West Jersey. The document effecting this division was signed by Carteret and four representatives of the Quakers' interests, and is called the Quintipartite Deed.

Through the powerful influence of William Penn, the doubtful title of the Quaker settlement was finally established by a definite grant from the Duke of York, who thereby relinquished title to the entire territory of New Jersey.

The beginning of proprietary rights in West Jersey, in which division our interest from this time centers, was in March, 1676, when by the "Concessions" a definite arrangement was made by which these rights could be obtained (New Jersey Archives, first series, Vol. I, p. 241, and Columbia University studies in History, etc., quoted above.) The entire province of West Jersey was divided into 100 equal parts to be known as "properties," and these were to be grouped into ten larger divisions known as "tenths." Repeated divisions and subdivisions of properties followed—the interests of the Quakers predominating, until the time of the death of Byllenge in 1687, when four years later his entire holdings passed by purchase into the hands of Dr. Daniel Coxe, who had been physician to the Queen of Charles II and also to Anne. "He was an energetic and ambitious man whose object at this time was apparently to imitate the achievements of William Penn," (Columbia University Studies in History, etc., vol. XXX, p. 16). Dr. Coxe's ambition went to the extent of claiming full jurisdiction over the whole extent of West Jersey, and on September 5, 1687, he wrote to the proprietors stating that though the concessions might be binding upon others, he had been assured upon the highest legal authority, they were in no way binding upon him. Further, he declared that his power of government was as absolute as that of Penn over Pennsylvania, that he had assumed the title of governor, and would exercise its duties with diligence. Dr. Beesley says of Dr. Coxe and his holdings:—"In April, May, and June, 1691, John Worlidge and John Budd, from Burlington, came down the bay in a vessel, and laid a number of proprietary rights, commencing at Cohansey, and so on to Cape May. They set off the larger portion of this county, consisting of 95,000 acres, to Dr. Daniel Coxe, of London, who had large proprietary rights in West Jersey. This was the first actual proprietary survey made in the county. In the copy of the original draft of these surveys, and of the county of Cape May, made by David Jameison, in 1713, from another made by Lewis Morris, in 1706, (which draft is now in my possession, and was presented by William Griffith, Esq., of Burlington, to Thomas Beesley, of Cape May, in 1812,) Egg Island, near the mouth of Maurice River, is laid off to Thomas Budd, for three hundred acres. Since this survey was made, the attrition of the waters has destroyed almost every vestige of it scarcely enough remaining to mark the spot of its former magnitude. Upon this map likewise is laid down Cape May Town, at Town Bank on the Bayshore, the residence of the whalers, consisting of a number of dwellings and a short distance above it we find Dr. Coxe's Hall, with a spire, on Coxhall Creek, a name yet retained by the inhabitants. As no other buildings or improvements are noted on this map, than those above mentioned, it is to be presumed that there were few, if any, existing except them, at this day. The only attraction then was the whale fishery; and the small town of fifteen or twenty houses marked upon this map, upon the shore of Town Bank, in close contiguity, would lead us to infer that those adventurous spirits, who came for that purpose, preferred in the way of their profession to be near each other, and to make common stock in the operations of harpooning, in which, according to Thomas, they seemed to be eminently successful.''

Dr. Coxe was a speculator to large extent in colonial land claims, but his attempted operations did not find sympathy in West Jersey. His claim to governmental control over the province met with opposition, and he decided to withdraw from the undertaking in that territory, and in 1691 sold out the greater part of his interest to a company known as the West Jersey Society. By deeds of lease and release, about 20 properties in West Jersey, together with interests in East Jersey and Pennsylvania and New England, passed over to the new investors in consideration of 4800 pounds. Sir Thomas Lane was its first president, Edmund Harrison its vice-president, and Robert Hackshaw treasurer. The purpose of the Society as stated in the articles of agreement was "our mutual benefit, profit, and advantage" and "the better and more orderly managing and improving of the said hereditary government, lands and tenements." The stock was divided into 1600 equal shares, and the holder of two of these was entitled to the privilege of voting at the annual meeting for the election of officers. The actual business management rested in the hands of a committee, which had power to sell and dispose of all lands. The operations of the Society were directed from London, and the Quakers were no longer a controlling majority (Columbia University Studies in History, etc., vol. XXX, pages 17, 18).

From this time the new settlers were able to obtain title to the land necessary for the development of the slowly increasing community.

"This sale," says Dr. Beesley, who makes the consideration 9,000 pounds and the date the 20th of January, 1692, "opened a new era for the people of Cape May. As no land titles had been obtained under the old regime of the proprietors, except five conveyances from George Taylor, as agent for Dr. Coxe, the West Jersey Society became the medium through which they could select and locate the choice of the lands, at prices corresponding with the means and wishes of the purchaser."

From Trenton and Cape May records Dr. Beesley gathered the following lists of purchasers of land, mostly previous to 1696, some few (of Dr. Coxe) as early as 1689:—

	Acres		Acres
Christopher Leamyeng	204	William Mason	150
William Jacoks	340	Henry Stites	200
Abigail Pine	200	Cornelius Skellinks	134
Humphrey Hughes	206	John Richardson	124
Samuel Matthews	175	Arthur Cresse	350
Jonathan Osborne	110	Peter Causon	400
Nathaniel Short	200	John Causon	300
Caesar Hoskins	250	John Townsend	640
Shamgar Hand	700	Wm. Golden and Rem Garretson	1016
Joseph Wheldon (Whilldin)	150		
Joseph Houlding	200	William Johnson	436

Dorothy Hewit	340	John Page	125
Thomas Hand	400	John Parsons	315
John Taylor	220	William Smith	130
John Curwith	55	George Taylor	175
John Shaw, 2 surveys	315	Dennis Lynch	300
Timothy Brandreth	110	William Whitlock	500
John Crawford	380	Jacob Spicer, 2 surveys	1000
Ezekiel Eldridge	90	Benjamin Godfrey	210
Oliver Russel	170	Randal Hewit	140
Samuel Crowell	226	Elizabeth Carman	300
John Carman	250	John Reeves	100
Thomas Gandy	50	Benjamin Hand	373
Caleb Carman	250	James Stanfield	100

The list is of the greatest genealogical interest, and the continuation of the same family names in the County to the present time is remarkable as contrasted with some parts of the County of Plymouth of the Pilgrims, where in many towns the names of the first comers have entirely disappeared. These persons had settled in the County previous to 1700, and the same authority (Dr. Beesley) gives an additional list of those who at that date were residing in the County, many of whom had acquired land by secondary purchase:—

Thomas Leamyeng	Thomas Hand
Alexander Humphries	Joseph Ludlam, Sen.
John Briggs	Anthony Ludlam
Abraham Hand	Jonathan Pine
Shamgar Hand, Jr.	John Wolredge
Benjamin Hand, Jr.	John Jervis
Daniel Johnson	Jonathan Foreman
Oliver Johnson	Thomas Goodwin
William Harwood	Jonathan High
Jacob Dayton	Edward Howell
Richard Haroo	George Crawford
Jonathan Crossle	Joseph Babcock
William Lake	William Dean
Theirs Raynor	Richard Jones
Thomas Matthews	John Howell
William Stillwell	Thomas Stanford
John Cresse	George Noble
Morris Raynor	John Wolly
Joshua Howell	Peter Cartwright
Arthur Cresse, Jr.	Abraham Smith
William Blackburry	John Hubard
Daniel Carman	Thomas Miller

Joseph Knight	Robert Crosby
John Stillwell	John Fish
John Else	Lubbart Gilberson
John Steele	Edward Marshall
James Cresse	Thomas Bancroft
William Simpkins	Edward Summis
Thomas Goodwin	Henry Gray
Thomas Clifton	Abraham Weston
Joshua Carman	Thomas Going
William Duboldy	Jonathan Edmunds
James Marshall	Nicholas Martineau
John Baily	John Garlick
William Richardson	Samuel Matthews, Jr.
Thomas Foster	William Shaw
Thomas Hewit	Robert French
George Taylor, Jr.	Jeremiah Miller
John Dennis	Zebulon Sharp
Isaac Hand	William Sharwood
Daniel Hand	John Story
Jeremiah Hand	Richard Townsend
Joseph Hand	Robert Townsend

It is quite possible we have in these lists New England ancestors of hitherto unsuspected interest. Whether "Lubbard Gilberson" is a corruption of some New England name which appears early in the history of Plymouth County, or whether the name Raynor is of the same family as that of the Plymouth pastor, are matters of speculation which we have not place to consider. Jacob Spicer's son of the same name married first Judith Hughes and second Deborah Hand, widow of Christopher Leaming, who was the son of Thomas and the Hannah Whilldin mentioned below. In the second list, Thomas Leamyeng (Leaming) married Hannah Whilldin[4] (Hannah Gorham[3], Desire Howland[2], John Howland[1] the Pilgrim), and had a family of seven children, from whom many in Cape May County are descended.

A John Garlick married Phebe Leaming, daughter of Thomas, and the name "Isacer Crafford (Crawford) appears among the grandchildren of Joseph Whilldin the second.

The first settlement was on the bay, and was called Cape May Town, the site of which, Dr. Beesley says, with adjoin-

24

ing land, has been washed away by the attrition of the water. Aaron Leaming the second gives a description of the first village, beginning with an account of his family.

"My father's father, Christopher Leaming, was an Englishman, and came to America in 1670, and landed near or at Boston; thence to East Hampton. There he lived till about the year 1691, and then leaving his family at Long Island, he came himself to Cape May, which, at that time, was a new county, and beginning to settle very fast, and seemed to promise good advantages to the adventurers. Here he went to whaling in the proper season, and at other times worked at the cooper's trade, which was his occupation, and good at this time by reason of the great number of whales caught in those days, made the demand and pay for casks certain. He died of a pleurisie in 1696. His remains were interred at a place called Cape May Town, was situated next above now New England Town Creek, and contained about thirteen houses; but, on the failure of the whale fishery in Delaware Bay, it dwindled into common farms, and the graveyard is on the plantation now owned by Ebenezer Newton. At the first settlement of the county, the chief whaling was in Delaware Bay, and that occasioned the town to be built there, but there has not been one house in that town since my remembrance. In 1734 I saw the graves; Samuel Eldredge showed them to me. They were then about fifty rods from the Bay, and the sand was blown to them. The town was between them and the water. There were some signs of the ruins of houses."

It is probable the first graves were not marked by stones, and the first village of the settlers of Cape May has long been swallowed up by the encroaching sea.

Before the death of the last survivor of the Pilgrim band descendants of the Mayflower had built homes and established themselves in Cape May County. Mrs. Mary Allerton Cushman, the last of the Pilgrims, died in 1699, at the age of 90. She was the wife of Elder Thomas Cushman, the second of the three succeeding ruling elders of the Pilgrim Church, namely, Elder Brewster, Elder Cushman, Elder Faunce, the office becoming extinct in the Pilgrim Church with the death of the last named in 1745, aged 99. Mary Allerton, afterward Mrs. Cushman, was eleven years of age when the Mayflower came to anchor in Plymouth Harbor. Her memory reached back to the first steps in the proposed migration from Holland, and she lived to see the union with Massachusetts Bay in 1692, when the Pilgrim Colony came to an end. By 1685 descendants of the Mayflower were settled on the coast of Maine and in Connecticut. Hannah Gorham, the granddaughter of John Howland with her husband, Joseph Whilldin, had settled in Cape May by 1690, and it is probable this was the most distant point colonized (in part) by Pilgrim descendants at this time.

Manuscripts, Deeds, Wills and Family Bibles
of the Early Days

Joseph Whilldin[4] (Hannah Gorham[3], Desire Howland[2], John Howland[1] the Pilgrim) made his will 16 March, 1748, naming his wife, Abigail; sons, Matthew, James and David; daughters, Hannah, Rachel and Loes; also deceased daughter Mercy's children, Ellis and Judith; grandsons, "Memukin" Hughes, Willman, and "Isecar" Crafford. Joseph Whilldin died two days after making the will and the instrument was proved 30 March, 1748, the inventory 26 April, and the accounting 19 May of the same year. Abigail, Joseph's second wife, was not the mother of the children named. His first wife was Mary Wilmon, born 1698, died 8 April, 1743. Hannah married Ellis Hughes, whose will names five children, Ellis, Memucan, Jesse, Constantine, David. The Rev. Daniel Lawrence Hughes, D. D., in an article on the "Hughes of Cape May," states that Ellis Hughes, whom he calls Ellis the first, and Memucan were the sons of John and Martha. The following deed shows that Ellis was the father of Jesse, that Jesse's wife was Mary or Molly, that at the time of the making of the deed, 20 August 1768, the Ellis who was living signed his name Ellis Hughes "Junior," and that Ellis Senior made a will of the date 9 May, 1751. The deed is in the possession of Mrs. Aaron W. Hand, of Cape May, who has kindly placed it in my hands for examination.

DEED OF JESSE HUGHES AND MARY HIS WIFE
TO MEMUCAN HUGHES

"This Indenture made this Twentieth Day of august in the Eighth year of Reign of George the third King of Great Britain and in the year of our Lorde one thousand Seven Hundred and Sixty Eight Between Jesse Hughes of the

County of Cape May of the one part and moley his wife the Same and Memucan Hughes of the other part Witnesseth That the Said Jesse Hughes and moley his wife for and In Consideration of the Sume of Seventy two Pounds in hand paid By the Said Memucan Hughes the Receipt Where of they the said Jesse and his Wife Mary doth her By (acknowledge) themself fully Satisfied——and By these presents doth Grant Bargain and sell Alien Enfeaf and Confirm unto the said Memucan Hughes his heirs and assigns for Eaver All that Messuage tenement which was Given him by the Death of his father Ellis Hughes whose will Baireing Date the Ninth day of May one thousand Seven Hundred and fifty one among other things Gaive unto his son Jesse Forty Eight Acre of upland and mash Which he Bought at Public Sale of the Estate of Levi Eldredge Late of Cape May deceased adjoining his other Land and to Land of James Whilldin Esquire to have and to hold to him the said Jesse his heirs and assigns for Eaver A Recital Being had to the said will Will more fully appear and By Vertue of a write derected to Jeremiah Hand high Sheriff he did take and Sell the Saime forty Eight acres of upland and mash Beginning at James Whilldin corner —————————————— Containing forty Eight acres of upland and mash Be the same more or Less With in the Above Bounderys and the said Jesse haith Sold and the Right and Estate title Interest Claime and Demand Whatsoever of them that the Said Jesse Hughes and mary his Wife of in and to the same premises of in and to Every parte and parcel their of to have and hold unto the Said Memucan Hughes his heirs and assigns for eaver together with all the mines Woodsunder Woods Hunting Hawking Fowling fishing Ways and Waters Watercourses in any ways Belonging theire to and also they

Jesse Hughes Now haith Good right full power and Lawful authority in his own Right to Grant Bargan and sell and Convey the Above premises unto Memucan Hughes his heirs and assigns————

Signed Sealed and Delivered
  in the presence of
    Silas Hand   Jesse Hughes (seal)
    Ellis Hughes Junior

                                heir
                        Mary X Hughes (seal) ''
                        marke

    The following is an abstract of the will of Ellis Hughes. The contention that Mary, sister of Hannah, was the mother of Ellis Hughes will be further discussed in the genealogical notes at the end of this volume. That Memucan and Ellis Hughes were grandchildren of Joseph Whilldin 2nd and are of Mayflower descent cannot be disputed.

    1751, May 16.—Hughes, Ellis, of Cape May, New Jersey, will of. Wife, Hannah. Children—Mecuman, Jesse, Ellis, Constant, David. "The plantation whereon I dwell, Lower Precinct of Cape May, near a place called New England." Witnesses—Mary Ross, Ellen Hand, Jacob Spicer, Nathan Eldredge.
    Proved, Feb. 4, 1752.
    Inventory—£149-11-5. Appraisors—John Eldredge, and James Whilldin.   Cape May Wills, 160 E.

    Samuel Eldredge, "Esq., of Cape May, yeoman," made his will 23 September, 1742, mentioning his wife, Mercy Leaming[5], (Hannah Whilldin[4], Hannah Gorham[3], Desire Howland[2], John Howland[1] the Pilgrim); his eldest son, Samuel, to whom he gives the plantation on which he lived, also one hundred acres of land, "and my negro man York." He further gives direction that ten pounds is to be paid to his

youngest daughter, Sarah Eldredge, "when she will be 17."
To sons Aaron and Jacob large tracts of land are given, and
provision is made for an unborn child. Dr. Hughes was mistaken when he stated at the beginning of the Eldredge genealogy that his grandfather, Aaron Eldredge was the son of
Jeremiah Eldredge, and the whole genealogy of the family
has been upset by this error, copied and repeated by others.
The Jeremiah Eldredge whom Dr. Hughes supposed to be his
great-grandfather never had children. He was the brother
of Aaron Eldredge (1st), and the son of Samuel Eldredge
and Mercy Leaming, and married his first cousin, Lydia
Leaming. The father of Aaron Eldredge who married Hannah Langdon was Aaron Eldredge 1st and not Jeremiah Eldredge, as stated in Dr. Hughes' work; in fact, Dr. Hughes
later acknowledged the error, and in a letter says: "Samuel
Eldredge and his wife, Mercy Leaming Eldredge, are said to
have come to Cape May with his father-in-law, Thomas Leaming, (date uncertain). Aaron Eldredge, their oldest son,
who married Elizabeth Stillwell the daughter of Richard
Stillwell, (an elder of Cold Spring Presbyterian Church,)
and Sarah Hand Stillwell, was my great-grandfather and not
Jeremiah Eldredge, their second son, who married his first
cousin Lydia Leaming, the daughter of Thomas Leaming,
and had no children."

In another letter Dr. Hughes says: "It is plain—Aaron
Eldredge 1st is our great ancestor." He further writes:
"Samuel Eldredge, our ancestor married Mercy Leaming.
They had three sons—Aaron 1st, Jeremiah (a Colonial Judge,
who married his first cousin, Lydia Leaming) and Eli Eldredge." It will be observed that the error of Dr. Hughes
in his "Divine Covenant Fulfilled in Pious Households" does
not affect the ancestry of the Eldredge family, as far as the
Mayflower line is concerned. It does not matter whether the
father of Aaron 2nd was Jeremiah, as Dr. Hughes first gave
it, or Aaron 1st as corrected by Dr. Hughes' later letter—in
either case Aaron 2nd was the grandson of Mercy Leaming,

but there was no third Aaron, as Dr. Hughes supposed at first.

Through the courtesy of Mrs. Irvin Eldredge, of Cape May, I have made an examination of the Eldredge Bible, now in her possession. The date is "London 1773," (first date before the Book of Common Prayer and administration of the Sacraments, bound up with the Bible in the same volume). The Holy Bible is of the date 1783, Clarendon Press, Oxford. The birth of Aaron Eldredge 2nd and that of his wife are the first entries:

"Aaron Eldredge was born the 13th day of June 1771.

"Hannah Eldredge was born December 22nd, 1774.

"Jeremiah Eldredge the first son of Aaron and Hannah Eldredge was born the 14th day of July, Sunday, 1793.

"Aaron Eldredge was born June 6th, Saturday, 1795.

"Aaron Eldredge and Hannah Langdon were married on the 17th day of October 1792. Joseph Eldredge and Ann West were married on the 22nd day of September 1830 —By the Rev. Israel Townsend at Cape May."

Then follows the record of the death of Aaron and Hannah Eldredge:

"Aaron Eldredge departed this life on August 21st, 1819.

"Hannah Eldredge departed this life 6 June 1836."

The earlier entries are evidently made by a quill pen, and are remarkable illustrations of the good penmanship of the forefathers.

The other entries agree with the record given in Dr. Hughes' work, and are included in the genealogical tables of this work.

That Aaron Eldredge, husband of Hannah Langdon, was the son of Aaron the first is proved by a deed of Parsons Leaming, Charlotte (Eldredge) his wife, Aaron Eldredge and Sarah Eldredge to Aaron Edmunds and Lydia

(Eldredge) his wife, dated August 30, 1792, of which the following is an extract (Recorded at Cape May Court House):—

To all persons to whome these presents shall come or may concern.

Know ye this thirtieth day of August in the year of Our Lord One Thousand seven hundred and Ninety two Between Persons Leaming Charlotte his wife Aaron Eldredge and Sarah Eldredge all of the County of Cape May and State of New Jersey of the one part and Aaron Edmunds and Lydia his wife of the same place of the other part. Whereas Aaron Eldredge of the Lower Precinct of the County of Cape May and Elizabeth his Wife, late deceased, both Dying Intestate, and being Posessed of Lands in their own fee Simple Right Situate in the Lower Precinct of the County aforesaid (to say) the said Aaron Eldredge now Deceased was in his lifetime Posessed of the plantation whereon he lived at the time of his Death Situate at Cold Spring * * * * which his Heirs agreed mutually to sell, and the said Elizabeth his Wife died Posessed of a Plantation Situate * * * * all which said Land Descended to their four Children, viz., to Charlotte the wife of Persons Leaming, to Lydia the wife of Aaron Edmunds, to Aaron Eldredge and Sarah Eldredge agreable to a Law of New Jersey * * * *.

Aaron Edmunds married first Lydia Eldredge, date of marriage, 25 June, 1790; he married second Sarah, older sister of Lydia, date of marriage, 3 June, 1798.

Mrs. Dr. Mecray has kindly permitted the author to examine the following record from a family Bible in her possession. The Bible was printed in Worcester, Mass., by Isaiah Thomas, and the date is 1801. At the foot of the first page of the New Testament the following note of the death of Thomas Eldredge is written: "Thomas Eldredge died January 29th, A. D. 1849, aged 51 years 8 days old."

On the following page the record proper begins, with a list of births: "William Eldredge was born November the 1st day, in the year of Our Lord A. D. 1759.

"Judith Corson was born August, the 8th day—A. D. 1759."

"Births of the Children:

"Enoch Eldredge was born on Monday the 22nd day of March, A. D. 1779. Jeremiah Eldredge was born on Saturday, December the 16th, 1780. Mary Eldredge was born on Friday, the 25th day of February, 1785. Hannah Eldredge was born on Saturday, the 20th October—1787. Judith Eldredge was born on Saturday, the 1st day of May—1790. William Eldredge was born on Sunday, the 25 day of December 1791. Elizabeth Eldredge was born May the 21st day—1794. Thomas Eldredge was born January the 21st—1798. John Bennett was born Friday, September the 7th—1798."

On the opposite page of the beginning of St. Matthew's Gospel the following is written: "Harriet W. Eldredge was born Thursday December 20, 1857;" and a note pinned to the page reads: "Married, Hannah, daughter of William and Judith Eldredge to John Mecray, April 2nd, 1805." A note at the side of the same page reads: "Judith Eldredge died August 26, 1831."

As seen from the above record, John Mecray married Hannah Eldredge, 2 April, 1805. James Mecray, their son, married Mary Ann Mulford; their son, James, married 8 November, 1865, Elizabeth Schellenger Hughes, who was born 4 April, 1844, her husband, Dr. James Mecray, was born 21 February, 1842. Elizabeth Schellenger Hughes is a descendant of John Howland, the Pilgrim, the line running back to the Mayflower through the generations following: The mother of Eilzabeth Schellenger Hughes was Elizabeth Schellenger, born 7 May, 1817, died 14 April, 1844, married 9 March 1839, to Albert Henry Hughes, who was born 8 January, 1812. The last named was the son of Humphrey Hughes and Hetty Williams, the Pilgrim ancestry running back through the mother of Humphrey Hughes, Jane Whilldin (widow of Humphrey Hughes, Sr.), Jane Whilldin[6], James Whilldin[5], Joseph Whilldin[4], Hannah Gorham[3], Desire Howland[2], John Howland the Pilgrim.

Descendants of Priscilla Leaming

On the Sugar Company's property, facing Holly Beach, between Taylor's Creek and Wildwood bridge, beyond Bennett station, near Rio Grande, there is near the meadows, surrounded by the scrubby second growth, a grave and a stone bearing the inscription:—

MARGARET LEAMING
OCTOBER 22ND, 1764
AGED 24

The mother of Margaret was Priscilla Leaming, whose ancestors run back to the Pilgrim John Howland as follows: Hannah Whilldin[4], mother of Priscilla, who married the first Thomas Leaming, born at South Hampton, L. I., 9 July, 1674, died 31 December, 1723, Hannah Gorham[3], Desire Howland[2], John Howland[1]. Priscilla Leaming, mother of Margaret, married twice, first John Stites, second Jacob Hughes, the ancestor of Dr. Daniel Hughes, and many now living in the county. By her first marriage (to John Stites) she had a daughter, Margaret Stites, who on the 3rd of March, 1763, married Jonathan Leaming, son of Aaron the 2nd, as shown the Diary of Aaron Leaming the 2nd, 1770:—

"My oldest child married March 3rd, 1763, to Margaret Stites, the only child of John and Priscilla Stites (both deceased) by her he had a daughter Priscilla, born the 9th of October, 1764 at 45 minutes past ten o'clock in the night and the 22nd of October, 1764 about 3 in the morning the said Margaret died."

This is the history of Margaret Leaming, who lies in the neglected grave. How remarkably the names of the early settlers are repeated through the intermarriages of the few families of the first years evidently without injury to the stock is shown by the marriage of Margaret's daughter, Priscilla, whose marriage to Humphrey Stites, in three generations, brings the family name back to the starting point.

From an earlier entry in the diary we have the following account of the family of Thomas Leaming:—

"Thomas Leaming married Hannah daughter of Joseph Whilldin the Elder, and had—

Esther, married William Eldredge.

Mercy, married Samuel Eldredge.

Jane, married William Doubleday.

Phebe, married John Garlick.

Priscilla, married first John Stites, and after his death, Jacob Hughes.

Christopher, married Deborah Hand.

Thomas, Mary Elizabeth Leaming."

But the interesting fact we have discovered is this, that the grandmother of Priscilla, who married Humphrey Stites, married as her second husband Jacob Hughes, the great-grandfather of the Rev. Dr. Daniel L. Hughes. Mrs. Priscilla Hughes, wife of Jacob Hughes, was buried in Cold Spring Cemetery, the inscription on her tomb reading: "Died September 21, 1758, aged 48." Dr. Hughes reckoned back from the date of her death, making her birth in the year of 1710.

In Thomas Leaming's Anecdotes, printed in Stillwell, 432 (Vol. 3) we find the date of the birth of Priscilla, daughter of Thomas and Hannah Leaming, confirming our conclusions as to the identity of the two Priscillas, Priscilla Leaming was born 15 June, 1710, and is the Mrs. Priscilla Hughes who lies in Cold Spring Cemetery, the ancestress of Dr. Hughes and many of that name now living in Cape May County.

Jacob Hughes, son of Jacob and Priscilla Leaming Hughes, born 9 August, 1746, died 20 March, 1796, married Ann Lawrence (daughter of Rev. Daniel Lawrence) who was born in August 1753. She married second Jeremiah Edmonds, and died 27 November, 1817.

The Wife of Ellis Hughes

The author has received the following note accompanying a copy of the record of the family Bible of Franklin Davenport Edmunds and Ann Marshall Edmunds, his wife:

"Rev. Dr. Howe:—

"The following is written on a fly-leaf between the old and new Testaments of the family Bible of Franklin D. and Ann M. Edmunds, in front of the Registry of 'Marriages,' 'Births,' and 'Deaths'; it is written in the hand of my grandfather, Franklin D. Edmunds.

"The Bible is not dated, but was published by Joseph N. Lewis, at Baltimore. After the marriage of Mary Jane Edmunds, daughter of Franklin D. and Ann M. Edmunds, to Joel Cook, Jr., the family records are in the handwriting of the latter, up until the last two years when I have made the entries.

Very truly,

FRANKLIN D. EDMUNDS,

son of Henry Reeves and Ann (Welsh) Edmunds; grandson of Franklin D. and Ann M. Edmunds."

The following is the memorandum referred to above:—
"Ellis Hughes departed this life
on the 16th day of April, 1817,
in his 72nd year.
His father's name was Ellis
and his mother's name was
Hannah, of Welsh descent.
I have understood they
first settled on Long Island and

finally on Cape May at 'New
England'' on what is now better
known as 'Town Bank.'
Memo of
Thomas H. Hughes,
grandfather to
F. D. Edmunds.''

The involved problem of the genealogical interpretation
of the will of Joseph Whilldin[2] will be further discussed in
the genealogical notes at the end of this volume; briefly the
facts of the record, agreeing with the conclusions of the late
Major Charles Welsh Edmunds, whose careful work has been
consulted, are as follows, resting upon the foregoing documents:—Joseph Whilldin[4], (Hannah Gorham[3], Desire Howland[2], John Howland[1]), names in his will (see page 27) his
daughter Hannah and his grandson Memucan (Memukin)
Hughes. The will of Ellis Hughes (page 29) names his wife
Hannah and his son Memucan Hughes. Hannah survived her
husband, and Ellis, born after Memucan, and expressly called
by Rev. Dr. Hughes the brother of Memucan, was also the son
of Hannah.

The Will of Jacob Hughes, 2nd

Jacob Hughes 2nd was born on the 9 of August, 1746, and died on the 20 of March, 1796, and was buried in Cold Spring Cemetery. Through the courtesy of Mr. Harry Hughes the writer has been permitted to examine Jacob Hughes' will, an instrument of great interest in confirming the Pilgrim genealogical record. (See page 36.)

The will begins: "The Will of Jacob Hughes of the County of Cape May," and the date is 1795, but the last page is missing. Mention is made of his wife Ann (Lawrence), his sons, Jacob, Jeremiah, James R., Daniel; and of his daughters, Mary and Elizabeth. The testator was a man of large wealth and influence in the community, as shown by the disposition of his several plantations, and the evident extent of his household. Except in the case of his son Daniel, the several plantations are given to the son named and his male heirs forever, to daughters and heirs. The following extracts show the unusual wealth of the testator and throw light upon a little known fact in the domestic life of the ancestors:

"I give unto my daughter Mary Hughes a Legacy of One Hundred and Fifty Pounds and my negro wench Patience.

"I give unto my daughter Elizabeth Hughes a Legacy of Two Hundred and Fifty Pounds, and my negro wench Dinah.

"I give unto my son Daniel Hughes One Hundred and Fifty Pounds and my negro boy Julius.

"I give unto my son Jacob Hughes my negro man Zedebiah (Zebediah).

"I give unto my son James R. Hughes a Legacy of One Hundred and fifty pounds and my negro Toney."

The mother of Jacob Hughes 2nd was Priscilla Leaming, daughter of Hannah Whilldin[4] (Hannah Gorham[3], Desire Howland[2], John Howland[1] the Pilgrim), as already given. (See page 36).

Ann Lawrence, wife of Jacob Hughes 2nd was born in August, 1753, died 27 November, 1817, (tombstone in Cold Spring Cemetery). She was the daughter of the Rev. Daniel Lawrence and his wife Sarah, whose tombstones are in the above named cemetery. A biographical history of the family is given on page 14 of "The Divine Covenant Fulfilled in Pious Households" by the Rev. Daniel Lawrence Hughes, and in the notes following the genealogical record of the family will be given.

The Session Book of the Lower Township of Cape May, New Jersey

On the occasion of the one hundred and seventy-fifth anniversary of the origin and founding of the Cold Spring Presbyterian Church, Cape May County, New Jersey, on September 26th, 1889, the Rev. Daniel Lawrence Hughes, who delivered the historical address said:—

" Unfortunately we cannot tell exactly the date of the origin or founding of the Cold Spring Presbyterian Church. It is greatly to be regretted that no church or sessional records can be found for over one-third of a century from its beginning until the installation there of the Rev. Daniel Lawrence in 1754. We are told that the first records of the church available date from this period and that after 1808, the church records were preserved; but where they are with others that have been misplaced or consumed, I know not."

The historical address was afterwards published with "A Chronological List of Persons Buried at Cold Spring Cemetery", and in a footnote on the sixth page we read: "On May 12th, 1804, under the pastorate of Rev. David Edwards, he having accepted a call presented to him from the Cape May Church in 1804. The session was composed of Rev. David Edwards and Messrs. Matthew Whilldin, James Whilldin, Robert Edmunds, John Stites, and John Yates, Elders.

"The minutes in this small 'copy book' closed with some baptisms on May 19th, 1804, and the session unanimously agreed to procure another book, better fitted for the purpose, which was done, said to be 'quarto bound with parchment'.

Signed by David Edwards.

41

"There has been no knowledge of this 'quarto bound with parchment,' since the death of Mr. Edwards in 1813, but that it was faithfully kept is now known, for in the winter of 1903 the workmen who were moving the house formerly occupied by the Rev. Moses Williamson, for forty-four years a beloved pastor of the church, found the book with others, under the eaves where it had lain many years.

"It was my privilege to see this book in February 1904, and recognizing at once its value to the Presbyterian Church, and also to all descended from the people mentioned therein, I made a literal copy of the entire book so it could be published and reach a larger number of those interested.

"Mr. Edwards wrote in a clear flowing hand, no blots nor erasures marring the entire book.

"The entry of marriages and his own signature vary but little until the year 1812, when there is so much variety that one may suspect that the warlike times affected even Session Books.

"He recorded three deaths in December, 1813, including his wife's on December seventh: and his own death on December thirtieth of the same year, was recorded by another hand."

The Rev. Dr. Daniel Lawrence Hughes failed in his evident purpose of publishing this valuable genealogical record and did not suspect that the material contained therein was largely a record of Pilgrim descendants in the County, but the importance of the Session Book was recognized by the Massachusetts Society of Mayflower Descendants, and in 1906 published at Boston in the official quarterly magazine of that Society, having been contributed by Mrs. Annie Crowell Rand. It is now for the first time printed in this State.

The Record of Marriages

DAVID EDWARDS, Pastor.

The record of marriages solemnized by David Edwards in the Lower Township of Cape May. And this record has peculiar reference to those belonging to his own congregation—directly or indirectly, that is to say, that one or the other of the parties belonging to, and resided within the bounds of the congregation.

11 Married by D. E. Febry 2nd 1804 Stephen Pierson Jun to Elizabeth Reeve.

12 March 15th Married Robert Hanley to Ella Bradford —D. E.

13 May 16th Married Zacheus Ray to Ann Pierson—D. E.

14 May 17th Married Joseph Smith to Ronami Shaw—D. E.

15 July 30th Married Robert Corgee to Phebe Schellenger —D. E.

16 August 17th Married George Cresse to Judith Swain —D. E.

17 Nov 4th Thos Hand (Married) to Laviza Hand—D. E.

18 Nov 12th Married Dr. Dl. Hughes to Charlotte Bennet —D. E.

19 Nov 20th Married Reuben Foster to Nancy Edmunds —D. E.

20 Nov 21st Married Samuel Thomas to Sarah Swain—D. E.

21 Febry 9th, 1805, Married Enoch Eldridge to Elizabeth Eldridge—D. E.

22 Feb 24th Married Elisha Hand to Phebe Willis—D. E.

23 March 18th Married George Hand to Experience Smith —D. E.

24 April 9th Married John Marcay (sic) to Hannah Eldredge—D. E.

25 July 3rd 1805 Married Ezra Hand to Mary White—D. E.

26 Nov 30th Married Phillip Bennet to Susannah Weithman —D. E.

27 Dec 24th Married Elijah Hays to Hannah Foster—D. E.

28 Janry 29th Married John Church to Elizabeth Hughes —D. E.

29 Febry 1st 1806 Married Glasco Wms to Emy Frederick —D. E.—Colored People.

30 Ditto Married Wm Coachman to Bina Almer—D. E.

31 Feb 8th Married Nathl Hand to Rachel Hughes—D. E.

32 May 15th Married Caleb Woolson to Nancy Reeve—D. E.

33 Jan 28th 1807 Married Dd Russel to Sarah Robinson —D. E.

34 Feb 13th Married John Shaw to Hannah Wicks—D. E.

35 March 10th Married Dd Yates to Elizabeth Hughes —D. E.

36 Oct 9th Married George Taylor to Naomi Hughes—D. E.

37 Nov 28th Married Wm Hughes to Elizabeth Buck—D. E.

38 Jan 14th 1808 Married Isaac Vanmeter to Sarah Buck —D. E.

39 Feb 17th Married Jacob Hand to Laviza Clark—D. E.

40 March 22nd Married James Schellinger to Lydia Whilldin—D. E.

41 April 13th Married Thos. Pierson to Sarah Reeve—D. E.

42 April 22nd Married Jacob Epler to Mary Clark—D. E.

43 April 26th Married Downs Edmunds to Elizabeth Stilwell—D. E.

44 June 10th 1808 Married Joseph Ware to Harriet Whilldin—D. E.

45 Aug 24th Married John Ames to Sarah Connell—D. E.

46 Oct 20th Married Dd Reyons to Nancy Almer—D. E.

47 Jan 16th 1809 Married Gideon Palmer to Ruth Hand —D. E.

48 Feb 2nd Married Harvey Teal to Sarah Bacon—D. E.

49 March 7th Married Isaac Whilldin to Mahala Edmunds —D. Edwards

50 May 14th Married Stephen Stimpson to Sophia Corgee

51 June 18th Married James Thompson to Mary Swain
—D. Edwards

52 Ditto Married David Swain to Elizabeth Corson—D. E.

53 Aug 5th Married Saml Richardson to Elizabeth Eldridge
—D. E.

54 Dec 5th Married Lieutenant Joshua Townshend to Sarah
Schellenger—

55 Dec 12th Married by D. Edwards James Townshend to
Elizabeth Schellenger.

56 Dec 17th 1809 Married Jonathan Crawford to Hannah
Crowell—D. E.

57 Feb 10th 1810 Married Capn James Swain to Elizabeth
Swain—D. E.

58 March 10th 1810 Married Enos Schellenger to Eliza Mills
—D. E.

59 April 1st, 1810 Married Peter Humphreys to Marriah Cox
—people of colour

60 May 15th 1810 Married John Ross to Rachel Hand—D. E.

61 June 21st 1810 Married Stevens Stimpson to Phebe Corgee—D. E.

62 July 11th 1810 Married Harvey Hand to Catherine Swain
—D. E.

63 Aug 20th 1810 Married Evin Edmonds to Anna Hand
—D. E.

64 Nov 13th 1810 Married Thos Pierson to Nancy Bancroft
—D. E.

65 Nov 20th 1810 Married John Steward to Harriet Hand
—D. E.

66 Dec 18th 1810 Married Robert Parsons to Elizabeth Edmunds—D. E.

67 April 8th 1811 Married Thomas Buck to Luzinda Gilbert
—D. E.

68 Sept 24th, 1811, Married Reuben Swain to Sarah Reeds
(sic)—D. E.

69 March 16th 1812 Married Isaac Smith Esq to Miss Judith Hand—D. E.

70 April 8th 1812 Married John Bancroft, Junr to Deborah Kent—D. E.

71 May 6th 1812 Married Jacob Corson to Lois Yates—D. E.

72 May 18th 1812 Married Jesse Crammer to Sarah Rankins —D. E.

73 June 25th Married John Church to Mary Taylor—D. E.

74 Married Ezekiel Stevens on Monday the 15th of June 1812 to Lois Higgins—D. E.

75 Married Matthew Hand on the 21st of July 1812 to Rhodda Hughes,—D. E.

76 Married by the subscriber Rd Schellenger to Hannah Buck on the 24th of Oct 1812.

77 Married on the 24th of Dec 1812 Stephen Pierson to Christiana High—D. E.

78 Dec 25th 1812 Married John Shaw to Martha Clark—by me David Edwards.

79 Married Dec 31st 1812 Richard Edmonds to Lydia Hughes—by me D. E.

80 Jan 8th 1813 Married Virgil Davis to Elizabeth Crowell —by me D. E.

81 Jan 19th 1813 Married Bat to Emy—people of colour— by me D. E.

82 Married Black Abraham to Susan—people of colour —D. E.

83 July 11th 1813 Married Thos J. Curtis to Philomela Shaw —D. E.

84 Oct 9th 1813 Married John Shaw to Mary Swain—D. E.

85 Oct 16th 1813 Married Ellis Hughes Junr to Sarah Higgins—D. E.

Quarto 2nd.

[A continuance of quarto 1st]

The Records of marriages are to be found at the close of this Quarto.

The asterisk mark is for the dead. *

The obelisk for dismissed by certificate. ‡

[P 1]   September 24th 1808.   The session of the Presbyterian church of Cape May met at the Parsonage house, according to appointment and constituted with prayer.

Members present Messr Matthew Whilldin, John Stites Jr, Robert Edmunds, Elders.

David Edwards, minister.

John Bencroft, Mary Buck, ‡Ann Ways, Elizabeth Edmunds, Martha Thomas, and Abigail Schellenger applied for admission into the church [who being examined were admitted to the sealing Ordinances of the church of Christ.

Concluded with prayer.

[P 2]   Martha Thomas and Mary Buck having not been baptized in their infancy were baptized the 1st of October, the day preceding the Sacrament.

At different Sessions appointed on Nov 12th 1808. March 24th 1809—May 5th 1809—And met at the Parsonage house.

Members present, Matthew Whilldin, John Stites, Robert Edmunds, Elders.

David Edwards.

Constituted with prayer.

The following persons applied for admission to the sealing ordinances of the church.

[P 3]   Thomas Stillwell
Lavisa Bennet
Judith Hughes
Abigail Bencroft ‡
Ester Rankins
Rachel Crawford
Amelia Eldridge
Henry Stevens [to be restored]
Abigail Hughes
Tryphena Edmunds
George Baker
Martha Baker
Uriah Hand
Edmund Ireland
Mary Bennet
Samuel Eldridge

Jane Eldridge ‡
Levi Eldridge
Elizabeth Eldridge
John Clark
Patience Clark *
Laviza Schellenger
Sarah Ames
Philomela Stevens
Charlotte Stites
James Smith ‡
Tabitha Whilldin ‡
Abigail Stites
Harriet Beyers ‡
Stephen Stimptson
Samuel Watson   recd by
Catherine Watson letter

[P 4]   Who being examined were considered as worthy objects of admission and accordingly were admitted.

Concluded with prayer.

———————

Thomas Stilwell, Laviza Bennet, Judith Hughes, Abigail Bencroft, Esther Rankins, Rachel Crawford, Uriah Hand, George Baker, Edmund Ireland, Laviza Schellenger, Sarah Ames, Philomela Stevens, James Smith, Charlotte Stites, Abigail Stites, Stephen Stimptson, having not been baptized in their infancy were introduced into the church by the Ordinance of Baptism—16.

48

[P 5]   November 20th 1808 were baptized

1	John Edwards	Children of
2	Alexander Edwards	Dl & Jane Edwards

3	Elizabeth Bencroft	
4	Phebe Bencroft	
5	Roberts Edmunds Bent	Children of
6	Thos Hand Bencroft	Miller & Abigal Bencroft.
7	Miller Bencroft	
8	Abigail Bencroft	

9	Joseph Ways	
10	William Ways	Children of
11	Harriet Ways	Joseph & Ann Ways.
12	John Ways	

13	Hetty Schellenger	
14	Washington Schellenger	Children of
15	Samuel Schellenger	Dl & Abigal Schellenger
16	Daniel Schellenger	

[P6] 17 William Buck   Son of Wm & Mary Buck.

18 Daniel Bencroft   A child of John and
                             Elizabeth Bencroft.

Until April Presbytery 1809.

May 7th 1809, Baptized—

1	John Beyers	Children of
2	Joseph Beyers	——— and Harriet Beyers

May 14th 1809, The sacrament of the Lord's supper was administered and the above name Thos Stilwell, Laviza Bennet were received into the full communion of the Church. Total 32.

[P. 7.]   June 4th 1809.   Were baptized the following children.

3 Elizabeth Eldridge
4 Levi Eldridge
5 Ester Eldridge   The children of
6 Jeremiah Edmunds Ege   Levi & Elizabeth Eldridge

7 'George Schellenger   A child of
    James & L. Schellenger.

8 Jonathan Whilldin   A child of
    Jon & Tabitha Whilldin.

9 George Bennet
10 William Bennet   The children of
11 Mary Ann Bennct   John and Mary Bennet.

12 Hannah Stites
13 Rachel Stites   The children of
14 Wm Stites   Nathan & Charlotte Stites
15 Lois Stites

[P. 8.]   Baptized Sept 10th 1809

16 Richard Smith
17 Martha Smith   The children of
18 Judith Smith   James Smith.

19 Anna Foster   A child of
    Dd Foster & his wife.

20 Joseph Hays   The children of
21 Hannah Hays   Elijah & Hannah Hays

22 Elizabeth Schellenger   A child of Jn Schellenger

At the different Sessions held on August 4th, October 8 & 13 1809. The following persons applied for admission into the church thro its sealing ordinances.

—who being examined were received and admitted into full communion Octr 15th, Viz;

[P 9] 1 Hannah Foster *
2 Sarah Schellenger
3 Tabitha Buck
4 Mary Miller
5 John Ames *
6 Judith Hand
7 Hannah Hays ‡
8 Mary Hughes
9 Harriet Ware
10 Ester Edmunds
11 Richd Edmunds
12 Sarah Leaming *
13 Phebe Hand
14 Daniel Crowell
15 Daniel Andrew
16 Hannah Andrew
17 Frederick Buck
18 Rebecca Weithman
19 Zereviah Schenck
20 Judith Cresse
21 Jane Edwards
22 Stilwell Shaw
23 Sarah Crowell
24 Sarah Smith *
25 Sarah Hand
26 Sarah Vanmeter
27 Rebecca Merret
28 Elizabeth Hand
29 Hannah Eldridge
30 Martha Stites *
31 Aaron Schellenger
32 Isaac Vanmeter
33 John Crowell
34 Fany Schellenger
35 Ann Hand
36 Johanna Bencroft
37 Emi Williams

[P. 10] The following of the above named persons (adults) were baptized, October 14th 1809.

1 Hannah Foster
2 Ester Edmunds
3 Richard Edmunds
4 Tabitha Buck
5 Daniel Crowell
6 Hannah Andrew
7 Phebe Hand
8 Zereviah Schenck
9 Judith Cresse
10 Hannah Hays
11 Mary Hughes
12 Harriet Ware
13 Elizabeth Hand
14 Martha Stites
15 Hannah Eldredge
16 Isaac Vanmeter
17 John Crowell
18 Stilwell Shaw
19 Sarah Smith
20 Sarah Crowell
21 Sarah Vanmeter
22 Fany Schellenger
23 Ann Hand
24 Johanna Bencroft

On the same day October 14th the following children were dedicated unto the Lord by baptism.

[P. 11.] 23 Hannah Stevens
24 Wm Stevens
25 Rebecca Stevens   The children of
26 Henry Stevens   Dl & Philomela Stevens.
27 Daniel Stevens
28 Stilwell Stevens

29 Margaret Buck
30 Isaac Buck
31 Frederick Buck   The children of
32 Hannah Buck   Frederick Buck.
33 Mary Buck

34 Art Hughes   The children of
35 Mary Ann Hughes   Israel & Mary Hughes.

36 Tryphene Edmunds A child of
         Downs & Elizath Es.

37 David Edwards   A child of
         Dd & Jane Edwards.

38 Richard Crawford The children of
39 Joseph Crawford   Richd & Rachel Crawford.

[P 12] On the aforesaid day, October 14th, three ruling elders were also set apart to said office having been chosen and propounded at a suitable season before hand—Namely Stephen Pierson Samuel Watson and Ephriam Kent. On October the 15th, 1809 the Sacrament of the Lord's supper was administered to upwards of 100 communicants.

[P. 13]   Novr 5th 1809 were baptized

40 Aaron Eldredge	
41 Eliza Eldredge	The children of
42 Joseph Eldredge	Aaron & Hannah Eldredge
43 Wm Eldredge	
44 Stilwell Eldredge	

45 Sarah Schellenger	
46 Mary Schellenger	The children of
47 Judith Schellenger	Aaron Schellenger.
48 Aaron Schellenger	

49 John Vanmeter	A child of
	Isaac & S. Vanmeter.

50 Anna Merret	The children of
51 Elizabeth Merret	John & Rebecca Merret.

52 Zabitha Hand[1]	
53 Zabbiah Hand[3]	The children of
54 Jacob Stites Hand[2]	Thos & Sarrah Hand.

[P. 14]   Novr 12th 1809 Were baptized

55 Catherine Hughes Andrew	The children of
56 Jesse Hughes Andrews	Dl & Hannah Andrew
57 Lois Andrews	

58 Mary Ann Taylor	Under the care of H. Ware

59 Saml Fithian Ware	The children of
60 Deborah W. Ware	Joseph & Deborah Ware.
61 James Whilldin Ware	

62 Joseph Ware	of Joseph & Harriet Ware.

63 Nathan Moestander	Under the care of
	Dl & Lydia Crowell.

Novr 19th 1809

| 64 Franklin Williams | The children of |
| 65 George W. Williams | Glasco & Emi Williams. |

[P. 15]   Dec 12th 1809 Baptized.

66 Charlotte Stites	The children of
67 Mary Stites	Thos & Martha Stites.
68 Smith Stites	

Decr 17th 1809

| 69 John Crowell | A child of |
| | John & Abigal Crowell. |

March 16th 1810

| 70 Thomas Clark | The children of |
| 71 James B. Clark | John & Patience Clark. |

Ending April 1810

Dismissed by letters 5 of those adults received into the communion of the church between April 1809 & 1810— Namely, Harriet Beyers, James Smith, Samuel Eldredge, Jane Eldredge and Tabitha Whilldin, April 1810.

[P. 16]   March 30th 1810.   The Session met according to appointment at the parsonage-house and was constituted with prayers.   Members present

Messrs Matthew Whilldin, John Stites, Robert Edmunds, Stephen Pierson, Samuel Watson, Ephriam Kent, Elders.
David Edwards, Pastor.

The following applied for admission into the church, thro' its sealing ordinances, Viz, Lydia Corgee, Drusilla Schellenger, Pryssilla Schellenger, Hannah Leaming.

[P. 17]   Rhoda Teal, Silas Matthias, Eleanor Matthias, Sarah Woolson, Abigal Crowell, Gyls Cox, Rheum (the two last people of color)—All the above were baptized by adult baptism, except Eleanor Matthews & Abigal Crowell who had been baptized in their infancy.   And all were returned as above described at the last stated meeting of Presbytery April 1810.   Concluded with prayer.

May 3rd 1810.   Baptized.

1	Robert Corgee	Children of
2	Anna Sophia Corgee	George Corgee & his wife.

[P. 18]   May 15th 1810.   Baptized.

3	———— Weithman	The children of
4	———— Weithman	Mrs. Weithman.
5	Bennet Weithman	
6	Sarah Williams	A child of
		Glasco & Emi Williams.

May 16th the session met according to appointment and was constituted with prayer.

Members present, Messrs Matthew Whilldin, John Stites, Robert Edmunds, Stephen Piersons, Samuel Watson, Ephriam Kent, Elders.

David Edwards, Pastor.

[P.19]   The following persons applied for admission into the church; Viz,

Pena Shaw, Mercy Foster, Debro Isard, Sarah Teal, Lazinda Gilbert, Deborah Borney, Sarah Brown, Richd Crofford*, Joel Brown, Jeremiah Ewing, Joan (a woman of colour)—11. Who were after examination received. Concluded with prayer.   9 of the above were baptized on Saturday, 26,

Viz, Deborah Barney, Deborah Isard, Pena Shaw, Lazinda Gilbert, Sarah Brown, Richd Crawford, Joel Brown, Jeremiah Ewing, Joan.   In all 9.

The sacrament of the Lord's supper was [P. 20] administered unto the church.

The number of communicants in all, 131.

Between April 1809 & 1810, 5 were dismissed by certificates; Viz, Herriet Beyers, James Smith, Samuel and Jane Eldredge & Tabitha Whilldin.

Hannah Hays an absentee! ! !

[P. 21]   Baptized, May 20th.

7 Ann Eliza Ways	A child of Joseph & Ann Ways.
8 Mary Mills	A child of Ephriam & Mary Mills.

Baptized, June 17th.

9 Jane White Eldridge	A child of Levi & Elizth Eldredge.
10 Wm Bacon Teal	A child of Harvey & Sarah Teal.
11 Charlotte Swain	of Samuel & Judith Swain
12 George Cresse	of George & Judith Cresse.
13 John Hand Cresse	
14 Art Bencroft	The children of Miller Bencroft.
15 Samuel Swain Bencroft	

[P. 22] 16 Wm Matthews
17 Eleanore Matthews The children of
18 Hannah Matthews Silas & Eleanr Matthews.
19 Thos Matthews

20 Swain Shaw
21 Mary S. Shaw The children of
22 Parsons E. Shaw Stillwell and Phena Shaw.
23 William Shawe

24 Jacob Teal
25 Clarissa Teal The children of
26 Jeremiah Teal Eli and Rhodda Teal.
27 David Teal
28 Levi Teal

29 James Hand A child of Abi Bencroft.

 October 1, 1810.

30 Isaac Vanmeter A child of
    Isaac & Sarah Vanmeter.

[P. 23] 31 James Hand The children of
32 Martha Hand George & Elith Hand.

33 Charlotte Bennet A child of
    John & Mary Bennet.

October 12, 1810. The session met according to appointment. Members present

Matthew Whilldin John Stites, Robert Edmunds, Stephen Pierson, Ephriam Kent, Samuel Watson, Elders.

David Edwards, Minister, constituted with prayer.

The following persons applied for [P.24] admission into the church, Viz, Miller Bencroft, Elizabeth Church (Daniel Church's wife), Elizabeth Church (John Church's wife, a pilot), and Theti, a black woman, the wife of James Lively. Who after being examined and the session having obtained satisfaction of their experience, knowledge and motives were admitted into full communion of the church on the 21st of

October, being the day appointed for the celebration of the Lord's supper. The Rev. Nathl Irvin assisted on said day. [P. 25] Theti Lively, having not been baptized in her infancy, was introduced into the church privileges thro' the ordinances of baptism on Oct 20th the day preceeding the administration of the Lord's supper.

Novr 13th 1810. Died, Richard Crawford a communicating member of this church. March 15th 1811, The session of this church met according to appointment and constituted with prayer. Members present, Matthew Whilldin, John Stites, Robert Edmunds, Stephen Pierson, Ephriam Kent, David Edwards.

[P. 26] Priscilla Ireland and Thomas Hand applied for admission to the full communion of the church, who after being examined, were accordingly admitted. Concluded with prayer.

Baptized on Sunday March 17th 1811, the following children.

34 Priscilla   A child of
Thos & Sarah Hand.

35 Daniel Crowell   A child of
Joseph & Harriet Ware.

36 Memucan   A child of
Israel & Mary Hughes.

37 George   A child of
Aaron & Hannah Eldredge

38 Thomas   A child of
Thos & Martha Stites.

39 ———— ————   A child of
Frederick & Tabitha Buck.

40 Samuel
41 Seth   The children of
42 Constant   Aaron and Mary Miller.
43 Mary

[P. 27] 44 Sarah   The children of
45 Aaron   Aaron & Mary Miller.

46 Henry
47 Elizabeth
48 Sarah   The children of
49 Mary   Henry & Deborah Isard.
50 Isaac
51 ——————

March 24th 1811.   Baptized Thos Hand and Pricilla Ireland, adults; and also the following infants

Susie Bennet *   The children of
Phebe Smith   Jerh & Martha Thomas.
Sarah

                       A child of
52 Mason   John & Abigal Crowell.

[P. 28] 53 Elizabeth   Children of
54 George   Jacob & Nancy Foster.
55 Rachel

56 Lucy Bennet   Children of
57 Phebe Smith   Jeremiah & Martha Thos.
58 Sarah

Regularly returned and recorded in the minutes of Presbytery.

April 17th 1811.

May 10th 1811. The Session met according to appointment and constituted with Prayer. Members present, Robert Edmunds, Stephen Pierson, Samuel Watson, Elders, & D. Edwards, Minister. Absent Matthew Whilldin, John Stites & Ephriam Kent.

[P. 29] The following named persons applied for admission into the church, namely, Naomi Taylor, Mary Hand,

and Hannah Leaming, the last one named although having been examined & received about a year past, Did not come forward to the Lord's supper now applied de Novo and is admitted as well as the other two to the ordinances of God's house.   Concluded with prayer.

Adjourned to meet the 18th of May, at the Parsonage-house, at 10 O'Clock, A. M.

[P. 30]   May 18th 1811.   Met according to adjournment. Present, Messrs. John Stites, Robert Edwards, Stephen Piersons, Ephrim Kent & Samuel Watson, Elders and David Edwards, pastor.

Rachel Hughes and Elizabeth Hughes, applied for admission into the church which was granted.

May 19th 1812.   Were baptized, Mary Hand & Elizabeth Hughes.   2 were baptized and also,

1	Alfred	The children of
2	Ruth	Henry Pierson & wife.

[P. 31] 3	————	Children of
4	————	Dnl and Elizabeth Church.
5	————	

6	Abigal Stites	A child of
		Downs & Elizth Edmunds.

7	Charlotte	A child of
		Nathn & Charlotte Stites.

July 21st Baptized by Revd James K. Birch.

8	Anna Robertson Edwards	A child of
		E. D. & Jane Edwards.

9	Rhodda Corgee	Children of St Stimpson &
10	Robert Corgee Stimpson	Phebe, his wife.

11	Nancy	Children of
12	Joanna	James & Theter Lively.

60

[P. 32]   Patience Clark, a member of this church died. Lios Higgins, a member of a long standing in this church died triumpant in the Lord on the 5th of Sept 1811.   John Ames also a member of this church was removed from time into eternity on the 15th of Sept 1811.   Went to bed as well as usual, and in one hour after any indisposition was perceived, was a breathless corpse ! ! !

Baptized the same fall John Macray and Mrs. Lydia Hughes.

[P. 33]   Sept 25th 1811.   Died Sarah Smith, the consort of Isaac Smith, Esqr. a member of this church.   Be ye therefore ready for the hour ye know not, the Son of man cometh. May the memory of this worthy woman be perserved.

Andrew Higgins, the husband of Lois Higgins whose decease is noticed on the opposite page, died the 26th of Dec 1811, and left after him 3 protectless daughters.   A member in full communion.   Sarah Leaming, died a member of this church.

[P. 34]   October 29th 1811.   The Session of this church met according to appointment.   Members present, Matthew Whilldin, Robert Edmunds, Stephen Pierson and John Stites, Elders & David Edwards, pastor.

The following persons applied for admission into the privileges of the church, which upon an examination was granted, namely, Judith Eldredge, Hannah Macray, Nancy Foster.

April 5th 1812.   Baptized.

13 Franklin Lively   A child of
                                 James & Hety Lively.

13 children, 5 adults—18.   Reported to Presbytery.

[P. 35] May 8th 1812 The Session met according to appointment. Members present Matthew Whilldin, Rbt Edmunds, Stephen Pierson and E. D. Edwards.

The following persons applied for admission into the full communion of the church. Mrss Jeremiah Ewing Senr and Clarissa Foster.

May 17th Baptized, Clarissa Foster. 1 adult, Clarissa Foster.

Infants.

| 1 Jeremiah Eldredge Foster | Children of |
| 2 James Macray | John & Hannah Macray. |

[P. 36] 3 ———————	Children of
4 ———————	John & Elizth Church.
5 ———————	

10 O'clock A. M. May 23rd 1812. The Session met at the Parsonage-house agreeably to adjournment when and where Mrs. Jacob Foster applied for admission into the church, which was granted. On the ensuing day, May 24th the Sacrament at the Lord's supper was administered to about a hundred & fifty communicants in the presence of a numerous assembly.

[P. 37] Died June the 10th 1812. Mary Pierson the consort of Stephen Pierson, Senr.

The Session of the church met agreeably to appointment, the 30th of October 1812. The following persons applied for admission into the full communion of the church, Viz; Lydia Hughes, Eliza Richardson, and Rhodda Hand, to be readmitted after being a wandering Methodist.

In the month of October 1812, Martha Stites, a communicating member of this church, departed this life. Also Hannah Foster, 71 years old, died on the 29th October, 1812.

[P. 38] Adjourned to meet at the Parsonage house on the 6th of Novr 1812, 10 o'clock when and where Elijah Eldredge, Martha Hand applied for admission into the church, which request was granted. Elizabeth Richardson and Mrs. Hand were baptized on the date above written and also 6th, Isaac Merret, a child of Jn & Rebecca Merret.

Elijah Eldredge, departed this life on the 11th of Novr 1812, after a standing of only 5 days in the fellowship of the church.

[P. 39] Departed this life Henry Stephens, a member of this church in full communion, a sensible and worthy man.

May 13th 1813. Died Major Joseph Hughes, who altho' not a member of this church, was a useful member of the congregation having been a member of the corporation for a great many years, and a clerk and treasurer for seven years past, which office he discharged with fidelity and satisfaction to the church and congregation. Dd Edwards.

[P. 40] May 14th 1813. The Session of this church met according to appointment. Members present, Matthew Whilldin, John Stites, Robert Edmunds, Ephraim Kent, Stephen Pierson, Elders, Dd Edwards, Pastor.

May 14th, 1813. Applied for admission into the full communion of the church the following persons, Viz; Isaac Whilldin, Mahalla Whilldin, Amelia Ewing, Elizath Parsons, Catherine Schenck, and Judith Eldredge.

[P. 41] May 22nd 1813. The Session met agreeably to adjournment at the Parsonage house; members present as before. The following persons applied for church privileges, namely, David Hughes, Phebe Stimpson, William Hughes, Elizath Eldredge, Mary Bennet. In all 16. Mary Bennet,

63

By certificate 6—22. Sarah Mulford, Hannah Thos. Last fall 5—27. Ruenni Foster, Hannah Crawford.

[P. 42] May 22nd 1813. Baptized the following,

Named adults.	Infants on the same day.
Amelia Ewing	7 Albert Henry, Cap Huhges.
Elizabeth Parsons	8 Johanna Edmunds
Wm Hughes	9 Sarah Hand
Mary Bennet	10 Jane Edmunds
Nancy Bennet	11 Silas Matthews
Sarah Mulford	12 Caroline Hughes
Catherine Schenck	14 Ester Wms Hughes
Reuemmi Foster	15 Aaron Teal
Hannah Thos	16
Judith Eldridge	

[P. 43] December 7th 1813. Died, Jane Edwards the consort of David Edwards, the pastor of the church to which this session book belongs, aged 34, abruptly taken from time into eternity, leaving behind her a disconsolate husband and 4 helpless children!!! A communicating member—102.

December 10th died David Whilldin a promising young man, (the son of Matthew Whilldin, Esqr. a ruling elder of this church for many years) indisposed. Alas! the brittle thread of life.

[P. 44] Died on the 17th Charlotte Hughes, the consort of Dr Daniel Hughes, in the bloom of life, aged 33.

Received into full communion since the Death of Rev. David Edwards, Sarah Edmunds, October 1814.

Jesse Hughes
Hannah Hughes
Sarah Hughes   May 19th Day, 1815.
Aaron Teal, Senr

Children Bin Baptized.

Lot Buck, sun of Th Buck.

Thomas Stites, sun of T. Hand.

Elizabeth Edmunds, Dautor of T. Hand.

Elizabeth Parsons. The above was baptized by the Rev. Mr Reeves.

[P. 45]   Thursday, August 24th 1815.   The Session met agreeably to appointment at the house of Daniel Crowell and constituted with prayer by George W. Janvier, Pastor of the church in Pitts Grove, who being appointed to supply the church here on the ensuing Sabbath moderated the meeting of session.

Thomas Ross, Jonathan Crawford & Aaron Shaw, applied for admission into the full communion of the church & the two last for Baptism.   And on Saturday Aug 26th 1815, the said Jonathan Crawford & Aaron Shaw were upon profession of the Faith baptized by the said George W. Janvier, after devine service.   At the same time the following children were baptized, Viz;

[P. 46]   Jonathan, William and Elizabeth the three infant children of Jonathan Crawford above named and Hannah his wife.   Also John Schellinger infant child of John Schellinger and Catharine his wife.

[P. 47]   The sessional Records.

John Howland, the Pilgrim

The general history of the men who founded Plymouth Colony in New England begins with the events described in Bradford's manuscript History of Plymouth Plantation, pages 11 to 14, ending with the words, "Seeing they could no longer continue in yt condition they resolved to get over into Holland as they could which was in ye year 1607 & 1608." The sufferings of the Pilgrims in England is a part of general history which it is not the purpose of this introduction to discuss. The general history of the colony comes to an end with the last meeting of the Board of Assistants, April 15, 1692. From this time Plymouth is merged with Massachusetts Bay and ceases to exist as an independent colony.

The word "Pilgrim" is often used to include the early settlers who came to Plymouth in the three ships, the Mayflower, 1620, the Fortune, 1621, and the Ann, 1623. The word is here limited to those men, women and children who came in the Mayflower in 1620. The high resolution of the colony of Separatists from the Church of England to leave Holland and seek a home for themselves and their children in the New World made them pilgrims from that time.

The history of the Pilgrim Fathers properly begins early in 1620 with the visit to the band of Separatists at Leyden of Mr. Thomas Weston, of London, who offered to furnish funds for the proposed migration to the New World. Mr. Weston associated with him some seventy merchants who, as a matter of speculation, offered to take stock at ten pounds per share for the purpose of promoting the enterprise. (Bradford's Manuscript, page 54.) This offer made the migration possible.

The account of the life at Scrooby, the escape to Amsterdam and the removal to Leyden, is preliminary to the great drama whose epic period is the subject of this short outline. Briefly, the introductory facts are as follows: In 1607 a large

THE MAYFLOWER AT ANCHOR, 1620

ship was hired by members of the congregation at Scrooby, which was to take a portion of the company to Holland. They embarked during the night, but in spite of caution, were forced to return, and their leaders were imprisoned. (Bradford, pages 16, 17.) In the spring of 1608 another attempt was made; Bradford and a few others landed at Flushing at this time. By August, 1608, the whole company were in Amsterdam. After about a year, according to Bradford (nine months, actually), one hundred removed to Leyden, "A fair & bewtifull citie and of sweete situation, but made more famous by ye Universitie."

Their pastor, John Robinson, was honored by the University, and the congregation grew to "not much fewer than three hundred communicants." (Young's Chronicles; but Goodwin, in The Pilgrim Republic, page 35, where Young is quoted, places the number at not less than five hundred.) It is remarkable that neither Bradford, Mourt or other manuscripts mention the exact place of residence in England. That this was Scrooby was the discovery of the Rev. Joseph Hunter, whose work, "The Founders of New Plymouth," was published in 1849.

The Pilgrims did not leave Holland because of persecution or disability, civil or religious. Under the wise policy of Prince Maurice, civil and religious liberty was granted all, and the salaries of the clergy of all religions were paid in part by the state, with the exception of the Separatists, whom the Dutch ignored out of deference to the King of England, while personally respecting and honoring them. (Bradford, page 26; Goodwin. page 34.)

The agreement between the Merchant Adventurers and the expectant Pilgrims was signed July 1, O. S., 1620, and was on the basis of an equal division of the colony's possessions at the end of seven years between the Adventurers and the colonists. This included all the property of the colonists, houses and garden plots, and the hardness of the terms imposed was immediately a cause of controversy. As a matter of fact, this division was never made; in 1627 the colonists bought out the Adventurers. (Bradford, pages 56, 57, 75.)

On or near the last day of July, the younger and stronger of the congregation left Leyden for Delft-Haven, the place of embarkation. Robinson's famous sermon on the text, Ezra 8: 21, was preached at this time: "And there at the river by Ahava I proclaimed a fast, that we might humble ourselves before our God, and seek of him a right way for us, and for all our children, and all our substance." So affecting was the scene of the parting of old and young, of husbands and wives, that the people of Delft-Haven held it in memory twenty-five years later. (Goodwin, page 59.)

"So they lefte yt goodly & pleasante citie which had been ther resting place near 12 years; but they knew they pilgrims & looked not much on those things, but lift up their eyes to ye heavens, their dearest cuntrie and quieted their spirits."

The next morning the colonists embarked on the Speedwell, a ship of sixty tons burden, and proceeded to Southampton. Here Weston, representing the Adventurers, declined to make further advances, alleging that the Pilgrims had broken their agreement in insisting upon the right to retain their houses and garden plots at the division, and to have a part of the working days of the week for their own improvement. This was a part of the original contract which, without the consent of the Pilgrims, had been modified by their agent, Thomas Cushman. They remained at Southampton one week for the purpose of securing the necessary stores, but, Weston having failed them, it was necessary to sell provisions brought from Holland to obtain money for port dues. On August 15, the emigrants proceeded in two ships, the Speedwell and the Mayflower, the latter of one hundred and eighty tons burden. When four days out of port, the Speedwell began to leak, and it was decided that the two ships should put in at Dartmouth, where sixteen days were spent in making repairs.

Again the voyage was begun, but when three hundred miles beyond Lands End, the Speedwell showed such signs of unseaworthiness that the passengers were compelled to abandon hope of continuing the voyage with her, and both ships returned to harbor at Plymouth—the exact date is not known. The Speedwell returned to her owners at London, carrying with her eighteen of her thirty passengers, who now abandoned the undertaking, through fear or discontent, among them Robert Cushman. The twelve remaining were added to the ninety of the Mayflower list, making the total number one hundred and two at the time of sailing. The final departure of the Mayflower was on September 16, O. S. The ship came to anchor at Cape Cod sixty-seven days after the final embarking at Plymouth, ninety-nine days after leaving Southhampton, one hundred and thirty-three days after leaving Delft-Haven, and it was many months before the last of the passengers were released from the ship.

A great storm beset the ship in the middle of the ocean, and it is at this time that the chronicler of the voyage, William Bradford, afterward governor of the colony, makes the first mention of John Howland the Pilgrim:—

"After they had injoyed faire winds and weather for a season, they were incountred many times with crosse winds, and mette with many feirce stormes, with which ye shipe was shroudly shaken, and her upper works made very leakie; and one of the maine beames in ye mid ships was bowed & craked, which put them in some fear that ye shipe could not be able to perform ye vioage. So some of ye cheefe of ye company, perceiveing ye mariners to feare ye suffisiencie of ye shipe, as it appeared by their mutterings, they entred into serious consultation with ye mr. & other officers of ye ship, to consider in time of ye danger; and rather to returne then to cast them selves into a desperate & inevitable perill. And truly ther was great distraction & differance of opinion amongst ye mariners them selves; faine would they doe what could be done for their wages sake, (being now half the seas over), and on ye other hand they were loath to hazard their lives too desperately. But in examening of all opinions, the mr. & others affirmed they knew ye ship to be stronge & firme under water; and for the buckling of ye maine beame, ther 'was a great iron scrue ye passengers brought out of Holland, which would raise ye beame into his place; ye which being done, the carpenter & mr. affirmed that with a post put under it, set firme in ye lower deck, & otherways bounde, he would make it sufficiente. And as for ye decks & uper workes they would calke them as well as they could, and though with ye workeing of ye ship they would not longe keep stanch, yet ther would otherwise be in no great danger, if they did not overpress her with sails. So they comited them selves to ye will of God, & resolved to proseede.

In sundrie of these stormes the winds were so feirce, & ye seas so high, as they could not beare a knote of saile, but were forced to hull, for divorce days togither. And in one of them, as they thus lay at hull, in a mighty storme, a lustie yonge man (called John Howland) coming upon some occasion above ye grat-tings, was, with a seele of ye shipe throwne into ye sea; but it pleased God yt he caught hould of ye top-saile halliards, which hunge over board, & rane out at length; yet he held his hould (though he was sundrie fadomes under water) till he was hald up by ye same rope to ye brime of ye water, and then with a boat hooke & other means got into ye shipe againe, & his life saved; and though he was something ill with it, yet he lived many years after, and became a probtable member both in church & commone wealthe."

This is the first mention in history of the Pilgrim John Howland.

The Number and Character of the Mayflower Passengers

The number of passengers is variously given—one hundred, one hundred and one, one hundred and two. In computing the number who are entitled to be enrolled in the list of Mayflower passengers, it must be remembered that five of those who sailed on the Mayflower did not land at Plymouth, and two landed at Plymouth who did not sail in the Mayflower. The ages of the passengers, as far as known, and the dates of death have been collected from records, deeds, wills, depositions and other documents, and are given in Goodwin, page 183. It was a migration of families—men, women and children—and not a mere fishing expedition or commercial undertaking, as some have attempted to show. (Note, quoting error of Hutchinson in Young, page 81.) Jones, captain of the ship, and the crew were no part of the Pilgrim band; but two seamen, under contract to remain a year, were included in the number of colonists. Of the total number, eighteen were women; nine were servants, probably minors; thirty-three were children, of whom twenty-two were boys and eleven girls. Two dogs—a spaniel and a mastiff—were brought over in the ship. For genealogical qualifications, William Butten, who died on the voyage; Oceanus Hopkins, who was born on the voyage; Peregrine White, who was born while the ship lay at anchor at Cape Cod; as well as the two seamen, who were considered by the Pilgrims a part of the colony (Bradford, page 534), must be included in the list of Mayflower passengers.

Prince, in his New England Chronology, makes the mistake of excluding the two seamen, while rightly retaining the names of William Butten and Oceanus Hopkins, thus making the number one hundred and one. Young says the servant of

William White, who died at Cape Cod before the ship came into Plymouth Harbor, should be excluded, making the number one hundred (page 122, where quotation from Prince is given in note). This further error is repeated by Russell in Pilgrim Memorials, page 43, and is widely copied in popular histories.

All of the histories, including Bradford's list, omit the name of Peregrine White, yet the child of Pilgrim parents, born on the Mayflower, is surely entitled to be included in the Pilgrim band. Furthermore, the two seamen who undertook the hardships of the first year, as well as the unfortunate servant of William White, are in the number of those "who for an undefiled conscience and the love of pure Christianity, first left their native and pleasant Land and encountered the Toils and Hazzards of the tumultuous Ocean." (Prince.) The exact number of the Pilgrims is, therefore, one hundred and four, and the full list of names is given in Pilgrim Notes and Queries, a publication of the Massachusetts Society of Mayflower Descendants. It is interesting to note that of the whole number of one hundred and four, only fifty are known to have left descendants.

The high character of the Pilgrims is shown by their ability to attract to their number men of the type of Standish, who was not a member of the congregation. and the aristocratic Winslow. During the sojourn at Leyden, the townsmen gave them credit freely and were never defrauded. Their peaceful, upright life was publicly acknowledged by the magistrates of the city. They lived after the pattern of the early church, and the Communion was celebrated each Sabbath. (Bradford, pages 26, 27 and 194—in answer to objections to Pilgrims.)

Manuscripts and Sources of Pilgrim History for the First Two Years and Preceding Events

(1) First of all in importance is Bradford's Manuscript History of Plymouth Plantation, sometimes called "The Log of the Mayflower."

The autographic manuscript, the most precious historical document in the United States, is in the Massachusetts State Library at Boston, and with proper care may be seen by the historical investigator. The famous manuscript is a folio 7½ inches by 12, backed with parchment. In scope, the history extends from 1602 to 1646, with a list of Mayflower passengers at the end, under the date 1650.

Prince, in his New England Chronology, thus describes the manuscript: "The manuscripts I have opportunity to search (1736)—In folio, Gov. Bradford's History of Plimouth People and Colony from 1602 to 1646, in 270 pages, with some account of the Increase of those who came over with Him, from 1620 to 1650, and all in his own handwriting." Preface to Chronology, Vol. I, vi, Boston, 1736. (Copy in library of author of this volume.)

Governor Hutchinson also used the manuscript in the preparation of the second volume of his history, 1657. From that time the manuscript disappeared; no trace of it was left behind, and after nearly a century, to the despair of investigators, the mystery was as great as ever. In 1855, a lover of antiquities, John Wingate Thornton, while lounging in a London book-shop, chanced to pick up a book by Wilberforce, Bishop of Oxford, published in 1844, entitled, History of the Episcopal Church in America. On page 56 he found a reference to a "Ms. History of the Plantation of Plymouth,—in Fulham Library." Thus the long-lost manuscript was recovered and identified from the description of Prince. The stu-

73

dent of Pilgrim history must begin by mastering this manuscript—a task of some years. A working copy has been issued by the State of Massachusetts (1898), and the references in this introduction are to this official copy. On a flyleaf there is written by the grandson of the Governor:

"This book was rit by govener William Bradford and given to his son mager (major) William Bradford and by him to his son mager John Bradford. rit by me Samuel bradford, mach 20, 1705."

The great struggle of the early colonists was not against Indians, famine or "muskeetos" (Bradford, 196), but against illiteracy. The Bradford of 1705 was inferior in education to the Bradford of 1620.

(2) Mourt's Relation, including:

(*a*) A daily journal of Governor Bradford extending from November 20, 1620, to April 2, 1621.

(*b*) Four narratives of Winslow, detailing chief events of the colony to the return of the Fortune, December 21, 1621 This ship carried the manuscript to England, where it was published in 1622. From the signature in the preface, "G. Mourt" (probably George Morton), the publication took its name.

(3) Winslow's Brief Narration, containing Robinson's Farewell Address to the Pilgrims, printed in London, 1646.

These documents, Mourt's Relation and Winslow's Brief Narration, are included in Dr. Young's Chronicles of the Pilgrims, 1844. The references are to this collection. Thus, Mourt, page 209, refers to page 209 in Young's Chronicles.

(4) Plymouth Colony Records, printed by the State of Massachusetts.

(5) Bradford's Letter Book, a fragment of a collection of letters pertaining to the early days of the colony. This complete collection was at one time in the possession of Prince. Lost at the time of the Revolution (probably), a fragment was found in a grocer's shop in Halifax, N. S., in 1793. The text used here is that of the Massachusetts His-

torical Society Collections, Vol. III, 1794, pages 27 to 76, the whole reprinted by the Massachusetts Society of Mayflower Descendants, 1906.

(6) Founders of New Plymouth, by Rev. Joseph Hunter, 1849. This work identifies the place of residence of the Pilgrims in England.

(7) Pilgrim Memorials and Guide to Plymouth, Russell, 1855 (containing errors as to the number of Mayflower passengers).

(8) History of Plymouth, Thacher, 2nd edition, 1835, (containing errors as to the ancestry of John Howland).

(9) Goodwin's Pilgrim Republic. This is the most complete work on the subject to the date of the death of the author, 1884 (published 1888). The fact that Goodwin admits that he has found nothing new makes him absolutely reliable. He was of Pilgrim stock, and had access to all the sources.

(10) The publication of the Massachusetts Society of Mayflower Descendants, edited by G. E. Bowman. Here new matter has been found, and the editor is the greatest authority on the subject of Pilgrim history and genealogy. The twenty volumes of the publication, The Pilgrim Descendant, have been used in preparing this introduction. Pilgrim Notes and Queries is an additional publication of this society.

Cape Cod and Plymouth

The Mayflower came to anchor at what is now called Provincetown, Cape Cod, on Saturday, November 21 (11, O. S.), 1620. On the next day the Sabbath was observed on the ship, and on Monday the life in the New World began. Some, in their eagerness to land, jumped from the landing boat into the shallow surf, and contracted coughs and colds, laying the foundation for the severe mortality of the following winter. On Saturday preceding, the Compact had been signed, forming the Pilgrim band into a body politic, with authority to make and execute laws. That this coast was not the intended destination of the colonists, and the legal significance of the compact, are matters of general history, too lengthy to be discussed here. John Carver, who had been appointed governor of the ship, continued, by election, in that office.

Immediately an exploring expedition was organized, and now appears for the first time one of the most famous of the Pilgrim band, Captain Myles Standish. That, having a commission under Elizabeth, he had served in Flanders, and was of distinguished family, so much we know, but how he became associated with the Pilgrims is unknown. He was not, and never was, a member of the Pilgrim church. (Young, page 125, note.) Under the command of Standish, with Bradford, Stephen Hopkins and Edward Tilley, brother of John Tilley, as advisers, the exploring party set out on Wednesday, November 25. When they had proceeded along the shore a mile, they saw five or six Indians with a dog. Seeing the party, the Indians whistled the dog after them, and ran away. The explorers followed ten miles, without overtaking them, but the next day made a discovery which saved the life of the colony, namely, a cellar of Indian corn. The ethical question in-

76

MONUMENT TO CAPTAIN MYLES STANDISH, CAPTAIN'S
HILL, DUXBERRY, MASS.

By permission of A. S. Burbank, Plymouth

volved in appropriating a part of the corn will be referred to later. A number of Indian graves were also found.

On the return the next day, Bradford became entangled in a deer trap baited with acorns. The identification of the trap by Hopkins, and his knowledge of Indian skill, confirms the belief that he had been in this part of the world before. (Goodwin, pages 76, 435.) Thomas Snell Hopkins, Esq., governor general of the Society of Mayflower Descendants, said to the author: "Hopkins was an all-round adventurer." He was a lay minister of the Church of England; a leader of insurrection; a member of Governor Bradford's Council; a trusted ambassador to Massasoit; a tavern-keeper who more than once was fined, as shown by the colony records.

Ten days later, a large boat called the shallop had been put together, and in company with the ship's long boat, began the second exploring expedition under the command of Jones, the captain of the ship, with nine sailors. A cold, blustering snowstorm compelled them to put in at East Harbor and wade ashore in the freezing weather. "Some of our people that are dead took the original of their death here." (Mourt.)

The following day, Tuesday, December 8, the party rejoined the shallop and sailed to the mouth of a supposed river, which they named Cold Harbor. Landing here, the party proceeded along the shore, the shallop following. (The vagueness of Bradford in writing here, "4 or 5 miles," is especially illustrated in the list of Mayflower passengers given at the end of his manuscript, page 534: "These being about a hundred sowls, came over in the first ship." He did not take the pains to add up his own figures.)

For supper that night they had three fat geese and six ducks, which they ate with "soldiers' stomachs." The next day they revisited the corn cellar, now covered with snow and ice, and Bradford notes the "spetiall providence of God and great mercie to this poore people," that the corn was discovered before the fall of snow. (Bradford, 100.)

77

Those who were sick from exposure were now sent back in the shallop. The remaining members, eighteen in number, made an interesting discovery the next day. A grave, covered by a board carved and painted with three tynes like a crown, containing the body of a blond-haired man and the bones of a little child, a little bow and child's trinkets. The wreck of a French ship on this coast four years before, and the probable marriage of a European and a native, seem to explain this grave. (Bradford, 119.)

After finding an Indian village, the party returned to the ship. The question was now discussed as to whether they should settle here or make further explorations. It was necessary to make haste, as disease had broken out in the narrow quarters of the ship; Edward Thompson, servant of William White, had died, and the orphan boy Jasper Moore, adopted by the Pilgrims, was dying. The question of the future site of the colony was settled by Robert Coppin, pilot of the Mayflower, who said that there was a good harbor and a navigable river on the other headland, and that he had been there.

The third exploring party set out in the shallop late in the afternoon of Wednesday, December 16. The party was composed of eighteen men, and the names are given by Mourt: Captain Myles Standish, Governor Carver, William Bradford, Edward Winslow, John Tilley, Edward Tilley and John Howland, all from the Leyden congregation, the following from those who joined the emigrants in England: Richard Warren, Stephen Hopkins, Edward Doty. John Allerton and Thomas English, seamen of the Pilgrims, accompanied them, and Jones sent six of his men, including Clark, the mate, Coppin, the pilot, and the master-gunner of the Mayflower. This is the second time the name of John Howland appears.

It was such freezing weather that the spray froze on their garments, making them like coats of iron. Edward Tilley, brother of John, became insensible from cold; the master-gunner was sick unto death (neither survived the winter). The shallop put in at the place afterward known as

First Encounter, on the interior side where the arm of the Cape begins to widen out. Here they saw ten or twelve Indians busy over the carcass of a grampus which had washed up on the shore. That night, as they were encamped, they saw the fires of Indian camps. Thursday, December 17, the bay and adjoining land were explored, and graves and corn fields discovered. Their rest that night was disturbed by great cries, which at the time they supposed to be wolves.

Friday, December 18, was a memorable day in Pilgrim history. The party rose at 5, beginning the day with the accustomed prayer. Some, fearing no danger, carried their arms down to the boat, but at breakfast the strange cry of the night was heard again, and the men ran to recover their arms. Then occurred the First Encounter with the Indians, in which no one was killed, and the Indians ran away, badly frightened. Some of the arrows shot by the Indians were tipped with eagles' claws, some with deers' horn, and some with brass. Bradford relates, as an incident of the affray, that a certain lusty Indian was wounded by one of the Pilgrims. Edward Johnson, in his Wonder-working Providence (London, 1624), says that "the lustie man" was the stoutest sachem of the Indians, and that Standish struck the sachem's right arm with a shot from his fowling piece. (Young, 158, note.) There is no authority for this statement, and it is an illustration of the mythological element which early appears in Pilgrim history. They now set sail for the good harbor, which Coppin assured them they would reach before night, "of which they were glad, for it begane to be foule weather," and by afternoon a heavy storm of snow and rain settled upon them; the rudder was broken by the force of the waves, and two men had difficulty in steering with a "cupple of oares." As the night drew on, Pilot Coppin bade them be of good cheer, for he saw the harbor. The storm increasing, the mast fell down, broken in three pieces, but having the flood tide with them, they rowed by the point, called the Gurnet, at the entrance to Plymouth Harbor. As they rounded the point, Pilot Coppin exclaimed: "Ye Lord be mercifull unto us, for my eyes never saw yt place before." With difficulty, as it became dark, they rowed along the stretch between the Gurnet and Saquish, coming to safe anchorage between the latter point and Clark's Island, where later, as it grew colder, the whole company spent the night around the watch fire.

Saturday, December 19, was a "faire sunshining day," and as the equipment was wet, the day was spent in drying and putting it in order. "And this being the last day of ye weeke they prepared to keepe ye Sabbath." (Bradford.) "On the Sabbth day we rested." (Mourt.)

Monday (Forefathers' Day) was the date of the landing on Plymouth Rock, yet no account of the exact place and manner of landing is given in the original manuscripts. The words of Bradford and Mourt are the same, Bradford in the third person, Mourt in the first.

"On Munday they sounded ye harbor, and founde it fitt for shipping; and marched into ye land, & found diverse cornfeilds, & litle runing brooks, a place (as they supposed) fitt for situation; at least it was ye best they could find, and ye season, & their presente necessitie, made them glad to accepte of it. So they returned to their shipp againe with this news to ye rest of their people. which did much comforte their harts."

To Elder Faunce, the third and last of the ruling elders, we owe the identification of the famous rock as the landing place of the Pilgrims. It must be understood that the popular belief that the passengers landed directly from the ship on the rock is mistaken; there was no general landing of the passengers in a body. The Mayflower never came nearer than one and one-half miles of the rock, and the landing was made in the shallop, or the ship's boat. Only eighteen in all landed on the rock on Forefathers' Day, and the names are given in Mourt. (See ante, page 78). Elder Faunce was born in 1646, and was ten years old when Standish died, eleven when Bradford died, forty-one when Alden died, fifty-three when Mary Allerton died, in 1699, at the age of ninety. John Soule and Priscilla Mullins were still living when he was approaching early manhood. In 1741, four years before his death at the age of ninety-nine, hearing that a wharf was to be built over the rock, Elder Faunce visited the landing place for the last time, and in the presence of many hearers declared that to his certain knowledge this was the rock on which the Pilgrims landed. (Russell, page 31.)

Five days later the Mayflower came to anchor in the harbor.

THE REMAINDER OF THE YEAR 1620.

From November 21, the date of the landing on the rock, the time was spent in making explorations of the new country, and on December 30, urged on by the increasing sickness, it was decided by common vote to settle at the "first place." On Monday following the work of the settlement was under way, and Mourt takes pains to tell us that, though it was Christmas Day by the old reckoning, "no man rested that day." Bradford says: "And ye 25 began to erecte ye first house for common use and to receive them and their goods." The workmen returned to the ship at night, and it was many days before the little village was ready for the families of the infant colony. Not only was there no general landing of men, women and children, as represented in popular pictures, but some died on the ship, among others William Mullins, father of Priscilla, who afterward married John Alden, and this fact, established by the recent discovery of Mr. Mullin's will, is an important contribution to our knowledge of Pilgrim history. (Mayflower Descendants, 1916, Vol. 1, page 13.)

On the first page of the Colony Records a plan of the settlement, with the explanation, "The meersteads & garden plotes of those which came first layd out 1620", gives us an idea of the location and form of the village. Seven houses only are indicated on this plan, and it is possible that the loss by death was so great that the families into which the colony was divided were, for a time, crowded into these buildings, little more than one-story huts.

From now on to the end of the year (March 24, O. S.) the history of the settlement is a record of sickness and death, with exploring parties intervening. January 11, Degory Priest, died; January 18, Mr. Cristopher Martin, treasurer of the ship, died; February 9, Rose, wife of Myles Standish, died; March 5, Mr. William White, Mr. William Mullins, "with two more," died; "March 5, dies Mary, the wife of Mr. Isaac Allerton." Two—Dorothy, wife of Bradford, and James Chilton—had died at the Cape, in addition to those already mentioned. "This month 17 of our number died."

With distressing lack of particularity, Bradford tells us that in two or three months half of the company died, through exposure and "scurvie," so that "ther died sometimes 2 or 3 of a day." So severe was the infection that at the time of greatest distress but six or seven sound persons were left to care for the sick, of whom Standish and Elder Brewster are honorably mentioned by both Bradford and Mourt.

The first building completed was the Common House, a structure twenty feet square, in which religious services were held Sunday, January 31. Saturday, February 17, Standish was elected captain, with authority of command, a step hastened by the appearance of Indians, on one occasion twelve in number.

The winter on the whole was mild, and the great mortality was due to lack of proper food rather than to extreme cold. Monday, January 8, was a fair day, and during the week Bradford worked out of doors without discomfort. The next week began with rain, but Tuesday, Wednesday and Thursday were bright and mild "as it had been April." A week later it was fair (but cold and frosty weather in the middle of February). On March 3 the wind was south, and toward noon it was warm and fair, and the birds sang in the woods most pleasantly. In the afternoon it thundered. (Mourt, 181.)

The First Communication With the Indians

On March 26, "a fair warm day," the Pilgrims were astonished at the appearance of a naked Indian, who fearlessly walked down the street of the new village, and addressed the colonists in broken English, one word being unmistakable in its import, "Welcome." The "Welcome Englishmen" of the text books is an amplification of history, and without authority. The story of Samoset, the sachem who had learned English from fishermen on the Maine coast, and the subsequent visit of Massasoit, Grand Sachem of the Pokanoket Confederacy, is narrated in all works on American history. There are three overlooked facts in this first friendly contact of the colonists and the Indians which throw sidelights upon the Pilgrims and their character.

(1) Samoset appears abruptly in Pilgrim history, and after eight days as abruptly disappears, yet his service to the colonists as the peaceful intermediary between them and the Sachem Massasoit was of incalculable value. He was, nevertheless, a troublesome visitor, fond of eating and strong drink, and when the night of March 26 came, his entertainers were in a quandary as to the disposal of their guest, in whom they did not have full confidence. An attempt was made to row out to the ship with him, but the roughness of the sea made this impossible. Finally, he was foisted upon the hopitality of Stephen Hopkins. This is further evidence that Hopkins had previous experience with the Indians. (See ante, page 77.)

(2) Samoset brought to the colonists an Indian, Tisquantum, who henceforth becomes their adviser and spends the two remaining years of his life with them, hoping as he dies to go to the white man's heaven. He was the sole surviving member of the Patuxets that formerly inhabited the territory of Plymouth, and had been enticed on shipboard by Captain Hunt, 1614, who intended to sell him with divers

others into slavery. (Bradford, 116.) Somehow he "got away for England, and was entertained by a marchant in London—& lastly brought hither to into these parts by one Mr. Dermer." The great plague of 1617-18 had swept away his tribe, and he readily joined the white men whom he found, after six years, occupying the territory of his race. He who most of all might object to the presence of the Pilgrims became their friend from the first.

(3) The legal significance of the famous treaty between Massasoit and the Pilgrims cannot be discussed here. The important fact for us to note is that the treaty was not forced upon the Indians, but was a willing alliance made by Massasoit to assure the assistance of the colonists for himself and his tribes, decimated by the plague, under him, against the Narragansetts, his powerful and dangerous neighbors. (Bradford, 123-4.)

The first year of Pilgrim history ends with the re-election of Governor Carver on March 23, O. S. Here the first division of Mourt's Relations, written by Governor Bradford, ends. The remainder of this important collection of documents is the work of Winslow. On the very last day of the year, Mrs. Winslow died—the year ending by Old Style reckoning on March 24th.

THE SECOND YEAR.

Winslow's Relations, contained in Mourt down to December 21, 1621, and Bradford, are our authorities for this period, "yet many historians neglect their writings, and by relying on Morton, Hubbard, Baylies, Bancroft, the second Freeman, and so on, are led into many errors of detail, and the setting forth of an amount of false history that is amazing." (Goodwin, 127.)

Cushman's Discourse in Young and one letter in Bradford's Letter Book, are documents to be read in connection with this year.

The Mayflower sailed out of Plymouth Harbor April 5, O. S., and reached England in thirty-one days. In spite of sickness and hardship, no one of the colonists accepted the opportunity to return.

"The spring now approaching, it pleased God the mortalitie begane to cease amongst them, and ye sick and lame recovered apace, which put as it were new life into them; though they had borne their sadd affliction with much patience and contedness, as I thinke any people could doe." (Bradford, 119.)

After the departure of the ship, with the aid of Tisquantum, who showed them the use of fish as a fertilizer, twenty acres of corn were planted. Governor Carver, being taken suddenly ill as he was working in the fields, died shortly after, and Bradford was elected governor, in which office he continued, with the exception of five years, until his death thirty-five years later.

We now come to the important embassy of Winslow and Hopkins to Massasoit in the early summer. The purpose of the visit was to strengthen the alliance between the colonists and the Indians, to pay for the corn taken at the Cape, and furthermore, the Pilgrims had the prudence to wish to know more of their ally, his strength and influence. The two Pilgrims, with Tisquantum as guide, set out on Tuesday, July 3. ('Goodwin, 163, for date, the Mss. do not agree.) The first resting place was Nemasket, now Middleborough, a distance of fifteen miles, where they were cordially entertained by the natives. Proceeding, the night was spent at the present village of Titicut, four or five miles further on. The next afternoon they arrived at Massasoit's principal seat, Sowams, the present Warren, Rhode Island, a distance of forty miles from Plymouth.

The ambassadors saluted the great chief with the discharge of their muskets, and having been received by him, declared the purpose of their visit. Massasoit was requested to find the owner of the corn taken from the cellar in the

Cape, and to make known the wish of the Pilgrims to make payment. An exchange of seed corn was also arranged, and an agreement to open up trade in skins.

The Sachem arrayed himself in the red coat and copper chain and medal brought by the Pilgrims as presents, "and was not a little proud to see himself so bravely attired." The Sachem having just returned from a journey, there was no food in the larder, and as Winslow and Hopkins had generously given their stock to importunate natives, the problem of supper became pressing. Neither the Chief nor his retainers regarded this requirement of hospitality, and they slept supperless that night on the Sachem's own bed of planks, a foot above the ground, with a mat upon them. The royal bed was also occupied by Massasoit, his wife, and two of the chief men who pressed in upon them, "So that we were worse weary of our lodging than of our journey." (Mourt, 210.)

Thursday there were games and shooting exhibitions, but no breakfast or dinner, until at one o'clock, Massasoit himself shot with bow and arrow two fish, and of the forty who partook of this meal, not the least hungry were the two Pilgrims, and this was the only meal they had for two nights and a day, save a partridge which they bought. The proper title of Massasoit and his son, the famous or infamous Philip, is Grand Sachem, the appellation "king" given to the verminous Massasoit is a magnifying of titles.

After another night of discomfort, the Chief pressed them to continue their stay, but the two Pilgrims declined, fearing that the mosquitoes without and the more domesticated insects within would so wear them out that they "should not be able to recover home for want of strength." Furthermore, they wished to keep the Sabbath at Plymouth.

On Friday the messengers took leave, spending the night again at Tuticut, and on Saturday reached Plymouth by night, "though wet, weary and surbated" (footsore).

The owner of the corn was finally discovered, during an expedition in search of a son of John Billington, who had become lost in the Cape woods. The boy had been well treated by the Indians with whom he had taken refuge. Full payment was made for the corn taken by the Pilgrims, to the satisfaction of the Pilgrim conscience and the claims of the owner.

Hobomok, one of Massasoit's chief counsellors, now joins the colonists and continues to serve them, until at an advanced age he dies at Duxbury, at the home of Standish, cared for in his last days by the Captain, who was kindly as well as valiant.

A report that Tisquantum had been killed by a suspected chief, Corbitant, led to another expedition to Middleborough, and although the report was not true, the severe threat of the Pilgrims that any misconduct on his part would be followed by the overthrow of Corbitant and his followers so impressed the natives that nine sachems signed a document declaring themselves to be loyal subjects of the King of England. (Names given in Morton's Memorials quoted by Young, 232.)

September 28, an expedition in the shallop set out to explore the neighborhood of Boston, and establish trade with the Indians. A considerable stock of beaver skins was secured, and the trade in this commodity became the foundation of the wealth of the colony, a pound of beaver skin being worth in London a pound sterling. (Goodwin, 178, note.)

On November 20, just one year after the Mayflower sighted land at Cape Cod, the ship Fortune arrived with thirty-five new colonists, and in their number, Robert Cushman, who came on behalf of the Adventurers. The new colonists had been two months on the ocean and had been detained in the English Channel two more by adverse winds. They brought little food with them, and the added burden made futile the happy anticipation of Thanksgiving Day, celebrated at the return of the harvest.

Of the one hundred and four who are entitled to be enrolled in the list of Mayflower passengers, fifty were now living. The total number of the inhabitants of Plymouth was therefore eighty-five Europeans and two native Indians.

We have seen that John Howland is first mentioned on the voyage across the Atlantic and that he was a member of the volunteer party who made the third exploring expedition, ending with the landing on Plymouth Rock on Forefathers' Day.

"The 'lustie young man' whom the Mayflower's people fished out of the sea with a boat-hook soon became a leader. He was an assistant in 1633-4-5, and so late as 1670 served his seventeenth year as deputy from Plymouth. He is credited with a military turn, and at the Hocking affair showed himself a chivalrous commander. As in the height of the Quaker troubles he was dropped from the General Court, there is reason to think that he, like the other Howlands, was found too liberal for the times. Yet his high standing in their church was shown at Cotton's ordination in 1669, when four visiting clergy conducted the exercises and Elder Cushman preached, while the church members appointed Howland as their proxy to join in the laying-on of hands."

"This old Pilgrim died March 5, 1673 (N. S.), at the age of eighty. Two days later he was buried 'with honor,' says the record, which adds that he was 'a godly man' who had proved 'a useful instrument of good in his place.' The graves of his posterity forming a clue to his own, a stone was erected there half a century ago (1888) by his great-great-grandson, John Howland, a soldier of the Revolution, and long the honored president of the Rhode Island Historical Society. Unfortunately, the good man was led by tradition into the misstatement that the Pilgrim's wife was Governor Carver's daughter. It will be remembered that she was the child of John and Bridget Tilley, and was left an orphan when she was fourteen years old, which was thirteen years

THE HOWLAND HOUSE, PLYMOUTH, MASS., built 1667
By permission of A. S. Burbank, Plymouth

less than Howland's age. She was married before the land-division of 1624, and her son John was born February 24, 1626 (N. S.). She survived her husband, and spent the last of her days with her children, James and Lydia Brown, of Swansea, where she was buried in 1687. Howland was the last signer of the 'Compact' who remained at Plymouth; but at Duxbury, Soule and Alden both survived. * * * The descendants of the Pilgrim pair are many, and not a few of them honorably bear the family name. It has been fondly supposed that they generally show in an usual degree certain genial traits of character which are a legacy from the May-flower. At all events they are sure that their stalwart an-cestor was brave, honorable, cheerful, and godly.'' (Good-win's Pilgrim Republic, page 507.)

The circumstances of the ''Hocking affair,'' in which John Howland played an honorable part, are as follows:

In 1630 the Council for New England sent over a new patent of the Pilgrim territory, defining the grant as practi-cally co-extensive with the present counties of Plymouth, Barnstable and Bristol, with a tract of land for trade on the Kennebec River, reaching from the present city of Augusta, thirteen miles down the stream, and extending fifteen miles each side of the river. This patent, in the name of Bradford, known as the ''Warwick Patent,'' is still in the Registry of Deeds at Plymouth. Governor Bradford surrendered the Warwick Patent to the freemen of Plymouth Colony in 1640.

As the spring trade opened in 1634, John Hocking, of Piscataqua, agent for Lords Say and Brook, came into the river and attempted to interrupt the trade of the Pilgrims at this post. John Howland, who was in charge of the business of the territory, directed Hocking to remain outside the limits of the Pilgrim Colony, declaring his intrusion a trespass upon rights which were secured to Plymouth by a formal patent under seal. Hocking refused to acknowledge the Pilgrim claim, and proceeded to interrupt the trade of the post, al-though twice visited by Howland, with renewed entreaties to regard the rights of the colony. Howland, as commander of the post, made a further attempt to persuade the intruder to withdraw, the attempt drawing further abuse and defiance from Hocking. A canoe was then sent out to cut the cable of the intruding craft, which was accomplished by Moses Talbot, one of Howland's men. As the craft began to drift down stream, Hocking, aiming a carbine at Talbot, was hailed by Howland, who demanded that his man should not be hurt, as he had only obeyed orders, and that if anyone was to be shot, it was himself, adding that he would make an excellent mark. Unfortunately, Howland's gallantry did not save his employee, who was shot through the head, and in turn Hocking was killed by one of Talbot's friends, "that loved him well." The whole affair and its sequel is a painful episode in early colonial history, resulting in the arrest and imprisonment at Boston of John Alden, who was present, but took no part in the matter, and Myles Standish, as a member of the Plymouth government, was put under bonds, upon his appearance at Boston on Alden's behalf. Delegates from the plantations, including the clergy, after reviewing the case, formally and fully exonerated the Plymouth men and declared that Hocking alone had been to blame.

The record of the will of the Pilgrim Howland as exhibited to the court held at Plymouth March 5, 1763, is as follows:

The Last Will and testament of Mr. John Howland of Plymouth late deceased exhibited to the Court held att Plymouth the fifth day of March Anno: Dom. 1672 on the oath of Mr. Samuel Fuller and Mr. William Crow as followeth:

Know all men to whom these presents shall Come that I, John Howland, senr, of the town of New Plumouth, in the Colony of New Plymouth in New England in America, this twenty ninth day of May one thousand six hundred seventy and two being of whole mind and in Good and Perfect Memory and Remembrance praised be God; being now Grown aged: having many infirmities of body vpon mee; and not Knowing how soon God will call mee out of this world, doe make and ordaine these presents to be my testament containing heerin my last Will in manor and forme following:

BURIAL HILL, PLYMOUTH, MASS.

By permission of A. S. Burbank, Plymouth

Imp   I will and bequeath my body to the dust, and my soule to God that gave it, in hopes of a joyful Resurrection vnyo Glory; and as concerning my temporall estate, I dispose thereof as followeth

Item   I doe giuve and bequeath vnto John Howland my eldest sonne besides what lands I haue alreddy giuen him, all my Right and interest in that one hundred acres of land granted mee by the Court, lying on the eastern side of Taunton River, between Titicutt and Taunton, bounds and all the appurtenances and Priviledges therevnto belonging, to belonge to him and his heires and assignes forever; And if that tract should faile, then to haue all my Rights, title and Interest by and in that Last Court graunted to mee, in any other place, to belonge to him his heires and assignes forever;

Item   I giue and bequeath vnto my son, Jabez Howland, all those my vpland and Meadows that I now posesse att Satuckett and Paomett, and places adjacent, with all the appurtenances and privilidges belonging therevnto, and all my right title and interest therin, to belonge to him, his heires and assignes forever,

Item   I giue and bequeath vnto my son, Jabez Howland all that my one peece of land that I haue lying on the southsyde of the Mill:brook, in the town of Plymouth, aforesaid; be it more or lesse, and is on the northsyde of a tract that is now Gyles Richards, sen; to belonge to the said Jabez his heires and assignes forever,

Item   I giue and bequeath unto Isack Howland my youngest sonne all those my vplands and Meddows devided and undivided with all the appurtenances and priviledges vnto them belonging lying and being in the towne of Middlebery, and in a tract of Land called the Majors purchase, neare Namaskett Ponds; which I haue bought and purchased of William White, of Marshfield, in the colonie of New Plymouth; which may or shall appear by any deed or writing that is Giuen vnder the said White's hand all such deeds and writinges together with the aforementioned peticular & to belonge to the said Isack, his heires and assignes forever.

Item   I giue and bequeath vnto my said son, Isack Howland, the one half of my twelve acree lott of Meddow that I now haue att Winnetussett River within the towne of Plymouth aforesaid to belonge to him the Said Isack Howland his heires and assignes forever.

Item   I Will and bequeath vnto my deare and louing wif Elizabeth Howland the Vse and benifit of my now dwelling house in Rockey Nook in the township of Plymouth aforesaid, with the outhousing lands, that is vplands and meddow lands, and all appurtenances and priviledges therevnto belonging in the towne of Plymouth and all other lands housings and meddows that I haue in said towne of Plymouth, excepting what meddow and vpland I have before given to my sonnes Jabez and Isack Howland during her naturall life, to injoy make vse of and improve for her benefit and comfort.

Item   I giue and bequeath to my son, Joseph Howland after the decase of my louing wife Elizabeth Howland my aforesaid dwelling house at Rocky Nook together with all the out housing vplands and meddowes appurtenances and priviledges belonging thervnto, and all other housing vplands and meddowes that I haue within the aforesaid towne of New Plymouth excepting what lands and meddowe I haue before Given to my two sonnes Jabez and Isack to belonge to him the said Joseph Howland to him and his heires and assignes forever.

Item   I giue and bequeath vnto my daughter, Desire Gorham, twenty shillings

Item   I giue and bequeath vnto my daughter, Hope Chipman, twenty shillings

Item   I giue and bequeath vnto my daughter Elizabeth Dickenson, twenty shillings.

Item   I giue and bequeath vnto my daughter Lydia Brown, twenty shillings

Item   I giue and bequeath to my daughter Hannah Bosworth, twenty shillings

Item   I giue and bequeath vnto my daughter, Ruth Cushman, twenty shillings

Item   I giue and bequeath to my grand child Elizabeth Howland the daughter of my son John Howland twenty shillings

Item   My will is that these legacies Giuen to my daughters, pe payd by my executrix in such space as shee thinketh meet

Item   I will and bequeath to my louing wife Elizabeth Howland—my debts and legacies being first payd—my whole estate, viz: lands, houses goods chattels, or any thinge else that belongeth or appertaineth vnto mee, undisposed of be it either in Plymouth, Duxburrow, Middlebery or any other place whatsoever I do freely and absolutely giue and bequeath to my deare and loving wife Elizabeth Howland whom I do by these presents make ordaine and constitute to be the sole executrix of this my Last will and Testament to see the same truely and faithfully pformed according to the tenour therof; In witness wherof I the said John Howland, senior, haue heervnto sett my hand and seale the aforesaid twenty ninth day of May, one thousand six hundred and seventy and two. 1672.

JOHN HOWLAND
and a [Seale]

Signed and sealed
  in the Presence of
            Samuel Fuller
            William Crow

Evidently the Pilgrim had unlimited confidence in his wife's ability to undertake the settlement of his affairs. She spent her last days at the home of her daughter, Lydia Brown, at Swansea, as has been said. What communications pasesd between the grandmother and granddaughter, Hannah Gorham, as she grew into womanhood, we can only surmise. No record of such communications are found at Cape May. While the granddaughter and her husband, Joseph Whilldin,

THE TOMBSTONE OF JOHN HOWLAND, THE PILGRIM,
Burial Hill, Plymouth

were building their first home at Cape May, two of the Pilgrim band were still living—John Cook, who died in 1694, and Mrs. Mary Allerton Cushman, wife of Elder Cushman, who died in 1699, at the age of ninety. She was the last surviving member of those who sailed from Europe in the Mayflower. The colony of New Plymouth continued its independent jurisdiction and life until after the settlement at Cape May, coming to an end in 1692, when the colonies of Massachusetts Bay and Plymouth became united.

The devout character of Elizabeth Tilley Howland is shown in the beginning and ending of her will, dated at Swansea, 17 December, 1686.

"Being seventy nine years of age, but of good & perfect memory thanks be to Almighty God, and calling to Remembrance ye uncertain Estate of this transitory Life—that all flesh must yield vnto Death when it shall please God to call: Doe make, constitute, etc——————— and first being penitent and sorry from ye bottom of my heart for all my sinns past, most humbly desiring forgivness for ye same, giue & comit my soule vnto Almighty God my Savior and Redeemer in whome & by ye meritts of Jesus Christ I trust and believe assuredly to be saved & to full remission & forgiveness of all my sins, & that my Soule wh my Body at the Generall Day of Resurrection shall rise again wh joy, & through ye meritts of Christ's Death & Passion possesse & inherit ye Kingdom of heaven prepared for his Elect & Chosen; & my Body to be buryed in such place as it shall please my Executr————."

Elizabeth had learned her catechism when a child, and was evidently well grounded in Effectual Calling, Assurance, and the familiar words learned in her youth came to her mind when she made her last will and testament. The last item in the will is an admonition that it is her "Will and charge to all the Children that they walke in ye Feare of Ye Lord."

Genealogical Record of Mayflower Descendants

JOHN HOWLAND THE PILGRIM

JOHN HOWLAND of the Mayflower was born in England in 1592, died at Plymouth, Plymouth Colony, 23 February, 1672, Old Style, married ELIZABETH TILLEY, who came with her father, JOHN TILLEY, in the company of the Pilgrims in 1620. (See introduction page 88).

Their daughter, DESIRE HOWLAND, born at Plymouth, 1624, died at Barnstable, Plymouth Colony, 13 October, 1683, married 1643 Captain John Gorham, who was baptized at Benefield, Northamtonshire, England, 28 January, 1621, died at Swansey, Plymouth Colony, 5 February, 1675, Old Style.

Issue known to have descendants in Cape May County:—

(1) DESIRE GORHAM, born 20 May, 1644, died 30 June, 1700, married at Barnstable, Plymouth Colony, 7 October, 1661, John Haws. (For descendants see page 320).

(2) HANNAH GORHAM, born at Barnstable, Plymouth Colony, 28 November, 1663, died at Cape May, New Jersey, circa 1728, married, circa 1683, Joseph Whilldin, of Yarmouth, Plymouth Colony, born circa 1656-60, died at Cape May, circa 1725, and with her husband removed to Cape May. (For descendants see page 98). For an account of the Gorham family and the removal to Cape May of Joseph Whilldin (Wheelding) and his wife, HANNAH GORHAM, see "WAST BOOK" of Colonel John Gorham, page 7 of this volume.

The will of JOHN HOWLAND is given in full on page 90, and an account of the last days and death of Elizabeth Tilley Howland on page 92. See also Otis, Barnstable Families, page 413.

HANNAH GORHAM

For ancestors leading back to the Mayflower see page 97.

HANNAH GORHAM[3], (Desire Howland[2], JOHN HOWLAND[1] THE PILGRIM), was born at Barnstable, Plymouth Colony, 28 November, 1663, died at Cape May, New Jersey, circa 1728, married, circa 1683, Joseph Whilldin of Yarmouth, Plymouth Colony, born circa 1656-1660, died at Cape May, circa 1725, and with her husband moved before 1690 to Cape May. (See "Wast Book" of Colonel John Gorham, page 7 of this volume).

Issue:—

(1) HANNAH WHILLDIN, born at Yarmouth, Plymouth Colony, 1683, died 1728, married first at Cape May, 18 June, 1701, Thomas Leaming, born at Southampton, Long Island, 9 July, 1674, died at Cape May, 31 December, 1723. (For descendants see page 99. HANNAH WHILLDIN married second Philip Syng of Philadelphia, no issue by this last marriage.

(2) JOSEPH WHILLDIN, born circa 1690, died at Cape May, 18 March, 1748, aged 58 years, (tombstone in Cold Spring Cemetery), married first Mary Wilmon, born 1689, died at Cape May, 8 April, 1743, aged 54 years, (tombstone in Cold Spring Cemetery). For descendants see page 100.

(3) MARY WHILLDIN, married Josiah Crowell, (date of marriage 17 December, 1708).

(4) EXPERIENCE WHILLDIN, married W i l l i a m Foster.

(5) ISAAC WHILLDIN.

For history of the settlement of the Leaming family in Cape May see Diary of Thomas Leaming quoted on page 14, and also Diary of Aaron Leaming second on page 25.

HANNAH WHILLDIN

For ancestors leading back to the Mayflower see page 98.

HANNAH WHILLDIN[4], (Hannah Gorham[3], Desire Howland[2], JOHN HOWLAND[1] THE PILGRIM), was born at Yarmouth, Plymouth Colony, 1683, died at Cape May, 1728, married first at Cape May, 18 June, 1701, Thomas Leaming, born at Southampton, Long Island, 9 July, 1674, died at Cape May, 31 December, 1723. She married second Philip Syng of Philadephia.

Issue:—

(1) ESTHER LEAMING, born at Cape May, 3 July, 1702, married William Eldredge.

(2) MERCY LEAMING, born at Cape May, 10 September, 1704, married Samuel Eldredge. (For descendants see page 101).

(3) JANE LEAMING, born at Cape May, 15 October, 1706, married William Doubleday.

(4) PHEBE LEAMING, born at Cape May, 4 November 1708, married John Garlick.

(5) PRISCILLA LEAMING, born 15 June, 1710, died at Cape May, 21 September, 1758, aged 48 years, (tombstone in Cold Spring Cemetery), married first at Cape May, John Stites, who died at Cape May before 1 August, 1743, (for descendants see page 102); married second at Cape May Jacob Hughes, who was born 1711, died at Cape May, 28 September, 1772, (for descendants see page 103).

(6) CHRISTOPHER LEAMING, born at Cape May, 1714, died at Cape May, 31 December, 1751, married Deborah Hand, born at Cape May, 14 November, 1716, died at Cape May, 27 February, 1784. (For descendants see page 105).

(7) THOMAS LEAMING, born at Cape May, 31 March, 1718, Old Style, married Elizabeth Leaming. (For descendants see page 106).

JOSEPH WHILLDIN

For ancestors leading back to the Mayflower see page 98.

JOSEPH WHILLDIN[4], (Hannah Gorham[3], Desire Howland[2], JOHN HOWLAND[1] THE PILGRIM), was born circa 1690, died at Cape May, 18 March, 1748, aged 58 years, (tombstone in Cold Spring Cemetery), married first Mary Wilmon, who was born 1689, died at Cape May, 8 April, 1743, aged 54 years, (tombstone in Cold Spring Cemetery). His will made 16 March, 1747, proved 8 June, 1748, recorded in Book of Wills V, 454, at Trenton, New Jersey, names his wife, Abigail then living, and the following children.

Issue :—

(1) MATTHEW WHILLDIN, first mentioned in will.

(2) JAMES WHILLDIN, born at Cape May, 1714, died at Cape May, 5 November 1780, (tombstone in Cold Spring Cemetery), married first Jane Hand, born at Cape May, 1719, died at Cape May, 8 November, 1760, (tombstone in Cold Spring Cemetery); married second by license of 20 July, 1761, Jane Izzard; married third by license of 13 January, 1766, Susannah Hand, who survived him, and is mentioned in his will. (For descendants see page 196).

(3) HANNAH WHILLDIN, born at Cape May circa 1719, married before 1739, Ellis Hughes, who was born at Cape May, 1708, died at Cape May, 8 February, 1762. (For descendants see page 197). She married second ———— Eldredge.

(4) DAVID WHILLDIN, born 1725, died 17 March, 1762, aged 37 years, (tombstone in Cold Spring Cemetery).

(5) RACHEL WHILLDIN, mentioned in will.

(6) LOES WHILLDIN, mentioned in will.

(7) MARY WHILLDIN, deceased at time of making of will. (See page 27).

MERCY LEAMING

For ancestors leading back to the Mayflower see page 99.

MERCY LEAMING[5], (Hannah Whilldin[4], Hannah Gorham[3], Desire Howland[2], JOHN HOWLAND[1] THE PILGRIM), was born at Cape May, 10 December, 1704, died at Cape May, 1769, married at Cape May Samuel Eldredge, who died at Cape May in 1745. (For marriage see Diary of Aaron Leaming second quoted on page 36; for will of Samuel Eldredge see page 29. The date of the birth of MERCY LEAMING is given in the above mentioned manuscript of Aaron Leaming the second).

Issue:—

(1) SAMUEL ELDREDGE, named in will of his father Samuel, see above.

(2) SARAH ELDREDGE, named in will of father.

(3) AARON ELDREDGE, born at Cape May, 2 February, 1735, married at Cape May, 29 January, 1761, Elizabeth Stillwell, born at Cape May, 27 June, 1735. (For descendants see page 107).

(4) JACOB ELDREDGE, named in will of father.

(5) JEREMIAH ELDREDGE, born at Cape May, 5 August, 1745, died at Cape May, 28 April, 1795, (tombstone in Cold Spring Cemetery), married at Cape May, 9 September, 1775, Lydia Leaming, born at Cape May, 22 August, 1751, died 5 July, 1798, no issue, (see page 30). Lydia Leaming married second, 15 May, 1797, Anthony Van Mannerick, and is buried in Cold Spring Cemetery. (See also page 106).

PRISCILLA LEAMING

For ancestors leading back to the Mayflower see page 99.

PRISCILLA LEAMING[5], (Hannah Whilldin[4], Hannah Gorham[3], Desire Howland[2], JOHN HOWLAND[1] THE PILGRIM), was born at Cape May, 15 June, 1710, died at Cape May, 21 September, 1758, aged 48 years, (tombstone in Cold Spring Cemetery), married first at Cape May, John Stites, who died at Cape May, 1743, will proved 1 August of that year.

Issue:—

(1) MARGARET STITES, born at Cape May, 1740, died at Cape May, 22 October, 1764, married at Cape May, 3 March, 1763, Jonathan Leaming, (son of Aaron Leaming the second), born 1738, and had one child, PRISCILLA LEAMING, born at Cape May, 9 October, 1764, who married Humphrey Stites. (For descendants see page 143).

PRISCILLA LEAMING (first) married second at Cape May, Jacob Hughes, who was born 1711, died at Cape May, 28 September, 1772. (For descendants see page 103).

For the date of the birth of PRISCILLA LEAMING (first), her marriage to John Stites, and subsequent marriage to Jacob Hughes, see Diary of Aaron Leaming the second, date of 1770, quoted on page 36 of this volume, and on page 35 an account of the death and grave of her daughter, MARGARET STITES. See also abstract of will of John Stites in New Jersey Archives, First Series, vol. XXX, page 459—''Wife Priscilla to have use of lands—until my daughter Margrit will be 20.''

PRISCILLA LEAMING

For ancestors leading back to the Mayflower see page 99.

PRISCILLA LEAMING[5], (Hannah Whilldin[4], Hannah Gorham[3], Desire Howland[2], JOHN HOWLAND[1] THE PILGRIM), was born at Cape May, 15 June, 1710, died at Cape May, 21 September 1758, aged 48 years, married second at Cape May, after August 1st, 1743, Jacob Hughes, born 1711, died at Cape May, 28 September, 1772, (tombstones in Cold Spring Cemetery).

Issue:—

(1) JACOB HUGHES, born 9 August, 1746, died 22 March, 1796, married by license of 24 November, 1773, (see Pennsylvania Marriages), Ann Lawrence, born August, 1753, died 27 November, 1817, and had the following children:

(1) JACOB HUGHES, born about 1777, died about 1830, married at Cape May, 28 July, 1800, Sophia Stillwell, (for record of marriage see Cape May County Records, Book A of Marriages, page 12), and had: JACOB STILLWELL HUGHES, born 1803, died 1835, married 6 February, 1833, Rebecca Crawford, and had MARY HIGBEE HUGHES, who married Joseph Russell, and had: JOSEPH RUSSELL; MARY RUSSELL, who married William Rutherford; CHARLES RUSSELL; and GEORGE RUSSELL.

(2) DANIEL HUGHES, M. D., born 1779, died 3 July, 1815, (tombstone in Cold Spring Cemetery), married 12 November, 1804, Charlotte Bennett, (see Session Book of the Cold Spring Presbyterian Church in this volume, page 43), and had: BENJAMIN RUSH HUGHES, born 4 June, 1807; HENRY FISHER HUGHES, born 7 January, 1810.

(Continued on next page)

103

(3) MARY HUGHES, born 1780, married 17 February, 1800, John Bennett, marriage recorded in Book A of Marriages, Cape May County. (For descendants see page 148).

(4) JEREMIAH HUGHES, born at Cape May, 1783, died 23 February, 1815, (tombstone in Cold Spring Cemetery), married Rhoda Taylor, born 11 April, 1778, died 11 September, 1843; she married second, 11 May, 1820, Edward Price. (For descendants of Jeremiah and Rhoda Taylor Hughes see page 149).

(5) ELIZABETH HUGHES, married 29 January, 1806, John Church, (Cape May County Records, Book A of Marriages), and had SOPHIA CHURCH, RHODA CHURCH and ARABELLA CHURCH, (See "The Divine Covenant Fulfilled in Pious Households" by REV. DANIEL LAWRENCE HUGHES, D. D., page 20). See also page 44 of this volume.

(6) JAMES RAINY HUGHES, born at New England, Lower township, Cape May County, New Jersey, 6 July, 1791, died at Cape May, 13 March, 1865, (tombstone in Cold Spring Cemetery), married at Cape May, 9 January, 1815, ELIZA ELDREDGE[8], (Aaron Eldredge[7], Aaron Eldredge[6], Mercy Leaming[5], Hannah Whilldin[4], Hannah Gorham[3], Desire Howland[2], JOHN HOWLAND[1] THE PILGRIM), born at Cold Spring, New Jersey, 15 December, 1796, died at Unionville, Pennsylvania, 6 January, 1876, (tombstone in Cold Spring Cemetery). For descendants see page 150.

For marriage of PRISCILLA LEAMING and Jacob Hughes, see Diary of Aaron Leaming the second, quoted on page 36 of this volume.

The REV. DANIEL LAWRENCE HUGHES, D.D., author of "The Divine Covenant Fulfilled in Pious Households, From 1711 to 1891," was the son of JAMES RAINY and ELIZA ELDREDGE HUGHES; the record of his family and descendants is given on page 157 of this volume.

CHRISTOPHER LEAMING

For ancestors leading back to the Mayflower see page 99.

CHRISTOPHER LEAMING[5], (Hannah Whilldin[4], Hannah Gorham[3], Desire Howland[2], JOHN HOWLAND[1] THE PILGRIM), was born at Cape May, 18 April, 1712, died at Cape May, 31 December, 1751, married Deborah Hand, born at Cape May, 14 November, 1716, died at Cape May, 27 February, 1784, and had: CHRISTOPHER LEAMING, born at Cape May, died at Cape May, 1788, married by license of 8 August, 1761, Sarah Spicer, who died about 1797, and had the following children:—

(1) SPICER LEAMING, born 14 April, 1762, married Hannah Swain. (For descendants see page 177).

(2) DEBORAH LEAMING, born 11 September, 1764.

(3) HANNAH LEAMING, born 23 February, 1768, married first Edward Rice, married second Amos C. Moore. (For descendants see page 179).

(4) JACOB LEAMING, born 31 October, 1771.

(5) CHRISTOPHER LEAMING, born 5 July, 1775, married Ann Mecray, and had EDWIN LEAMING.

(6) ESTHER LEAMING, born 9 February, 1778, married Eli Foster and moved to Ohio in 1806. She died at Lebanon, Ohio.

(7) HUMPHREY LEAMING, born 6 December, 1780, married Mary Stites. (For descendants see page 178).

(8) ALLISON LEAMING, born 25 September, 1784.

The tombstone of Christopher Leaming, son of Hannah Whilldin, gives his age as 39 years. (Leaming burial ground at Clermont, N. J.)

THOMAS LEAMING

For ancestors leading back to the Mayflower see page 99.

THOMAS LEAMING[5], (Hannah Whilldin[4], Hannah Gorham[3], Desire Howland[2], JOHN HOWLAND[1] THE PILGRIM), was born at Cape May, 31 March, 1718, Old Style, (See Diary of Aaron Leaming the second quoted on page 36), died at Cape May, 19 December, 1795, married 29 April, 1740, Elizabeth Leaming, born at Cape May, 18 September, 1721, died at Cape May, 26 January, 1769.

Issue:—

(1) THOMAS LEAMING, born in Cape May County, 20 August, 1748, Old Style, died at Philadelphia, Pennsylvania, 29 October, 1797, married at Philadelphia, Pennsylvania, 19 August, 1779, Rebecca Fisher, born 31 October, 1757, Old Style, died at Philadelphia, Pennsylvania, 9 September, 1833, and had the following children:—ELIZA LEAMING, born 13 August, 1780, died 1835, married 3 January, 1799, Charles Caldwell, M.D., and had, THOMAS LEAMING CALDWELL, M.D., born 9 November, 1799, who married 13 May, 1822, Mary Jane Clifford; THOMAS FISHER LEAMING, born at Philadelphia, Pennsylvania, 14 July, 1786, died at Philadelphia, Pennsylvania, 23 June, 1839, married Susan Murgatroyde, and had, STEVENSON M. LEAMING, born 16 February, 1822, died 8 August, 1890; LYDIA LEAMING, born 28 August, 1789, married J. Somers Smith, (for descendants see page 188); JEREMIAH FISHER LEAMING, born at Philadelphia, Pennsylvania, 8 October, 1795, married Rebecca Waln, (for descendants see page 189).

(2) LYDIA LEAMING, born 22 August, 1751, married first Jeremiah Eldredge, married second Anthony Van Mannerick—she died 16 July, 1798, and is buried in Cold Spring Cemetery. No issue.

AARON ELDREDGE

For ancestors leading back to the Mayflower see page 101.

AARON ELDREDGE[6], (Mercy Leaming[5], Hannah Whilldin[4], Hannah Gorham[3], Desire Howland[2], JOHN HOWLAND[1] THE PILGRIM), was born at Cape May, 2 February, 1735, died at Cape May, 2 July, 1785, married at Cape May, 29 January, 1761, Elizabeth Stillwell, born 27 June, 1735, died 23 April, 1790.

Issue :—

(1) CHARLOTTA ELDREDGE, born at Cape May, 5 April, 1765, married by license of 21 October, 1782, Persons Leaming. (For descendants see page 108).

(2) SARAH ELDREDGE, born at Cape May, 20 February, 1767, married as his second wife, 3 June, 1798, Aaron Edmunds; his first wife was LYDIA, younger sister of SARAH. He was born at Cape May, 14 September, 1766, died 23 June, 1844. (For descendants see page 109).

(3) LYDIA ELDREDGE, born at Cape May, 4 March, 1769, died at Cape May, 29 January, 1794, married at Cape May, 25 June, 1780, Aaron Edmunds. (For descendants see page 110).

(4) AARON ELDREDGE, born at Cape May, 13 June, 1771, died at Cape May, 21 August, 1819, (tombstone in Cold Spring Cemetery), married at Cape May, 17 June, 1792, Hannah Langdon. (For descendants see page 111).

CHARLOTTA ELDREDGE

For ancestors leading back to the Mayflower see page 107.

CHARLOTTA ELDREDGE[7], (Aaron Eldredge[6], Mercy Leaming[5], Hannah Whilldin[4], Hannah Gorham[3], Desire Howland[2], JOHN HOWLAND[1] THE PILGRIM), was born at Cape May, 5 April, 1765, died at Cape May, 12 December, 1812, married 24 October, 1782, Persons Leaming, born at Cape May, 23 July, 1756, died at Cape May, 29 March, 1807, (tombstone in Cold Spring Cemetery).

Issue:—

(1) AARON LEAMING, born 15 May, 1784, married HANNAH STITES[8], (Priscilla Leaming[7], Margaret Stites[6], Priscilla Leaming[5], Hannah Whilldin[4], Hannah Gorham[3], Desire Howland[2], JOHN HOWLAND[1] THE PILGRIM). For descendants see page 144).

(2) FURMAN LEAMING, born at Cape May, 27 September, 1786, died 18 March, 1832, married Hannah Ludlam. (For descendants see page 113).

(3) MARY LEAMING, born at Cape May, 1778, died 5 February, 1861, married Robert M. Holmes.

(4) PERSONS LEAMING, born at Cape May, 3 September, 1790, died at Cape May, 20 November, 1820, unmarried, (tombstone in Cold Spring Cemetery).

(5) JEREMIAH LEAMING, born at Cape May, 25 May, 1792, died at Dennisville, New Jersey, 26 April, 1839, married 3 October, 1814, Abigail Falkenburge. (For descendants see page 114).

(6) JAMES RAINY LEAMING, born at Cape May, 6 June, 1794, married at Cape May, 7 August, 1814, Sarah Irwin, and had: JAMES LEAMING, died 1838; JONATHAN LEAMING, and SOMERS LEAMING.

MAYFLOWER DESCENDANTS IN CAPE MAY COUNTY

SARAH ELDREDGE

For ancestors leading back to the Mayflower see page 107.

SARAH ELDREDGE[7], (Aaron Eldredge[6], Mercy Leaming[5], Hannah Whilldin[4], Hannah Gorham[3], Desire Howland[2], JOHN HOWLAND[1] THE PILGRIM), was born at Cape May, 20 February, 1767, died at Cape May, 20 January, 1846, (tombstone in Cold Spring Cemetery), married at Cape May, 3 June, 1798, Aaron Edmunds, (his first wife was LYDIA ELDREDGE, younger sister of SARAH ELDREDGE). He was born at Cape May, 14 September, 1766, died at Cape May, 23 June, 1844, (tombstone in Cold Spring Cemetery).

Issue :—

(1) EPHRIAM ELDREDGE EDMUNDS, born at Cape May, 7 June, 1789, died 30 August, 1812, (tombstone in Cold Spring Cemetery).

(2) REV. JAMES EDMUNDS, born at Cape May, 19 December, 1799, married Harriet Howe Whittlemore, and had WILLIAM W. EDMUNDS, born 2 May, 1825, "died of cholera on a business trip from Philadelphia to St. Paul, leaving a wife and daughter residing in Philadelphia," (Rev. Dr. Hughes , REV. JAMES M. EDMUNDS, born at Cold Spring, New Jersey, 1 June, 1827, died 23 March, 1858, married 18 March, 1858, Isabella B. Work; EMILY J. EDMUNDS, born 30 December, 1830, married Rev. William R. Work—"she died, and her children also, several years ago," (Dr. Hughes)—date of death 19 November, 1866.

(3) LYDIA EDMUNDS, born 22 January, 1803, died in infancy.

(4) LYDIA EDMUNDS, born at Cape May, 3 June, 1805, married Robert Foster. (For descendants see page 118).

LYDIA ELDREDGE

For ancestors leading back to the Mayflower see page 107.

LYDIA ELDREDGE[7], (Aaron Eldredge[6], Mercy Leaming[5], Hannah Whilldin[4], Hannah Gorham[3], Desire Howland[2], JOHN HOWLAND[1] THE PILGRIM), was born at Cape May, 4 March, 1769, died at Cape May, 29 January, 1794, (tombstone in Cold Spring Cemetery, with variations in dates), married at Cape May, 25 June, 1790, Aaron Edmunds, born at Cape May, 14 September, 1766, died at Cape May, 23 June, 1844, (tombstone in Cold Spring Cemetery). He married second SARAH ELDREDGE, sister of his first wife, LYDIA ELDREDGE, (see page 109).

Issue :—

(1) ELIZABETH EDMUNDS, born at Cape May, 25 May, 1791, died at Cape May, 15 February, 1847, (tombstone in Cold Spring Cemetery), married at Cape May, 10 December, 1810, Robert Parsons, born at Cape May, 14 September, 1785, died at Cape May, 7 August, 1860, (tombstone in Cold Spring Cemetery), and had, JOHN SMITH PARSONS, born 22 March, 1828, died at Cold Spring, New Jersey, 2 February, 1893, married 6 November, 1860, HARRIET ELDREDGE[9], (Jeremiah Leaming Eldredge[8], Aaron Eldredge[7], Aaron Eldredge[6], Mercy Leaming[5], Hannah Whilldin[4], Hannah Gorham[3], Desire Howland[2], JOHN HOWLAND[1] THE PILGRIM), who was born 20 December, 1841, died 14 December, 1903. (For descendants see page 120).

(2) AARON EDMUNDS, born at Cape May, 22 June, 1793, died at Cape May, 25 November, 1856, (tombstone in Cold Spring Cemetery), married at Cape May, 2 November, 1816, Roxanna Hildreth, born 18 January, 1795, died at Linwood, New Jersey, 26 September, 1876. (For descendants see page 121).

AARON ELDREDGE

For ancestors leading back to the Mayflower see page 107.

AARON ELDREDGE[7], (Aaron Eldredge[6], Mercy Leaming[5], Hannah Whilldin[4], Hannah Gorham[3], Desire Howland[2], JOHN HOWLAND[1] THE PILGRIM), was born at Cape May, 13 June, 1771, died at Cape May, 21 August, 1819, (tombstone in Cold Spring Cemetery), married at Cape May, 17 June, 1792. Hannah Langdon, born 21 December, 1774, died 6 June, 1836, (tombstone in Cold Spring Cemetery).

Issue:—

(1) JEREMIAH LEAMING ELDREDGE, born at Cape May, 14 July, 1793, married 16 August 1821, Harriet Tomlin. (For descendants see page 124).

(2) AARON ELDREDGE, born 6 June, 1795, married 29 April, 1824, Hannah Eldredge. (For descendants see page 120).

(3) ELIZA ELDREDGE, born at Cape May, 15 December, 1796, married 9 January, 1815, JAMES RAINY HUGHES[7], (Jacob Hughes[6], Priscilla Leaming[5], Hannah Whilldin[4], Hannah Gorham[3], Desire Howland[2], JOHN HOWLAND[1] THE PILGRIM), for descendants see page 150).

(4) JOSEPH ELDREDGE, born at Cape May 7 August, 1798, married 22 September, 1830, Mrs. Ann Morgan Coxe West. (For descendants see page 127).

(5) WILLIAM ELDREDGE, born at Cold Spring, New Jersey, 30 April, 1804, died at Cold Spring, 29 June, 1886, married at Somers Point, New Jersey, 6 September, 1828, Esther A. Ireland, born at Somers Point, New Jersey, 8 July, 1811, daughter of Elijah and Rachel Somers Ireland. (For descendants see page 128).

(Continued on next page)

AARON ELDREDGE

(6) STILLWELL ELDREDGE, born at Cape May, 6 August, 1806, died at Philadelphia, Pennsylvania, 14 July, 1849, married 2 September, 1830, Mary Benner, born at Philadelphia, 18 December, 1812, died 24 November, 1882. (For descendants see page 129).

(7) GEORGE M. ELDREDGE, born at Cold Spring, New Jersey, 6 December, 1810, died at Abbeville, Louisiana, 27 April, 1886, married 1842, Emma Elizabeth Frierson. (For descendants see page 130).

(8) EPHRIAM ELDREDGE, born at Cape May, 6 October, 1812, died at West Chester, Pennsylvania, 13 August, 1887, married Sarah Payran. (For descendants see page 131)

A full biography of the family of AARON ELDREDGE and his wife Hannah Langdon, extending to the year 1891, is given in "The Divine Covenant Fulfilled in Pious Households from 1711-1891" by the Rev. Daniel Lawrence Hughes, D. D., son of ELIZA ELDREDGE, the third child of AARON ELDREDGE and Hannah Langdon. See pages 21 to 37 of that record of the Eldredge family; but it should be carefully noted that the title of this division of Dr. Hughes record of the Lawrence-Hughes and Eldredge families is an error and should read AARON ELDREDGE instead of JEREMIAH ELDREDGE, who died without issue (see pages 10 and 30 of this volume), and the third paragraph should read: "My grandfather, Aaron Eldredge, Jr., son of my great grandfather, Aaron Eldredge."

FURMAN LEAMING

For ancestors leading back to the Mayflower see page 108.

FURMAN LEAMING[8], (Charlotta Eldredge[7], Aaron Eldredge[6], Mercy Leaming[5], Hannah Whilldin[4], Hannah Gorham[3], Desire Howland[2], JOHN HOWLAND[1] THE PILGRIM), was born at Cape May, 22 September, 1786, died 18 March, 1832, married at Cape May, 14 May, 1809, Hannah Ludlam, born 29 November, 1789, died 6 July, 1836.

Issue:—

(1) MARY LEAMING, born at Philadelphia, Pennsylvania, 31 March, 1810, died at Philadelphia, Pennsylvania, in her eighty-seventh year, unmarried.

(2) SARAH LEAMING, born 15 March, 1813, married Edmund Throckmorton.

(3) FURMAN LEAMING, born 30 August, 1815, married Mary Curwen. (For descendants see page 116).

(4) LEWIS LEAMING, born 31 January, 1820, married Rachel Fox.

(5) ELIZABETH LEAMING, born 9 November, 1821, died 1889, married 22 July, 1844, Charles D. Meigs, born 1817, died 1893, and had:—MARY LEAMING MEIGS, born at Philadelphia, 25 February, 1845, died at Indianapolis, Indiana, 24 April, 1918, unmarried; CHARLES D. MEIGS, born at Philadelphia, 20 September, 1846, married Anna Allen; MONTGOMERY C. MEIGS, born near Romney, Indiana, 1 April, 1848, died 1904, married Mary Matthews, and had: ELIZABETH MEIGS, born 1879, MONTGOMERY MEIGS, born 1881, EMILY BIDDLE MEIGS, born 1883, JAMES MATTHEWS MEIGS, born 1888; LEWIS LEAMING MEIGS, (son of Charles and Elizabeth) born March, 1850, died in infancy; HARRY L. MEIGS, born 1851, died 1878; EMILY BIDDLE MEIGS, born 28 August, 1853, married Warwick H. Ripley, and had: CHARLES MEIGS RIPLEY; ELIZABETH MEIGS, born 1855, died in infancy; SARAH THROCKMORTON MEIGS, born 13 August, 1857; JOHN FORSYTH MEIGS, born 1 June 1860, died 1878; SAMUEL MEIGS, born 1863, died 1880.

(6) HENRY LEAMING, born 25 November, 1825, married first Ellen Jones, married second Bessie Eichelburger.

(7) EMMA LEAMING, born 26 March, 1829, married George Forman.

(8) HANNAH LEAMING, died young.

JEREMIAH LEAMING

For ancestors leading back to the Mayflower see page 108.

JEREMIAH LEAMING[8], (Charlotta Eldredge[7], Aaron Eldredge[6], Mercy Leaming[5], Hannah Whilldin[4], Hannah Gorham[3], Desire Howland[2], JOHN HOWLAND[1] THE PILGRIM), was born at Cape May, 25 May, 1792, died at Dennisville, New Jersey, 26 April, 1839, married at Dennisville, New Jersey, 3 October, 1814, Abigail Falkenburg, born at Dennisville, New Jersey, 16 February, 1796, died at Philadelphia, Pennsylvania, 4 December, 1865.

Issue:—

(1) JOSEPH FALKENBURG LEAMING, born 23 September, 1815, married Isabella Thompson, and had ISABELLA LEAMING, born 21 January, 1859, married Dr. Forman.

(2) DR. COLEMAN FISHER LEAMING, born at Dennisville, New Jersey, 6 June, 1818, died at Cape May Court House, New Jersey, 13 May, 1900, married at Cape May Court House, New Jersey, 23 August, 1846, Hannah Holmes Thompson, born at Cape May Court House, New Jersey, 12 January, 1829, died at Cape May Court House, 30 January, 1910, and had: JOSEPHINE LEAMING; EMMA LEAMING, died 1883; EDWIN THOMPSON LEAMING, born 13 August, 1857, died 1868.

(3) ABIGAIL LEAMING, born at Dennisville, New Jersey, 26 November, 1820, died at Woodbury, New Jersey, 4 September, 1907, married at Dennisville, New Jersey, 23 June, 1846, Robert Kennedy Matlock, born at Woodbury, New Jersey, 22 January, 1804, died at Woodbury, New Jersey, 27 April, 1877, and had: ELIZABETH BROWNING MATLOCK, born 16 August, 1847; MARY LEAMING MATLOCK, born 3 October, 1849, died 30 May, 1907; LEAMING MATLOCK, born 26 March, 1854, died 28 April, 1909; ELLEN LEAMING MATLOCK, born 15 September, 1858; ROBERT KENNEDY MATLOCK, born 31 October, 1860, married 15 May, 1912, Elizabeth Dickinson Green; CHARLOTTE LEAMING MATLOCK, born 22 May, 1865.

(4) CHARLOTTE LEAMING, born 1 January, 1826, married J. McKnight.

(Continued on next page)

114

JEREMIAH LEAMING

(5) RICHARD S. LEAMING, born at South Dennis, New Jersey, 16 July, 1828, died at Dennisville, New Jersey, 25 May, 1895, married 8 December, 1849, Amelia Ludlam, born 15 September, 1827, died 8 November, 1895, and had: EMMA LEAMING, died in infancy; COLEMAN FISHER LEAMING, born 19 September, 1850, married Hulda Cresse, and had, RICHARD S. LEAMING, born 17 February, 1882, LEWIS C. LEAMING, born 13 November, 1883, who married 8 February, 1913, Georgie H. Wells, and had, COLEMAN F. LEAMING, born 10 August, 1913, LEWIS C. LEAMING, born 14 August, 1915; FRANK LEAMING, (son of RICHARD and AMELIA), born 10 March, 1857, died 7 August, 1916, married 11 February, 1888, Anna M. Edwards.

(6) JEREMIAH LEAMING, born 20 January, 1831, died 30 January, 1908, married 20 August, 1856, Harriet H. Scoville, and had: —JOSEPH FALKENBURG LEAMING, born 1857, married first, 1889, Cora Lockwood, who died in 1895, and had, HARRIET LOUISE LEAMING, born 1891, who married John McGuire, and had, John LEAMING McGUIRE, born 1918, MARJORIE LEAMING, born 1894; —married second, 1901, Katherine Cropsy Hess, and had JEREMIAH CROPSY LEAMING, born 1902; ALDEN CORTLAND LEAMING, born, 1858, died in fancy; ANNA LEAMING, born 1861, died 1898; ELLEN LEAMING, born 1863, died in infancy; SUSAN FALKENBURG LEAMING, born 1865; KATHARINE LEAMING, born 1867, married 1890, Walter Livingstone Lee, and had, WALTER LIVINGSTONE LEE, born 1894, died in infancy; CHARLOTTE LEAMING, born 1871; HARRIET LEAMING, born 1873, died in infancy.

(7) SUSAN FALKENBURG LEAMING, born 8 July, 1836, married 25 March, 1855, Redman Abbott and had:—ELLEN FALKENBURG ABBOTT, married 12 August, 1880, Count Magawly Cerati de Calry, and had, ROSE, born 27 June, 1881, married September, 1908, Christopher J. P. Banon, Broughall Castle, Kings County, Ireland, and had, CHRISTOPHER, born 1912, EDWARD, ROSEMARY, GILBERT, GERTRUDE, born 1918, VALERIO AWLY, born 25 August, 1883, killed in action near Arras, France, 10 May, 1917, having rank of Lt. Col., married 1 June, 1912, Sheila Cameron, and had, PATRICIA, ROBERT LOUIS, born 11 July, 1898; WILLIAM LOUIS ABBOTT, M. D., born 23 February, 1860; GERTRUDE ABBOTT, 8 July, 1866.

FURMAN LEAMING

For ancestors leading back to the Mayflower see page 113.

FURMAN LEAMING[9], (Furman Leaming[8], Charlotta Eldredge[7], Aaron Eldredge[6], Mercy Leaming[5], Hannah Whilldin[4], Hannah Gorham[3], Desire Howland[2], JOHN HOWLAND[1] THE PILGRIM), was born 30 August, 1815, died 1 April, 1891, married 28 September, 1843, Mary Curwen, born 29 October, 1823, died 12 February, 1903.

Issue:—

(1) HENRY LEAMING, born 20 January, 1845, married 1 November, 1870, Martha F. Fox, who died 1902, and had the following children:—MARY CURWEN LEAMING, born 15 December, 1871, married Samuel C. Malsbary, and had MIL-DRED MALSBURY and DALE MALSBURY; LEWIS LEAMING, born 10 May, 1873, married Alice Newman, and had LOUISE LEAMING, ELINOR LEAMING, and LUTHER LEAMING; EMILY LEAMING, born October, 1874, died 1901; CHARLOTTE LEAMING, born June, 1876, married Samuel S. Kirkpatrick, and had LEAMING S. KIRKPAT-RICK, FRANCIS KIRKPATRICK and JOHN KIRKPAT-RICK; HUNTER BELL LEAMING, born 18 December, 1881, married Ruby Zion, and had JAMES LEAMING.

(2) JOSEPH CURWEN LEAMING, born 1 January, 1847, died 29 June, 1849.

(3) ELINOR EWING LEAMING, born 13 September, 1850, married 6 February, 1873, William J. Inskeep, and had the following children: FURMAN LEAMING INSKEEP, died in infancy; ELINOR CURWEN INSKEEP, born January, 1876; HENRY INSKEEP, died 1901; WILLIAM INSKEEP, married Cora Simison, and had HENRY INSKEEP and WIL-LIAM INSKEEP; GEORGE INSKEEP and FURMAN LEAMING INSKEEP.

(Continued on next page)

FURMAN LEAMING

(4) GEORGE CURWEN LEAMING, born 9 August, 1853, married 25 December, 1879, Alice Stewart, and had the following children:—ANNE STEWART LEAMING, married Warren Booker; EMMA HOLMES LEAMING, married Elmer Waters; JAMES STEWART LEAMING, married ———— Johnston, and had ————————; GEORGE CURWEN LEAM-ING, married Ruth Riston, and had MARION LEAMING; ALICE STEWART LEAMING.

(5) MARY ELMER LEAMING, born 8 September, 1857, married 10 February, 1887, Preston R. Austin, and had the following children: ELINOR CURWEN AUSTIN, born 15 February, 1888, married 13 July, 1918, John H. Atherton; MARY LEAMING AUSTIN, born 12 June, 1890, married 30 May, 1917, Frank M. Sinison; ROWLAND AUSTIN, born 8 August, 1892, married 23 November, 1918, Alice Bossart, who died 20 March, 1919; JOHN HARRIS AUSTIN, born 5 July, 1895, married 30 June, 1918, Laura M. Hoch.

(6) ELIZABETH MEIGS LEAMING, born 10 January, 1861, married 29 December, 1881, Dr. Albert D. Pyke, and had the following children: MARGARET PYKE, born October, 1883, deceased; FURMAN LEAMING PYKE, born 14 February, 1889, married Inez ————————; DAVID PYKE, married Fern Field; ALBERT PYKE, married Ruth Stafford.

(7) FURMAN MASKELL LEAMING, born 3 January, 1865, married 16 October, 1890, Flora M. Fox, and had ELINOR CURWEN LEAMING and MABEL LEAMING.

LYDIA EDMUNDS

For ancestors leading back to the Mayflower see page 109.

LYDIA EDMUNDS[8], (Sarah Eldredge[7], Aaron Eldredge[6], Mercy Leaming[5], Hannah Whilldin[4], Hannah Gorham[3], Desire Howland[2], JOHN HOWLAND[1] THE PILGRIM), was born at Cape May, 3 May, 1805, died at Cape May, 24 December, 1837, (tombstone in Cold Spring Cemetery), married at Cape May, 25 February, 1829, Robert Edmunds Foster, born at Cape May, 19 September, 1805, died 31 March, 1890.

Issue:—

(1) SAMUEL M. FOSTER, born at Fishing Creek, New Jersey, 9 March, 1831, married at Philadelphia, Pennsylvania, 18 February, 1854, Emily Jane Hughes, born at Fishing Creek, New Jersey, 25 January, 1830, died at Fishing Creek, 22 July, 1897, and had the following children: ROBERT EDMUNDS FOSTER, born at Philadelphia, Pennsylvania, 19 June, 1855, died at Norfolk, Virginia, 8 February, 1875; ELLA V. FOSTER, born at Philadelphia, Pennsylvania, 12 August, 1857, married Daniel Woolson, (for descendants see page 119); EDGAR HUGHES FOSTER, born at Philadelphia, Pennsylvania, 24 March, 1865, married at Camden, New Jersey, 14 March, 1886, Abigail Virginia Hoeflich, and had EDGAR C., EDNA VIRGINIA, EARL HOEFLICH, and FLORENCE EDNA FOSTER.

(2) JANE CROWELL FOSTER, born 28 November, 1833, died at Fishing Creek, 14 February, 1897, married at Fishing Creek, 14 December, 1853, James H. Shaw, born 4 May, 1830, died September, 1911.

ELLA V. FOSTER

For ancestors leading back to the Mayflower see page 118.

ELLA V. FOSTER[10], (Samuel L. Foster[9], Lydia Edmunds[8], Sarah Eldredge[7], Aaron Eldredge[6], Mercy Leaming[5], Hannah Whilldin[4], Hannah Gorham[3], Desire Howland[2], JOHN HOWLAND[1] THE PILGRIM), was born at Philadelphia, Pennsylvania, 12 August, 1857, married at Cape May, 5 July, 1875, Daniel Woolson, born at Fishing Creek, New Jersey, 23 December, 1855, died at Fishing Creek, New Jersey, 30 December, 1910.

Issue :—

(1) EMILY HUGHES WOOLSON, married Harry Bennett Thompson.

(2) EDGAR WOOLSON, born at Fishing Creek, New Jersey, 23 November, 1878, married 25 November, 1910, Grace S. Ross.

Grace S. Ross, wife of EDGAR F. WOOLSON, was born at Brooklyn, New York, 30 March, 1885.

(3) MEDORA WOOLSON, married Claude Eldredge, and had, MELVIN ELDREDGE.

(4) EDNA MAY WOOLSON, born at Fishing Creek, New Jersey, 30 August, 1884, married Fred G. Raff, and had, MARION E. RAFF, and CLARENCE F. RAFF.

(5) CHARLES LESLIE WOOLSON, born at Fishing Creek, New Jersey, 24 October, 1885.

(6) JENNIE WOOLSON, born at Fishing Creek, New Jersey, 29 April, 1888.

(7) EARL SHANNON WOOLSON, married Theresa Chester.

(8) ROBERT EDMUNDS WOOLSON, born at Fishing Creek, New Jersey, 4 June, 1892.

JOHN SMITH PARSONS

For ancestors leading back to the Mayflower see page 110.

JOHN SMITH PARSONS[9], (Elizabeth Edmunds[8], Lydia Eldredge[7], Aaron Eldredge[6], Mercy Leaming[5], Hannah Whilldin[4], Hannah Gorham[3], Desire Howland[2], JOHN HOWLAND[1] THE PILGRIM), was born at Cape May, 22 March, 1828, died at Cold Spring, New Jersey, 2 February, 1893, married 6 November, 1860, HARRIET ELDREDGE[9], (Jeremiah Leaming Eldredge[8], Aaron Eldredge[7], Aaron Eldredge[6], Mercy Leaming[5], Hannah Whilldin[4], Hannah Gorham[3], Desire Howland[2], JOHN HOWLAND[1] THE PILGRIM), born 20 December, 1841, died at Merchantville, New Jersey, 14 December, 1903. (Burial at Cold Spring Cemetery).

Issue:—

(1) ELIZABETH PARSONS, born at Cold Spring, New Jersey, 31 May, 1861, married at Cold Spring, New Jersey, 12 November, 1885, William H. Ritter, born at Philadelphia, Pennsylvania, 13 June, 1860, and had: HIRAM RITTER, born at Philadelphia, 24 October, 1886; CHARLES EDMUND RITTER, born at Philadelphia, 8 November, 1889, married at Philadelphia, 27 June, 1917, Bessie Gregg, and had, CHARLES EDMUNDS and WILLIAM DAVID RITTER, twin children, born 20 September, 1919; MARY RITTER, born at Philadelphia, 14 February, 1892.

(2) MARGARET PARSONS, born at Cold Spring, New Jersey, 17 April, 1863, married at Cold Spring, 26 August, 1886, Frank Taylor, born at Philadelphia, 3 December, 1861, and had: HELEN PARSONS TAYLOR, born at Philadelphia, 26 March, 1889, married 9 May, 1914, David Jamison Timmons, and had, DAVID J. TIMMONS, born 22 October, 1915, and FRANK TAYLOR TIMMONS, born 2 December, 1916.

(3) EMMA PARSONS, married Isaac Smith.

(4) ROBERT PARSONS, born 6 September, 1868, died 17 November, 1914.

(5) AUGUSTUS LENGERT PARSONS, born at Cold Spring, 5 June, 1874, died at Cape May, 22 October, 1915, married 2 January, 1896, Lillian Stevens, and had, EDLA PARSONS, born 2 May, 1898, died 7 September, 1907; HARRIET ELDREDGE PARSONS, born 29 July, 1900, married 6 January, 1919, Bert Elmer Dares, and had, BERT ELMER DARES.

AARON EDMONDS

For ancestors leading back to the Mayflower see page 110.

AARON EDMONDS[8], (Lydia Eldredge[7], Aaron Eldredge[6], Mercy Leaming[5], Hannah Whilldin[4], Hannah Gorham[3], Desire Howland[2], JOHN HOWLAND[1] THE PILGRIM), was born at Cape May, 22 June, 1793, died at Cape May, 25 November, 1856, (tombstone in Cold Spring Cemetery), married at Cape May, 2 November, 1816, Roxanna Hildreth, born 18 January, 1795, died at Linwood, New Jersey, 26 September, 1878.

Issue:—

(1) MARY EDMONDS, born at Cape May, 12 January, 1820, died at Cape May, 11 May, 1868, married at Cold Spring, New Jersey, 26 January, 1841, Luther Cummings Edmunds, born 12 August, 1815, died at Cape May, 14 May, 1874, and had ROXANNA HILDRETH EDMUNDS, who married Nathan Cozens Price.   (For descendants see page 122).

(2) JOSEPH STILLWELL HILDRETH EDMONDS, born 30 January, 1824, married Margaret McCann.   (For descendants see page 123).

(3) AARON EDMONDS, born at Cold Spring, 1826, died 1859.

(4) SAMUEL COMPTON EDMONDS, born 27 October, 1829, died at Linwood, New Jersey, 17 September, 1901, married 11 January, 1853, Judith Frambes, and had: MARY EDMONDS, JOSEPH EDMONDS, LAURA EDMONDS, ARFE EDMONDS, and MINNIE EDMONDS.   Judith Frambes was born at Linwood, 30 June, 1830.

(5) MATTHEW WHILLDIN EDMONDS, M. D., born 20 August, 1831, died at Delphi, Indiana, 4 May, 1906, married 2 September, 1862, Katherine M. Haigh, and had, MARY M. EDMONDS.

ROXANNA HILDRETH EDMUNDS

For ancestors leading back to the Mayflower see page 121.

ROXANNA HILDRETH EDMUNDS[10], (Mary Edmonds[9], Aaron Edmonds[8], Lydia Eldredge[7], Aaron Eldredge[6], Mercy Leaming[5], Hannah Whilldin[4], Hannah Gorham[3], Desire Howland[2], JOHN HOWLAND[1] THE PILGRIM), was born Philadelphia, Pennsylvania, 15 December, 1841, died 18 October, 1899, married at Cold Spring, New Jersey, 27 December, 1865, Nathan Cozens Price, born at Tuckahoe, New Jersey, 23 March, 1828, died at Cape May, 9 April, 1906, (tombstone in Cold Spring Cemetery).

Issue :—

(1) and (2) LUTHER EDMUNDS PRICE and WILLIAM COZENS PRICE, born at Town Bank, Cape May County, New Jersey, 27 September, 1866. LUTHER EDMUNDS PRICE married at Montclair, New Jersey, 30 October, 1900, Gertrude Agnes Evans, daughter of William Thomas Evans and his wife Mary Jane Hinman, and had: WILLIAM EVANS PRICE, born at New York City, 19 May 1902; NATHAN COZENS PRICE, born at Montclair, New Jersey, 20 December, 1904.

WILLIAM COZENS PRICE married at Philadelphia, Pennsylvania, 18 November, 1895, Caroline Marqueze Halliday, born at Philadelphia, Pennsylvania, and had: MARION HALLIDAY PRICE, born at Philadelphia, Pennsylvania, 6 November, 1896, died at Philadelphia, Pennsylvania, 12 March, 1909.

For record of the ancestors of the Cape May branch of the Price family, see notes following the genealogical record of this volume.

JOSEPH STILLWELL EDMONDS

For ancesters leading back to the Mayflower see page 121.

JOSEPH STILLWELL EDMONDS[9], (Aaron Edmonds[8], Lydia Eldredge[7], Aaron Eldredge[6], Mercy Leaming[5], Hannah Whilldin[4], Hannah Gorham[3], Desire Howland[2], JOHN HOWLAND[1] THE PILGRIM), was born at Cold Spring, Cape May County, New Jersey, 30 January, 1834, died at Philadelphia, 9 November, 1879, married at Philadelphia, Margaret McCann.

Issue :—

(1) JOSEPH PARK EDMONDS, born 22 November, 1847, died 27 March, 1850.

(2) AARON HILDRETH EDMONDS, born 20 June, 1846, died 2 December, 1850.

(3) ANNA BELLE EDMONDS, born at Philadelphia, 27 December, 1849, married at Philadelphia, 1 September, 1871, Isaac Miller, and had : MARY EMMA MILLER and AMELIA C. MILLER, who married Isaac Strang.

(4) AMELIA CULP EDMONDS, born at Philadelphia, 12 February, 1851, died 24 September, 1902, married at Philadelphia, 25 November, 1871, William Johnson, and had: EVA JOHNSON, who married Edward Westerfield; AMELIA CULP EDMONDS married second Albert Lowery.

(5) FRANK SCOFFIN EDMONDS, born at Philadelphia, 20 December, 1852, married at Willimantic, Connecticut, 28 September, 1878, Emily Josephine Atwood, born at Cleveland, Ohio, 28 September, 1853, died at Norwich, Connecticut, 10 May, 1909, and had son, ARTHUR GARFIELD EDMONDS.

JEREMIAH LEAMING ELDREDGE

For ancestors leading back to the Mayflower see page 111.

JEREMIAH LEAMING ELDREDGE[8], (Aaron Eldredge[7], Aaron Eldredge[6], Mercy Leaming[5], Hannah Whilldin[4], Hannah Gorham[3], Desire Howland[2], JOHN HOWLAND[1] THE PILGRIM), was born at Cape May, 14 June, 1793, died 10 July, 1849, married at Goshen, Cape May County, New Jersey, 16 August, 1821, Harriet Tomlin, born in Cumberland County, New Jersey, 3 December, 1805, died at Cape May, 23 October, 1863. (Tombstones in Cold Spring Cemetery).

Issue:—

(1) WILLIAM TOMLIN ELDREDGE, born at Cape May, 19 October, 1822, died 4 December, 1888, married Arabella Corson. (For descendants see page 132).

(2) SAMUEL ELDREDGE, born at Cape May, 30 March, 1824, died 26 April, 1824.

(3) ELIZA ELLEN ELDREDGE, born at Cape May, June, 1825, died in infancy.

(4) ELIZA ELDREDGE, born at Cape May, 7 August, 1826, married at Cape May, HUMPHREY HUGHES[8], (Humphrey Hughes[7], Jane Whilldin[6], James Whilldin[5], Joseph Whilldin[4], Hannah Gorham[3], Desire Howland[2], JOHN HOWLAND[1] THE PILGRIM). (For descendants see page 133).

(5) CHARLES ELDREDGE, born 18 February, 1830, married Elizabeth Tomlin. (For descendants see page 134).

(Continued on next page)

124

JEREMIAH LEAMING ELDREDGE

(6) JEREMIAH LEAMING ELDREDGE, born 21 November, 1831, married Mary Marshall, and had: ALONZO ELDREDGE, born 3 May, 1856, died 31 August, 1862; IDA MAY ELDREDGE, born 12 September, 1858, died unmarried; JOHN MARSHALL ELDREDGE, born 21 February, 1860; FRANK HILWORTH ELDREDGE, born 15 September, 1862, died 4 March, 1867; GEORGE HORN ELDREDGE, born 7 December, 1872.

(7) NELSON TOMLIN ELDREDGE, born at Cape May, 13 October, 1833, died 16 June, 1886, (tombstone in Cold Spring Cemetery), married Deborah V. B. Hand, daughter of Aaron Hand of New England, Cape May County, New Jersey. (For descendants see page 135).

(8) FRANCIS SPRINGER ELDREDGE, born at Cape May, 22 April, 1836, married ELIZABETH EDMUNDS JOHNSON[9], (Jane White Eldredge[8], Elizabeth Edmunds[7], Jane Whilldin[6], James Whilldin[5], Joseph Whilldin[4], Hannah Gorham[3], Desire Howland[2], JOHN HOWLAND[1] THE PILGRIM), born 1 February, 1840. (For descendants see page 136).

(9) JAMES SMITH ELDREDGE, born 28 September, 1839, married Latitia Stimpson, and had: CHARLES STIMPSON ELDREDGE; AUGUSTUS ELDREDGE and CLARA ELDREDGE.

(10) HARRIET ELDREDGE, born 20 December, 1841, married John Smith Parsons. (For descendants see page 120).

(11) GEORGE EMMA ELDREDGE, born 23 September, 1845, married William C. Town. (For descendants see page 137).

AARON ELDREDGE

For ancestors leading back to the Mayflower see page 111.

AARON ELDREDGE[8], (Aaron Eldredge[7], Aaron Eldredge[6], Mercy Leaming[5], Hannah Whilldin[4], Hannah Gorham[3], Desire Howland[2], JOHN HOWLAND[1] THE PILGRIM), was born at Cape May, 6 June, 1795, died 10 August, 1832, (tombstone in Cold Spring Cemetery), married at Cape May, 29 April, 1824, Hannah Eldredge, born 14 June, 1800, died 21 April, 1831, (tombstone in Cold Spring Cemetery).

Issue:—

(1) ELI HICKMAN ELDREDGE, born at Cape May, 3 March, 1825, died at Philadelphia, Pennsylvania, at the age of thirty-nine years, married at Philadelphia, 21 July, 1846, Mary Moore Brunner, and had the following children:

ANNA MAY ELDREDGE, died at the age of fourteen; ELLA VIRGINIA ELDREDGE, married William Stuart King; ELIZABETH BRUNNER ELDREDGE, died at the age of five years; ELI HICKMAN ELDREDGE, married Helen Mar Van Dyke; ABRAHAM BRUNNER ELDREDGE, died at the age of five years; EDWARD LANGDON ELDREDGE; EMMA SHEPHERD ELDREDGE, married John Franklin Soby.

See "The Divine Covenant Fulfilled in Pious Households," by Rev. Daniel Lawrence Hughes, D. D., pages 25 and 26 for biographical notes upon the families of Aaron Eldredge and his son Eli Hickman Eldredge. The authority for the above record was obtained from this source.

JOSEPH ELDREDGE

For ancesters leading back to the Mayflower see page 111.

JOSEPH ELDREDGE[8], (Aaron Eldredge[7], Aaron Eldredge[6], Mercy Leaming[5], Hannah Whilldin[4], Hannah Gorham[3], Desire Howland[2], JOHN HOWLAND[1] THE PILGRIM), was born at Cape May, 7 August, 1798, died at Cape May, 21 March, 1879, (tombstone in Cold Spring Cemetery), married at Cape May, 22 September, 1830, Mrs. Ann Morgan Coxe West, born 18 May, 1800, died at Cape May, 20 July, 1880. (Tombstone in Cold Spring Cemetery).

Issue :—

(1) HARRIET ANN WALES ELDREDGE, born at Cape May, 17 June, 1831, married JAMES LEAMING, (see page 180) and had: JOSEPH ELDREDGE LEAMING, born 21 January, 1854, died at Washington, D. C., 2 February, 1917, married at Cape May, 17 May, 1904, Florence Whitney, and had: DOROTHY LEAMING, born 27 September, 1906.

(2) SARAH EDMONDS ELDREDGE, born at Cape May, 22 August, 1833, died 11 October, 1856.

(3) JOSEPH COXE ELDREDGE, born at Cape May, 9 July, 1836, married at Cape May, 9 June, 1869, OCIE BENNETT. (For descendants see page 138).

(4) ELIZA THERESA ELDREDGE, born at Cape May, 13 December, 1839, died at Cape May, 12 April, 1883.

(For Pilgrim Ancestry of OCIE BENNETT see page 258.)

WILLIAM ELDREDGE

For ancestors leading back to the Mayflower see page 112.

WILLIAM ELDREDGE[8], (Aaron Eldredge[7], Aaron Eldredge[6], Mercy Leaming[5], Hannah Whilldin[4], Hannah Gorham[3], Desire Howland[2], JOHN HOWLAND[1] THE PILGRIM), was born at Cold Spring, New Jersey, 30 April, 1804, died 29 June, 1886, married at Somers Point, New Jersey, 6 September, 1828, Esther Ann Ireland, born at Somers Point, New Jersey, 8 July, 1811.

Issue :—

(1) RACHEL SOMERS ELDREDGE, born 1829, married first George Higbee Stevens, married second James Mecray. (For descendants see page 139).

(2) SARAH W. ELDREDGE, married Constantine Somers, who died 8 January, 1891. MAHLON ELDREDGE, son of SARAH, died 16 September, 1885, married 6 November, 1884, Ella Sayre Stevens, and had: FREDERICK DODSON ELDREDGE, born 20 August, 1885, who married Mary Bland, and had JOHN C. ELDREDGE, born 22 March, 1918.

(3) MARY BENNER ELDREDGE, married Frederick G. Dodson.

(4) HANNAH A. ELDREDGE, born 22 May, 1836, died at Norwich, Connecticut, 16 March, 1920, married DEWITT CLINTON CROWELL. (For descendants see page 140).

(5) AARON ELDREDGE died in infancy.

(6) JOHN SOMERS ELDREDGE, married first Mary Collier Gibson of Richmond, Virginia, and had DEWITT C. ELDREDGE, who married Eleanor Reeves Schellenger, and had MABEL ESTHER ELDREDGE; married second May Brown of Seaford, Delaware; married third Sarah Janney of Baltimore, Maryland, and had JOHN SOMERS ELDREDGE and PEMBERTON ELDREDGE, who married Lillian ———— and had PEMBERTON ELDREDGE, Jr.

(7) EMILINE VANGILDER ELDREDGE.

(8) WILLIAM AGUSTUS ELDREDGE, who married Mary Stewart, and had: HUGH GWYNE ELDREDGE and WILLIAM ELDREDGE.

(9) ELIZA LANGDON ELDREDGE.

STILLWELL ELDREDGE

For ancestors leading back to the Mayflower see page 112.

STILLWELL ELDREDGE[8], (Aaron Eldredge[7], Aaron Eldredge[6], Mercy Leaming[5], Hannah Whilldin[4], Hannah Gorham[3], Desire Howland[2], JOHN HOWLAND[1] THE PILGRIM), was born at Cape May, 6 August, 1806, died at Philadelphia, Pennsylvania, 14 July, 1849, married 2 September, 1830, Mary Benner, born at Philadelphia, Pennsylvania, 18 December, 1812, died 24 November, 1882.

Issue:—

(1) CHARLES HOOVER ELDREDGE, born at Philadelphia, Pennsylvania, 13 June, 1831, died at Wayne, Pennsylvania, September, 1911, married at Philadelphia, 27 November, 1855, Sarah Ann Bavington, born at Philadelphia, 23 August, 1832, died at Wayne, May, 1896, and had: MARIA FLORENCE ELDREDGE, born at Philadelphia, 14 November, 1856, married Oliver Sloan Haines, M. D.; CHARLES STILWELL ELDREDGE, born at Philadelphia, 20 November, 1859, married at Philadelphia, December, 1880, Helen Montgomery, and had CHARLES H. ELDREDGE, born 23 December, 1881, died September, 1887, HOWARD MONTGOMERY ELDREDGE, born at Philadelphia, 19 August, 1884, who married Mabel French, and had GEORGE FRENCH ELDREDGE.

(2) JAMES HENRY ELDREDGE, born at Philadelphia, 12 September, 1835, married 16 February, 1861, Eliza F. Linerd, born at Philadelphia, Pennsylvania, 26 June, 1837, and had: JOSEPH LINERD ELDREDGE, born at Philadelphia, Pennsylvania, 26 November, 1861; ANNA LINERD ELDREDGE, born at Philadelphia, 5 June, 1866.

(3) GEORGE PATTERSON ELDREDGE, born at Philadelphia, Pennsylvania, 1 September, 1838, died 17 August, 1917, married Lizzie Wallace of Sinking Valley, Blair County, Pennsylvania.

(4) EMMA L. ELDREDGE, born at Philadelphia, Pennsylvania, 25 August, 1833, died at Somers Point, New Jersey, at the age of sixty-eight years.

(5) MARY ADELAIDE ELDREDGE, born at Philadelphia, Pennsylvania, 27 December, 1840.

GEORGE M. ELDREDGE

For encestors leading back to the Mayflower see page 112.

GEORGE M. ELDREDGE[8], (Aaron Eldredge[7], Aaron Eldredge[6], Mercy Leaming[5], Hannah Whilldin[4], Hannah Gorham[3], Desire Howland[2], JOHN HOWLAND[1] THE PILGRIM), was born at Cold Spring, New Jersey, 6 December, 1810, died at Abbeville, Louisiana, 27 April, 1886, married 1842, Emma Elizabeth Frierson, born at Charleston, South Carolina, 5 July, 1819, died at Abbeville, Louisiana, 1 January, 1890.

Issue :—

(1) MARY EMMA ELDREDGE, born 4 March, 1846, at Lowndes County, Alabama.

(2) MARION LANGDON ELDREDGE, born at Lowndes County, Alabama, 24 May, 1848, married at De Soto Parish, Louisiana, 19 December, 1878, Daisy Allison, born at De Soto Parish, Louisiana, 15 September, 1857, and had the following children:

LANGDON MARION ELDREDGE, born at Vermilion Parish, Louisiana, 25 September, 1879.

HARTWELL ALLISON ELDREDGE, born at Vermilion Parish, Louisiana, 6 July, 1881.

GEORGE M. ELDREDGE, born at Vermilion Parish, Louisiana, 11 August, 1883.

ANNIE LUCILE ELDREDGE, born at Vermilion, Parish, Louisiana, 2 July, 1886.

(For a biographical account of GEORGE M. ELDREDGE, and his family, see ''The Divine Covenant Fulfilled'' by Rev. DANIEL HUGHES, D.D., page 33.)

MAYFLOWER DESCENDANTS IN CAPE MAY COUNTY

EPHRIAM ELDREDGE

For ancestors leading back to the Mayflower see page 112.

EPHRIAM ELDREDGE⁸, (Aaron Eldredge⁷, Aaron Eldredge⁶, Mercy Leaming⁵, Hannah Whilldin⁴, Hannah Gorham³, Desire Howland², JOHN HOWLAND¹ THE PILGRIM), was born at Cape May, 6 October, 1812, died at West Chester, Pennsylvania, 13 August, 1887, married 22 September, 1835, Sarah Payran, born at Philadelphia, Pennsylvania, 8 March, 1813, died near Pennington, New Jersey, 13 January, 1898.

Issue:—

(1) LIVINGSTON AARON ELDREDGE, born 5 August, 1836, died in infancy.

(2) LIVINGSTON AARON ELDREDGE, born 1 January, 1838, married 5 October, 1869, Rachel Freason, and had, IDA MAY ELDREDGE.

(3) SALONIA IMLAH ELDREDGE, born 25 May, 1840, married 20 August, 1863, William Bernshouse. (For descendants see page 141.)

(4) BARRINGTON SANFORD ELDREDGE, born at Cape May, 26 March, 1843, married first Ettie Blanche McDowell, married second 7 November, 1887, Sallie A. McLean. Children, FLORENCE BEATRICE ELDREDGE and HARRY BARRINGTON ELDREDGE.

(5) REV. WILLIAM HENRY ELDREDGE, born 3 July, 1848, died 7 April, 1920, married Maurie Annie Souder, and had: CLARA HENSON ELDREDGE, born 22 March, 1886, who married 29 June, 1918, Jasper Thomas Perry; WILLIAM PAYSON ELDREDGE, born 14 May, 1893, married 5 October, 1915, Edna Esther Moss; ADA ELDREDGE, born 27 November, 1894.

(6) SAMARIA ANNA ELDREDGE, born 13 December, 1851, at Philaelphia, married at Trenton, New Jersey, 12 April, 1894, Charles Henry Burd, and had: HELEN ELDREDGE BURD, born near Pennington, New Jersey, 22 March, 1896, married at Philadelphia, 10 July, 1918, Francis C. Jobson, and had CHARLES REUBEN JOBSON, born 1 January, 1920.

WILLIAM TOMLIN ELDREDGE

For ancestors leading back to the Mayflower see page 124.

WILLIAM TOMLIN ELDREDGE[9], (Jeremiah Leaming Eldredge[8], Aaron Eldredge[7], Aaron Eldredge[6], Mercy Leaming[5], Hannah Whilldin[4], Hannah Gorham[3], Desire Howland[2], JOHN HOWLAND[1] THE PILGRIM), was born at Cape May, 19 October, 1822, died 4 December, 1888, (tombstone in Cold Spring Cemetery), married Arabella Corson.

Issue :—

(1) STILLWELL ELDREDGE, married Ella Hand, no Issue :—

(2) ELLIS CORSON ELDREDGE, married Emma Robinson and had: FLORA KEELER ELDREDGE, married Bishop Oliver; ELSIE DINSMORE ELDREDGE, who married Thomas Halpin.

(3) LEWIS ELDREDGE, married first May Harris, and had: HAROLD ELDREDGE and IDA MAY ELDREDGE; married second Hannah Weeks and had WILLIAM ELDREDGE and LILLIAN ELDREDGE.

(4) WALTER ELDREDGE, married Mrs. Kate Cresse Worth, no issue.

(5) LIVINGSTON ELDREDGE, born 27 April, 1862, married Judith Hoffman and had: FLORENCE ELDREDGE, who married Thomas Stillwell Sayre; REUBEN ELDREDGE, who married Florence Brown and had EDNA ELDREDGE, born 21 May, 1916, and EMMA ELDREDGE, born 10 May, 1917; STILLWELL ELDREDGE.

(6) ELIZABETH ELDREDGE, married William Hemsley, and had: MAY HEMSLEY; RALEIGH HEMSLEY; JOSEPH HEMSLEY; HARRIET HEMSLEY; and WILLIAM HEMSLEY.

See "Divine Covenant Fulfilled" by Rev. Dr. Daniel Lawrence Hughes, page 22, for a biographical notice of the family of WILLIAM TOMLIN ELDREDGE.

MAYFLOWER DESCENDANTS IN CAPE MAY COUNTY

ELIZA ELDREDGE

For ancesters learding back to the Mayflower see page 124.

ELIZA ELDREDGE[9], (Jeremiah Leaming Eldredge[8], Aaron Eldredge[7], Aaron Eldredge[6], Mercy Leaming[5], Hannah Whilldin[4], Hannah Gorham[3], Desire Howland[2], JOHN HOWLAND[1] THE PILGRIM), was born at Cape May, 7 August, 1826, married 31 December, 1846, HUMPHREY HUGHES[8], (Humphrey Hughes[7], Jane Whilldin[6], James Whilldin[5], Joseph Whilldin[4], Hannah Gorham[3], Desire Howland[2], JOHN HOWLAND[1] THE PILGRIM), who was born at Cape May, 2 May 1882. (See page 202.)

Issue:—

(1) ADRIAN BATEMAN HUGHES, born at Cape May, 6 December, 1848, married and had two children. (See Divine Covenant Fulfilled" by Rev. Daniel Lawrence Hughes, D. D., page 23.)

(2) HARRIET ELDREDGE HUGHES, born at Cape May, 26 December, 1850, married at Cape May, 18 April 1871, Michel Augustus Lengert, born at Philadelphia, Pennsylvania, 15 June, 1848, and had the following children:

GEORGE ELDREDGE LENGERT, born 22 February, 1872, married Florence Prichert, and had, EDITH CRESSON LENGERT; HARRIET HUGHES LENGERT, who married Philip Mercer Maloney, and had, MERCER SHERWOOD MALONEY and GORDON ELDREDGE MALONEY; M. AUGUSTUS LENGERT, married CHARLOTTE RUTHERFORD; LIDA FRANCESCA LENGERT.

For Pilgrim Ancestry of Charlotte Rutherford, see page 232.

CHARLES ELDREDGE

For ancestors leading back to the Mayflower see page 124.

CHARLES ELDREDGE[9], (Jeremiah Leaming Eldredge[8], Aaron Eldredge[7], Aaron Eldredge[6], Mercy Leaming[5], Hannah Whilldin[4], Hannah Gorham[3], Desire Howland[2] JOHN HOWLAND[1] THE PILGRIM), was born at Cold Spring, New Jersey, 18 February, 1830, died at Shiloh, New Jersey, 11 April, 1911, married Elizabeth Tomlin, born at Goshen, New Jersey, 4 May, 1831, died 6 November, 1898, at Shiloh, New Jersey.

Issue:—

(1) HENRY H. ELDREDGE, born 2 December, 1852, died 18 August, 1889.

(2) LINDA M. ELDREDGE, born 10 December, 1854, died 1 April, 1858.

(3) VIRGINA ELDREDGE, born 25 August, 1857, married 24 Decmber, 1878, Samuel Craig. She died 7 April, 1904.

(4) JUDITH T. ELDREDGE, born 3 July, 1859, married 16 March, 1892, Robert Spence.

(5) JEREMIAH L. ELDREDGE, born 7 March, 1861, died 29 September, 1863.

(6) HARRIET ELDREDGE, born 30 May, 1864, married 6 June, 1892, Rev. Raymond M. West, D. D.

(7) ABBIE P. ELDREDGE, born 30 July, 1866, married 10 March, 1887, John Harris, and had: LAWRENCE FITHIAN HARRIS, born 3 March, 1892, married Merle Fitz Randolph, and had KATHERINE MARIE HARRIS, born 6 October, 1919. LINDA E. HARRIS, born 22 March, 1896; FLOYD D. HARRIS, born 6 February, 1899.

(8) PAUL ELDREDGE, born 17 December, 1870, married 31 December, 1891, Rachel Elwell.

NELSON TOMLIN ELDREDGE

For ancesters leading back to the Mayflower see page 124.

NELSON TOMLIN ELDREDGE[9], (Jeremiah Leaming Eldredge[8], Aaron Eldredge[7], Aaron Eldredge[6], Mercy Leaming[5], Hannah Whilldin[4], Hannah Gorham[3], Desire Howland[2], JOHN HOWLAND[1] THE PILGRIM.), was born at Cape May, 13 October, 1833, died at Cape May, 16 June, 1886, (tombstone in Cold Spring Cemetery), married at Cape May, 6 December, 1854, Deborah V. B. Hand, born at Cape May, 24 March, 1834.

Issue :—

(1) MARIETTA ELDREDGE, born 11 August, 1856, died 30 August, 1875, (tombstone in Cold Spring Cemetery).

(2) ELLA ELDREDGE, born 26 February, 1858, died in infancy, (tombstone in Cold Spring Cemetery).

(3) SOUTHARD HAND ELDREDGE, born 20 August, 1861, married at Cape May, 28 April, 1892, Amanda de Prefontaine Ewing, born at Cape May, 19 March, 1872, and had: SOUTHARD SMALLWOOD ELDREDGE, born 3 February, 1893, died in infancy; MARY EWING ELDREDGE, born at Cape May, 23 September, 1894, married 4 December, 1918, Harrison Wainwright Batchelder, and had HARRISON EWING BATCHELDER, born 23 October, 1919.

(4) ELIZA HAND ELDREDGE, born at Cape May, 11 May, 1863.

(5) JACOB SMALLWOOD ELDREDGE, born at Cape May, 28 February, 1871, married at Cape May, LOUISA HAND, (see page 209) and had, ELIZABETH SMALLWOOD ELDREDGE and FRANCES ELDREDGE, the latter died in infancy.

(6) WOODRUFF ELDREDGE, born 13 August, 1875, married LAURA STITES.

(For Pilgrim Ancestry of LAURA STITES see page 221.)

135

FRANCIS SPRINGER ELDREDGE

For ancestors leading back to the Mayflower see page 124.

FRANCIS SPRINGER ELDREDGE[9], (Jeremiah Leaming Eldredge[8], Aaron Eldredge[7], Aaron Eldredge[6], Mercy Leaming[5], Hannah Whilldin[4], Hannah Gorham[3], Desire Howland[2], JOHN HOWLAND[1] THE PILGRIM), was born at Cape May, 22 April, 1836, married at Cape May, 30 January, 1860, ELIZABETH EDMUNDS JOHNSON[9], (Jane White Eldredge[8], Elizabeth Edmunds[7], Jane Whilldin[6], James Whilldin[5], Joseph Whilldin[4], Hannah Gorham[3], Desire Howland[2], JOHN HOWLAND[1] THE PILGRIM), born at Cape May, 6 February, 1840. (See page 224.)

Issue:—

(1) LORING BREWSTER ELDREDGE, born at Cape May, 9, January, 1861, married at Covington, Kentucky, 27 December, 1893, Julia Winter Wolverton, born at Covington, Kentucky, 28 November, 1874, and had: VINCENT SYDNEY ELDREDGE, born at Philadelphia, Pennsylvania, 1 November, 1894, EMMA LORAINE ELIZABETH ELDREDGE, born at Covington, Kentucky, 18 September, 1897, BEATRICE ALBERTA ELDREDGE, born at Philadelphia, 14 February, 1902, died at Laurel Springs, New Jersey, 27 January, 1904.

(2) JOSEPH JOHNSON ELDREDGE, born at Cape May, 26 September, 1863, died 17 February, 1915, married at Philadelphia, Pennsylvania, 26 April, 1885, Hannah Hand, born at Cape May, 24 March, 1866, and had: FRANCIS SPRINGER ELDREDGE, born at Philadelphia, Pennsylvania, 9 October, 1886, married at Camden, New Jersey, 31 December, 1913, Emma V. Davis, and had, BLANCHE L. ELDREDGE, born at Laurel Springs, New Jersey, 20 April, 1915, FRANCIS SPRINGER ELDREDGE, born at Laurel Springs, New Jersey, 5 January, 1917, and JOSEPH JOHNSON ELDREDGE, born at Laurel Springs, New Jersey, 12 May, 1918.

(3) FRANCIS GOODELL ELDREDGE, born at Cape May, 30 April, 1878, married at Philadelphia, 9 June, 1901, Bertha May Woodmansee, and had MERLE ANDERSON ELDREDGE, born 25 May, 1902.

GEORGE EMMA ELDREDGE

For ancestors leading back to the Mayflower see page 124.

GEORGE EMMA ELDREDGE[9], (Jeremiah Leaming Eldredge[8], Aaron Eldredge[7], Aaron Eldredge[6], Mercy Leaming[5], Hannah Whilldin[4], Hannah Gorham[3], Desire Howland[2], JOHN HOWLAND[1] THE PILGRIM), was born at Cape May, 23 September, 1845, died at Cape May, 2 August, 1920, married at Cape May, 20 September, 1867, William Corgie Town, born at Cape May, 17 February, 1844.

Issue:—

(1) HARRIET ELDREDGE TOWN, born at Cold Spring, New Jersey, 22 February, 1870, married at Cold Spring, April, 1888, Lot Buck Cresse, and had: EMLYN TOWN CRESSE, born at Cold Spring, New Jersey, 1 September, 1889; NORMAN CRESSE, born at Cold Spring, New Jersey, 27 September, 1891, died 11 February, 1914; GILBERT STIMSON CRESSE, born at Cold Spring, New Jersey, 2 September, 1893; ADRIAN HUGHES CRESSE, born at Erma, New Jersey, 29 February, 1896, died 25 August, 1903; AUGUSTUS JOHNSON CRESSE, born at Erma, New Jersey, 2 February, 1898; HELEN CRESSE, born at Erma, New Jersey, 27 April, 1900; LOTTIE CRESSE, born at Erma, New Jersey, 9 May, 1903, died 20 August, 1903; MARY EMMA CRESSE, born at West Cape May, May, 22 August, 1904.

(2) ELIZABETH SMALLWOOD TOWN, born at Cold Spring, New Jersey, 15 November, 1871, married at Cold Spring, New Jersey, 12 September, 1894, Sidney Racket Goff, born at Eldora, New Jersey, 20 March, 1866, and had: HENRIETTA GOFF, born at Tuckahoe, New Jersey, 8 February, 1899.

(3) CHARLES ELDREDGE TOWN, born at Cold Spring, New Jersey, 19 March, 1874, married Mary Emma Leycock.

(4) ADA CORGIE TOWN, born at Cold Spring, New Jersey, 17 October, 1884, married George Bernard Hess.

JOSEPH COXE ELDREDGE

For ancestors leading back to the Mayflower see page 127.

JOSEPH COXE ELDREDGE[9], (Joseph Eldredge[8], Aaron Eldredge[7], Aaron Eldredge[6], Mercy Leaming[5], Hannah Whilldin[4], Hannah Gorham[3], Desire Howland[2], JOHN HOWLAND[1] THE PILGRIM), was born at Cape May, 9 July, 1836, died at Trenton, New Jersey, 17 August, 1913, married at Cape May, 9 June, 1869, OCIE BENNETT[9], (Sophia Hughes[8], Israel Hughes[7], Memucan Hughes[6], Hannah Whilldin[5], Joseph Whilldin[4], Hannah Gorham[3], Desire Howland[2], JOHN HOWLAND[1] THE PILGRIM), born at Cape May, 20 August, 1846. (See page 258.)

Issue:—

(1) IRVIN HOWARD ELDREDGE, born at Cold Spring, New Jersey, 22 March, 1875, married at Philadelphia, Pennsylvania, 10 November, 1898, Marie Louise Benton, born at Cannonsburg, Pennsylvania, 17 November, 1869, and had: ALLEN BENNETT ELDREDGE, born at Cold Spring, New Jersey, 10 September, 1899; LAURENCE HOWARD ELDREDGE, born at Cold Spring, New Jersey, 18 March, 1902; MARY LOUISE ELDREDGE, born at Cape May, 22 November, 1903; ESTHER FORBES ELDREDGE, born at Cape May, 20 February, 1905; ELEANORE ANDREW ELDREDGE, born at Cold Spring, New Jersey, 19 September, 1911; MARJORIE BENTON ELDREDGE, born at Cold Spring, New Jersey, 26 April, 1913.

(2) OCIE MAY ELDREDGE, born at Cold Spring, New Jersey, 11 May, 1876, married at Cold Spring, 1 July, 1896, George E. Walter, and had: JOHN GEORGE WALTER, born 18 July, 1897, married at Darby, Pennsylvania, 11 February, 1920, Helen Tyler Levergood.

MAYFLOWER DESCENDANTS IN CAPE MAY COUNTY

RACHEL SOMERS ELDREDGE

For ancestors leading back to the Mayflower see page 128.

RACHEL SOMERS ELDREDGE[9], (William Eldredge[8], Aaron Eldredge[7], Aaron Eldredge[6], Mercy Leaming[5], Hannah Whilldin[4], Hannah Gorham[3], Desire Howland[2], JOHN HOWLAND[1] THE PILGRIM), was born at Cape May, 1829, died at Cape May, 24 December, 1870, (tombstone in Cold Spring Cemetery), married first George Higby Stevens, son of Ezekiel Stevens, of Cold Spring, New Jersey.

Issue:—

(1) LOIS H. STEVENS, married first William Eldredge, of Cape May County, and had GEORGE ELDREDGE; married second, D. E. Mathis, of New Gretna, Burlington County, New Jersey.

(2) ALBERT STEVENS.

RACHEL SOMERS ELDREDGE married second James Mecray, born at Cape May, 24 August, 1808, died at Camden, New Jersey, 12 January, 1892, and had:

(3) RACHEL SOMERS MECRAY, who married at Philadelphia, Pennsylvania, 29 April, 1890, Joseph Thomson Dolby, born at Philadelphia, Pennsylvania, 5 February, 1864, died at Philadelphia, Pennsylvania, 16 January, 1909, and had the following children: IRENE MARTIN DOLBY, born at Philadelphia, Pennsylvania, 12 October, 1896; JAMES LOUIS DOLBY, born at Philadelphia, Pennsylvania, 20 June, 1900; JOSEPH THOMSON DOLBY, born at Philadelphia, Pennsylvania, 31 March, 1904, died at Cape May, 4 August, 1904.

139

HANNAH A. ELDREDGE

For ancestors leading back to the Mayflower see page 128.

HANNAH A. ELDREDGE[9], (William Eldredge[8], Aaron Eldredge[7], Aaron Eldredge[6], Mercy Leaming[5], Hannah Whilldin[4], Hannah Gorham[3], Desire Howland[2], JOHN HOWLAND[1] THE PILGRIM), was born at Cape May, 22 May, 1836, died at Norwich, Connecticut, 16 March, 1920, married at Cold Spring, New Jersey, 8 February, 1859, DeWITT CLINTON CROWELL[9], (Hannah Matthews[8], Eleanor Hughes[7], Ellis Hughes[6], Hannah Whilldin[5], Joseph Whilldin[4], Hannah Gorham[3], Desire Howland[2], JOHN HOWLAND[1] THE PILGRIM), see page 266, who was born at Philadelphia, Pennsylvania, 5 February, 1828, died at Norfolk, Virginia, 25 November, 1874.

Issue:—

(1) MARY CECILIA CROWELL, born at Cape May, 3 December, 1859.

(2) DESSA WILLIAMSON CROWELL, born at Cape May, 30 September, 1861, married at Philadelphia, Pennsylvania, 19 October, 1882, John Browning Clement, born at Philadelphia, Pennsylvania, 9 July, 1859, and had: DESSA CROWELL CLEMENT, born at Philadelphia, Pennsylvania, 20 November, 1883; JOHN BROWNING CLEMENT, born at Philadelphia, Pennsylvania, 4 December, 1886; GREGORY CLEMENT, born at Haverford, Pennsylvania, 28 November, 1890; DeWITT CROWELL CLEMENT, born at Philadelphia, Pennsylvania, 22 December, 1894.

(3) EVA JANE CROWELL, born at Norfolk, Virginia, 17 August, 1867, married at Philadelphia, Pennsylvania, October, 1901, Leonard Owen Smith, and had: ELOISE CROWELL SMITH, born at Philadelphia, Pennsylvania, 8 December, 1903, and EVA VIRGINIA SMITH, born at Philadelphia, Pennsylvania, 23 December, 1904.

(4) HANNAH MATTHEWS CROWELL, born at Norfolk, Virginia, 7 September, 1869.

SALONIA IMLAH ELDREDGE

For ancestors leading back to the Mayflower see page 131.

SALONIA IMLAH ELDREDGE[9], (Ephriam Eldredge[8], Aaron Eldredge[7], Aaron Eldredge[6], Mercy Leaming[5], Hannah Whilldin[4], Hannah Gorham[3], Desire Howland[2], JOHN HOWLAND[1] THE PILGRIM), was born at Philadelphia, Pennsylvania, 25 May, 1840, married at Hammonton, New Jersey, 20 August, 1863, William Bernshouse, born at Fathinga, Prussia, 30 March, 1834, son of Peter and Christine Bernshouse.

Issue:—

(1) WILLIAM HENRY BERNSHOUSE, born at Winslow, New Jersey, 3 July, 1864, married at Perryman, Maryland, 29 May, 1890, Fannie Rosabelle Taylor, born at Perryman, 7 September, 1864, daughter of Richard M. and Margaret J. Taylor, and had: HELEN BERNSHOUSE, born at Hammonton, New Jersey, 5 January, 1892, married at Hammonton, New Jersey, 6 November, 1915, Charles Alfred Smith, born at Philadelphia, Pennsylvania, 3 February, 1889, son of William Hinds and Clarissa Gay Smith, and had CHARLES ALFRED SMITH, JR., born at Philadelphia, Pennsylvania, 27 February, 1919; ETHEL BERNSHOUSE, born at Hammonton, New Jersey, 9 January, 1894, married at Hammonton, New Jersey, 15 November, 1919, Robert Clinton Cronin, Jr., of Perryman, Maryland, son of Robert Clinton and Mary Catherine Cronin.

Fannie Rosabelle Taylor, wife of WILLIAM HENRY BERNSHOUSE, died at Hammonton, New Jersey, 26 June, 1917.

(2) ALBERT LIVINGSTONE BERNSHOUSE, born at Winslow, New Jersey, 11 December, 1866, married at Houston, Texas, 19 May, 1897, Devene Bourgeois, born at Houston, Texas, 9 February, 1879, daughter of Joseph D. and Salize Bourgeois.

(Continued on next page)

141

SALONIA IMLAH ELDREDGE

Children of ALBERT LIVINGSTONE BERNSHOUSE and Devene Bourgeois, his wife: ANDREW KESSLER BERNS-HOUSE, born at Houston, Texas, 12 April, 1898; MABEL DE-VENE BERNSHOUSE, born at Houston, Texas, 13 August, 1899; WILLIAM HENRY BERNSHOUSE, born at Houston, Texas, 3 August, 1904, died at Hamilton, Texas, 18 November, 1907; GEORGE ALBERT BERNSHOUSE, born at Houston, Texas, 20 January, 1906; LEON and SALONIA LORENE BERNSHOUSE (twins), born at Brady, Texas, 13 July, 1914.

(3) ANDREW KESSLER HAY BERNSHOUSE, born at Winslow, New Jersey, 9 November, 1868, married first at Sumter, South Carolina, 29 May, 1904, Selma Nash, (daughter of B. R. and Maria Nash), who died at Sumter, South Carolina, 17 June, 1908, without issue; married second at Summerton, South Carolina, 14 December, 1911, Elizabeth Holladay, born at Summerton, South Carolina, 1 August, 1891, daughter of James and Susie Holladay, and had: WILBERT BERNS-HOUSE, born at Sumter, South Carolina, 10 September, 1913; SELMA BERNSHOUSE, born at Sumter, South Carolina, 29 March, 1916.

(4) SALONIA IMLAH BERNSHOUSE, born at Wins-low, New Jersey, 16 June, 1870, died at Winslow, New Jersey, 19 July, 1871.

(5) SAMARIA ANNA BERNSHOUSE, born at Winslow, New Jersey, 28 February, 1872, married at Pitman Grove, New Jersey, 17 November, 1907, John Winzer Goforth, born at Woodstown, New Jersey, 4 July, 1876, died at Denver, Colorado, 15 March, 1910, (son of William Stanley and Julia Wells Go-forth.)

PRISCILLA LEAMING

For ansectors leading back to the Mayflower see page 102.

PRISCILLA LEAMING[7], (Margaret Stites[6], Priscilla Leaming[5], Hannah Whilldin[4], Hannah Gorham[3], Desire Howland[2], JOHN HOWLAND[1] THE PILGRIM), was born at Cape May, 9 October, 1764, died at Cape May, 4 April, 1821, married Humphrey Stites. (See Diary of Aaron Leaming second quoted on page 35 of this volume.)

Issue:—

(1) HANNAH STITES, born 12 November, 1788, married AARON LEAMING. (For descendants see page 144).

(2) ELIZA STITES, born 21 June, 1798, died 18 March, 1868, married Jeremiah Cresse, and had: HUMPHREY CRESSE, born 1828, married Ruhama Ludlam, and had LENA CRESSE, died 1897, unmarried, and ELIZA CRESSE, who married 16 February, 1904, George H. Peirce; MARGARET CRESSE, born 1830, married George Downs, and had FRANK P. DOWNS, and LIZZIE DOWNS, who married E. K. Godschalk, and had HELEN GODSCHALK and CLARENCE GODSCHALK; MAURICE CRESSE, born at Cape May, 1835, married first Lydia Hildreth, and had ADELAIDE CRESSE, who married Morgan Hand, JERE LILBURN CRESSE, who married Irene Stover, and had LYDIA CUMMINGS CRESSE; EDMUND CRESSE, son of Jeremiah, married Hannah Bennett, and had ORILLA CRESSE, who married Gilbert Dunn. MAURICE CRESSE married second LENA WARE. (See page 220.)

(3) MARGARET STITES, married 2 February, 1806, Philip Cresse, and had: PRISCILLA CRESSE, married John Townsend, and had MARGARET TOWNSEND; CHARLES CRESSE; HANNAH CRESSE; and AMOS CRESSE.

(4) MARY STITES, married Eli Townsend, and had: PRISCILLA TOWNSEND, who married Rev. Edward Swain; EDMUND TOWNSEND, died in Civil War.

(5) HUMPHREY STITES, died without issue.

143

HANNAH STITES

Far ancestors leading back to the Mayflower see page 143.

HANNAH STITES[8], (Priscilla Leaming[7], Margaret Stites[6], Priscilla Leaming[5], Hannah Whilldin[4], Hannah Gorham[3], Desire Howland[2], JOHN HOWLAND[1] THE PILGRIM), was born at Cape May, 12 November, 1788, died at Cape May, 12 April, 1862, married at Cape May, 20 August, 1809, AARON LEAMING (see page 108), who was born at Cape May, 15 May, 1784, died at Cape May, 7 January, 1836.

Issue :—

(1) CHARLOTTE LEAMING, born 28 May, 1810, died 30 July, 1854, married SILAS MATTHEWS, no issue. (See page 252).

(2) PARSONS LEAMING, born 22 November, 1811, married Lydia Hand, and had: HANNAH and AUGUSTA LEAMING, both died in childhood.

(3) LYDIA LEAMING, born 29 September, 1813, married LEMUEL LEAMING (see page 177).

(4) ELIZA LEAMING, born 21 November, 1815, died 24 August, 1894, married George Hoffman. (For descendants see page 145).

(5) HANNAH LEAMING, born 15 October, 1817, died 20 November, 1882, married Jeremiah Richardson, and had: FURMAN RICHARDSON, who married Minnie Hildreth, and had, FRANK RICHARDSON, EDITH RICHARDSON; SOPHIA RICHARDSON, who married Brook Goble, and had EMILY LEAMING GOBLE; CHARLES W. RICHARDSON, married LIZZIE H. LEE, and had MABEL G. RICHARDSON, who married John T. Hewitt, (see page 280).

(6) PRISCILLA LEAMING, born 8 January, 1820, married Daniel Buzby Hughes, (For descendants see page 146).

(7) EMILY LEAMING, born 5 February, 1822, married REV. ALBERT MATTHEWS. (For descendants see page 300).

(8) AARON LEAMING, born 29 April, 1824, unmarried.

(9) HUMPHREY LEAMING, born 1 March, 1826, married Amelia Augusta Woodruff. (For descendants see page 147).

(10) MARY LEAMING, born 16 February, 1828, died 31 July, 1862, married Furman Compton, and had FURMAN COMPTON.

(11) JOHN QUINCY LEAMING, born 18 February, 1830, died 21 November, 1857, unmarried.

ELIZA LEAMING

For ancestors leading back to the Mayflower see page 144.

ELIZA LEAMING[9], (Hannah Stites[8], Priscilla Leaming[7], Margaret Stites[6], Priscilla Leaming[5], Hannah Whilldin[4], Hannah Gorham[3], Desire Howland[2], JOHN HOWLAND[1] THE PILGRIM), was born at Cape May, 21 November, 1815, died 24 August, 1894, married 23 March, 1841, George Hoffman. Issue:—

(1) HARRIET HOFFMAN, born 11 January, 1842, died April, 1915, married 11 December, 1861, Socrates Shaw, and had: LIZZIE SHAW, born January, 1862, married Edwin Morton, and had, MYRON MORTON, CLAUDE MORTON, JULIUS MORTON, HARRIET SHAW MORTON, LESLIE MORTON and CLARA MORTON; ELLA VIRGINIA SHAW, born 23 June, 1865, married John Morton, and had, HAROLD MORTON, LEROY MORTON and BERNICE MORTON.

(2) FRANCIS HOFFMAN, born 17 April, 1848, died 21 May, 1916, married 17 July, 1876, Mary Helen Sheets, and had: ELIZA LEAMING HOFFMAN, born at Philadelphia, 6 November, 1878, married Jesse M. Brown, and had, FRANCES BROWN, born 22 July, 1900, and KENNARD EARL BROWN, born 30 March, 1905; ELLA SHAW HOFFMAN, born at Philadelphia, 18 December, 1880, married John William Stidworthy, and had WILLIAM McNAUGHTON STIDWORTHY; GEORGE SHEETS HOFFMAN, born at Philadelphia, 20 February, 1883, married Nevada Turner, and had, HERBERT HOFFMAN, MARY ELMA HOFFMAN and GEORGE HOFFMAN; LEWIS SHEETS HOFFMAN, born at Cape May County, 3 March, 1885, married Miranda Reeves Dickinson; JACOB CRESS HOFFMAN, born at Cape May, 29 April, 1887; CHARLES RICHARD HOFFMAN, born at Cape May, 21 December, 1896, married Emily Jane Jones.

(3) EDMUND MATTHEWS HOFFMAN, born 2 May, 1855, died 3 August, 1913, married Lydia Foster Shaw, born 10 April, 1855, died 13 October, 1915, and had, CHARLES SMITH HOFFMAN, born 26 July, 1893.

(4) JULIA HOFFMAN, born 27 July, 1859, married 28 October, 1893, Dennis Peterson, and had, ETHEL MAY PETERSON, born 4 June, 1895, married 4 June, 1916, John Van Dover Muncey.

PRISCILLA LEAMING

For ancestors leading back to the Mayflower see page 144.

PRISCILLA LEAMING[9], (Hannah Stites[8], Priscilla Leaming[7], Margaret Stites[6], Priscilla Leaming[5], Hannah Whilldin[4], Hannah Gorham[3], Desire Howland[2], JOHN HOWLAND[1] THE PILGRIM), was born at Rio Grande, New Jersey, 8 January, 1820, died 29 June 1915, married Daniel Busby Hughes, born 25 July, 1816, died 1 June, 1888.

Issue:—

(1) JULIA HUGHES, born 24 May, 1841, married at Cape May, 1865, SILAS MATTHEWS, and had CLARENCE H. MATTHEWS, born at Fishing Creek, New Jersey, 8 February, 1867, and ALICE MATTHEWS, born at Cold Spring, New Jersey, 23 February, 1873. (See page 265.)

(2) EMILY LEAMING HUGHES, born 2 October, 1842, married at Cold Spring, New Jersey, 15 November, 1865, Samuel Townsend, born at Cold Spring, 7 September, 1838, and had MARY EMMA TOWNSEND, born at Cold Spring, 21 February, 1872, married at Cold Spring, 4 June, 1901, Lewellyn Hildreth, born at Rio Grande, New Jersey, 12 March, 1869.

(3) ELLEN HUGHES, born 12 November, 1844, died at Cold Spring, November, 1881, married John M. Russell, and had: EVA MAY RUSSELL, married Howard M. Swalley,; BERTHA LEAMING RUSSELL, married J. Allan Odaniel; DANIEL HUGHES RUSSELL, married Mabel Foster. (For descendants see page 327).

(4) CHARLOTTE HUGHES, died in infancy.

(5) BEULAH HUGHES, died in infancy.

(6) MARY JANE HUGHES, born 17 May, 1851, married John Bate, and had: E. MORRIS BATE, who married Ella Craig, and had, MORRIS BATE and MARY BATE; BEULAH BATE, who married GEORGE O. CUMMINGS, (see page 172); JOHN HERBERT BATE; WILLIAM BATE, who married Alma Corson.

(7) HARRIET N. HUGHES, married Edwin J. Cummings, and had FLORENCE H. CUMMINGS, who married Luther Peck.

(8) LEAMING ELLSWORTH HUGHES, born at Cold Spring, 26 March, 1862, married 21 August, 1886, Isabella Reeves Cresse, and had MARY LEAMING HUGHES.

146

MAYFLOWER DESCENDANTS IN CAPE MAY COUNTY

HUMPHREY LEAMING

For ancestors leading back to the Mayflower see page 144.

HUMPHREY LEAMING[9], (Hannah Stites[8], Priscilla Leaming[7], Margaret Stites[6], Priscilla Leaming[5], Hannah Whilldin[4], Hannah Gorham[3], Desire Howland[2], JOHN HOWLAND[1] THE PILGRIM), was born at Rio Grande, New Jersey 1 March, 1826, died at Patchogue, New York, 28 August, 1866, married at Medford, New York, 4 March, 1860, Amelia Augusta Woodruff, born at Bellport, New York, 16 June, 1838.

Issue:—

(1) INEZ LEAMING, born at Patchogue, New York, 27 February, 1864, married at Patchogue, New York, 4 December, 1890, Walter Husted Jaycox, born at Amenia Union, Dutchess County, New York, 3 September, 1863, and had DOROTHY LEAMING JAYCOX, born 28 September, 1891, died 12 May, 1892.

(2) BYRON LEAMING, born at Patchogue, New York, 30 October, 1867, married at New York City, 1 January, 1906, Bessie Bayles, born 1888, and had: FRANK B. LEAMING, born at Stony Brook, New York, 14 October, 1906; DONALD WOODRUFF LEAMING, born at Stony Brook, New York, 3 June, 1908; THELMA LEAMING, born at Stony Brook, New York, 1 July, 1910; MARY ELIZABETH LEAMING, born at Stony Brook, New York, 7 January, 1913.

(3) AMELIA AUGUSTA LEAMING, born at Patchogue, New York, 1 July, 1872, married 16 November, 1892, Walter Scott Rose, born 28 December, 1871, and had: INEZ MADELEINE ROSE, born at Patchogue, New York, 1 July, 1895, married 29 September, 1919, Carlton Raphael McCarthy, born April, 1893; HENRIETTA LEAMING ROSE, born at Patchogue, New York, 22 February, 1899.

147

MARY HUGHES

For ancestors leading back to the Mayflower see page 103.

MARY HUGHES[7], (Jacob Hughes[6], Priscilla Leaming[5], Hannah Whilldin[4], Hannah Gorham[3], Desire Howland[2], JOHN HOWLAND[1] THE PILGRIM[1]), was born at Cape May, 1780, died at Philadelphia, Pennsylvania, 30 January, 1862, aged 82 years, (tombstone in Old Swedes Church Yard, Philadelphia, Pennsylvania,) married at Cape May, 17 February, 1800, John Bennett, (Cape May Marriages, Book A),who was born at Cape May, 1780, died at Philadelphia, 5 October, 1834, and was buried beside his wife in Old Swedes Church Yard. (See also ''The Divine Covenant Fulfilled'' by Rev. Dr. Lawrence Hughes, page 20.)

Issue :—

(1) WILLIAM BENNETT, born at Cape May, 4 October, 1803, died 29 December, 1886, married at Cape May, 28 August, 1830, Phebe Schellenger. (For descendants see page 152.)

(2) SOPHIA HUGHES BENNETT, married 20 March, 1831, Enoch Jackson, and had: OLIVIA JACKSON, born 1 November, 1832, who married 16 March, 1853, Robert Jones.

(3) GEORGE BENNETT, lost at sea.

(4) LOUISA STEVENS BENNETT, born at Cape May, 15 October, 1817, died at Philadelphia, Pennsylvania, 3 June, 1900, married at Cape May, 1 May, 1833, Isaac Printz Merritt. (For descendants see page 153.)

(5) MARY ANN BENNETT, married John Rowland, and had ADELAIDE ROWLAND, who married John Murphy.

(6) CHARLOTTE BENNETT, married John Sinclair.

JEREMIAH HUGHES

For ancestors leading back to the Mayflower see page 104.

JEREMIAH HUGHES[7], (Jacob Hughes[6], Priscilla Leaming[5], Hannah Whilldin[4], Hannah Gorham[3], Desire Howland[2], JOHN HOWLAND[1] THE PILGRIM), was born at Cape May, 23 February, 1815, (tombstone in Cold Spring Cemetery), married about 1805, Rhoda Taylor, born at Cape May, 11 April, 1778, died at Cape May, 11 September, 1843. She married second Edward Price, 11 May, 1820, who died 21 January, 1825.

Issue:—

(1) RACHEL HUGHES, born at Cape May, 16 February, 1808, unmarried.

(2) MARIA HUGHES, born at Cape May, 28 October, 1810, died 13 November, 1852, married Zerubbabel Gaskill, and lived in Camden, New Jersey.

(3) SARAH HUGHES, born at Cape May, 21 October, 1811, died about 1880, married Jacob Middleton. No issue.

(4) JEREMIAH TAYLOR HUGHES, born at Cape May, 5 April, 1815, died 1893, married at Cape May, 27 December, 1843, Mary Ann Wheatley, born 1820, died 1873, and had WILLIAM W. HUGHES, RHODA A. HUGHES, CHARLES M. HUGHES, MARY RUTH HUGHES and DAVID HUGHES. (See page 154.)

JAMES RAINY HUGHES

For ancestors leading back to the Mayflower see page 104.

JAMES RAINY HUGHES[7], (Jacob Hughes[6], Priscilla Leaming[5], Hannah Whilldin[4], Hannah Gorham[3], Desire Howland[2], JOHN HOWLAND[1] THE PILGRIM), was born at New England, Lower Township, Cape May County, New Jersey, 6 July, 1791, died at Cape May, 13 March, 1865, married at Cape May, 9 January, 1815, ELIZA ELDREDGE[8], (Aaron Eldredge[7], Aaron Eldredge[6], Mercy Leaming[5], Hannah Whilldin[4], Hannah Gorham[3], Desire Howland[2], JOHN HOWLAND[1] THE PILGRIM),born at Cold Spring, New Jersey, 15 December, 1796, died at Unionville, Pennsylvania, 6 January, 1876, (tombstone in Cold Spring Cemetery).

Issue :—

(1) JEREMIAH ELDREDGE HUGHES, born at Cape May, 10 December, 1815, died at Gainesville, Texas, 23 June, 1884, married at Gainesville, 29 March, 1857, Sophronia Sparks, born at Nilson County, Tennessee, 31 July, 1834, died at Gainesville, 25 April, 1880, and had: GEORGE ELDREDGE HUGHES, died in infancy; ADELAIDE HUGHES, born 15 November, 1864, married at Gainesville, Texas, 15 September, 1887, Cyrus Ritchie, born in Texas, 7 November, 1862, and had, ANNIE HUGHES RITCHIE, born 6 September, 1888; JAMES R. HUGHES, born 29 January, 1867; CLARA HUGHES, born 9 November, 1869.

(2) ANN LAWRENCE HUGHES, born 9 November, 1817, married Downs E. Foster. (For descendants see page 155).

(3) REV. DANIEL LAWRENCE HUGHES, D. D., born 8 January, 1820, married ELMIRA WILLIAMS HUGHES[8], (Humphrey Hughes[7], Jane Whilldin[6], James Whilldin[5], Joseph Whilldin[4], Hannah Gorham[3], Desire Howland[2], JOHN HOWLAND[1] THE PILGRIM). (For descendants see page 157.)

(4) JOSEPH ELDREDGE HUGHES, born at Cape May, 31 July, 1821, married 28 November, 1842, Experience Somers, born at Somers Point, New Jersey, 23 October, 1824, died at Cape May, 28 January, 1886, (tombstone in Cold Spring Ceme-

(Continued on next page)

150

JAMES RAINY HUGHES

tery), and had: WILLIAM SOMERS HUGHES, born 29 July, 1843, died in infancy; LAURA SOMERS HUGHES, born 2 February, 1848, married 1867 Jonathan Hoffman, and had, EDWARD HOFFMAN, deceased, HOWARD SOMERS HOFFMAN and BEULA HOFFMAN (died in infancy); JOSEPH HENRY HUGHES, married at Moorestown, New Jersey, 28 February, 1878, Emma Thackra Bennett, daughter of Abraham and Sarah Bennett, and had, SALLIE KENNEDY HUGHES and JENNIE WALKER HUGHES. JOSEPH ELDREDGE HUGHES married second, 14 September, 1886, Mrs. Mary A. Farrow, of Cape May.

(5) HARRIET NEWELL HUGHES, born 23 July, 1825, married Rev. Charles M. Oakley. (For descendants see page158.)

(6) REV. JAMES POTTER HUGHES, born 15 December, 1827, married Emily Wiltsie Roberts. (For descendants see page 159.)

(7) HANNAH ELIZA HUGHES, born 21 February, 1830, married Thomas McMinn. (For descendants see page 161.)

(8) MARY BENNETT HUGHES, born at Cape May, 25 March, 1833, married at Pacific City, Iowa, 15 November, 1860, Charles Hollister Fletcher, born at Springfield, Ohio, 7 September, 1837, died at Keosauqua, Iowa, 2 January, 1877, and had HOLLIS HUGHES FLETCHER, born at Burlington, Iowa, 22 August, 1861, died at Chicago, Illinois, 11 April, 1888.

(9) EMMA MILINDA HUGHES, born 22 January, 1836, married Rev. John Sinclair Roberts. (For descendants see page 162.)

(10) AMELIA FOSTER HUGHES, born 7 June, 1839, married Rev. John Kershaw. (For descendants see page 163.)

(11) REV. JACOB VAN RENSSELAER HUGHES, born at Cape May, 11 September, 1844, married at Canonsburg, Pennsylvania, 27 July, 1870, Elizabeth Catherine McGinnes, born at Lewiston, Illinois, 2 May, 1843, died at Shawano, Wisconsin, 11 May, 1888, and had: MARY FLETCHER HUGHES, born at Unionville, Pennsylvania, 22 February, 1874; HAROLD DALRYMPLE HUGHES, born at Unionville, 16 May, 1876; ALICE McGINNES HUGHES, born at Unionville, 4 July, 1877. The Rev. JACOB VAN RENSSELAER HUGHES married second Mary A. Ayers, and had: MARGARET HUGHES; ARTHUR HUGHES; CAROLYN HUGHES.

WILLIAM BENNETT

For ancestors leading back to the Mayflower see page 148.

WILLIAM BENNETT[8], (Mary Hughes[7], Jacob Hughes[6], Priscilla Leaming[5], Hannah Whilldin[4], Hannah Gorham[3], Desire Howland[2], JOHN HOWLAND[1] THE PILGRIM), was born at Cape May, 4 October, 1803, died 29 December, 1886, married at Cape May, 28 August, 1830, Phebe Schellenger, born at Cape May, 8 August, 1811, died 29 June, 1886.

Issue:—

(1) WILLIAM JACKSON BENNETT, born 24 April, 1832, married HENRIETTA HAND. (For descendants see page 164.)

(2) LOVENIA BENNETT, born 30 September, 1833, married Robert Chambers, and had: ABIGAIL CHAMBERS, married Michael Holland, and had BERTA HOLLAND, who married Edward Benezet; WILLIAM CHAMBERS, born 16 May, 1869, married Lizzie Chambers, and had, FLORENCE CHAMBERS, born 22 September, 1900, and FREDERICK CHAMBERS, born 20 January, 1902; ELWOOD CHAMBERS, died in infancy.

(3) EMMA LEAMING BENNETT, born 31 October, 1837, married John Gilbert, and had, WILLIAM GILBERT and ALBERT GILBERT.

(4) ALBERT G. REED BENNETT, born 24 October, 1839, married first Martha A. Naves, married second Elizabeth Smallwood. (For descendants see page 165.)

(5) GEORGE BENNETT, born 1 January, 1841, married at Cape May, 22 May, 1865, Sarah Richardson, born 25 July, 1841, and had: MARY LOUISE BENNETT, born at Cape May, 23 December, 1866, married at Cape May, 24 December, 1902, George Wicks, born 11 July, 1868, died 17 May, 1906, and had, RUTH WICKS, born at Cape May, 2 April, 1904; SOPHIA BENNETT, born at Cape May, 27 March, 1880, married at Cape May, 24 September, 1902, Joseph Dougherty, and had, GEORGE DOUGHERTY, born 19 February, 1903, and WISTAR DOUGHERTY, born 8 April, 1904; FREDERICK BENNETT, born at Cape May, 25 November, 1883, married 1 July, 1903, Martha Gile, born 2 May, 1884, (daughter of Augustine Charles Gile and Mary Schreiner Gile) and had, EMMA BENNETT, born 20 July, 1904.

LOUISA STEVENS BENNETT

For ancestors leading back to the Mayflower see page 148.

LOUISA STEVENS BENNETT[8], (Mary Hughes[7], Jacob Hughes[6], Priscilla Leaming[5], Hannah Whilldin[4], Hannah Gorham[3], Desire Howland[2], JOHN HOWLAND[1] THE PILGRIM), was born at Cape May, 15 October, 1817, died at Philadelphia, Pennsylvania, 3 June, 1900, married at Cape May, 1 May, 1853, Isaac Printz Merritt, born at Cape May, 14 April, 1811, died at Philadelphia, 3 June, 1888.

Issue:—

(1) GEORGE MERRITT, died in infancy.

(2) JOHN BENNETT MERRITT, born 2 August, 1835, married 11 October, 1858, Fannie Antoine, who died 29 December, 1891, and had: JAMES ROBB MERRITT, born at Philadelphia, 30 December, 1860, married Maxamelia Douglas Taylor. (For descendants see page 322.)

(3.) ALEXIS GRASSON MERRITT, born 9 January, 1838, died 13 November, 1916, married first 26 April, 1858, Susannah Dale, who died 16 June, 1888; married second, 19 March, 1891, Cynthia B. Atkins. (For descendants see page 176.)

(4) ISAAC PRINTZ MERRITT, born 21 February, 1842.

(5) LOUISA BENNETT MERRITT, born 8 January, 1845, died 17 November, 1872, married 15 August, 1861, Jeremiah Bennett Schellinger, and had: ISAAC MERRITT SCHELLINGER, born 9 December, 1863, married 7 May, 1887, Jane Farrow, born 28 February, 1868; JOSEPH SCHELLINGER, born at Cape May, 16 March, 1865, married at Cape May, 7 October, 1886, Electra H. Edmunds, and had, LOUISA BENNETT SCHELLINGER, born 2 November, 1887, who married 8 April, 1907, William McCalla Bland, and had, LOUISA S. BLAND, born 9 October, 1907, and ALICE McCALLA BLAND, born 9 January, 1909.

(6) AMANDA VIRGINIA MERRITT, born 4 April, 1847.

(7) ELLA OLIVER MERRITT, born 5 October, 1850.

JEREMIAH TAYLOR HUGHES

For ancestors leading back to the Mayflower see page 149.

JEREMIAH TAYLOR HUGHES[8], (Jeremiah Hughes[7], Jacob Hughes[6], Priscilla Leaming[5], Hannah Whilldin[4], Hannah Gorham[3], Desire Howalnd[2], JOHN HOWLAND[1] THE PILGRIM), was born at Cape May, 5 April, 1815, died at Cape May, 1893, married at Cape May, 27 December, 1843, Mary Ann Wheatley, born 1820, died 1873.

Issue:—

(1) WILLIAM WHEATLEY HUGHES, born at Fishing Creek, New Jersey, 25 July, 1845, died at Green Creek, New Jersey, 1 March, 1912, married Annie Mixner, and had ARTHUR HUGHES, who married Charlotte Lever, of Brooklyn, New York.

(2) RHODA ANN HUGHES, born at Fishing Creek, New Jersey, 31 March, 1848, died 5 November, 1907, without issue.

(3) CHARLES MILLER HUGHES, born at Fishing Creek, New Jersey, 18 October, 1849, married Hannah Maria Oliver. (For descendants see page 167.)

(4) MARY RUTH HUGHES, born at Fishing Creek, New Jersey, 25 June, 1852, married at Fishing Creek, New Jersey, 2 November, 1873, Richard Somers Sapp, who died at Beesley's Point, New Jersey, 30 December, 1897, and had, MARY ELMA SAPP, born at West Cape May, New Jersey, 10 June, 1874, married at Bridgeton, New Jersey, 10 April, 1898, Thomas F. Hemingway, son of Washington and Emma Hemingway of Fishing Creek, New Jersey, and had FRANK HUGHES HEMINGWAY, born at Ocean City, New Jersey, 6 December, 1905, died at Ocean City, New Jersey, 13 December, 1905.

(5) DAVID HUGHES, born at Fishing Creek, New Jersey, 8 December, 1856, married ANNIE M. RUTHERFORD. (For descendants see page 168.)

154

ANN LAWRENCE HUGHES

For ancestors leading back to the Mayflower see page 150.

ANN LAWRENCE HUGHES[8], (James Rainy Hughes[7], Jacob Hughes[6], Priscilla Leaming[5], Hannah Whilldin[4], Hannah Gorham[3], Desire Howland[2], JOHN HOWLAND[1] THE PILGRIM), was born at Cape May, 9 November, 1817, died at Cape May, 16 February, 1865, (tombstone in Cold Spring Cemetery), married at Cape May, 19 December, 1838, Downs E. Foster, born at Fishing Creek, New Jersey, 20 October, 1807, died at West Cape May, New Jersey, 20 October, 1886, (tombstone in Cold Spring Cemetery).

Issue:—

(1) REUBEN FOSTER, born at Cape May, 28 October, 1839, married Sarah Louisa Hand. (For descendants see page 169).

(2) JANE ANN FOSTER, born 8 May, 1841, married Aaron D. E. Crowell. (For descendants see page 170.)

(3) SAMUEL LAWRENCE FOSTER, born 22 February, 1843, married Marion Upham. (For descendants see page 171.)

(4) DOUGLASS FOSTER, born at Cape May, 28 November, 1844, married at Philadelphia, Pennsylvania, 11 November, 1875, Mary E. Crowell, and had LESLIE D. FOSTER, born 6 August, 1877, and NELLIE FOSTER, born 27 August, 1880, married Edwin Warren and had ELEANOR WARREN.

(5) JAMES HEWITT FOSTER, born 8 January, 1847, died 10 June, 1852.

(Continued on next page)

ANN LAWRENCE HUGHES

(6) RHODA FOREST FOSTER, born 12 July, 1848, married at Cold Spring, New Jersey, 13 October, 1868, William Leonard Cummings, born 11 June, 1845, son of Leonard and Lydia Cummings. (For descendants see page 172.)

(7) ELIZA ELDREDGE FOSTER, born 22 August, 1850, died 4 June, 1851.

(8) ELLEN EDMUNDS FOSTER, born 7 January, 1853, married at Cold Spring, New Jersey, 12 November, 1876, LAFAYETTE MILLER HALL[9], (Jane Edmunds[8], Mahalah Edmunds[7], Jane Whilldin[6], James Whilldin[5], Joseph Whilldin[4], Hannah Gorham[3], Desire Howland[2], JOHN HOWLAND[1] THE PILGRIM). (For descendants see page 173.)

(9) MARY CARLL FOSTER, born 3 May, married JAMES WARE ELDREDGE[10], (Daniel C. Eldredge[9], Deborah Whilldin Ware[8], Deborah Whilldin[7], Jonathan Whilldin[6], James Whilldin[5], Joseph Whilldin[4], Hannah Gorham[3], Desire Howland[2], JOHN HOWLAND[1] THE PILGRIM). (For descendants see page 246.)

ELIZA ELDREDGE, mother of ANN LAWRENCE HUGHES, was a descendant of the Pilgrim JOHN HOWLAND through the Eldredge line as follows: ELIZA ELDREDGE[8], (Aaron Eldredge[7], Aaron Eldredge[6], Mercy Leaming[5], Hannah Whilldin[4], Hannah Gorham[3], Desire Howland[2], JOHN HOWLAND[1] THE PILGRIM). Mercy Leaming, fifth from HOWLAND in the Eldredge line, was the sister of Priscilla Leaming, fifth from HOWLAND in the Hughes line. The latter married first John Stites. (See pages 36, 101, 102.)

REV. DANIEL LAWRENCE HUGHES, D. D.

For ancestors leading back to the Mayflower see page 150.

REV. DANIEL LAWRENCE HUGHES, D. D.[8], (James Rainy Hughes[7], Jacob Hughes[6], Priscilla Leaming[5], Hannah Whilldin[4], Hannah Gorham[3], Desire Howland[2], JOHN HOWLAND[1] THE PILGRIM), was born at Cape May, 8 January, 1820, married 19 October, 1843, ELMIRA WILLIAMS HUGHES[8], (Humphrey Hughes[7], Jane Whilldin[6], James Whilldin[5], Joseph Whilldin[4], Hannah Gorham[3], Desire Howland[2], JOHN HOWLAND[1] THE PILGRIM), born at Cape May, 1 January, 1820, died at Traer, Tama County, Iowa, 5 October, 1886.

Issue:—

(1) DANIEL LAWRENCE HUGHES, born 30 March, 1846, died in infancy.

(2) ELLA THOMAS HUGHES, born 19 December, 1847, died in infancy.

(3) WILLIAM WILLIAMS HUGHES, born at Cape May, 17 August, 1849.

(4) ELMIRA FLORENCE HUGHES, born at Cape May, 23 July, 1851, married at Vinton, Iowa, 29 April, 1874, George Taylor Rock. (For descendants see page 174).

(5) GEORGE WASHINGTON HUGHES, born 22 February, 1854, married Mrs. Elizabeth Wilson.

(6) ANNA LYON HUGHES, born at Spruce Creek, Huntingdon County, Pennsylvania, 26 November, 1855, married 24 August, 1876, Clinton Orville Harrington, born at Chenango County, New York, 14 October, 1843, and had, CLINTON OAKLEY HARRINGTON, born at Vinton, Iowa, 7 June, 1881.

(7) JAMES LAWRENCE HUGHES, born 18 May, 1859, died in infancy.

(8) LOUISA EDMUNDS HUGHES, born 2 February, 1861, married 18 October, 1881, L. Williston Kinney, and had: FLORENCE LUCILE KINNEY, born at Traer, Iowa, 15 January, 1885; HERBERT HUGHES KINNEY, born at Lake CHARLES, Louisiana, 15 July, 1888; ANNA HARRINGTON KINNEY, born at Lake Charles, Louisiana, 20 April, 1891.

HARRIET NEWELL HUGHES

For ancestors leading back to the Mayflower see page 150.

HARRIET NEWELL HUGHES[8], (James Rainy Hughes[7], Jacob Hughes[6], Priscilla Leaming[5], Hannah Whilldin[4], Hannah Gorham[3], Desire Howland[2], JOHN HOWLAND[1] THE PILGRIM), was born at Cape May, 23 July, 1825, married at Cape May, 24 July, 1844, Rev. Charles M. Oakley, born at New York City, 2 July, 1815, died at Northport, Long Island, 16 February, 1882.

Issue :—

(1) CHARLES PAYSON OAKLEY, born 3 July, 1845, married 20 June, 1872, Elizabeth DeBow Oakley, and had MARY FOREST OAKLEY, born 30 August, 1876, and ISABEL DeBOW OAKLEY, born 28 December, 1883.

(2) ROBERT S. OAKLEY, born 16 April, 1848, married 3 March, 1868, Margaretta J. Shields, and had: JENNIE SHIELDS OAKLEY, born 26 October, 1868, married 23 December, 1889, Daniel J. Conhey; HARRIET NEWELL OAKLEY, born 28 October, 1870, married 20 June, 1889, Edward A. Laws; HENRY SHIELDS OAKLEY, born 29 August, 1874; KATIE MEAD OAKLEY, born 18 September, 1878; ROBERT STRONG OAKLEY, born 3 November, 1880; WILLIE FRENCH OAKLEY, born 26 September, 1885.

(3) ENDORA SMITH OAKLEY, born 2 April, 1849, died in infancy.

(4) GEORGE WARNER OAKLEY, born 26 March, 1850, died 3 August, 1882, married 20 January, 1881, Emily Bell Thompson.

(5) MARY ELLEN OAKLEY, born 19 August, 1851, married 27 June, 1877, Arthur Butler and had: ALBERT BOARDMAN BUTLER, born 12 September, 1878; MARGARET OAKLEY BUTLER, born 14 April, 1880; HAROLD LOCKWOOD BUTLER, born 7 February, 1882; HARRIET ELLEN BUTLER, born 10 March, 1884; BESSIE ADELAIDE BUTLER, born 19 May, 1886.

REV. JAMES POTTER HUGHES

For ancestors leading back to the Mayflower see page 150.

REV. JAMES POTTER HUGHES[8], (James Rainy Hughes[7], Jacob Hughes[6], Priscilla Leaming[5], Hannah Whilldin[4], Hannah Gorham[3], Desire Howland[2], JOHN HOWLAND[1] THE PILGRIM), and (ELIZA ELDREDGE[8], Aaron Eldredge[7], Aaron Eldredge[6], Mercy Leaming[5], Hannah Whilldin[4], Hannah Gorham[3], Desire Howland[2], JOHN HOWLAND[1] THE PILGRIM), was born in Cape May county, New Jersey, 15 December, 1827, died 8 February, 1920, married at Williamsburg, Long Island, 27 June, 1861, Emily Wiltsie Roberts, born 6 September, 1840, died at Bellefonte, Pennsylvania, 8 June, 1889.

Issue :—

(1) EMMA SINCLAIR HUGHES, born at Princeton, New Jersey, 13 January, 1863, married 1903 at Dover, Delaware, James Adams Dunkel.

(2) JAMES ROBERT HUGHES, born at Cape May, 29 December, 1864, married at Bellefonte, Pennsylvania, 12 July, 1899, Mary Green Hughes.

(3) ELIZABETH RUSHTON HUGHES, born at Tipton, Iowa, 13 November, 1867, married James Q. Carrell, and had MARY GLADYS CARRELL.

(4) CHARLES STONE HUGHES, born at Bellefonte, Pennsylvania, 2 April, 1870, married at Mt. Washington, Maryland, 21 March, 1901, Emma V. Graham, and had JAMES POTTER HUGHES, born 13 December, 1905; VIRGINIA GRAHAM HUGHES, born 23 October, 1909; JOSEPH GRAHAM HUGHES, born 1 July, 1911; DAISY CLARK HUGHES, born 17 October, 1912.

(Continued on next page)

159

REV. JAMES POTTER HUGHES

(5) MARION FOSTER HUGHES, born at Bellefonte, Pennsylvania, 16 November, 1872, married at Bellfonte, Pennsylvania, 17 July, 1890, Frank P. Bassett, and had the following children:—

EMILY HAMLIN BASSETT, born 17 May, 1891, married 24 April, 1912, Colonel Theodore Hugh Winter, place of marriage, Society Hill, South Carolina; their son, THEODORE HUGH WINTER, was born 11 March, 1913.

JAMES EUGENE BASSETT, born 29 October, 1892, at Bellefonte, Pennsylvania.

MELVIN HUGHES BASSETT, born 12 June, 1899, at Covington, Virginia.

(6) EDWARD LAWRENCE HUGHES, born at Bellefonte, Pennsylvania, 25 February, 1876, married at Columbus, Ohio, 19 September, 1901, Hattie Peitsmeyer Hughes, and had FREDERICK PERDUE HUGHES, born 24 March, 1907.

(7) LUTHER ELDREDGE HUGHES, born at Bellefonte, Pennsylvania, 26 March, 1878, married at Baltimore, Maryland, Sophia Hermon Hughes, and had OTTILIE GLADYS HUGHES, born 22 January, 1901; CHARLES LAWRENCE HUGHES, born 29 November, 1908.

(8) OTTILE ROBERT HUGHES, born at Bellfonte, Pennsylvania, 9 March, 1881, married 16 November, 1906, Chester Kent Irvine and had MARION FOSTER IRVINE, born 15 October, 1907; CHESTER KENT IRVINE, born 5 October, 1909; OTTILIE HUGHES IRVINE, born 18 November, 1914.

HANNAH ELIZA HUGHES

For ancestors leading back to the Mayflower see page 151.

HANNAH ELIZA HUGHES[8], (James Rainy Hughes[7], Jacob Hughes[6], Pricilla Leaming[5], Hannah Whilldin[4], Hannah Gorham[3], Desire Howland[2], JOHN HOWLAND[1] THE PILGRIM), was born at Cape May, 21 February, 1830, died at Altoona, Pennsylvania, 15 August, 1861, married 7 July, 1852, Thomas McMinn.

Issue :—

(1) CHARLES W. McMINN, born at Altoona, Pennsylvania, 16 August, 1853, died at Altoona, Pennsylvania, 7 June, 1854, aged nine months and twenty-two days.

(2) JAMES H. McMINN, born at Altoona, Pennsylvania, 25 August, 1855, died at Altoona, Pennsylvania, 19 September, 1856, aged one year and twenty-five days.

(3) LAWRENCE H. McMINN, born at Altoona, Pennsylvania, 7 June, 1857, died at Altoona, Pennsylvania, 10 October, 1858, aged one year, four months and three days.

(4) ELIZABETH McMINN, born at Altoona, Pennsylvania, 20 June, 1859, married at Chicago, Illinois, 12 September, 1889, William F. Tucker, born at Enford, Wiltshire, England, 29 September, 1849.

(5) JOHN CALVIN McMINN, born at Altoona, Pennsylvania, May, 1861, died at Altoona, Pennsylvania, July, 1861.

EMMA MELINDA HUGHES

For ancestors leading back to the Mayflower see page 151.

EMMA MELINDA HUGHES[8], (James Rainy Hughes[7], Jacob Hughes[6], Priscilla Leaming[5], Hannah Whilldin[4], Hannah Gorham[3], Desire Howland[2], JOHN HOWLAND[1] THE PILGRIM), was born at Cape May, 22 January, 1836, married at Edgehill, Princeton, New Jersey, 31 July, 1861, Rev. John Sinclair Roberts, born at New York City, 25 July, 1859.

Issue:—

(1) LIDA HUGHES ROBERTS, born at Shanghai, China, 16 May, 1862, died at Tung Chow, China, 8 September, 1863, aged one year, three months and twenty-three days.

(2) ALICE OAKLEY ROBERTS, born at Cape May, 1 December, 1865, died at Glen Cove, New York, 2 December, 1870, aged five years and one day.

(3) JOHN SINCLAIR ROBERTS, born at Glen Cove, New York, 7 March, 1870.

(4) EVA DURYEA ROBERTS, born at Bellefonte, Pennsylvania, 31 May, 1872.

(5) ETHEL WINN ROBERTS, born at Shanghai, China, 10 December, 1875, died at Shanghai, China, 4 February, 1876, aged one month and twenty-four days.

For Pilgrim ancestry of ELIZA ELDREDGE, mother of EMMA MELINDA HUGHES, see page 111.

See "Divine Covenant Fulfilled in Pious Households," page 70 for a biography of this family, and in the same work by Rev. Dr. D. L. Hughes, page 38 and following, an account of the other children of JAMES RAINY HUGHES.

AMELIA FOSTER HUGHES

For ancestors leading back to the Mayflower see page 151.

AMELIA FOSTER HUGHES[8], (James Rainy Hughes[7], Jacob Hughes[6], Priscilla Leaming[5], Hannah Whilldin[4], Hannah Gorham[3], Desire Howland[2], JOHN HOWLAND[1] THE PILGRIM), was born at Cape May, 7 June, 1839, married 9 July, 1862, Rev. John Kershaw, born at Patterson, New Jersey, 14 May, 1842.

Issue:—

(1) ELIZA GORDON KERSHAW, born 19 November, 1866, married at New York City, 18 September, 1908, Matthias Woolley Conrow, M. D., born at Long Branch, New Jersey, 7 December, 1878, son of Luke and Lavinia Woolley Conrow.

(2) JOHN ALFRED KERSHAW, born 26 August, 1870, married at Coxackie, New York, 24 May, 1892, Margaret Miller, born at New York City, 9 May, 1871, and had:—JOHN DONALD KERSHAW, born at New York City, 21 April, 1893; ALBERT CARMEN KERSHAW, born at New York City, 31 December, 1894, married at New York City, 10 March, 1914, Christine Coomey, and had, JOHN ALBERT KERSHAW, born at New York City, 8 November, 1914, JEREMIAH HUGHES KERSHAW, born at New York City, 26 February, 1916, ALBERT DONALD KERSHAW, born at New York City, 23 November, 1920.

(3) ALBERT VAN HOUTEN KERSHAW, born at Brookdale, New Jersey, 25 July, 1876, married at Bound Brook, New Jersey, 1 March, 1902, Clara Van Doren, born 15 January, 1877, and had, ALBERT VAN DOREN KERSHAW, born at Brooklyn, New York, 2 October, 1902, RICHARD KERSHAW, born July, 1905, died in infancy.

(4) EVA ROBERTS KERSHAW, born at Brookdale, New Jersey, 26 April, 1879, married at New York City, 15 September, 1912, Edward Joseph Donlon, and had, MARY ELDREDGE DONLON, born at Springfield, Massachusetts, 20 March, 1916.

(5) ADA LOUISA KERSHAW, born at Bound Brook, New Jersey, 15 October, 1882.

WILLIAM JACKSON BENNETT

For ancestors leading back to the Mayflower see page 152.

WILLIAM JACKSON BENNETT[9], (William Bennett[8], Mary Hughes[7], Jacob Hughes[6], Priscilla Leaming[5], Hannah Whilldin[4], Hannah Gorham[3], Desire Howland[2], JOHN HOWLAND[1] THE PILGRIM), was born at Cape May, 24 April, 1932, died at Cape May, 25 January, 1904, married at Cape May, 12 February, 1855, HENRIETTA HAND[9], (Nancy Schenck[8], Zeruiah Hughes[7], Memucan Hughes[6], Hannah Whilldin[5], Joseph Whilldin[4], Hannah Gorham[3], Desire Howland[2], JOHN HOWLAND[1] THE PILGRIM), see page 255.

Issue :—

(1) JUDSON BENNETT, married LILLIAN JOHNSON. (For descendants see page 241).

(2) REBECCA BENNETT, born at Cape May, 16 May, 1863, married 27 December, 1889, Dr. Walter S. Leaming, who was born March 4, 1854, and had, REBECCA LEAMING and HENRIETTA LEAMING.

(3) ELIZABETH H. BENNETT, born at Cape May, 26 May, 1869, married 14 January, 1896, J. Ashton Williams, born 22 April, 1864, and had: ANNE CORRY WILLIAMS, born 23 March, 1899; SARA ELIZABETH, born 22 April, 1902, died 29 May, 1906; MARGARET L., born 29 June, 1907.

(4) GEORGE W. BENNETT, born 29 May, 1871, deceased.

(5) WILLIAM HENRY BENNETT, born at Cape May, 30 August, 1874, married Elizabeth M. Bohm, and had: THEODORE G. BENNETT, born 14 November, 1899; PAUL L. BENNETT, born 25 October, 1900; MARY BENNETT, born 18 May, 1902; HENRY B. BENNETT, born July, 1906; FLORENCE BENNETT, born 18 April, 1908.

(6) LEWIS S. BENNETT, born 19 December, 1877, married Maude Thompson, who died, 17 June, 1921.

HENRIETTA HAND BENNETT, died at Cape May, 18 July, 1910, aged 76 years.

ALBERT G. REED BENNETT

For ancestors leading back to the Mayflower see page 152.

ALBERT G. REED BENNETT[9], (William Bennett[8], Mary Hughes[7], Jacob Hughes[6], Priscilla Leaming[5], Hannah Whilldin[4], Hannah Gorham[3], Desire Howland[2], JOHN HOWLAND[1] THE PILGRIM), was born at Cape May, 24 Octoper, 1839, married first at Cape May, 11 September, 1864; MARTHA A. NAVES; married second at Cape May, 16 September, 1873, Elizabeth Smallwood, born at Lower Bank, Burlington County, New Jersey, 5 June, 1851, died at Cape May, 8 May, 1920.

Issue by first wife:—
(1) MARTHA L. BENNETT, born at Cape May, 1 July, 1865, married Charles York. (For descendants see page 175).

Children by second marriage:—
(1) SAMUEL WALTER BENNETT, born at Cape May, 1874, married Mary G. Bowker, and had DONALD P. BENNETT.

(2) IDA HAND BENNETT, born at Cape May, 6 January, 1877.

(3) HARRY GILMORE BENNETT, born at Cape May, 2 January, 1878, married at Philadelphia, Pennsylvania, 24 June, 1903, Bessie Patchell, born at Philadelphia, Pennsylvania, 9 January, 1879, and had:—

AGNES ELIZABETH BENNETT, born at Cape May, 25 May, 1904; MABEL KNEASS BENNETT, born at Cape May, 19 November, 1905; MILDRED IRENE BENNETT, born at Cape May, 28 September, 1907; HARRY GILMORE BENNETT, born at Cape May, 2 September, 1909; BESSIE

(Continued on next page)

ALBERT G. REED BENNETT

PATCHELL BENNETT, born at Cape May, 3 July, 1911; CHARLES WEEKS BENNETT, born at Cape May, 27 July, 1913.

(4) CLARENCE G. BENNETT, born at Cape May, 12 September, 1881.

(5) ETTA MAY BENNETT, born 13 November, 1883, married HENRY E. BELLANGY, and had CHARLES A. BELLANGY, DOROTHY S. BELLANGY, CATHARINE R. BELLANGY and ELIZABETH BELLANGY. (see page 297 for the Pilgrim ancestry of HENRY E. BELLANGY).

(6) GEORGIANNA BENNETT, born 3 February, 1885, died in infancy.

(7) ALICE GRAY BENNETT, born at Cape May, 2 June, 1887, married James B. Rock, and had MELVIN B. ROCK and BENNETT A. ROCK.

(8) FRANK LEE BENNETT, born at Cape May, 5 August, 1889, married Reba Oliver, and had FRANK LEE BENNETT.

(9) ALBERT ALLEN BENNETT, born at Cape May, 7 November, 1891, died in infancy.

(10) JESSIE IRENE BENNETT, born at Cape May, 3 October, 1892, married Herbert Johnson.

(11) GEORGE A. McILVAIN BENNETT, born at Cape May, 9 April, 1894, died in infancy.

MARTHA S. NAVES the first wife of ALBERT G. REED BENNETT was a descendant of JOHN HOWLAND in the line following:

MARTHA A. NAVES[10], Achsah Hand[9], Martha Schenck[8], Zeruiah Hughes[7], Memucan Hughes[6], Hannah Whilldin[5], Joseph Whilldin[4], Hannah Gorham[3], Desire Howland[2], JOHN HOWLAND[1] THE PILGRIM. (See page 278).

166

CHARLES MILLER HUGHES

For ancestors leading back to the Mayflower see page 154.

CHARLES MILLER HUGHES[9], (Jeremiah Taylor Hughes[8], Jeremiah Hughes[7], Jacob Hughes[6], Priscilla Leaming[5], Hannah Whilldin[4], Hannah Gorham[3], Desire Howland[2], JOHN HOWLAND[1] THE PILGRIM), was born at Fishing Creek, New Jersey, 18 October, 1849, married at Fishing Creek, New Jersey, 21 January, 1872, Hannah Maria Oliver.

Issue :—

(1) SARAH EMILY HUGHES, born at West Cape May, New Jersey, 4 December, 1872, married first, Harry Chester, and had HARRY CHESTER, born 2 October, 1890; married second, 27 November, 1896, Edward M. Cherry, born 9 December, 1872, and had WILLIAM W. CHERRY, born 7 August, 1897, FRANCIS LEON CHERRY, born 28 January, 1899, EDWARD MORRIS CHERRY, born 3 January, 1904.

(2) CLARA HUGHES, born 23 December, 1874, married 3 March, 1895, WILLIAM PRICE MATTHEWS and had IRENE MATTHEWS, born 4 December, 1895, married ORION H. REEVES, (see page 302).

(3) CHARLES EDWARD HUGHES, born 13 November, 1877, married 29 November, 1899, at Cape May, New Jersey, Justina Heritage, and had WALTER PHILIPS HUGHES, born 21 November, 1907.

(4) RALPH EMERSON HUGHES, born 27 September, 1882, married 16 August, 1903, Wilhelmina Roseman, and had FLORENCE MAY HUGHES, born 12 August, 1904.

(5) FLORENCE HUGHES, born 18 November, 1884, married 10 February, 1902, Alfred Matthews, and had CHARLES ALFRED MATTHEWS, born 2 November, 1905.

(6) FLOYD LISTON HUGHES, born 2 December, 1895, married 1 October, 1915, LULU HUGHES, and had HARRY HUGHES, died 28 February, 1916.

DAVID HUGHES

For ancestors leading back to the Mayflower see page 154.

DAVID HUGHES[9], (Jeremiah Taylor Hughes[8], Jeremiah Hughes[7], Jacob Hughes[6], Priscilla Leaming[5], Hannah Whilldin[4], Hannah Gorham[3], Desire Howland[2], JOHN HOWLAND[1] THE PILGRIM), was born at Cape May, 8 December, 1856, married 1 May, 1877, ANNIE MECRAY RUTHERFORD[10], Ann Eliza Ware[9], Samuel Fithian Ware[8], Deborah Whilldin[7], Jonathan Whilldin[6], James Whilldin[5], Joseph Whilldin[4], Hannah Gorham[3], Desire Howland,[2], JOHN HOWLAND[1] THE PILGRIM), who was born at Fishing Creek, New Jersey, 30 April, 1858.

Issue:—

(1) FRANKLIN RAMSDELL HUGHES, M. D., born at Cold Spring, New Jersey, 8 August, 1879, graduated from Hahnemann Medical College, Philadelphia, Pennsylvania, 24 May, 1906, married at Eldora, New Jersey, 5 June, 1907, Lulu Lee Bishop, born at Eldora, New Jersey, 11 July, 1880, and had the following children:—

SAMUEL BISHOP HUGHES, born at West Cape May, New Jersey, 6 June, 1909.

HAROLD FRANKLIN HUGHES, born at West Cape May, 23 December, 1912.

DAVID WHEATLEY HUGHES, born at West Cape May, 4 February, 1918.

(2) BERTHA MAY HUGHES, born 17 January, 1884, died 4 January, 1887.

For the genealogical history of the family of ANNIE MECRAY RUTHERFORD, wife of DAVID HUGHES, see Family and Descendants of ANN ELIZA WARE on page 233 of this volume.

REUBEN FOSTER

For ancestors leading back to the Mayflower see page 155.

REUBEN FOSTER[9], (Ann Lawrence Hughes[8], James Rainy Hughes[7], Jacob Hughes[6], Priscilla Leaming[5], Hannah Whilldin[4], Hannah Gorham[3], Desire Howland[2], JOHN HOWLAND[1] THE PILGRIM), in one line; and ANN LAWRENCE HUGHES[9], (Eliza Eldredge[8], Aaron Eldredge[7], Aaron Eldredge[6], Mercy Leaming[5], Hannah Whilldin[4], Hannah Gorham[3], Desire Howland[2], JOHN HOWLAND[1] THE PILGRIM), in the other line; was born at Cape May, 28 October, 1839, married at Cape May, 6 November, 1866, Sarah Louise Hand, born at Cape May, 8 June, 1843.

Issue:—

(1) ENOCH EDMUNDS FOSTER, born at Cape May, 2 September, 1867, married at Baltimore, Maryland, 25 October, 1894, Mary Celeste Saulsbury, born at Baltimore, Maryland, 28 December, 1868, and had REUBEN FOSTER, born at Baltimore, Maryland, 1 December, 1897.

(2) ARTHUR DOUGLASS FOSTER, born at Baltimore, Maryland, 9 November,1872, died 6 April, 1917, married at Snow Hill, Worcester County, Maryland, 30 November, 1898, Georgie Richardson Smith, and had, JOHN WALTER SMITH FOSTER, born at Baltimore, Maryland, 27 November, 1900, and ARTHUR DOUGLASS FOSTER, born at Maryland, 27 March, 1903.

(3) REUBBEN CARLL FOSTER, born at Baltimore, Maryland, 10 July, 1875, died 27 January, 1908, married at Boston, Massachusetts, Effie Tuttle.

(4) GILBERT FOSTER, born at Baltimore, Maryland, 29 October, 1877, died 30 June, 1878.

(5) FREDERICK FOSTER, born at Baltimore, Maryland, 5 October, 1879, married at Boston, Massachusetts, 31 January, 1912, Clara Bruce, and had: SARAH HALL FOSTER, born 31 May, 1913; HELEN FOSTER; and BRUCE FOSTER.

JANE ANN FOSTER

For ancestors leading back to the Mayflower see page 155.

JANE ANN FOSTER[9], (Ann Lawrence Hughes[8], James Rainy Hughes[7], Jacob Hughes[6], Priscilla Leaming[5], Hannah Whilldin[4], Hannah Gorham[3], Desire Howland[2], JOHN HOWLAND[1] THE PILGRIM), was born at Cold Spring, New Jersey, 8 May, 1841, married at Cold Spring, New Jersey, 13 September, 1859, Aaron D. E. Crowell, born at Philadelphia, Pennsylvania, 20 August, 1834.

Issue :—

(1) THOMAS S. CROWELL, born at Fishing Creek, New Jersey, 8 June, 1860, married at Philadelphia, 9 December, 1878, Emma M. Herring, born 10 June, 1860, and had WILLIE H. CROWELL, born 23 August, 1880.

(2) EDWARD M. CROWELL, born at Fishing Creek, New Jersey, 25 March, 1852, married 9 June, 1883, Orilla Whilden, born November, 1864, and had: ANNA FOSTER CROWELL, born 18 December, 1884, AARON DOWNS CROWELL, born 20 March, 1895, and THEODORE WHILDEN CROWELL, born 28 June, 1902.

(3) TRYPHENA P. CROWELL, born at Fishing Creek, New Jersey, 15 April, 1864, married 30 August, 1882, William G. Essen, and had WILLIS G. ESSEN and JOHN R. ESSEN.

(4) ANNA FOSTER CROWELL, born 5 January, 1866, married 9 February, 1886, George Chester Germon, who died 9 January, 1890, and had: RALPH GERMON, and EDWARD M. GERMON, who married Edith Smith, and had, FRANCIS GERMON.

(5) SARAH E. CROWELL, born 8 May, 1867, married, 1890, John Snyder, and had MARY SNYDER, born 17 January, 1900, married Alfred Sheets, 10 October, 1920.

SAMUEL LAWRENCE FOSTER

For ancestors leading back to the Mayflower see page 155.

SAMUEL LAWRENCE FOSTER[9], (Ann Lawrence Hughes[8], James Rainy Hughes[7], Jacob Hughes[6], Priscilla Leaming[5], Hannah Whilldin[4], Hannah Gorham[3], Desire Howland[2], JOHN HOWLAND[1] THE PILGRIM), was born at Cold Spring, New Jersey, 22 February, 1843, married at Philadelphia, Pennsylvania, 31 August, 1871, Marion Upham, born at Philadelphia, Pennsylvania, 8 April, 1848, (daughter of Samuel Curtis Upham, born 2 February, 1819, and his wife, Ann Eliza Bancroft, born at Fishing Creek, New Jersey, 22 April, 1829). She died 29 March, 1909. For a second line of descent from the Mayflower see page 150).

Issue:—

(1) CURTIS UPHAM FOSTER, born at Philadelphia, Pennsylvania, 4 May, 1874, married 16 June, 1897, Harriet Eugenia Houtz, and had: LAWRENCE HOUTZ FOSTER, born 16 April, 1897, and BYRON LEIGH FOSTER, born 22 March, 1903.

(2) LILLIAN FOSTER, born at Philadelphia, Pennsylvania, 26 July, 1876, married 20 November, 1901, James Thomas Reed, and had, FREDERICK FOSTER REED, born 30 August, 1902.

(3) HOWARD LAWRENCE FOSTER, born at Philadelphia, Pennsylvania, 14 July, 1879, died 15 February, 1910.

(4) MARION UPHAM FOSTER, born at Philadelphia, Pennsylvania, 19 May, 1882, married 17 October, 1906, James Albert Mears, and had: JAMES ALBERT MEARS, born 23 September, 1907; HOWARD FOSTER MEARS, born 11 August, 1910; SAMUEL FOSTER MEARS, born 20 November, 1911; JOHN CARR MEARS, born 20 December, 1913, died in infancy.

(5) HERBERT WARREN FOSTER, born 2 September, 1885, died in infancy.

(6) WILMER STRONG FOSTER, born 30 November, 1887, married Anne C. Frailey (12 October, 1910), and had: SAMUEL LAWRENCE FOSTER, born 18 August, 1911, died in infancy; WILMER STRONG FOSTER, born 11 November, 1913; PETER LINCOLN FOSTER, born June, 1918.

RHODA FOREST FOSTER

For ancestors leading back to the Mayflower see page 155.

RHODA FOREST FOSTER[9], (Ann Lawrence Hughes[8], James Rainy Hughes[7], Jacob Hughes[6], Priscilla Leaming[5], Hannah Whilldin[4], Hannah Gorham[3], Desire Howland[2], JOHN HOWLAND[1] THE PILGRIM), in one line, and (ANN LAWRENCE HUGHES[9], Eliza Eldredge[8], Aaron Eldredge[7], Aaron Eldredge[6], Mercy Leaming[5], Hannah Whilldin[4], Hannah Gorham[3], Desire Howland[2], JOHN HOWLAND[1] THE PILGRIM) in the other line, was born 12 July, 1848, married at Cold Spring, New Jersey, 13 October, 1868, William Leonard Cummings, born at Fishing Creek, New Jersey, 11 June, 1845.

Issue:—

(1) HARRY EDMUNDS CUMMINGS, born at Cape May, 11 May, 1870, died 3 March, 1875.

(2) GEORGE OGDEN CUMMINGS, born at Cape May, 25 January, 1873, married at Cape May, 15 October, 1901, BEULAH ESTELA BATE, and had EDWIN JONES CUMMINGS, born at Cape May, 26 December, 1903; GEORGE HERBERT CUMMINGS, born at Cape May, 27 December, 1913. (See page 146 for Pilgrim ancestry of BEULAH E. BATE).

(3 EMMA ELDREDGE CUMMINGS, born at Cape May, 13 February, 1875, died 14 September, 1887.

(4) RALPH LEE CUMMINGS, born at Cape May, 9 Decmber, 1878, married at Cape May, 2 January, 1907, Ella Stevens Wheaton, and had DOROTHY WHEATON CUMMINGS, born 30 June, 1911.

ELLEN EDMUNDS FOSTER

For ancestors leading back to the Mayflower see page 155.

ELLEN EDMUNDS FOSTER[9], (Ann Lawrence Hughes[8], James Rainy Hughes[7], Jacob Hughes[6], Priscilla Leaming[5], Hannah Whilldin[4], Hannah Gorham[3], Desire Howland[2], JOHN HOWLAND[1] THE PILGRIM), was born at Cape May, 7 January, 1853, married at Cape May, 12 November, 1876, LAFAY-ETTE MILLER HALL[9], (Jane Edmunds Whilldin[8], Mahalah Edmunds[7], Jane Whilldin[6], James Whilldin[5], Joseph Whilldin[4], Hannah Gorham[3], Desire Howland[2], JOHN HOWLAND[1] THE PILGRIM), born at Cape May, 19 June, 1849, died at Cape May, 23 April, 1907), (tombstone in Cold Spring Cemetery). See page 226.

Issue:—

(1) HARRIET SHAW HALL, born at Cape May, 3 February, 1878.

(2) MARY ELDREDGE HALL, born at Cape May, 3 May, 1880.

(3) WILLIAM CUMMINGS HALL, born at Cape May, 14 January, 1883, married at Summit, New Jersey, 8 February, 1910, Felicie Pauli, born at Brooklyn, New York, October, 1888, and had the following children: FELICIE ANTOINETTE HALL, born at Haworth, New Jersey, 24 January, 1913; ELLEN GRACE HALL, born at Haworth, New Jersey, 17 June, 1914; WILLIAM AUGUSTUS HALL, born at Haworth, New Jersey, 6 November, 1917.

ELLEN EDMUNDS FOSTER is also a descendant of JOHN HOWLAND in another line as follows:—ELLEN ED-MUNDS FOSTER[10], (Ann Lawrence Hughes[9], Eliza Eldredge[8], Aaron Eldredge[7], Aaron Eldredge[6], Mercy Leaming[5], Hannah Whilldin[4], Hannah Gorham[3], Desire Howland[2], JOHN HOW-LAND[1] THE PILGRIM). See page 156.

ELMIRA FLORENCE HUGHES

For ancestors leading back to the Mayflower see page 157.

ELMIRA FLORENCE HUGHES[9], (Rev. Daniel Lawrence Hughes, D. D.[8], James Rainy Hughes[7], Jacob Hughes[6], Priscilla Leaming[5], Hannah Whilldin[4], Hannah Gorham[3], Desire Howland[2], JOHON HOWLAND[1] THE PILGRIM), and in the following line of descent on her mother's side, (ELMIRA WILLIAMS HUGHES[8], Humphrey Hughes[7], Jane Whilldin[6], James Whilldin[5], Joseph Whilldin[4], Hannah Gorham[3], Desire Howland[2], JOHN HOWLAND[1] THE PILGRIM), was born at Cape May, 23 July, 1851, married at Vinton, Iowa, 29 April, 1874, George Taylor Rock, born at Cedar Rapids, Iowa, 12 May, 1851.

Issue:—

(1) HERMAN WILLIAMS ROCK, born at Vinton, Iowa, 3 March, 1875.

(2) TAYLOR LAWRENCE ROCK, born at Vinton, Iowa, 27 February, 1876.

(3) GEORGE HORRIDGE ROCK, born at Vinton, Iowa, 29 July, 1877.

(4) CLINTON HARRINGTON ROCK, born at Vinton, Iowa, 2 November, 1878, died 29 July, 1879.

(5) ELIZABETH TAYLOR ROCK, born at Vinton, Iowa, 25 December, 1880.

(6) HAROLD HUGHES ROCK, born at Vinton, Iowa, 11 February, 1882.

(7) RAYMOND ROCK, born at Vinton, Iowa, 7 February, 1884.

(8) HAZEL ELMIRA ROCK, born at Vinton, Iowa, 13 February, 1886.

(9) KINGSLEY CARLETON ROCK, born at Vinton, Iowa, 6 January, married at Lake Charles, Louisiana, 25 August, 1917, Madge L. Patterson.

MAYFLOWER DESCENDANTS IN CAPE MAY COUNTY

MARTHA LAVELLE BENNETT

For ancestors leaing back to the Mayflower see page 165.

MARTHA LAVELLE BENNETT[10], (Albert G. Reed Bennett[9], William Bennett[8], Mary Hughes[7], Jacob Hughes[6], Priscilla Leaming[5], Hannah Whilldin[4], Hannah Gorham[3], Desire Howland[2], JOHN HOWLAND[1] THE PILGRIM), was born at Cape May, 1 July, 1865, died at Cape May, 8 August, 1913, married at Cape May, 16 January, 1887, Charles York, born at Swain, New Jersey, 11 October, 1865.

Issue:—

(1) SADIE YORK, born at Cape May, 21 October, 1887, married at Cape May, 29 November, 1906, HORACE FITHIAN CHURCH[11], Mary A. Rutherford[10], Ann Eliza Ware[9], Samuel Fithian Ware[8], Deborah Whilldin[7], Jonathan Whilldin[6], James Whilldin[5], Joseph Whilldin[4], Hannah Gorham[3], Desire Howland[2], JOHN HOWLAND[1] THE PILGRIM), who was born at Cape May, 19 November, 1882, and had: HORACE KENNETH CHURCH, born 25 July, 1907; MARY EVELINE CHURCH, born 16 May, 1915; HELEN MARTHA CHURCH, born 20 January, 1919. (See page 233).

(2) EDNA YORK, born at Cape May, 13 June, 1889, married at New York City, 7 August, 1905, WALTER CHURCH[11], (William Church[10], Mary Bennett Hall[9], Jane Edmunds Whilldin[8], Mahalah Edmunds[7], Jane Whilldin[6], James Whilldin[5], Joseph Whilldin[4], Hannah Gorham[3], Desire Howland[2], JOHN HOWLAND[1] THE PILGRIM), and had: EVELINA FENNER CHURCH, born 27 September, 1906; and WALTER LEROY CHURCH, born 4 August, 1912.

(3) HELEN YORK, born at Cape May, 21 February, 1894, married 28 October, 1913, Charles Shields.

175

ALEXIS GRASSON MERRITT

For ancestors leading back to the Mayflower see page 153.

ALEXIS GRASSON MERRITT[9], (Louisa Stevens Bennett[8], Mary Hughes[7], Jacob Hughes[6], Priscilla Leaming[5], Hannah Whilldin[4], Hannah Gorham[3], Desire Howland[2], JOHN HOWLAND[1] THE PILGRIM), was born at Philadelphia, Pennsylvania, 9 January, 1838, died at Westmont, New Jersey, 13 November, 1916, married first at Philadelphia, Pennsylvania, 26 April, 1858, Susannah Dale, born at Philadelphia, Pennsylvania, 24 June, 1841, died at Philadelphia, Pennsylvania, 16 June, 1888; married second, 19 March, 1891, Cynthia B. Atkins.

Issue by first wife:—

(1) AMANDA LOUISA MERRITT, born at Philadelphia, Pennsylvania, 6 July, 1859, married at Philadelphia, 12 May, 1880, Bascom Worthington Melvin, born at Kent County, Delaware, near Whitleysburg, Maryland, 25 August, 1850, and had: ALEXIS MERRITT MELVIN, born at Philadelphia, Pennsylvania, 8 December, 1880; FRANK WORTHINGTON MELVIN, born at Philadelphia, Pennsylvania, 7 August, 1884, married 24 June, 1911, Bertha Priscilla Haines; IRMA HERNDON MELVIN, born at Philadelphia, Pennsylvania, 13 December, 1886, married 20 November, 1916, William Cunningham Jackson Trimble, born at Philadelphia, 26 September, 1879; SUE HARDCASTLE MELVIN, born at Philadelphia, Pennsylvania, 15 January, 1891, married 4 June, 1913, Jacob Frederick Woeffreim Schmidt, born at Philadelphia, Pennsylvania, 19 September, 1886, and had, PHYLLIS WOEFFREIM SCHMIDT, born at Philadelphia, Pennsylvania, 26 June, 1914.

(2) JOHN BENNETT MERRITT, born at Philadelphia, Pennsylvania, 10 September, 1860.

SPICER LEAMING

For ancestors leading back to the Mayflower see page 105.

SPICER LEAMING[7], (Christopher Leaming[6], Christopher Leaming[5] Hannah Whilldin[4], Hannah Gorham[3], Desire Howland[2], JOHN HOWLAND[1] THE PILGRIM), was born at Cape May, 14 April, 1762, died at Cape May, 1 October, 1838 (record of family bible), married Hannah Swain, born 3 March, 1767, died 11 September, 1857, (tombstones in Cold Spring Cemetery).

Issue :—

(1) SWAIN LEAMING, born 22 June, 1787, died 1850, married Sarah Dixon, and had: SPICER LEAMING, born 1834, died 1890, unmarried; JAMES SMITH LEAMING, born 4 June, 1838 at Newbern, North Carolina, died at Philadelphia, Pennsylvania, 25 July, 1911, married at Philadelphia, 20 September, 1860, Josephine MacNamee, born 6 May, 1841, and had, FRANK SPICER LEAMING, born 28 March, 1862, died 26 July, 1877; FLORENCE MARCELLA LEAMING, born at Philadelphia, 29 October, 1869, married at Philadelphia, 25 April, 1888, Louis Julian Gregory, born at Winsted, Connecticut, 2 September, 1862, and had, FLORENCE LEAMING GREGORY, born at Philadelphia, 8 April, 1895.

(2) JAMES LEAMING, born 19 February, 1789, married first MRS. LYDIA SCHELLENGER, married second Sarah Bennett. (For descendants see page 180).

(3) MARIA LEAMING, born 4 August, 1806, married David Cresse. (For descendants see page 181).

(4) ISRAEL LEAMING, born 14 February, 1808, married Judith E. Hughes, and had ABIGAIL HUGHES LEAMING, married William Rose Sheppard, M. D. (For descendants see page 182).

(5) LEMUEL LEAMING, born 2 October, 1809, died 3 May, 1879, married LYDIA LEAMING, and had HANNAH LEAMING, who married WILMON WHILLDIN.

(6) JACOB LEAMING, born 16 January, 1812, married Melvina Eldredge. (For descendants see page 183).

HUMPHREY LEAMING

For ancestors leading back to the Mayflower see page 105.

HUMPHREY LEAMING[7], (Christopher Leaming[6], Christopher Leaming[5], Hannah Whilldin[4], Hannah Gorham[3], Desire Howland[2], JOHN HOWLAND[1] THE PILGRIM), was born at Cape May, 6 December, 1780, died at Asbury, New Jersey, on 28 August, 1851, married at Cape May, 19 January, 1809, Mary Stites, daughter of Philip and Rachel Stites.

Issue—:

(1) MARY LEAMING, born 15 September, 1811, died 9 February, 1874, unmarried.

(2) HUMPHREY LEAMING, born 12 October, 1813, married Sarah Ludlam, and had: ANNIE LEAMING; HANNAH LEAMING, married Henry T. Corson; EMMA LEAMING, married Lawrence C. Kandle, and had ELWOOD KANDLE.

(3) RACHEL LEAMING, born 30 November, 1815, married Levi Ludlam, and had: HUMPHREY LUDLAM; LEAMING LUDLAM, lost at sea, unmarried; REUBEN LUDLAM; HANNAH S. LUDLAM, born 18 May, 1842, who married 1860, Amos Wentzell, and had: LIZZIE L. WENTZELL, born 28 January, 1861, married Alonzo Brower, and had, LULU S. BROWER, born 7 January, 1883; LEVI S. WENTZELL, born 19 March, 1863, married Ella G. Crawford, and had: LEAMING L. WENTZELL, born 5 October, 1886, MABEL WENTZELL, born 19 May, 1889, RAYMOND WENTZELL, born 14 February, 1892, died in infancy, HANNAH WENTZELL, born 27 November, 1894, CLARA WENTZELL, born 13 July, 1898, MARY WENTZELL, born 3 June, 1901; RACHEL L. WENTZELL, daughter of Amos, born 12 September, 1865, married Hiram W. Godfrey, and had, JOHN SWAIN GODFREY, born 18 April, 1894; DEBORAH LUDLAM, daughter of Levi, married Warren Mitchell.

(4) PHILIP STITES LEAMING, born 30 May, 1819, died 28 December, 1890, married Elizabeth Bartlett Bunker, and had: ABBIE ELIZABETH LEAMING; EMILY BARTLETT LEAMING; GEORGE PHILIP HUMPHREY LEAMING; FLORENCE LUCILE LEAMING.

(5) DEBORAH LEAMING, born 17 February, 1821, died in infancy.

(6) CHRISTOPHER LEAMING, born 1 July, 1827, unmarried.

178

HANNAH LEAMING

For ancestors leading back to the Mayflower see page 105.

HANNAH LEAMING[7], (Christopher Leaming[6], Christopher Leaming[5], Hannah Whilldin[4], Hannah Gorham[3], Desire Howland[2], JOHN HOWLAND[1] THE PILGRIM), was born at Cape May, 23 February, 1768, died 1 September, 1835, married first at Philadelphia, 21 October, 1799, Edward Rice, born at Boston, Massachusetts, 23 March, 1756, died at sea, 1803, and had, EDWARD RICE, born 14 February, 1803, died 3 December, 1853, married 7 October, 1826, Jane S. Diverty, born 16 July, 1806, died 8 December, 1885, and had: LEAMING M. RICE, born 25 March, 1828, who married Maria Swain Ludlam, (for descendants see page 330); DEBORAH RICE, died in infancy; JAMES D. RICE, born 31 December, 1831, died 8 May, 1906, married Rebecca Johnson, and had one son who died in infancy.

HANNAH LEAMING married second 18 July, 1806, Amos C. Moore, and had, SARAH LEAMING MOORE, who married 2 May, 1831, Maurice Beesley, M. D., born at Dennisville, New Jersey, 16 May, 1804, died 13 January, 1882.

Issue:—

(1) JULIA BEESLEY, born 25 January, 1838, died 12 January, 1907, married 31 May, 1857, Jeremiah H. Townsend, born 23 January, 1827, died 29 January, 1897, and had: FLORA MAY TOWNSEND, born 26 August, 1860, married Walter Scott, and had, EDWARD MAURICE BEESLEY SCOTT, born 24 February, 1882, married Emma Kromer; FRANK TOWNSEND, born 8 April, 1864.

(2) HANNAH MOORE BEESLEY, born 14 April, 1840, died 11 January, 1889, married 18 April, 1866, Eugene Kendall, no issue.

(3) RHODA BEESLEY, born 23 March, 1842, died 29 November, 1919.

(4) EDWARD MAURICE BEESLEY, M. D., born 22 June, 1845, died 17 September, 1906, married 11 November, 1873, Carrie A. Harris, born 26 July, 1853, died 26 March, 1903, and had: ELEANOR E. BEESLEY, M. D., born 19 September, 1874; MARY TUFT BEESLEY, born 6 April, 1876, married 1 June, 1898, F. S. Matthews, and had, FRANCIS MATTHEWS, born 22 October, 1900, and MARY ELIZABETH MATTHEWS, born 23 January, 1902; ISRAEL HARRIS BEESLEY, born 21 December, 1878, died 10 January, 1882; MAURICE E. BEESLEY, born 9 October, 1882, married 28 June, 1912, Lena Bair, and had, EDWARD MAURICE BEESLEY, born 11 January, 1915.

JAMES LEAMING

For ancestors leading back to the Mayflower see page 177.

JAMES LEAMING[8], (Spicer Leaming[7], Christopher Leaming[6], Christopher Leaming[5], Hannah Whilldin[4], Hannah Gorham[3] Desire Howland[2], JOHN HOWLAND[1] THE PILGRIM), was born at Cape May, 19 February, 1789, died at Cape May, 12 August, 1870, (tombstone in Cold Spring Cemetery), married first Mrs. Lydia Schellenger, whose maiden name was LYDIA WHILLDIN, a descendant of the Mayflower in the following line: LYDIA WHILLDIN[7], (Matthew Whilldin[6], James Whilldin[5], Joseph Whilldin[4], Hannah Gorham[3], Desire Howland[2], JOHN HOWLAND[1] THE PILGRIM). She died 13 February, 1856. (Tombstone in Cold Spring Cemetery). (See page 200 under family of her father, MATTHEW WHILLDIN). JAMES LEAMING married second Sarah Bennett.

Issue:—
 (1) LYDIA LEAMING, married JOSEPH WARE[8], (Harriet Whilldin[7], Jonathan Whilldin[6], James Whilldin[5], Joseph Whilldin[4], Hannah Gorham[3], Desire Howland[2], JOHN HOWLAND[1] THE PILGRIM), who was born 16 May, 1809. (For descendants see page 220).
 (2) JANE LEAMING, married ROBERT S. HAND[9], (Nancy Schenck[8], Zeruiah Hughes[7], Memucan Hughes[6], Hannah Whilldin[5], Joseph Whilldin[4], Hannah Gorham[3], Desire Howland[2], JOHN HOWLAND[1] THE PILGRIM), who was born 1821, (for descendants see page 272).
 (3) MARY F. LEAMING, born 10 March, 1821, married William Townsend, who was born 26 November, 1818. For descendants see page 184).
 (4) JAMES LEAMING, married HARRIET ANN WALES ELDREDGE[9], (Joseph Eldredge[8], Aaron Eldredge[7], Aaron Eldredge[6], Mercy Leaming[5], Hannah Whilldin[4], Hannah Gorham[3], Desire Howland[2], JOHN HOWLAND[1] THE PILGRIM), who was born 17 June, 1831. (For descendants see page 127).
 (5) HANNAH LEAMING, married Enoch Cresse, and had: RHODA CRESSE and EMMA CRESSE.

MARIA LEAMING

For ancestors leading back to the Mayflower see page 177.

MARIA LEAMING[8], (Spicer Leaming[7], Christopher Leaming[6], Christopher Leaming[5], Hannah Whillin[4], Hannah Gorham[3], Desire Howland[2], JOHN HOWLAND[1] THE PILGRIM), was born at Cape May, 4 August, 1806, died at Cape May, 28 February, 1875, (tombstone in Cold Spring Cemetery), married at Cape May, 1828, David Cresse, born at Cape May, 19 December, 1799, died at Cape May, 18 October, 1849, (tombstone in Cold Spring Cemetery).

Issue :—

(1) JOSEPH CRESSE, born at Cold Spring, New Jersey, 18 January, 1831, married Elizabeth Gregory. (For descendants see page 185).

(2) JANE CRESSE, born at Cold Spring, New Jersey. 21 December, 1834, married James Crowell. (For descendants see page 186.)

(3) HANNAH M. CRESSE, born at Cold Spring, New Jersey, 1 April, 1837, married CLEMENT B. REEVES[9], (Isabella Matthews[8], Eleanor Hughes[7], Ellis Hughes[6], Hannah Whilldin[5], Joseph Whilldin[4], Hannah Gorham[3], Desire Howland[2], JOHN HOWLAND[1] THE PILGRIM), born at Cape May, 20 August, 1935. (See page 267).

(4) ANTHONY CRESSE, born at Cold Spring, 11 May, 1839, married MARY ELIZABETH REEVES, born 15 July, 1841, sister of CLEMENT B. REEVES, see above.

(5) ELLEN CRESSE, born at Cold Spring, 24 December, 1846, married at Cold Spring, 11 August, 1867, Clinton Hand, born at Rio Grande, New Jersey, 27 March, 1845. (For descendants see page 187).

ABIGAIL HUGHES LEAMING

For ancestors leading back to the Mayflower see page 177.

ABIGAIL HUGHES LEAMING[9], (Israel Leaming[8], Spicer Leaming[7], Christopher Leaming[6], Christopher Leaming[5], Hannah Whilldin[4], Hannah Gorham[3], Desire Howland[2], JOHN HOWLAND[1] THE PILGRIM), was born at Cape May, 28 January, 1840, died at Cape May, 14 April, 1889, married at Cape May, 16 September, 1862, William Rose Sheppard, M. D., born at Cedarville, Cumberland County, New Jersey, 22 September, 1831, died at Cape May, 12 March, 1879 (tombstone in Cold Spring Cemetery).

Issue :—

(1) WILLIAM ROSE SHEPPARD, born at Cape May, 10 July, 1863, married ELIDA KIMBER ELDREDGE[10], (Thomas Eldredge[9], Deborah Whilldin Ware[8], Deborah Whilldin[7], Jonathan Whilldin[6], James Whilldin[5], Joseph Whilldin[4], Hannah Gorham[3], Desire Howland[2], JOHN HOWLAND[1] THE PILGRIM). See page 236.

(2) ISRAEL LEAMING SHEPPARD, born 15 November, 1864, married Mary Morris, and had DOROTHY MECRAY SHEPPARD; married Paul Langdon Cox, and had PAUL COX, Jr; MARY ESTHER SHEPPARD.

(3) ABBIE SHEPPARD, born 20 January, 1866, married Charles Gilmore Dunn, and had MARIN SHEPPARD DUNN.

(4) JUDITH FLORENCE SHEPPARD, born 15 February, 1867, married Samuel Addison Weishampel, and had JOHN ADDISON WEISHAMPEL.

(5) SARAH GENEVIEVE SHEPPARD, born 11 July, 1872, married CHARLES S. STEVENS. (See page 269).

(6) FRANK SPICER SHEPPARD, born 27 July, 1874, married Lulu I. Bailey, and had SAMUEL BAILEY SHEPPARD.

JACOB LEAMING

For ancestors leading back to the Mayflower see page 177.

JACOB LEAMING[8], (Spicer Leaming[7], Christopher Leaming[6], Christopher Leaming[5], Hannah Whilldin[4], Hannah Gorham[3], Desire Howland[2], JOHN HOWLAND[1] THE PILGRIM), was born at Lower township, Cape May County, 16 January, 1812, died at Cape May, 6 January, 1888, (tombstone in Cold Spring Cemetery), married at West Cape May, 16 March, 1842, Melvina Eldredge, born 21 March, 1823, died at Cape May, 13 January, 1899.

Issue:—

(1) THERESA ELDREDGE LEAMING, born at Cape May, 16 July, 1843, married Edward Fendel Townsend, and had ALICE MELVINA TOWNSEND, married Rudolph Koch; and GEORGE L. TOWNSEND, who married Edna Jones.

(2) AMANDA MELVINA LEAMING, born at West Cape May, 17 March, 1849, married at Cape May, 12 April, 1875, Furman Sidney Townsend, and had: CHARLES ELMER TOWNSEND, born 23 June, 1882, married 5 October, 1907, Helen Datesman, and had MARJORIE TOWNSEND; MELVINA TOWNSEND, born 24 July, 1887, married Carl Weber.

(3) JACOB SPICER LEAMING, born at Cape May, 16 November, 1853, married first Helen Leaming; married second, at Flemington, New Jersey, 17 May, 1911, Edna R. Daily, and had the following children: EDMUND SPICER LEAMING, born at Cape May, 26 August, 1912; JACOB SPICER LEAMING, born at Cape May, 26 July, 1913; RICHARD ELDREDGE LEAMING, born at Cape May, 2 February, 1915.

MARY F. LEAMING

For ancestors leading back to the Mayflower see page 180.

MARY F. LEAMING[9], (James Leaming[8], Spicer Leaming[7], Christopher Leaming[6], Christopher Leaming[5], Hannah Whilldin[4], Hannah Gorham[3], Desire Howland[2], JOHN HOWLAND[1] THE PILGRIM), in one line, and (Lydia Whilldin[7], Matthew Whilldin[6], James Whilldin[5], Joseph Whilldin[4], Hannah Gorham[3], Desire Howland[2], JOHN HOWLAND[1] THE PILGRIM), in the other, was born at Cape May, 10 March, 1821, died 5 February, 1884, married 26 November, 1884, William Townsend, born 26 November, 1818, died 23 August, 1906.

Issue:—

(1) LILBURN HARWOOD TOWNSEND, born 26 June, 1850, married 12 November, 1874, Sophia Elizabeth Leach, who died September, 1917, aged 68 years, and had, WILLIAM HERBERT TOWNSEND, born 9 September, 1877, married 18 January, 1905, Lillian May Scott, born 14 September, 1878, and had, LILLIAN SCOTT TOWNSEND, born 21 October, 1909.

(2) MARY ELVENA TOWNSEND, born 28 July, 1853, married first 28 October, 1875, THOMAS HUGHES WILLIAMSON, (see page 213), born 22 July, 1852, died 7 October, 1886; married second Dr. Theophilus Townsend Price, born 21 May, 1828, died 27 April, 1908. Issue by first husband—ERNEST TOWNSEND WILLIAMSON, born 15 August, 1876, married 25 November, 1911, Emeline Amy Oswell, born 15 August, 1879.

LYDIA WHILLDIN, mother of MARY F. LEAMING, married first at Cape May, 22 March, 1808, James Schellenger, (Session Book of Cold Spring Presbyterian Church), and had, FRANKLIN SCHELLENGER and PHEBE SCHELLENGER, who are mentioned in the will of MATTHEW WHILLDIN, father of LYDIA, as under age at the time of making the will. (See page 200).

JOSEPH CRESSE

For ancestors leading back to the Mayflower see page 181.

JOSEPH CRESSE[9], (Maria Leaming[8], Spicer Leaming[7], Christopher Leaming[6], Christopher Leaming[5], Hannah Whilldin[4], Hannah Gorham[3], Desire Howland[2], JOHN HOWLAND[1] THE PILGRIM), born at Cold Spring, New Jersey, 18 January, 1831, died 7 February, 1920, married at Cold Spring, New Jersey, 28 November, 1851, Elizabeth Gregory, born at Philadelphia, Pennsylvania, 16 May, 1831, died July, 1913.

Issue:—

(1) MILTON CRESSE, born at Cold Spring, New Jersey, 10 November, 1854, married at Cold Spring, New Jersey, 1885, Hannah Leaming, died April, 1917.

(2) JULIA MECRAY CRESSE, born at Cold Spring, New Jersey, 20 May, 1857, married Charles P. Eldredge, and had the following children: LORENA CRESSE ELDREDGE, born at Cape May, 6 February, 1884, married 11 October, 1905, at Cape May, Samuel S. Doak, and had MARY STILLWELL DOAK, born 2 February, 1908; WINFIELD SCOTT ELDREDGE, born 5 March, 1886, died 25 June, 1915; ELIZABETH CRESSE ELDREDGE, born at Cape May, 21 August, 1889, married 8 May, 1912, Chester Davis, and had DOROTHY LORENA DAVIS, born 2 July, 1914, and CHARLES HENRY DAVIS, born 7 August, 1916.

JULIA MECRAY CRESSE and Charles P. Eldredge were married at Cape May, 17 May, 1881.

JANE CRESSE

For ancestors leading back to the Mayflower see page 181.

JANE CRESSE[9], (Marie Leaming[8], Spicer Leaming[7], Christopher Leaming[6], Christopher Leaming[5], Hannah Whilldin[4], Hannah Gorham[3], Desire Howland[2], JOHN HOWLAND[1] THE PILGRIM), was born at Cold Spring, New Jersey, 21 December, 1834, married at Cold Spring, New Jersey, 1849, James Crowell, born at Cold Spring, New Jersey, 11 March, 1822, died at Cape May, 3 July, 1906, (tombstone in Cold Spring Cemetery).

Issue:—

(1)   JOHN BUNYON CROWELL, born 1849, no issue.

(2)   DAVID CRESSE CROWELL, born 1853, married Lizzie Shields, and had: JENNIE CROWELL, married HAROLD HAND, and had HAROLD HAND, and RALSTON HAND; FREDERICK JAMES CROWELL, married May Martin; DAVID CROWELL, born 23 August, 1883, married 30 March, 1904, Pauline Elwell, born 16 May, 1886, and had DOROTHY CROWELL, born 26 December, 1905.

(3)   MARIA LEAMING CROWELL, born 15 July, 1858, married 3 March, 1878, Edwin W. Sayre, born 12 July, 1853, died 28 October, 1918, and had the following children: MARY SCHELLENGER SAYRE, born 1879, died 1905, married Willis Johnson Benkert, and had ELEANOR BENKERT, died in infancy; LOUIS JAMES SAYRE, born 20 June, 1885, married 4 October, 1915, Gertrude Simkins, born 5 July, 1891, and had LOUIS EDWARD SAYRE, born 6 July, 1916, and NORMAN LEAMING SAYRE, born 4 October, 1918.

For Pilgrim ancestry of HAROLD HAND, husband of JENNIE CROWELL, see descendants of JOSEPH HAND on page 277.

ELLEN CRESSE

For ancestors leading back to the Mayflower see page 181.

ELLEN CRESSE[9], (Maria Leaming[8], Spicer Leaming[7], Christopher Leaming[6], Christopher Leaming[5], Hannah Whilldin[4], Hannah Gorham[3], Desire Howland[2], JOHN HOWLAND[1] THE PILGRIM), was born at Cold Spring, New Jersey, 24 December, 1846, married at Cold Spring, New Jersey, 11 August, 1867, Clinton H. Hand, born at Rio Grande, New Jersey, 27 March, 1845.

Issue:—

(1) JULIA SMITH HAND, born 2 September, 1869, married at Cold Spring, New Jersey, 25 July, 1888, James A. Needles, born at Felton, Delaware, 1 October, 1860, and had: HARRY HAND NEEDLES, born at Cold Spring, New Jersey, 17 March, 1891, married at Elmira, New York, 14 October, 1916, Leora Warden, born at West Grove, Pennsylvania, 7 October, 1891.

(2) ELSIE MAY HAND, born 24 November, 1884, married at Cold Spring, New Jersey, 22 June, 1904, Walter Y. Shaw, born at Fishing Creek, New Jersey, 12 August, 1879, and had: JAMES CLINTON SHAW, born 14 February, 1906; ELLEN HAND SHAW, born 31 March, 1910.

LYDIA LEAMING

For ancestors leading back to the Mayflower see page 106.

LYDIA LEAMING[7], (Thomas Leaming[6], Thomas Leaming[5], Hannah Whilldin[4], Hannah Gorham[3], Desire Howland[2], JOHN HOWLAND[1] THE PILGRIM), was born 28 August, 1789, died at Philadelphia, Pennsylvania, 26 October, 1869, married at Philadelphia, Pennsylvania, 9 November, 1808, James S. Smith, born at Philadelphia, Pennsylvania, 27 October, 1782, died at Philadelphia, Pennsylvania, 25 January, 1861.

Issue:

(1)   THOMAS LEAMING SMITH, born at Philadelphia, Pennsylvania, 8 December, 1809, died at Philadelphia, Pennsylvania, 5 April, 1841.

(2)   ELIZABETH SHUTE SMITH, born at Philadelphia, 27 May, 1811, died at Philadelphia, 17 January, 1870.

(3)   JAMES SOMERS SMITH, born 23 October, 1813, died 26 August, 1815.

(4)   HENRY HOLLINGSWORTH SMITH, M. D., born 10 December, 1815, died 11 April, 1890, married 4 October, 1843, Mary Edmonds Horner.   (For descendants see page 190).

(5)   RICHARD RUNDLE SMITH, born at Philadelphia, Pennsylvania, 9 June, 1817, died at Philadelphia, Pennsylvania, 28 October, 1903.

(6)   LYDIA LEAMING SMITH, born at Philadelphia, Pennsylvania, 23 August, 1819, died at Philadelphia, Pennsylvania, 6 January, 1899.

(7)   JAMES SOMERS SMITH, born at Philadelphia, Pennsylvania, 16 February, 1822, died 30 March, 1894, married 19 November, 1863, Anna Maria Welsh.   (For descendants see page 191).

(8)   FISHER COLEMAN SMITH, born at Philadelphia, Pennsylvania, 13 October, 1825, died at Philadelphia, Pennsylvania, 14 August, 1873.

(9)   REBECCA LEAMING SMITH, born at Philadelphia Pennsylvania, 29 October, 1827, died 5 June, 1828.

JEREMIAH FISHER LEAMING

For ancestors leading back to the Mayflower see page 106.

JEREMIAH FISHER LEAMING[7], (Thomas Leaming[6], Thomas Leaming[5], Hannah Whilldin[4], Hannah Gorham[3], Desire Howland[2], JOHN HOWLAND[1] THE PILGRIM), was born at Philadelphia, Pennsylvania, 8 October, 1795, died at Philadelphia, Pennsylvania, 5 February, 1888, married at Philadelphia, Pennsylvania, 6 December, 1821, Rebecca Waln, born at Philadelphia, Pennsylvania, 5 January, 1802,, died at Poughkeepsie, New York, 18 August, 1846.

Issue:

(1) ROBERT WALN LEAMING, born at Philadelphia, Pennsylvania, 12 November, 1824, married at Philadelphia, Pennsylvania, Julia Scott, born 21 March, 1828, and had: REBECCA WALN LEAMING, MARY EMELEN LEAMING, JULIA LEAMING and THOMAS LEAMING. (For descendants see page 192).

(2) THOMAS LEAMING, born at Philadelphia, 22 October, 1827, died 2 January, 1837.

(3) FRANCIS WALN LEAMING, born at Philadelphia, 1 November, 1828, died 29 April, 1872, unmarried.

(4) FISHER LEAMING, born at Philadelphia, Pennsylvania, 18 December, 1830, died in infancy.

(5) REBECCA LEAMING, born at Philadelphia, Pennsylvania, 26 January, 1835, died 13 March, 1888, married Charles Pendleton Tutt, M. D., born 2 November, 1832, died 11 May, 1866, and had:—

CHARLES PENDLETON TUTT, who married Josephine Thayer; REBECCA TUTT, married F. Ogleby Wood.

HENRY HOLLINGSWORTH SMITH, M. D.

For ancestors leading back to the Mayflower see page 188.

HENRY HOLLINGSWORTH SMITH, M. D.,[8] (Lydia Leaming[7], Thomas Leaming[6], Thomas Leaming[5], Hannah Whilldin[4], Hannah Gorham[3], Desire Howland[2], JOHN HOWLAND[1] THE PILGRIM), was born at Philadelphia, Pennsylvania, 10 December, 1815, died at Philadelphia, Pennsylvania, 11 April, 1890, married at Philadelphia, Pennsylvania, 4 October, 1843, Mary Edmonds Horner, born at Philadelphia, Pennsylvania, 5 August, 1821, died at Philadelphia, Pennsylvania, 1 February, 1903.

Issue :—

(1) THOMAS LEAMING SMITH, born 3 August, 1844, died at New York City, 14 February, 1895, married 27 October, 1870, Emily Vezin Grant, and had:—

LYDIA LEAMING SMITH, born 18 June, 1872, married 9 November, 1910, Henry Paul Busch, (son of Henry E. Busch, born 19 June, 1830, died 3 December, 1915, and his wife Eleanor K. Jefferies; born 25 July, 1840; married 1 January, 1862). EMILIE SMITH BUSCH, child of Henry Paul and LYDIA LEAMING BUSCH, was born at Philadelphia, Pennsylvania, 17 December, 1914.

EMILY GRANT SMITH, born 17 December, 1875, died February, 1897.

ALICE GRANT SMITH, born 20 November, 1878.

THOMAS LEAMING SMITH, born at New York City, 16 November, 1886.

(2) EUGENIA HORNER SMITH, born 25 May, 1847.

(3) WILLIAM HORNER SMITH, born 2 September, 1853, married Henrietta Constantia Wilkins. (For descendants see page 194).

(4) HARRY EDMONDS SMITH, born 10 September, 1855, died 9 March, 1874.

(5) JAMES RUNDLE SMITH, born 14 August, 1857, married first Ellen Hollingshead; married second Mary Gibb (Stokes) Harris; married third Gertrude Merryweather. (For descendants, see page 195).

(6) ALFRED SMITH, born 10 July, 1864, died in infancy.

JAMES SOMERS SMITH

For ancestors leading back to the Mayflower see page 188.

JAMES SOMERS SMITH[8], (Lydia Leaming[7], Thomas Leaming[6], Thomas Leaming[5], Hannah Whilldin[4], Hannah Gorham[3], Desire Howland[2], JOHN HOWLAND[1] THE PILGRIM), was born at Philadelphia, Pennsylvania, 16 February, 1822, died at Philadelphia, Pennsylvania, 30 March, 1894, married at Philadelphia, Pennsylvania, 19 November, 1863, Anna Maria Welsh, born at Philadelphia, Pennsylvania, died at Philadelphia, Pennsylvania, 30 January, 1904.

Issue:—

(1) JAMES SOMERS SMITH, born at Philadelphia, Pennsylvania, 26 May, 1866, married at Philadelphia, Pennsylvania, 19 April, 1888, Mary Nixon Smith, and had the following children:—

JAMES SOMERS SMITH, born at Philadelphia, Pennsylvania, 16 November, 1889, married at Wayne, Pennsylvania, 5 July, 1918, Katherine Hancock.

NANCY CORRY SMITH, born at Philadelphia, Pennsylvania, 22 October, 1894, married at Philadelphia, Pennsylvania, 17 June, 1915, Joseph Wood, Jr., son of Joseph and Jennie Boas Wood, and had, NANCY COOPER WOOD, born at Philadelphia, Pennsylvania, 1 May, 1916, HOPE COOPER WOOD, born at Abington, Pennsylvania, 23 December, 1917.

COOPER SMITH, born at Philadelphia, Pennsylvania, 13 January, 1900.

ROBERT WALN LEAMING

For ancestors leading back to the Mayflower see page 189.

ROBERT WALN LEAMING[8], (Jeremiah Fisher Leaming[7], Thomas Leaming[6], Thomas Leaming[5], Hannah Whilldin[4], Hannah Gorham[3], Desire Howland[2], JOHN HOWLAND[1] THE PILGRIM), was born at Philadelphia, Pennsylvania, 12 November, 1824, died at Philadelphia, Pennsylvania, 9 November, 1884, married at Philadelphia, Pennsylvania, March, 1849, Julia Scott, born at Philadelphia, 21 March, 1828, died at Wayne, Pennsylvania, 22 February, 1914.

Issue:—

(1) REBECCA WALN LEAMING, born March, 1850, married William W. Montgomery, and had: MARY SCOTT MONTGOMERY, born 26 June, 1876, married Edward Biddle Halsey; WILLIAM W. MONTGOMERY, born 6 October, 1877, married Fanny Brock; ROBERT LEAMING MONTGOMERY, born 1879, married Charlotte Hope Binney Tyler, and had, HELEN HOPE MONTGOMERY, born 1904, MARY BINNEY MONTGOMERY, born 1907, ALEXANDER MONTGOMERY, born 1911, CHARLOTTE IVES MONTGOMERY, born 1912.

(2) MARY EMLEN LEAMING, born 19 September, 1851, died 13 May, 1911, married R. Francis Wood. (For descendants see page 193).

(3) JULIA LEAMING, born Dec. 1855, died 14 December, 1913, married Nicholas Leaming.

(4) THOMAS LEAMING, born 29 May, 1858, died 14 December, 1911, married Josephine Lea Baker.

MARY EMLEN LEAMING

For ancestors leading back to the Mayflower see page 192.

MARY EMLEN LEAMING[9], (Robert Waln Leaming[8], Jeremiah Fisher Leaming[7], Thomas Leaming[6], Thomas Leaming[5], Hannah Whilldin[4], Hannah Gorham[3], Desire Howland[2], JOHN HOWLAND[1] THE PILGRIM), was born at Philadelphia, 19 September, 1851, married at Rosemont, Pennsylvania, Church of the Good Shepperd, 15 October, 1878, Richard Francis Wood, born 15 May, 1850, at Philadelphia.

Issue:

(1) CHARLES STEWART WOOD, born 26 November, 1879.

(2) JULIA LEAMING WOOD, born 29 June, 1881.

(3) REBECCA LEAMING WOOD, born at Philadelphia, 16 March, 1883, married at St. David's, Radnor, 21 January, 1905, Francis Gurney Okie, born 1 January, 1880, and have the following children: MARY EMLEN OKIE, RICHARDSON BROGNARD OKIE 2nd, ANN WOOD OKIE, FRANCIS GURNEY OKIE, Jr., and REBECCA LEAMING OKIE.

(4) RICHARD FRANCIS WOOD, Jr., born 1 January, 1885.

(5) ROBERT LEAMING WOOD, born 1 November, 1886, married Sophia Wilcox Wheeler, at St. Mark's Church, Philadelphia, 9 April, 1912, and have issue: MARY WHEELER WOOD, ROBERT LEAMING WOOD, Jr., ELEANOR PEACE WOOD.

(6) EMLEN WOOD, born 27 February, 1889.

(7) EDWARD FITZ RANDOLPH WOOD, born 25 December, 1890, married Marian Farnum Butler, 20 November, 1919, at St. Luke's Church, Germantown.

WILLIAM HORNER SMITH

For ancestors leading back to the Mayflower see page 190.

WILLIAM HORNER SMITH[9], (Henry Hollingsworth Smith[8], Lydia Leaming[7], Thomas Leaming[6], Thomas Leaming[5], Hannah Whilldin[4], Hannah Gorham[3], Desire Howland[2], JOHN HOWLAND[1] THE PILGRIM), was born 2 September, 1853, died at Ardmore, Pennsylvania, 30 December, 1889, married 24 April, 1880, Henrietta Constantia Wilkins.

Issue:

(1) HARRY WILKINS SMITH, born 1 June, 1881, died 30 June, 1882.

(2) MARIA WILKINS SMITH, born 21 June, 1884.

(3) WILLIAM HORNER SMITH, born 4 May, 1886, deceased.

(4) ELIZABETH WASHINGTON SMITH, born at Ardmore, Pennsylvania, 8 September, 1889, married at Radnor, Pennsylvania, 8 June, 1909, Dr. Henry Pleasants, Jr., and had the following children:—

HENRY PLEASANTS, 3rd, born 12 May, 1910.

WILLIAM WILKINS PLEASANTS, born 17 May, 1911.

HOWARD SPENCER PLEASANTS, born 21 November, 1912. RICHARD RUNDLE PLEASANTS, born 21 November, 1912.

CONSTANTIA ELIZABETH PLEASANTS, born 18 January, 1915.

DALLAS FRANKLIN PLEASANTS, born 11 June, 1917,

JAMES RUNDLE SMITH

For ancestors leading back to the Mayflower see page 190.

JAMES RUNDLE SMITH[9], (Henry Hollingsworth Smith[8], Lydia Leaming[7], Thomsa Leaming[6], Thomas Leaming[5], Hannah Whilldin[4], Hannah Gorham[3], Desire Howland[2], JOHN HOWLAND[1] THE PILGRIM), was born 14 June, died 30 December, 1908, married first, 1879, Ellen Hollingshead, who died January, 1880; married second 11 January, 1894, Mary Gibb (Stokes) Harris, widow of Dr. Charles McIlvaine Harris, she died 25 August, 1897; married third at Bayhead, New Jersey, 1 October, 1902, Gertrude Merryweather.

Issue:—

(1) ELLEN HOLLINGSHEAD SMITH, born 17 January, 1880, married at the Church of St. Martin's in the Fields, Philadelphia, Pennsylvania, 14 December, 1904, Cushman Newhall, and had the following children:—

ANNETTE WRIGHT NEWHALL, born 14 October, 1905.

HENRY SMITH NEWHALL, born 21 March, 1907.

MARJORIE NEWHALL, born 19 May, 1911.

ELLEN NEWHALL, born 25 June, 1914.

ROBERT CUSHMAN NEWHALL, born 1 April, 1917, died 29 August, 1918.

(2) REBECCA FISHER SMITH, born July, 1905, died in infancy.

JAMES WHILLDIN

For ancestors leading back to the Mayflower see page 100.

JAMES WHILLDIN[5], (Joseph Whilldin[4], Hannah Gorham[3], Desire Howland[2], JOHN HOWLAND[1] THE PILGRIM), was born at Cape May, 1714, died at Cape May, 5 November, 1780, (tombstone in Cold Spring Cemetery), married first, Jane Hand, born at Cape May, 1719, died at Cape May, 8 November, 1760, (tombstone in Cold Spring Cemetery), married second by license of 20 July, 1761, Jane Izard, married third by license of 13 January, 1766, Susannah Hand, who survived him, and is mentioned in his will.

Issue:

(1) JAMES WHILLDIN, born 20 August, 1742, married by license of 8 December, 1774, Rhoda Mulford. (For descendants see page 198.)

(2) MATTHEW WHILLDIN, born at Cape May, 1749, married at Cape May by license of 22 April, 1771, Phebe Hildreth, born 1753, died at Cape May, 14 June, 1798, married second 9 April, 1801, Ruhama Hand. (For descendants see page 200).

(3) JONATHAN WHILLDIN, born at Cape May, 1755, died at Cape May, 1796, married Hannah Crowell. (For descendants see page 201.)

(4) JANE WHILLDIN, born at Cape May, 15 June, 1756, died at Cape May, 26 December, 1790, married first, Humphrey Hughes; (for descendants see page 202), married second Jeremiah Edmunds, (for descendants see page 203.)

Daughters, MARY (HUGHES), LOIS (YEATS), RACHEL WHILLDIN are mentioned in will, and grandsons SETH WHILLDIN and HUMPHREY HUGHES.

HANNAH WHILLDIN

For ancestors leading back to the Mayflower see page 100.

HANNAH WHILLDIN[5], (Joseph Whilldin[4], Hannah Gorham[3], Desire Howland[2], JOHN HOWLAND[1] THE PILGRIM), was born at Cape May about 1719, married first at Cape May, before 1739, Ellis Hughes, born at Cape May, 1708, died at Cape May, 1752, will proved 4 February of that year, She married second, Eldredge ——————

Issue by first marriage :—

(1) MEMUCAN HUGHES, born at Cape May, 12 April, 1739, died at Cape May, 8 January, 1812, married first at Cape May, 10 March, 1761, Martha Hughes; married second, Rhoda Allen, who survived him and is named in his will. (For descendants see page 204.)

(2) ELLIS HUGHES, born at Cape May, 16 August, 1745, died at Cape May, 16 April, 1817, (tombstone in Cold Spring Cemetery), married at Cape May by license of 21 September, 1768, Elenor Hurst, born at Cape May, 5 March, 1747, widow of WILMON WHILLDIN. She died 11 April, 1786, aged 39 years, 1 month, (tombstone in Cold Spring Cemetery), "wife of Ellis Hughes, Junior. (For descendants see page 205.)

(3) JESSE HUGHES, married Moly ——————.

(4) CONSTANTINE HUGHES.

(5) DAVID HUGHES.

See Deed of Jesse Hughes and Mary his Wife to Memucan Hughes, page 27, the Will of Ellis Hughes on page 29, and "The Wife of Ellis Hughes," with reference to the will of Joseph Whilldin 2nd on page 37. See also Genealogical Notes at the end of this volume.

JAMES WHILLDIN

For ancestors leading back to the Mayflower see page 196.

JAMES WHILLDIN[6], (James Whilldin[5], Joseph Whilldin[4], Hannah Gorham[3], Desire Howland[2], JOHN HOWLAND[1]
THE PILGRIM), was born at Cape May, 20 August, 1742, married first by license of 8 December, 1774, Rhoda Mulford, born
1755, died at Cape May, 9 September, 1801, (tombstone in Cold
Spring Cemetery). After the death of his wife, Rhoda, JAMES
WHILLDIN married second Martha Hand and moved to Ohio,
where he died.

Issue:
    (1) DANIEL WHILLDIN, born 31 December, 1775, lost
at sea 23 December, 1811, (see inscription on stone in Cold
Spring Cemetery), married 7 March, 1802, Jane Stillwell, born
17 November, 1782, died 13 September, 1829, (she married
second Jacob Foster, and is buried in Cold Spring Cemetery).
    Children of DANIEL and Jane Stillwell WHILLDIN:—
    ALEXANDER WHILLDIN, born at Cape May, 1808.
    AMELIA STILLWELL WHILLDIN, born at Cape May,
29 October, 1809, died at Cape May, 9 July, 1889, married at
Cape May, 27 February, 1827, Samuel Springer, born 9 May,
1800, died at Cape May, 7 March, 1877, and had:—JANE
SPRINGER, born 1828, died 1909, unmarried. WHILLDIN
SPRINGER, born at Cape May, 1830, married Sarah Beatty,
and had HANNAH M. SPRINGER, born 25 November, 1860,
married first Horace Hance, married second Walter Smith;
SAMUEL SPRINGER, born 9 April, 1863, married Alice Tuthill, and had WHILLDIN SPRINGER, died 20 February,
1907, HELENE SPRINGER, born 4 August, 1889, CLARA
SPRINGER, born 15 January, 1891, MILDRED SPRINGER,
born 3 January, 1895; ALICE SPRINGER, born 20 June, 1906.
ELIZA C. SPRINGER, born 12 March, 1865, married Luther
Tuthill, and had, MARION TUTHILL, born 18 September,
1889, married C. C. Mays, IRENE TUTHILL, born 27 September, 1892, DOROTHY TUTHILL, born 12 August, 1895, MY-
RON B. and SAMUEL SPRINGER TUTHILL, born 3 July,
1897.

(Continued on next page)

JAMES WHILLDIN

ALEXANDER W. SPRINGER, son of AMELIA STILL-WELL WHILLDIN and her husband Samuel Springer, was born at Dias Creek, New Jersey, 5 April, 1835, died at Cape May, 14 December, 1896, married Mary Fifield. (For descendants see page 206).

MARGARET SPRINGER, daughter of AMELIA W. and Samuel Springer, married Miles Corson.

EDWARD D. SPRINGER, son of AMELIA STILLWELL WHILLDIN and her husband, Samuel Springer, born 2 March, 1838, married first 3 March, 1860, Lydia Edwards, who died 2 October, 1867, married second 3 October, 1873, Clara Williams, and had: FRANKLIN H. SPRINGER, born 19 August, 1874, WHILLDIN SPRINGER, born 21 January, 1876, EMMA H. SPRINGER, born 26 August, 1877, HARRY W. SPRINGER, born 16 August, 1879, EDNA SPRINGER, born 2 April, 1882, EVA W. SPRINGER, born 19 November, 1883, JOHN WALLACE SPRINGER, born 29 April, 1887, ANNIE E. SPRINGER, born 18 February, 1891.

MARY H. SPRINGER, born 5 May, 1844, died 8 September, 1903, married Edmund Thomas Benezet, son of Anthony and Julia Benezet (date of marriage 25 February, 1874), and had: RALPH ANTHONY BENEZET, born 4 January, 1875, married 26 September, 1901, Rae Reeves Carpenter, and had, MARY CARPENTER BENEZET, born 31 December, 1904; MAUD H. BENEZET, born 17 January, 1883. Edmund Thomas Benezet, husband of MARY H. SPRINGER, died 21 March, 1920.

DANIELIA SPRINGER, born 1847, died 1901, unmarried.

AMELIA SPRINGER, died 1918, unmarried.

DANIELIA WHILLDIN, born at Cape May, 27 February, 1812, (daughter of DANIEL WHILLDIN and his wife Jane Stillwell), died at Cape May, 7 June, 1886, married at Cape May, 29 December, 1831, Franklin Hand, who was born at Cape May, 1 January, 1809, died 4 February, 1857. (For descendants see page 207).

(2) RUTH WHILLDIN, daughter of James and Rhoda, born 1783, died 7 March, 1791, (tombstone in Cold Spring Cemetery).

(3) DAVID WHILLDIN.

(4) RHODA WHILLDIN, daughter of JAMES by his second wife, Martha Hand.

MATTHEW WHILLDIN

For ancestors leading back to the Mayflower see page 196.

MATTHEW WHILLDIN[6], (James Whilldin[5], Joseph Whilldin[4], Hannah Gorham[3], Desire Howland[2], JOHN HOWLAND[1] THE PILGRIM), was born at Cape May, 1749, died at Cape May, 16 July, 1828, (tombstone in Cold Spring Cemetery), married first at Cape May, by license of 22 April 1771, Phebe Hildreth, born 1753, died at Cape May, 14 June, 1798; (tombstone in Cold Spring Cemtery); married second 1 September, 1799, Ruhama Hand, widow of Nicholas Stillwell, who survived him. She died 24 February, 1839, in her eighty-fourth year, and was buried in the Methodist Cemetery, Cape May Court House, New Jersey.

Issue :—

(1) ISAAC WHILLDIN, born at Cape May, 20 February, 1784, died at Cape May, 13 May, 1867, married MAHALA EDMUNDS[7], (Jane Whilldin[6], James Whilldin[5], Joseph Whilldin[4], Hannah Gorham[3], Desire Howland[2], JOHN HOWLAND[1] THE PILGRIM). (For descendants see page 215).

(2) LYDIA WHILLDIN, born 19 January, 1790, died 13 February, 1856, (tombstone in Cold Spring Cemetery), married first at Cape May, 22 March, 1808, James Schellenger, (Session Book of Cold Spring Presbyterian Church on page 44), and had FRANKLIN SCHELLENGER and PHEBE SCHELLENGER, mentioned in will of MATTHEW WHILLDIN as under age at the time of making the will. She married second JAMES LEAMING[8], (Spicer Leaming[7], Christopher Leaming[6], Christopher Leaming[5], Hannah Whilldin[4], Hannah Gorham[3], Desire Howland[2], JOHN HOWLAND[1] THE PILGRIM). (See page 180).

(3) DAVID WHILLDIN, born at Cape May, 1792, died at Cape May, 10 December, 1813, in the twenty first year of his age, (tombstone in Cold Spring Cemetery). For exact date of death, see Session Book of Cold Spring Presbyterian Church, page 64.

JONATHAN WHILLDIN

For ancestors leading back to the Mayflower see page 196.

JONATHAN WHILLDIN⁶, (James Whilldin⁵, Joseph Whilldin⁴, Hannah Gorham³, Desire Howland², JOHN HOWLAND¹ THE PILGRIM), was born at Cape May, 1755, died at Cape May, 13 February, 1796, married at Cape May by license of 16 November, 1772, Hannah Crowell.

Issue :—

(1) WILMON WHILLDIN, born at Cape May, 1773, died at Philadelphia, Pennsylvania, 2 April, 1852.

(2) DEBORAH WHILLDIN, born at Cape May, 1780, died at Cape May before 10 June, 1808, married at Cape May, 1799, Joseph Ware, born in Cumberland County, New Jersey, 27 August, 1771, died at Cape May, 13 February, 1827, (tombstone in Cold Spring Cemetery). He married as his second wife HARRIET WHILLDIN, sister of his first wife. (See below). (For descendants see page 208).

(3) HARRIET WHILLDIN, born at Cape May, 1785, died at Cape May, 3 August, 1851, (tombstone in Cold Spring Cemetery), married at Cape May, 10 June, 1808, Joseph Ware, (see above). (For descendants see page 209).

For an account of the Ware family see "Descendants of Joseph Ware of Fenwick Colony," by Franklin Ware.

JANE WHILLDIN

For ancestors leading back to the Mayflower see page 196.

JANE WHILLDIN[6], (James Whillin[5], Joseph Whilldin[4], Hannah Gorham[3], Desire Howland[2], JOHN HOWLAND[1] THE PILGRIM), was born at Cape May, 15 June, 1756, died at Cape May, 26 December, 1790, married first, 1774, Humphrey Hughes, born at Cape May, about 1752, died at sea about 1777.

Issue:—

(1) HUMPHREY HUGHES, born 20 November, 1775, died 21 August, 1858, married 9 March, 1800, Hetty Williams, born 14 December, 1781, died 4 February, 1870, and had the following children:—LOUISA WILLIAMS HUGHES, born 9 January, 1806, married Enoch Edmunds, (for descendants see page 210); ALBERT HENRY HUGHES, born 8 January, 1812, married first Elizabeth Schellenger, married second Mary Whitaker Pierson, (for descendants see page 212); EMILY HURST HUGHES, born 19 November, 1817, married Rev. Moses Williamson, (for descendants see page 213); ELMIRA WILLIAMS HUGHES, born 1 January, 1820, married REV. DANIEL LAWRENCE HUGHES, D. D., (for descendants see page 157); HUMPHREY HUGHES, born 2 May, 1822, married ELIZA ELDREDGE, (for descendants see page 133); CHARLES PINCKNEY HUGHES, born 26 June, 1826.

JAMES WHILLDIN

For ancestors leading back to the Mayflower see page 196.

JANE WHILLDIN[6], (James Whilldin[5], Joseph Whilldin[4], Hannah Gorham[3], Desire Howland[2], JOHN HOWLAND[1] THE PILGRIM), was born at Cape May, 15 June, 1758, died at Cape May, 26 December, 1790, married second, 1 July, 1779, Jeremiah Edmunds, born at Cape May, 2 October, 1760, died 22 November, 1807.

Issue:—

(1) ELIZABETH EDMUNDS, born at Cape May, 4 December, 1780, died at Cape May, 11 January, 1868, (tombstone in Cold Spring Cemetery), married 10 April, 1799, Levi Eldredge, born 17 October, 1776, died at Cape May, 23 November, 1822, (tombstone in Cold Spring Cemetery). For descendants see page 214).

(2) MAHALAH EDMUNDS, born at Cape May, 10 January, 1783, died at Cape May, 12 November, 1840, (tombstone in Cold Spring Cemetery), married at Cape May, 11 March, 1809, ISAAC WHILLDIN, born at Cape May, 20 February, 1784, (record of family bible), died 13 May, 1867. (For descendants see page 215).

(3) JEREMIAH EDMUNDS, born 15 April, 1785, married Ruhama Tomlin. (For descendants see page 216). Date of marriage, 5 August, 1810.

MEMUCAN HUGHES

For ancestors leading back to the Mayflower see page 197

MEMUCAN HUGHES[6], (Hannah Whilldin[5], Joseph Whilldin[4], Hannah Gorham[3], Desire Howland[2], JOHN HOWLAND[1] THE PILGRIM), was born at Cape May, 12 April, 1739, died at Cape May, 8 January, 1812, married first at Cape May, 10 March, 1761, Martha Hughes; married second, Rhoda Allen who survived him and is mentioned in his will, (date of marriage 22 May, 1799).

Issue:—

(1) ZERUIAH HUGHES, born at Cape May, 19 April, 1776, died at Cape May, 7 November, 1818, married 1 August, 1792, Robert Cummings Schenck, M. D., born near Freehold, New Jersey, 11 January, 1772, died at Cape May, 13 January, 1833. (For descendants see page 248).

(2) ISRAEL HUGHES, born at Cape May, 9 May, 1778, died at Cape May, 7 February, 1833, married at Cape May, 3 August, 1806, Mary Eldredge, born at Cape May, 16 March, 1785, died at Cape May, 16 June, 1863. (For note on the date of birth of Mary Eldredge and descendants see page 249).

(3) MARTHA HUGHES.

(4) ELIJAH HUGHES, "who died early, and whose coffin Isaac Smith, Esq., charged to his father, March 13, 1811," article of Rev. Daniel Lawrence Hughes, D. D., on "The Hughes of Cape May."

The will of MEMUCAN HUGHES, dated 3 January, 1812, proved 17 January 1812, mentions: (1) Wife Rhoda Hughes, then living; (2) grandson, Memucan Hughes, son of Israel Hughes; (3) son of Israel Hughes, and son of Israel, Art Hughes, under age; (4) Martha Hughes, and children of "my daughter Zeruviah (Zeruiah in family bible) Schenck"; (5) daughter Zeruviah Schenck.

ELLIS HUGHES

For ancestors leading back to the Mayflower see page 197.

ELLIS HUGHES[6], (Hannah Whilldin[5], Joseph Whilldin[4], Hannah Gorham[3], Desire Howland[2], JOHN HOWLAND[1] THE PILGRIM), was born at Cape May, 16 August, 1745, died at Cape May, 16 April, 1817, (tombstone in Cold Spring Cemetery), married at Cape May, by license of 21 September, 1768, Elenor Hurst, widow of WILMON WHILLDIN. She died 11 April, 1786, aged 39 years, 1 month, (tombstone in Cold Spring Cemetery, with inscription "Wife of Ellis Hughes, Junior."

Issue:—

(1) WILLIAM HUGHES, first mentioned in will of father, possibly a previous marriage.

(2) THOMAS HURST HUGHES, born 10 January, 1769, married Lydia Page. (For descendants see page 250).

(3) JOSEPH HUGHES, born 17 November, 1772, married Judith Bennett. (For descendants see page 251).

(4) HANNAH HUGHES, (second in will), married Charles Ford.

(5) ELIZABETH HUGHES, married 10 March, 1807, David Yeates. (Cape May Marriages, Book A).

(6) RICHARD HUGHES.

(7) ELEANOR HUGHES, born 7 August, 1776, died 5 October, 1818, married Silas Matthews. (For descendants see page 252).

(8) MARTHA HUGHES, married —––––– Pritchard. She died before 2 February, 1818.

See note at the end of this volume on the supposed first marriage of Ellis Hughes, Sr.

ALEXANDER W. SPRINGER

ALEXANDER W. SPRINGER⁹, (Amelia Stillwell Whilldin⁸,⁹ Daniel Whilldin⁷, James Whilldin⁶, James Whilldin⁵, Joseph Whilldin⁴, Hannah Gorham³, Desire Howland², JOHN HOWLAND¹ THE PILGRIM), was born at Dias Creek, New Jersey, 5 April, 1835, died 14 December, 1896, married Mary Fifield, born 27 April, 1841.

For ancestors leading back to the Mayflower see page 199.
Issue :—

(1) JOSEPH SPRINGER, born 24 June, 1860, married ANNA MARIA ELDREDGE. (For descendants see page 234).

(2) CHARLES SPRINGER, born 1862, lost at sea 1880.

(3) ELLA SPRINGER, married Charles W. Keeler, and had:— CHARLES SPRINGER KEELER, born 22 January, 1883, married 15 December, 1903, Elizabeth Cawman, and had, CHARLES H. KEELER, born 8 April, 1904, ALBERT A. KEELER, born 15 September, 1907, FRANK W. MILLER KEELER, born 6 July, 1912, JOHN C. KEELER, born 6 April, 1915, JESSIE SPRINGER KEELER, born 17 March, 1918; JESSIE SPRINGER KEELER, daughter of ELLA SPRINGER and Charles W. Keeler, died at the age of five years; MARY SPRINGER KEELER, married Everett L. Smith, and had, ANNA ELIZABETH SMITH; JOHN GILBERT KEELER, married Myrtle Hawn and had HARVEY KEELER.

(4) EDWARD WHILLDIN SPRINGER, born at Cape May Court House, 18 December, 1866, married 1894, Fannie Dickenson.

(5) AMELIA SPRINGER, married Frank Rutherford, and had: CLARA RUTHERFORD, who married 11 November, 1914, John E. Huff, and had, GENEVIEVE HUFF, born 30 March, 1917, and JOHN E. HUFF, Jr., born 12 March, 1919; FRANK RUTHERFORD; GENEVIEVE RUTHERFORD; ROBERT RUTHERFORD.

(6) JOHN SPRINGER, born at Dias Creek, December, 1871, married at Cape May, 25 November, 1900, Harriet Stanton, and had, OSCAR SPRINGER, born 1 March, 1903, EVELYN STANTON SPRINGER, born 28 August, 1914.

(7) ANNA SPRINGER, married Percy Haldeman, and had:— ALEXANDER HALDEMAN, born 4 May, 1896; PERCY HALDEMAN, born 25 July, 1897; BEATRICE HALDEMAN, born 18 October, 1898, married S. F. Harding, and had BEATRICE HARDING, born 18 May, 1918; EDITH HALDEMAN, born 28 August, 1901; EMILY HALDEMAN, born 8 September, 1904; DONALD HALDEMAN, born 12 June, 1906; WILLIAM HALDEMAN, born 8 June, 1909; EDWARD HALDEMAN, born 8 August, 1915.

DANIELIA WHILLDIN

For ancestors leading back to the Mayflower see page 199.

DANIELIA WHILLDIN[8], (Daniel Whilldin[7], James Whilldin[6], James Whilldin[5], Joseph Whilldin[4], Hannah Gorham[3], Desire Howland[2], JOHN HOWLAND[1] THE PILGRIM), was born at Cape May, 27 February, 1812 died at Cape May, 7 June. 1886. married at Cape May. 29 December, 1831, Franklin Hand, born 1 January, 1809, died 4 February, 1857.

Issue:—

(1) JANE HAND, born 7 October, 1832, died 14 January, 1910, married 24 February, 1869, Richard Meigs, no issue.

(2) DANIEL WHILLDIN HAND, born 18 August, 1834, married 23 January, 1868, Susan Melville Egerton Freeman, born August, 1842, at Petersburg, Virginia, and had:— DANIEL WHILLDIN HAND, born 14 October, 1869, (now Colonel in U. S. Army), married 8 April, 1896, Elizabeth Metcalf, and had, DANIEL WHILLDIN HAND, born 8 May, 1897, died unmarried, 22 January, 1919, while Junior Lieutenant in U. S. Navy, AGNES M. HAND, born 30 December, 1899; EDITH HAND, born 15 May, 1872, at St. Paul, Minn., married 4 June, 1907, Edmund B. Leaming, born at Seaville, Cape May County, New Jersey, 24 May, 1857, and had EDMUND B. LEAMING, born at Moorestown, New Jersey, 26 January, 1913.

(3) FRANKLIN HAND, born 26 September, 1836, died 1 November, 1887, unmarried.

(4) AMELIA SPRINGER HAND, born 9 October, 1838, died 7 March, 1888, unmarried.

(5) RICHARD TOWNSEND HAND, born 18 May, 1841, married 29 April, 1874, Clara L. McCormick, and had, RICHARDINA HAND.

(6). LYDIA FIFIELD HAND, born 20 December, 1843, died 27 October, 1913, married 27 July, 1877, John Wiley, M. D., no issue.

(7) ELMIRA HAND, born 24 July, 1846, died 7 March, 1888, married 9 October, 1884, Joseph Hall, no issue.

(8) HENRY CLAY HAND, born 17 March, 1849, died 2 March, 1876, married 15 October, 1874, Emma V. Smith, no issue.

(9) ARABELLA HAND, born 19 February, 1852, died in infancy.

DEBORAH WHILLDIN

For ancestors leading back to the Mayflower see page 201.

DEBORAH WHILLDIN[7], (Jonathan Whilldin[6], James Whilldin[5], Joseph Whilldin[4], Hannah Gorham[3], Desire Howland[2], JOHN HOWLAND[1] THE PILGRIM), was born at Cape May, 1780, died at Cold Spring, New Jersey, before 10 June, 1808, married at Cape May, 8 May, 1798, Joseph Ware, born in Cumberland County, New Jersey, 27 August, 1771, died at Cape May, 13 February, 1827, (tombstone in Cold Spring Cemetery).

Issue:—

(1) SAMUEL FITHIAN WARE, born at Cape May, 16 October, 1800, married first Esther Teal, married second Lydia Thomas. (For descendants see page 217).

(2) DEBORAH WHILLDIN WARE, born at Cape May, 4 May, 1804, married Thomas Eldredge. (For descendants see page 218).

(3) JAMES WHILLDIN WARE, born at Cape May, 12 January, 1806, married Deborah Hampton. (For descendants see page 219).

JOSEPH WARE, married as his second wife HARRIET WHILLDIN, sister of DEBORAH WHILLDIN. (See page 209).

HARRIET WHILLDIN

For ancestors leading back to the Mayflower see page 201.

HARRIET WHILLDIN[7], (Jonathan Whilldin[6], James Whilldin[5], Joseph Whilldin[4], Hannah Gorham[3], Desire Howland[2], JOHN HOWLAND[1] THE PILGRIM), was born at Cape May, 1785, died at Cape May, 3 August, 1851, married at Cape May, 10 June, 1808, Joseph Ware, (see page 44), born in Cumberland County, New Jersey, 27 August, 1771, died at Cape May, 13 February. (For first marriage of Joseph Ware see page 208).

Issue:—

(1) JOSEPH WARE, born 16 May, 1809, married first ANN HUGHES, married second LYDIA LEAMING. (For descendants see page 220).

(2) DANIEL CROWELL WARE, born 1 November, 1809, married first Rachel C. Hughes, married second Louisa Ford. Issue by second wife:—ANN WARE, married Stillwell Hand, and had: FRANCES HAND, who married Joseph Brooks, and had, JOSEPH BROOKS, married Helen Reeves, and had, FRANCIS RALSTON BROOKS, born 5 May, 1920, MAURICE BROOKS, married Rita Schellenger, and had EMILIE BROOKS; LOUISA HAND, married Dr. J. SMALLWOOD ELDREDGE (see page 135); DR. ROBERT HAND, married Lily Gabel, and had, ROBERT HAND. HARRIET WARE married Elwood Rowland and had, ADELE ROWLAND, who married Stamford Vanaman.

(3) WILMON WHILLDIN WARE, born 1818, died July, 1886, married first Mary B. Schellenger, married second Eliza B. Schellenger, married third Belle West. Issue by first marriage: GEORGE SCHELLENGER WARE, married MARIETTA LEACH; HARRIET WHILLDIN WARE, married Samuel Richardson Stites. (See page 221).

(4) MASKELL WARE, born 1829, married first Leah Mathis, married second Mary Jane Warrick. For descendants see page 222).

(5) JOHN GEORGE WASHINGTON WARE, born 1825, died 8 September, 1894.

LOUISA WILLIAMS HUGHES

For ancestors leading back to the Mayflower see page 202.

LOUISA WILLIAMS HUGHES[8], (Humphrey Hughes[7], Jane Whilldin[6], James Whilldin[5], Joseph Whilldin[4], Hannah Gorham[3], Desire Howland[2], JOHN HOWLAND[1] THE PILGRIM), was born at Cape May, 9 January, 1806, died at Cape May, 21 August, 1860, (tombstone in Cold Spring Cemetery), married at Cape May, 16 July, 1822, Enoch Edmunds, born at Cape May, 1799, died at Cape May, 30 March, 1867, (tombstone in Cold Spring Cemetery).

Issue:—

(1) LOUISA HUGHES EDMUNDS, born at Cape May, 1824, died at Philadelphia, Pennsylvania, 13 January, 1857, aged thirty three years, married at Cape May, January, 1845, Waters Borrows Miller, born at Rangleboro, Atlantic County, New Jersey, 10 May, 1824, died at Trenton, New Jersey, 3 September, 1848, and had: RICHARD THOMPSON MILLER, born at Cape May, 16 December, 1845, died at Camden, New Jersey, 15 December, 1906, married at Philadelphia, Pennsylvania, 18 November, 1874, Mercedes Ysabel Ascarte, born at Havana, Cuba, 10 July, 1858; LAFAYETTE MILLER, born at Cape May, 18 September, 1848, died at Camden, New Jersey, 3 June, 1904, married at Philadelphia, Pennsylvania, 26 June, 1875, Caroline Marqueze Haseltine, born at Philadelphia, Pennsylvania, 4 December, 1855, and had, STANLEY AROZARENA MILLER, born at Philadelphia, Pennsylvania, 31 August, 1876, LOUIS EDMUNDS MILLER, born at Philadelphia, Pennsylvania, 9 January, 1881.

(Continued on next page)

LOUISA WILLIAMS HUGHES

MERCEDES YSABEL MILLER, (daughter of LAFAY-ETTE MILLER and Marqueze Haseltine Miller, granddaughter of Waters Borrows Miller and LOUISA HUGHES EDMUNDS MILLER, great-granddaughter of LOUISA WILLIAMSON HUGHES and her husband Enoch Edmunds), was born at Camden, New Jersey, 19 November, 1882; RICHARD STANBURY MILLER, her brother, born at Cape May, 7 May, 1885; RUS-SELL MILLER, born 7 April, 1897; JONAS STANBURY MILLER, son of Waters Borrows and LOUISA HUGHES ED-MUNDS. MILLER, born at Cape May, died at Camden, New Jersey, 12 May, 1906, married at Washington, D. C., Mary Mc-Kenna; ELIZABETH STILLWELL MILLER, sister of the foregoing JONAS STANBURY MILLER, born at Cape May, 17 October, 1850, married at Cape May, 23 October, 1873, HENRY ALBERT HUGHES[9], (Albert Henry Hughes[8], Humphrey Hughes[7], Jane Whilldin[6], James Whilldin[5], Joseph Whilldin[4], Hannah Gorham[3], Desire Howland[2], JOHN HOWLAND[1] THE PILGRIM), born at Cape May, 30 May, 1846, and had HENRY ALBERT HUGHES, Jr., born at Cape May, 7 August, 1874, married at Philadelphia, 16 October, 1902, Edna Burr Catlin, born at Jersey City, 12 May, 1878, and had ALBERT HENRY HUGHES, born at Philadelphia, 15 October, 1903, died 5 March, 1904; HORACE HENRY HUGHES, born at Philadelphia, 5 December, 1905; RIDGWAY CATLIN HUGHES, born at Haddon Heights, 16 October, 1910; HENRY ALBERT HUGHES, 3rd, born at Haddon Heights, 6 August, 1913.

MARY ELIZABETH HUGHES, (daughter of ALBERT HENRY and ELIZABETH STILLWELL MILLER HUGHES), born at Camden, New Jersey, 29 March, 1876; LOUISA MILLER HUGHES, born at Camden, New Jersey, 8 March, 1878, married at Philadelphia, Pennsylvania, 1 November, 1899, Jacob Rogers Horner, born 11 January, 1877, and had ARTHUR ROGERS HORNER, born 14 August, 1900.

(2) ELIZABETH S. EDMUNDS, born 1826, married Adrian Bateman. She died 29 July, 1848.

(3) ENOCH EDMUNDS, born 1829, died 1 May, 1855.

211

ALBERT HENRY HUGHES

For ancestors leading back to the Mayflower see page 202.

ALBERT HENRY HUGHES[8], (Humphrey Hughes[7], Jane Whilldin[6], James Whilldin[5], Joseph Whilldin[4], Hannah Gorham[3] Desire Howland[2], JOHN HOWLAND[1] THE PILGRIM), was born at Cape May, 8 January, 1812, died at Cape May, 18 August, 1893, married first at Cape May, 9 March, 1839, Elizabeth Schellenger, born at Cape May, 7 May, 1817, died 14 April, 1844, married second 6 May, 1845, Mary Whitaker Pierson, born at Cold Spring, New Jersey, 26 March, 1817, died at Cape May, 23 September, 1894, (tombstone in Cold Spring Cemetery).

Issue :—

(1) ABIGAIL COLLINS HUGHES, born at Cape May, 1 January, 1840, married at Cape May, ELDRIDGE JOHNSON. No issue.

(2) JANE SCHELLENGER HUGHES, born at Cape May, 5 August, 1841, died at Cape May, 21 March, 1888, married ELDRIDGE JOHNSON, as his first wife. (For descendants see page 242).

(3) ELIZABETH SCHELLENGER HUGHES, born at Cape May, 4 April, 1844, married James Mecray, M. D. (For descendants see page 223).

(4) HENRY ALBERT HUGHES, born at Cape May, 30 May, 1846, married ELIZABETH MILLER. (See page 108).

(5) HETTY WILLIAMS HUGHES, born at Cape May, 27 June, 1849, married at Cape May, 14 October, 1873, George Wilson Miller, born at Green Creek, New Jersey, 7 March, 1850, died 12 March, 1914.

EMILY HURST HUGHES

For ancestors leading back to the Mayflower see page 202.

EMILY HURST HUGHES[8], (Humphrey Hughes[7], Jane Whilldin[6], James Whilldin[5], Joseph Whilldin[4], Hannah Gorham[3], Desire Howland[2], JOHN HOWLAND[1] THE PILGRIM), was born at Cape May, 19 November, 1817, died at Cape May, 18 December, 1888, married 15 September, 1834, Rev. Moses Williamson, born at Newville, Pennsylvania, 7 May, 1802, died 30 October, 1880, (tombstones in Cold Spring Cemetery).

Issue :—

(1) HADASSA WILLIAMSON, born 1836, died 1916, married Southard Hand, who died 29 September, 1874, without issue, (tombstones in Cold Spring Cemetery).

(2) ELMIRA WILLIAMSON, married Dr. S. Downs, died without issue.(She died 1 February, 1895, aged 55 years).

(3) EMILY HUGHES WILLIAMSON, born 1845, died 1913, unmarried.

(4) MARY I. WILLIAMSON, born 1845, died 1917, unmarried.

(5) REBECCA KNIGHT WILLIAMSON, born 1848, died 1907, unmarried.

(6) THOMAS HUGHES WILLIAMSON, born 22 July, 1852, died 7 October, 1886, married 28 October, 1875, MARY ELVENA TOWNSEND, (for Pilgrim ancestry see page 184 under family of MARY F. LEAMING), and had: ERNEST TOWNSEND WILLIAMSON, born 15 August, 1876, married 25 November, 1911, Emeline Amy Oswell.

(7) WILLIAM ALEXANDER WILLIAMSON, born 5 February, 1854, died 17 April, 1916, married 15 November, 1877, Ida A. Fisler, born 31 January, 1853, and had: STANLEY WILLIAMSON, born 31 March, 1879, married 21 June, 1919, Imogene Harber and had MARJORY WILLIAMSON, born 25 October, 1920; JOHN LAUGHLIN WILLIAMSON, born 20 February, 1882, married 21 October, 1911, Beatrice Adams, and had CYNTHIA ANNE WILLIAMSON, born 16 September, 1912, MARY JEAN WILLIAMSON, born 3 December, 1913; SAMUEL FISLER WILLIAMSON, born 26 November, 1883.

ELIZABETH EDMUNDS

For ancestors leading back to the Mayflower see page 205.

ELIZABETH EDMUNDS[7], (Jane Whilldin[6], James Whilldin[5], Joseph Whilldin[4], Hannah Gorham[3], Desire Howland[2], JOHN HOWLAND[1] THE PILGRIM), was born at Cape May, 4 December, 1780, died at Cape May, 11 January, 1868, (tombstone in Cold Spring Cemetery), married at Cape May, 10 April, 1799, Levi Eldridge, born at Cape May, 17 October, 1776, died at Cape May, 23 November, 1822, (tombstone in Cold Spring Cemetery).

Issue:—

(1) ELIZA ELDRIDGE, born at Cape May, 2 September, 1800, married Page Stites, and had EDGAR PAGE STITES.

(2) HETTY ELDRIDGE, born 22 September, 1901, died in infancy.

(3) LEVI ELDRIDGE, born 9 June, 1804, died 23 December, 1822.

(4) HETTY ELDRIDGE, born 26 March, 1806, married Daniel McBride.

(5) JEREMIAH ELDRIDGE, born 9 May, 1808.

(6) JANE WHITE ELDRIDGE, born at Cape May, 10 May, 1810, married Noah White Johnson. (For descendants see page 224).

(7) DANIEL WHILLDIN ELDRIDGE, born at Cape May, 3 February, 1815, died at New York City, 23 October, 1894, married Louisa Harwood, born at Philadelphia, Pennsylvania, 4 September, 1835, died at New York City, 9 December, 1905, and had: LILLIE ELDRIDGE, born at Philadelphia, 14 January, 1853, married 7 May, 1877, Thomas Bett Ryan, and had, HARWOOD ELDRIDGE RYAN, born 25 August, 1882; HARRY ELDRIDGE, born 14 March, 1854, died in infancy; PRESTON WOODNUTT ELDRIDGE, born 14 February, 1855, married 3 August, 1876, Sophie Johnston, and had PRESTON WOODNUTT ELDRIDGE, Jr., born at Washington, D. C., 18 March, 1879, who married 22 June, 1907, Caroline Lowe Vorhis, born at Canisteo, New York, 14 February, 1884, and had, CAROLINE SANDIFORD ELDRIDGE, born 23 January, 1910, and JANE FOLSOM ELDRIDGE, born 2 July, 1915.

MAHALAH EDMUNDS

For ancestors leading back to the Mayflower see page 203.

MAHALAH EDMUNDS[7], (Jane Whilldin[6], James Whilldin[5], Joseph Whilldin[4], Hannah Gorham[3], Desire Howland[2], JOHN HOWLAND[1] THE PILGRIM), was born at Cape May, 10 January, 1783, died at Cape May, 12 November, 1840, married 7 March, 1809, ISAAC WHILLDIN, (see page 200), born 20 February, 1784, (record of family bible), died 13 May, 1867, (tombstone in Cold Spring Cemetery. (See page 44 for record of marriage).

Issue:—

(1) JANE EDMUNDS WHILLDIN, born 24 December, 1809, (record of family bible), married Joseph Acton Hall. (For descendants see page 226).

(2) DANIEL WHILLDIN, born 1812.

(3) MATHEW WHILLDIN, born 13 December, 1815, married first Gratian Rice, married second Olive Oreun, married third Sophia Schellenger. (For descendants see page 227).

(4) MARY WHILLDIN, born 1820, married Stephen Bennett, born 1815, died 5 July, 1871, (tombstone in Cold Spring Cemetery), and had: EMMA C. BENNETT; STEPHEN DECATUR BENNETT; ELIZA BENNETT; ALPHONZO BENNETT; LOUISA SAINT BENNETT, who married Charles Henry Rutherford; (for descendants see page 329); MARY BENNETT, who married J. Wesley Hughes, and had AUSTIN HUGHES, born 7 March, 1885.

(5) ISAAC WHILLDIN, born 1824, died 8 September, 1876, (tombstone in Cold Spring Cemetery), married 7 November, 1846, MARTHA HUGHES, (see page 249), and had: JAMES WHILLDIN; EVELINE WHILLDIN; MARTHA WHILLDIN; WILLIAM WHILLDIN; LOUISA N. WHILLDIN; JOSEPHINE WHILLDIN, who married Joseph Reynolds; MARTHA H. WHILLDIN, who married Charles Smith; LORING WHILLDIN; ISAAC WHLLDIN; MARY WHILLDIN, who married Reuben Johnson; EVELINA WHILLDIN.

JEREMIAH EDMUNDS

For ancestors leading back to the Mayflower see page 203.

JEREMIAH EDMUNDS[7], (Jane Whilldin[6], James Whilldin[5], Joseph Whilldin[4], Hannah Gorham[3], Desire Howland[2], JOHN HOWLAND[1] THE PILGRIM), was born at Cape May, 17 April, 1785, married at Cape May, 5 August, 1810, Ruhama Tomlin, born 21 November, 1792, died 1852.

Issue:—

(1) SILVIA EDMUNDS, born at Cape May, 5 October, 1811.

(2) JEREMIAH EDMUNDS, born 13 September, 1813, married Amarilla Shaw. (For descendants see page 228).

(3) ROBERT EDMUNDS, born 18 January, 1817, married Hannah Ann Church. (For descendants see page 230).

(4) HUGH H. EDMUNDS, born at Cape May, 30 September, 1820, died 26 March, 1863, married ——Weeks, and had ELIZABETH EDMUNDS.

(5) MAHALA WHILLDIN EDMUNDS, born 26 December, 1822, died in infancy.

(6) WASHINGTON B. EDMUNDS, born 20 April, 1826, died about 1860.

(7) LEVI L. EDMUNDS, born 6 December, 1828.

(8) ANDREW JACKSON EDMUNDS, born 10 February, 1831, died at Cold Spring, 25 July, 1865, married Emily Rutherford, born 25 December, 1834, died 10 March, 1907, and had, SAMUEL SHIELDS EDMUNDS, born at Cold Spring, New Jersey, 7 July, 1854, married Deborah N. Long, and had:—

DORA EDMUNDS, born at Cold Spring, New Jersey, 31 August, 1883, married at Cold Spring, 27 October, 1900, Elmer Willets Reeves, and had ETHEL MAY REEVES; ETHEL MAY EDMUNDS, born 27 June, 1886, married Charles Holmes; REBECCA JANE EDMUNDS, born 27 May, 1889, married Samuel Elwell, born 25 September, 1883.

SAMUEL FITHIAN WARE

For ancestors leading back to the Mayflower see page 208.

SAMUEL FITHIAN WARE[8], (Deborah Whilldin[7], Jonathan Whilldin[6], James Whilldin[5], Joseph Whilldin[4], Hannah Gorham[3], Desire Howland[2], JOHN HOWLAND[1] THE PILGRIM), was born at Cape May, 16 October, 1800, died at Cape May, 10 May, 1877, (tombstone in Cold Spring Cemetery), married at Cape May, 3 May, 1827, Esther Teal, born 17 February, 1801, died at Cape May, 3 September, 1868, (tombstone in Cold Spring Cemetery).

Issue:—

(1) ANN ELIZA WARE, born at Cold Spring, New Jersey, 12 October, 1829, died 21 October, 1905, married 28 March, 1847, John Rutherford, born 2 September, 1828, died 25 March, 1891. (For descendants see page 239).

(2) SAMUEL FITHIAN WARE, Jr., born 18 May, 1834, died 14 September, 1903, married first 5 July, 1858, Mary Stites, born 28 December, 1838, died 24 August, 1869, (tombstone in Cold Spring Cemetery), and had, FRANK H. WARE, born 15 June, 1859, died 16 September, 1888, (tombstone in Cold Spring Cemtery), ELIZA S. WARE, born 16 April, 1862, died 3 April, 1863, (tombstone in Cold Spring Cemetery).

SAMUEL FITHIAN WARE, Jr., married second 18 July, 1870, Fanny E. Weaver, and had, WILLIAM R. WARE, born 6 October, 1871, died in infancy, S. FITHIAN WARE, born 21 November, 1873, FANNIE E. WARE, born 10 August, 1878, JAMES G. WARE, born 18 October, 1882, died 2 March, 1900.

217

DEBORAH WHILLDIN WARE

For ancestors leading back to the Mayflower see page 208.

DEBORAH WHILLDIN WARE[8], (Deborah Whilldin[7], Jonathan Whilldin[6], James Whilldin[5], Joseph Whilldin[4], Hannah Gorham[3], Desire Howland[2], JOHN HOWLAND[1] THE PILGRIM), was born at Cape May, 4 May, 1804, died at West Cape May, 29 January, 1865, (tombstone in Cold Spring Cemetery), married at Cape May, 24 January, 1827, Thomas Eldredge, born at Cape May, 21 January, 1798, died at Cape May, 29 January, 1849, (tombstone in Cold Spring Cemetery).

Issue :—

(1)   DANIEL C. ELDREDGE, born 30 March, 1829, married Mary A. Hoffman. (For descendants see page 234).

(2)   HARRIET WARE ELDREDGE, born 20 December, 1830, married Henry W. Sawyer.

(3)   SOPHIA ELDREDGE, born 21 February, 1832, married Francis K. Duke. (For descendants see page 235).

(4)   THOMAS ELDREDGE, born 2 April, 1835, married Emma Tabitha Baker. (For descendants see page 236).

(5)   JOSEPH WARE ELDREDGE, born 22 January, 1838.

(6)   JUDITH WHILLDIN ELDREDGE, born 15 August, 1839, married William Hoffman.

(7)   DEBORAH WHILLDIN ELDREDGE, born 29 January, 1841, married Reuben Hoffman.

(8)   WILLIAM BROOKS ELDREDGE, born 8 March, 1843, married Sarah Bailey, and had EVA ELDREDGE and WILLIAM ELDREDGE.

JAMES WHILLDIN WARE

For ancestors leading back to the Mayflower see page 208.

JAMES WHILLDIN WARE[8], (Deborah Whilldin[7], Jonathan Whilldin[6], James Whilldin[5], Joseph Whilldin[4], Hannah Gorham[3], Desire Howland[2], JOHN HOWLAND[1] THE PILGRIM), was born at Cold Spring, New Jersey, 12 January 1806, died at Cape May, 14 March, 1890, married at Bridgeton, New Jersey, 12 January, 1828, Deborah Hampton, born in Cumberland County, New Jersey, 24 March, 1806, died at Bridgeton, New Jersey, 30 March, 1864, (tombstone in Cold Spring Cemetery).

Issue:—

(1) JEREMIAH STRATTON WARE, born 19 January, 1831, married MAHALAH JANE HALL. (For descendants see page 237).

(2) JAMES WHILLDIN WARE, born at Bridgeton, New Jersey, 22 December, 1832, married first Sally Eldredge, married second Margaret Nelson.

(3) HESTER TEAL WARE, born at Bridgeton, New Jersey, 22 July, 1842, died 29 January, 1907, married George Washington Moore, born at Philadelphia, Pennsylvania, 22 February, 1841, and had:— STRATTON W. MOORE, born at Bridgeton, New Jersey, 30 December, 1861, married at Bridgeton, 26 September, 1888, Mary Sinex Duffield, and had, SIDNEY BLAINE MOORE, born 31 May, 1892, and EUGENE STRATTON MOORE, born 30 April, 1901; ENOCH HAMPTON MOORE, M. D., born at Bridgeton, 28 November, 1864, married at Camden, New Jersey, March, 1887, Martha McGeegan, and had RALSTON HAMPTON MOORE, born 5 May, 1888; I. WHILLDIN MOORE, born at Bridgeton, February, 1866, married Irene Miller, and had ETHEL MOORE, and I. WHILLDIN MOORE; SAMUEL WARE MOORE, born at Bridgeton, 12 June, 1870, married May West, and had, GEORGE A. MOORE, JAMES W. MOORE and HAZEL MOORE; HENRY STEWART MOORE, born at Bridgeton, 10 April, 1869, married at Wilmington, Delaware, Frances A. Atkins, and had, GEORGE ROBERT MOORE, born at Atlantic City, New Jersey, 17 February, 1903; JENNIE GRIFFITH MOORE, born at Bridgeton, 1875, died 21 June, 1911, married William Ritter, M. D., no issue.

(4) SAMUEL FITHIAN WARE, M. D., born at Allowaystown, New Jersey, 23 July, 1848, married first at Cape May, 8 November, 1871, Louisa Eldridge Sawyer, born at Cape May, 9 September, 1852, died 1 November, 1895; married second Helen Nora Crites. (For descendants see page 238).

219

JOSEPH WARE

For ancestors leading back to the Mayflower see page 209.

JOSEPH WARE[8], (Harriet Whilldin[7], Jonathan Whilldin[6], James Whilldin[5], Joseph Whilldin[4], Hannah Gorham[3], Desire Howland[2], JOHN HOWLAND[1] THE PILGRIM), was born 16 May, 1809, died at Cape May, 30 April, 1890, married LYDIA LEAMING[8], (James Leaming[7], Christopher Leaming[6], Christopher Leaming[5], Hannah Whilldin[4], Hannah Gorham[3], Desire Howland[2], JOHN HOWLAND[1] THE PILGRIM).

Issue:—

(1) JOSEPHINE WARE, born 15 October, 1844, married JOSEPH HAND[9], (Nancy Schenck[8], Zeruiah Hughes[7], Memucan Hughes[6], Hannah Whilldin[5], Joseph Whilldin[4], Hannah Gorham[3], Desire Howland[2], JOHN HOWLAND[1] THE PILGRIM). (For descendants see page 277).

(2) WALTER SCOTT WARE, married 26 February, 1876, Mattie Hand Schellenger, born 3 January, 1857, and had: CORA LEAMING WARE, who married at York, Pennsylvania, 12 April, 1904, JOHN ALLEN WALES[10], (Thomas Roger Wales[9], Sarah Hughes[8], Thomas Hurst Hughes[7], Ellis Hughes[6], Hannah Whilldin[5], Joseph Whilldin[4], Hannah Gorham[3], Desire Howland[2], JOHN HOWLAND[1] THE PILGRIM,) and had, EDITH HELENE WALES; EDITH WARE, died 30 August, 1904, and HILDA WARE. (See page 317).

(3) LAMBERT WARE, married Josephine Grace.

(4) HOWARD L. WARE, married Emma Radelar.

(5) LENA B. WARE, born at Cape May, 7 April, 1851, married first William H. Benezet, and had WALTER LAWRENCE BENEZET, who married Mary Clothier; married second MAURICE CRESSE[9], (Eliza Stites[8], Priscilla Leaming[7], Margaret Stites[6], Priscilla Leaming[5], Hannah Whilldin[4], Hannah Gorham[3], Desire Howland[2], JOHN HOWLAND[1] THE PILGRIM). (See page 143).

HARRIET WHILLDIN WARE

For ancestors leading back to the Mayflower see page 209.

HARRIET WHILLDIN WARE[9], (Wilmon W. Ware[8], Harriet Whilldin[7], Jonathan Whilldin[6], James Whilldin[5], Joseph Whilldin[4], Hannah Gorham[3], Desire Howland[2], JOHN HOWLAND[1] THE PILGRIM), was born at Cape May, 30 August, 1844, died 27 October, 1918, married at Cape May, 1865, Samuel Richardson Stites, born at Cape May, 17 October, 1840.

Issue:—

(1) CHARLES LINFORD STITES, born at Cape May, 24 April, 1866.

(2) MARY ELIZABETH STITES, born at Cape May, 3 May, 1867, married at Cape May, 6 December, 1887, William Porter, born at Hereford, England, 26 May, 1855, and had daughter, HELEN LOUISE PORTER, born at Cape May, 26 April, 1893.

(3) JOSEPH SCHELLENGER STITES, born at Cape May, 29 December, 1868, married at Washington, D. C., Belfora Smith.

(4) ELLA MERRET STITES, born 17 February, 1871, married 18 January, 1893, Archibald Paul, and had: ELLA PAUL, born 28 June, 1894, married 1916, J. E. T. Benson, and had HARLEY P. BENSON, born 19 July, 1918; ARCHIBALD PAUL, born 14 August, 1895, died in England, U. S. Army, 11 October, 1918; MAE RICHARDSON PAUL, born 1 December, 1899, married 30 July, 1918, Harry Davenport.

(5) ANNIE TINDALL STITES, born 29 April, 1872, died in infancy.

(6) HATTIE WHILLDIN STITES, born at Cape May, 7 November, 1875, married GILBERT C. HUGHES, (see page 286), and had WALTER PHILLIPS HUGHES, born 2 April, 1899; married at Elkton, Maryland, 1 June, 1920, Frances Hazel Hebenthal, and MARION HUGHES, born 25 February, 1904.

(7) LAURA S. STITES, married WOODRUFF ELDREDGE. (See page 135).

MASKEL WARE

For ancestors leading back to the Mayflower see page 209.

MASKEL WARE[8], (Harriet Whilldin[7], Jonathan Whilldin[6], James Whilldin[5], Joseph Whilldin[4], Hannah Gorham[3], Desire Howland[2], JOHN HOWLAND[1] THE PILGRIM), was born at Cape May, 19 March, 1822, died at Cape May, 30 December, 1910, (tombstone in Cold Spring Cemetery), married first 16 April, 1845, Leah Mathis, died 1 June, 1864, (tombstone in Cold Spring Cemetery), married second, 4 September, 1865, Mary Jane Warrick, born at Dennisville, New Jersey, 16 May, 1841.

Issue:—

(1)   MARY WARE, born at Cape May, 26 July, 1849, died 19 December, 1867.

(2)   HORACE WARE, born at Cape May, 7 April, 1859, married Lizzie Erickson, and had LEAH WARE, born 20 September, 1894.

(3)   LIZZIE WARE.

(4)   SOPHIE SCULL WARE, married Alfred Adams Rose.

(5)   JOSEPH ROSENBAUM WARE, married Lillian Craig, and had EDITH WARE, born at West Cape May, New Jersey, 14 August, 1894, who married Herbert F. Smith, and had HERBERT F. SMITH, Jr., born at Collingswood, New Jersey, 10 February, 1917.

(6)   HERBERT WARE, married Maud Reed, and had IRENE WARE, born 29 June, 1900, at Camden, New Jersey.

(7)   HENRY BELTING WARE, married Lizzie Rose.

MAYFLOWER DESCENDANTS IN CAPE MAY COUNTY

ELIZABETH SCHELLENGER HUGHES

For ancestors leading back to the Mayflower see page 212.

ELIZABETH SCHELLENGER HUGHES[9], (Albert Henry Hughes[8], Humphrey Hughes[7], Jane Whilldin[6], James Whilldin[5], Joseph Whilldin[4], Hannah Gorham[3], Desire Howland[2], JOHN HOWLAND[1] THE PILGRIM), was born 4 April, 1844, married 8 November, 1865, James Mecray, M. D., born 21 February, 1842, died at Cape May, 9 February, 1916.

Issue:—

(1) ELIZABETH HUGHES MECRAY, born 13 August, 1866, married 5 November, 1885, Peter Logan Bockius, born 20 April, 1859, died 6 March, 1905, and had: ELIZABETH MECRAY BOCKIUS, born 7 September, 1886, died 13 June, 1888; DOROTHY MECRAY BOCKIUS, born 13 August, 1889, married 10 November, 1909, ELLWOOD SOUDER[11], (Ellwood Souder[10], Hester Ann Eldridge Johnson[9], Jane White Eldredge[8], Elizabeth Edmunds[7], Jane Whilldin[6], James Whilldin[5], Joseph Whilldin[4], Hannah Gorham[3], Desire Howland[2], JOHN HOWLAND[1] THE PILGRIM), born at Wilmington, Delaware, 22 September, 1887, and had ELIZABETH MECRAY SOUDER, born 10 January, 1911; LOGAN BOCKIUS, born 31 March, 1893.

(2) HULDAH SCHELLENGER MECRAY, born 29 December, 1869, died 18 February, 1870.

(3) PAUL MULFORD MECRAY, M. D., born 24 October, 1871, married 18 October, 1900, Jane Elizabeth Boyer, born 15 December, 1872, and had, HELEN BOYER MECRAY, born 1 October, 1901, and PAUL MULFORD MECRAY, born 8 July, 1908.

JANE WHITE ELDRIDGE

For ancestors leading back to the Mayflower see page 214.

JANE WHITE ELDRIDGE[8], (Elizabeth Edmunds[7], Jane Whilldin[6], James Whilldin[5], Joseph Whilldin[4], Hannah Gorham[3], Desire Howland[2], JOHN HOWLAND[1] THE PILGRIM), was born at Cape May, 10 May, 1810, died at Cape May, 28 November, 1881, married at Philadelphia, Pennsylvania, 15 May, 1828, Noah White Johnson, born at Georgetown, Delaware, 11 February, 1806, died at Cape May, 26 August, 1895.

Issue:—

(1) HENRY STOKLEY JOHNSON, born at Cape May, 1 March, 1829, married ———————— and had GEORGE JOHNSON.

(2) HESTER ANN ELDRIDGE JOHNSON, born 4 November, 1832, married Richard Cresse Souder. (For descendants see page 240).

(3) JACOB ELDRIDGE JOHNSON, born 16 July, 1834, married Elizabeth Conover. (For descendants see page 241).

(4) LEVI ELDRIDGE JOHNSON, born 4 March, 1836, died 6 November, 1914, married at Cape May, 6 December, 1864, Sarah Spencer, who died 30 October, 1917, and had ANNIE K. JOHNSON, who married at Cape May, 15 February, 1905, Walter Daniel Peck, and had VERNON JOHNSON PECK, WALTER L. PECK and PAUL THOMAS PECK.

(5) ELDRIDGE JOHNSON, born 1 January, 1838, married first JANE SCHELLENGER HUGHES, married second ABIGAIL COLLINS HUGHES. (For descendants see page 242).

(6) ELIZABETH EDMUNDS JOHNSON, born 6 February, 1840, married FRANCIS SPRINGER ELDREDGE. (For descendants see page 136).

(Continued on next page)

224

JANE WHITE ELDRIDGE

(7) JOSEPH WHITE JOHNSON, born at Cape May, 10 April, 1842, married at Fonda, New York, 10 July, 1867, Gertrude Schermerhorn, born at Fonda, New York, 5 September, 1845, and had PETER SCHERMERHORN JOHNSON, born 11 December, 1869, married Clara Von Gonton, born 30 December, 1879.

(8) ANNIE ELDRIDGE JOHNSON, born at Cape May, 22 July, 1844.

(9) JOHN JOHNSON, born at Cape May, 25 October, 1846, married Matilda Sparks, and had LEVI JOHNSON, M. D., EDWARD JOHNSON, JOHN JOHNSON, and BENTLEY JOHNSON.

(10) CHARLES STOKLEY JOHNSON, born at Cape May, 7 May, 1849, died at Longport, New Jersey, 2 January, 1919, married at Glassboro, New Jersey, 7 May, 1874, Anna Belle Lutz, born at Glassboro, New Jersey, 10 October, 1848, and had CARL BROWN JOHNSON, born at Cape May, 30 August, 1878, died at Glassboro, New Jersey, 7 February, 1886; EVA LUTZ JOHNSON, born at Cape May, 3 August, 1881, married at Atlantic City, New Jersey, 28 November, 1914, William S. Gilmore.

(11) FRANKLIN PIERCE JOHNSON, born at Cape May, 6 November, 1850, married Della Paterson.

(12) STOKLEY JOHNSON, born at Cape May, 6 April, 1852, married Rose McNeil, born at Cape May, 28 September, 1852, and had: CHARLES AUGUSTUS JOHNSON, born at Cape May, 10 September, 1877, married 30 October, 1901, Ida Virginia Millet, and had EVELYN MILLET JOHNSON, born 10 May, 1904; HARRIET ELDREDGE JOHNSON, (daughter of Stokley and Rose), born at Cape May, 23 January, 1880.

JANE EDMUNDS WHILLDIN

For ancestors leading back to the Mayflower see page 215.

JANE EDMUNDS WHILLDIN[8], (Mahalah Edmunds[7], Jane Whilldin[6], James Whilldin[5], Joseph Whilldin[4], Hannah Gorham[3], Desire Howland[2], JOHN HOWLAND[1] THE PILGRIM), was born at Cape May, 24 December, 1809, died at Cape May, 21 March, 1887, (tombstone in Cold Spring Cemetery), married 27 September, 1830, Joseph Acton Hall, born at Salem, New Jersey, 18 February, 1807, died at Cape May, 21 June, 1897, (tombstone in Cold Spring Cemetery).

Issue:—

(1) MATTHEW WHILLDIN HALL, born at Cape May Court House, New Jersey, 14 September, 1831, married ELEANOR EDMUNDS. (For descendants see page 242).

(2) JOSEPH HALL, born 4 March, 1833, died at Cape May, 2 August, 1901, married first Theresa Eldredge, married second Elmira Hand, married third Lorena Stanger. (No issue).

(3) MAHALA JANE HALL, born 3 September, 1835, married JEREMIAH STRATTON WARE. (For descendants see page 237).

(4) HARRIET ANN HALL, born 3 February, 1837, married Charles Alexander Shaw. (For descendants see page 244).

(5) ISAAC HALL, born 29 August, 1830, died in the Civil War.

(6) MARY BENNETT HALL, born 21 December, 1843, married John Church. (For descendants see page 245).

(7) LAFAYETTE MILLER HALL, born 9 June, 1849, married ELLEN EDMUNDS FOSTER. (For descendants see page 173).

MATTHEW WHILLDIN

For ancestors leading back to the Mayflower see page 215.

MATTHEW WHILLDIN[8], (Isaac Whilldin[7], Matthew Whilldin[6], James Whilldin[5], Joseph Whilldin[4], Hannah Gorham[3], Desire Howland[2], JOHN HOWLAND[1] THE PILGRIM), in one line, and (Mahala Edmunds[7], Jane Whilldin[6], James Whilldin[5], Joseph Whilldin[4], Hannah Gorham[3], Desire Howland[2], JOHN HOWLAND[1] THE PILGRIM), in the other, was born at Cape May, 13 December, 1816, died 15 March, 1875, (tombstone in Cold Spring Cemetery), married at Cape May, 13 March, 1840, Gratian Rice, born 1817, died 7 October, 1851, (tombstone in Cold Spring Cemetery).

Issue:—

(1) WILMON WHILLDIN, born at Cape May, 27 July, 1843, died at West Palm Beach, Florida, 25 January, 1908, married HANNAH LEAMING[9], (Lemuel Leaming[8], Spicer Leaming[7], Christopher Leaming[6], Christopher Leaming[5], Hannah Whilldin[4], Hannah Gorham[3], Desire Howland[2], JOHN HOWLAND[1] THE PILGRIM), and had, WILMON WHILLDIN.

(2) LOUISA EDMUNDS WHILLDIN, born at Cape May, 31 January, 1846, died 8 March, 1876, married at Florence, New Jersey, 12 August, 1874, Amos Johnson.

(3) EMMA C. WHILLDIN, born at Cape May, 25 August, 1848, died 5 October, 1907, married at Camden, New Jersey, 16 April, 1868, Benjamin Johnson, and had MAY LOUISE JOHNSON, who married Garrett Hynson, and had, EMMA DOROTHY HYNSON, born at Philadelphia, Pennsylvania, 7 December, 1892.

(4) MARY WHILLDIN, born at Cape May, 22 February, 1851, married at Camden, New Jersey, 8 July, 1869, William Harris, born at Philadelphia, 22 January, 1848, and had:— ELEANOR PROVOST HARRIS, born at Camden, 22 March, 1870; LOUISA WHILLDIN HARRIS, born at Camden, 8 July, 1874, married at Camden, 4 December, 1891, William Richman, born at Woodstown, New Jersey, 20 July, 1872, and had, WHILLDIN LIPPINCOTT RICHMAN, born at Camden, 24 June, 1894, died in infancy; WILLIAM WHILLDIN HARRIS, born at Florence, Kansas, 29 April, 1878, died at Palmyra, New Jersey, 29 August, 1899.

JEREMIAH EDMUNDS

For ancestors leading back to the Mayflower see page 216.

JEREMIAH EDMUNDS[8], (Jeremiah Edmunds[7], Jane Whilldin[6], James Whilldin[5], Joseph Whilldin[4], Hannah Gorham[3], Desire Howland[2], JOHN HOWLAND[1] THE PILGRIM), was born at Cape May, 13 September, 1813, died 1885, married at Cape May, 20 May, 1838, Amarilla Shaw, born at Cape May, 14 December, 1821, died at West Cape May, New Jersey, 23 May, 1901.

Issue :—

(1) CARSWELL EDMUNDS, born at West Cape May, New Jersey, 7 July, 1839, died 17 July, 1839, (tombstone in Cold Spring Cemetery).

(2) EMMA EDMUNDS, born at West Cape May, New Jersey, 31 July, 1840, died 24 March, 1845, (tombstone in Cold Spring Cemetery).

(3 ALFRED EDMUNDS, born at West Cape May, New Jersey, 25 September, 1842, died at Belleplain, New Jersey, 20 May, 1879, married at Green Creek, New Jersey, 11 June, 1868, Mary Ellen Whillets, who died at Green Creek, New Jersey, 4 October, 1888, and had: JESSE EDMUNDS, born at West Cape May, New Jersey, 16 February, 1869, married at Camden, New Jersey, 7 April, 1893, Florence Farrow, and had, MILDRED EDMUNDS, married WALTER BENNETT, (see page 241), and had, BETTY BENNETT, WALTER LEAMING BENNETT, Jr., WILLIAM JUDSON BENNETT; IDA MAY EDMUNDS and MERRITT SCHELLINGER EDMUNDS; ORILLA AYERS EDMUNDS, married WESTLEY ROGERS WALES, M. D., see page 317.

(4) MARY EDMUNDS, born at Cape May, 1 March, 1845, died at Cape May, 20 April, 1898, married at Cape May, 15 July, 1865, George Rabeau, born at Bordentown, New Jersey, 4 October, 1835, died at Atlantic City, New Jersey, 29

(Continued on next page)

JEREMIAH EDMUNDS

March, 1902, and had:—JEREMIAH EDMUNDS RABEAU, born at Cape May, 26 April, 1866, married at Camden, New Jersey, 17 December, 1889, Jennie Moore, and had EDNA MARY RABEAU, and GEORGE V. RABEAU.

ANNA RABEAU, daughter of MARY EDMUNDS, and her husband George Rabeau, was born at Cape May, 26 April, 1872, married at Philadelphia, Pennsylvania, 15 June, 1901, Alexander J. Freeman.

(5) ENOS SCHELLENGER EDMUNDS, born 20 June, 1847, died in infancy.

(6) ENOS SCHELLENGER EDMUNDS, son of Jeremiah and his wife Amarilla Shaw, was born at West Cape May, 8 May, 1849, died 23 June, 1899, married at Cape May Court House, New Jersey, 18 May, 1873, Eliza Crawford, born at Green Creek, New Jersey, 26 April, 1851, and had, GEORGE CRAWFORD EDMUNDS, born 13 March, 1874, married at Cape May Court House, New Jersey, 22 June, 1898, Helen M. Nichols, and had, THEODORE CRAWFORD EDMUNDS.

(7) WATERS BORROWS MILLER EDMUNDS, born at West Cape May, New Jersey, 20 February, 1853, married at West Cape May, New Jersey, 6 July, 1880, Linda Ross, born at Goshen, New Jersey, 21 August, 1859, and had ALFRED EDMUNDS, born at West Cape May, New Jersey, 20 October, 1881, married at Philadelphia, Pennsylvania, 1 November, 1904, Anna Lizette Claussen, and had WILLIAM ALFRED EDMUNDS; LOUISA STILLWELL EDMUNDS (daughter of WATERS BORROWS MILLER and his wife Linda Ross Edmunds, was born at West Cape May, New Jersey, 13 March, 1883, married at Haddonfield, New Jersey, 10 March, 1909, William Franklin Miller, born at Nescopeck, Pennsylvania, 2 April, 1868.

ROBERT EDMUNDS

For ancestors leading back to the Mayflower see page 216.

ROBERT EDMUNDS[8], (Jeremiah Edmunds[7], Jane Whilldin[6], James Whilldin[5], Joseph Whilldin[4], Hannah Gorham[3], Desire Howland[2], JOHN HOWLAND[1] THE PILGRIM), was born at Cape May, 18 January, 1817, died at Philadelphia, Pennsylvania, 31 March, 1888, married at Cape May, 20 April, 1844, Hannah Ann Church, born at Cape May, 26 January, 1823, died 11 June, 1874.

Issue:—

(1) EVAN B. EDMUNDS, born 3 February, 1845, married first Mary Hutchinson, and had: HARRY EDMUNDS, and ALBERTA EDMUNDS, who married William Burch, and had DANIEL BURCH. Married second Elizabeth ——— and had ALBERT EDMUNDS and BLANCHE EDMUNDS.

(2) LEVI ELDREDGE EDMUNDS, born at Cape May, 29 November, 1846, married at Camden, New Jersey, 1884, Annie Rosine Ulman, born at Chew's Landing, New Jersey, 24 January, 1864, and had: BESSIE DOROTHY EDMUNDS, born 25 November, 1885; LEVI GEORGE EDMUNDS, born 9 January, 1890, died in infancy; ALBERT ELLIS EDMUNDS, born at Camden, New Jersey, 12 December, 1891; ADA MILLS EDMUNDS, born 9 February, 1894; BLANCHE DANIELLA EDMUNDS, born 1 September, 1899, died in infancy; ALICE ANNIE EDMUNDS, born 12 October, 1901.

(3) DANIELIA MAHALAH WHILLDIN EDMUNDS, born at Cape May, 12 December, 1848, married Elias Ellis Stites.

(4) ROBERT GARY EDMUNDS, born 23 February, 1851, died in infancy.

(Continued on next page)

ROBERT EDMUNDS

(5) ROBERT HENRY EDMUNDS, born 13 January, 1852, died 9 December, 1888.

(6) LUTHER HUDSON EDMUNDS, born at Cape May, 31 March, 1855, married Mattie Addams and had, ROBERT EDMUNDS, who married Edith Reed; LUTHER HUDSON EDMUNDS, and EMMA EDMUNDS.

(7) JAMES WATTS EDMUNDS, born at Cape May, New Jersey, 13 August, 1857, married Alice Needles.

(8) STEPHEN A. DOUGLASS EDMUNDS, born 14 December, 1859.

(9) ALBERT AUGUSTUS EDMUNDS, born at Cape May, 27 December, 1861, died at Philadelphia, Pennsylvania, 15 February, 1896, married at Philadelphia, Pennsylvania, 28 January, 1882, Mary Babb Weidenhammer, born at Richmond Township, Berks County, Pennsylvania, 15 June, 1859, and had: FLORENCE ANNA EDMUNDS, died in infancy; MABEL ISABELLA EDMUNDS, born at Philadelphia, Pennsylvania, 15 December, 1883, married at Philadelphia, Pennsylvania, 13 June, 1906, Charles Egner, born at Philadelphia, Pennsylvania, 4 July, 1878; LILLIE IDA EDMUNDS, born at Philadelphia, Pennsylvania, 20 March, 1885, married at Philadelphia, Pennsylvania, 14 January, 1908, George W. Koehler, born at Philadelphia, Pennsylvania, 19 February, 1873; ALBERT LAWRENCE EDMUNDS, born at Philadelphia, Pennsylvania, 26 January, 1887, died 3 October, 1893.

(10) ANNIE LORUHAMAH EDMUNDS, born at Cape May, 10 January, 1864, married at Cape May, 12 September, 1881, Joseph Cooper Wilson, born at Philadelphia, Pennsylvania, 22 February, 1860, and had: DANELIA WILSON, born 12 August, 1882, died in infancy; JOSEPH WILSON, born 14 February, 1884, died in infancy; LILLIE EDMUNDS WILSON, born 20 March, 1895; SAMUEL COOPER WILSON, born 26 October, 1896; LUTHER EDMUND WILSON, born 6 December, 1898, died 17 January, 1911.

ANN ELIZA WARE

For ancestors leading back to the Mayflower see page 217.

ANN ELIZA WARE[9], (Samuel Fithian Ware[8], Deborah Whilldin[7], Jonathan Whilldin[6], James Whilldin[5], Joseph Whilldin[4], Hannah Gorham[3], Desire Howland[2], JOHN HOWLAND[1] THE PILGRIM), was born at Cold Spring, New Jersey, 12 October, 1829, died 21 October, 1905, (tombstone in Cold Spring Cemetery), married 28 March, 1847, John Rutherford, born 2 September, 1828, died 25 March, 1891. (Tombstone in Cold Spring Cemetery).

Issue:—

(1) HENRY S. RUTHERFORD, born 29 December, 1849, married 18 February, 1877, Priscilla Souder, born 15 July, 1855, and had:—CHARLOTTE R. RUTHERFORD, born 25 December, 1878, married M. AUGUSTUS LENGERT[11], (Harriet Eldredge[10], Eliza Eldredge[9], Jeremiah Leaming Eldredge[8], Aaron Eldredge[7], Aaron Eldredge[6], Mercy Leaming[5], Hannah Whilldin[4], Hannah Gorham[3], Desire Howland[2], JOHN HOWLAND[1] THE PILGRIM), (see page 133); CLINTON S. RUTHERFORD, born 29 January, 1883, married Amy Doyle; KEZIAH S. RUTHERFORD, born 7 February, 1886, died 15 December, 1888.

(2) SAMUEL F. RUTHERFORD, born 5 July, 1851, died 31 August, 1882, (tombstone in Cold Spring Cemetery), married 13 August, 1874, Bessie Tierney, born 19 October, 1850, died 26 October, 1913, and had:—IDA RUTHERFORD, born 7 July, 1875, died in infancy; HARRY R. RUTHERFORD, born 7 June, 1876, died 20 March, 1879; WALTER RUTHERFORD, born 26 December, 1877, married 30 July, 1918, Gertrude Redgreaves, born 14 October, 1876.

(Continued on next page)

ANN ELIZA WARE

(3)   JOHN RUTHERFORD, born 17 April, 1853, married 24 December, 1874, Carrie Ingersol, born 21 April, 1854, and and had:—SPENCER RUTHERFORD, born 2 February, 1877, died 6 November, 1878; BENTLY RUTHERFORD, born 25 November, 1879; JOHN I. RUTHERFORD, born 11 November, 1881, married Anna Corson; CARL RUTHERFORD, born 23 July, 1884, married Madaline Corson.

(4)   MARY A. RUTHERFORD, born 31 August, 1852, died 25 September, 1909, married 19 May, 1875, Alexander Church, born 11 December, 1851, and had:—HARRY R. CHURCH, born 7 July, 1879, died 25 April, 1881; HORACE F. CHURCH, born 19 November, 1882, married at Cape May, 29 November, 1906, SADIE YORK[11], (Martha Lavelle Bennett[10], Albert G. Reed Bennett[9], William Bennett[8], Mercy Hughes[7], Priscilla Leaming[6], Hannah Whilldin[5], Hannah Gorham[4], Desire Howland[3], JOHN HOWLAND[2] THE PILGRIM), born at Cape May, 21 October, 1887, and had HORACE KENNETH CHURCH, MARY EVELINE CHURCH, and HELEN MARTHA CHURCH.   (See page 175).

(5)   ANNIE MERCY RUTHERFORD, born 30 April, 1858, married 1 May, 1877, DAVID HUGHES[9], (Jeremiah Taylor Hughes[8], Jeremiah Hughes[7], Jacob Hughes[6], Priscilla Leaming[5], Hannah Whilldin[4], Hannah Gorham[3], Desire Howland[2], JOHN HOWLAND[1] THE PILGRIM), for descendants see page 168.

(6)   SPENCER RUTHERFORD, born 12 August, 1862, died 12 October, 1865.

DANIEL CROWELL ELDREDGE

For ancestors leading back to the Mayflower see page 218.

DANIEL CROWELL ELDREDGE[9], (Deborah Whill-din Ware[8], Doborah Whilldin[7], Jonathan Whilldin[6], James Whilldin[5], Joseph Whilldin[4], Hannah Gorham[3] Desire Howland[2], JOHN HOWLAND[1] THE PILGRIM), was born at Cape May County, Lower Township, 30 March, 1829, died at Cape May, 13 February, 1903, (tombstone in Cold Spring Cemetery), married at Cape May, 16 February, 1853, Mary Hoffman, born 30 November, 1829, died at Cape May, 9 March, 1919, (tombstone in Cold Spring Cemetery).

Issue:—

(1) JAMES WARE ELDREDGE, born at Cape May, 24 November, 1853, married 24 August, 1874, MARY CARLL FOSTER. (For descendants see page 246).

(2) ANNA MARIA ELDREDGE, born at Cape May, 19 November, 1858, married 22 March, 1882, JOSEPH SPRINGER, (see page 206), and had: MARY ELDREDGE SPRINGER, born 7 November, 1882; ALICE HOFFMAN SPRINGER, born 11 May, 1886; ELSIE GATES SPRINGER, born 3 February, 1893, married Harry Settle, and had, JOSEPH HARRISON SETTLE and EMMA GATES SETTLE; AMELIA FIFIELD SPRINGER, born 13 March, 1895, died in infancy.

(3) DANIEL FITHIAN ELDREDGE, born at Cape May, 21 January, 1866, married MELINDA STEVENS, and had: MARION ELDREDGE; CHARLES STEVENS ELDREDGE; BESSIE ELDREDGE; HARRIET W. ELDREDGE; EDNA ELDREDGE. (See page 269).

(4) CLEMENTINE FARR ELDREDGE, born 22 January, 1868.

MAYFLOWER DESCENDANTS IN CAPE MAY COUNTY

SOPHIA LOUISE ELDREDGE

For ancestors leading back to the Mayflower see page 218.

SOPHIA LOUISE ELDREDGE[9], (Deborah Whilldin Ware[8], Deborah Whilldin[7], Jonathan Whilldin[6], James Whilldin[5], Joseph Whilldin[4], Hannah Gorham[3], Desire Howland[2], JOHN HOWLAND[1] THE PILGRIM), was born at Cape May, 13 February, 1832, died at Cape May, 8 February, 1912, married at Chester, Pennsylvania, 13 October, 1853, Francis Kendrick Duke, born at Harper's Ferry, Virginia, 7 December, 1830, died at Cape May, 9 September, 1908.

Issue:—

(1) HARRIET LOUISA DUKE, born at Philadelphia, Pennsylvania, 31 July, 1854, married at Cape May, 18 June, 1910, Francis K. Shimada.

(2) MARY ELIZABETH DUKE, born at Bridgeport, New Jersey, 13 January, 1857, married at Cold Spring, New Jersey, 24 July, 1879, Samuel Gordon Smyth, born at Falls Township, Bucks County, Pennsylvania, 24 July, 1859, and had:—FRANCIS ALISON SMYTH, born at Philadelphia, Pennsylvania, 7 June, 1880, married at Cape May, 3 July, 1899, Florence May Cavanaugh; MARION MAY SMYTH, born at Philadelphia, Pennsylvania, 16 May, 1885, married at Norristown, Pennsylvania, 24 December, 1918, James J. Wertz, and had FRANCIS DUKE WERTZ, born at Norristown, Pennsylvania, 9 October, 1919; SAMUEL GORDON SMYTH, Jr., born at Philadelphia, Pennsylvania, 21 November, 1891.

(3) JOHN FRANCIS DUKE, born at West Philadelphia, Pennsylvania, 22 August, 1861, died at Somer's Point, New Jersey, 13 September, 1917, married at Cape May, 24 July, 1881, Kate Goodwin, born in Kentucky, 1861, died at Atlantic City, New Jersey, 24 November, 1905, and had: EARLE FRANCIS DUKE, born at Philadelphia, Pennsylvania, 12 December, 1882, died at Cape May, 8 February, 1888; LOUIS DUKE, born at Philadelphia, Pennsylvania, 2 July, 1886, married at Atlantic City, New Jersey, 1906, Mamie Llewellyn, and had: VIOLET CATHARINE DUKE, born 10 July, 1909; DOROTHY G. DUKE, born 1911; FRANCES MARION DUKE, born 24 July, 1918.

THOMAS ELDREDGE

For ancestors leading back to the Mayflower see page 218.

THOMAS ELDREDGE⁹, (Deborah Whilldin Ware⁸, Deborah Whilldin⁷, Jonathan Whilldin⁶, James Whilldin⁵, Joseph Whilldin⁴, Hannah Gorham³, Desire Howland², JOHN HOWLAND¹ THE PILGRIM), was born at West Cape May, New Jersey, 2 April, 1835, died 4 March, 1909, married 24 November, 1858, Emma T. C. Baker, died 8 February, 1913, daughter of Daniel Baker.

Issue:—

(1) HARRIET S. ELDREDGE, died 23 January, 1904, married Daniel E. Stevens, and had HARRY ELDREDGE STEVENS, M. D., married Hettie Hartranft, at Southold, Long Island; IDA ELDREDGE STEVENS married Frank Wallace Stevenson and had, FRANK WALLACE STEVENSON; DANIEL STEVENSON and CHARLES SIMMINGTON STEVENSON.

(2) HARRY S. ELDREDGE, died 12 March, 1888, married Lida Van Winkle.

(3) ELIDA K. ELDREDGE, married WILLIAM ROSE SHEPPARD¹⁰, (Abigail Hughes⁹, Israel Leaming⁸, Spicer Leaming⁷, Christopher Leaming⁶, Christopher Leaming⁵, Hannah Whilldin⁴, Hannah Gorham³, Desire Howland², JOHN HOWLAND¹ THE PILGRIM). (See page 182).

(4) THOMAS ELDREDGE, married Elizabeth Parsons, and had WILLIAM LEONE ELDREDGE.

(5) EMMA T. ELDREDGE, married Charles C. Simmington, and had HARRIET ELDREDGE SIMMINGTON and MARY TABITHA SIMMINGTON.

JEREMIAH STRATTON WARE

For ancestors leading back to the Mayflower see page 219.

JEREMIAH STRATTON WARE[9], (James Whilldin Ware[8], Deborah Whilldin[7], Jonathan Whilldin[6], James Whilldin[5], Joseph Whilldin[4], Hannah Gorham[3], Desire Howland[2], JOHN HOWLAND[1] THE PILGRIM), was born at Bridgeton, New Jersey, 19 January, 1831, died at Cape May, 25 August, 1902, married at Cape May, 22 December, 1853, MAHALAH JANE HALL[9], (Jane Edmunds Whilldin[8], Isaac Whilldin[7], Matthew Whilldin[6], James Whilldin[5], Joseph Whilldin[4], Hannah Gorham[3], Desire Howland[2], JOHN HOWLAND[1] THE GRIM), and (Mahalah Edmunds[7], Jane Whilldin[6], James Whilldin[5], Joseph Whilldin[4], Hannah Gorham[3], Desire Howland[2], JOHN HOWLAND[1] THE PILGRIM), born at Delaware City, Delaware, 3 September, 1835, died at Cape May, 21 January, 1920.

Issue:—

(1) MARY JANE WARE, born 5 November, 1854, married Lemuel Eldredge Miller. (For descendants see page 239).

(2) EDWARD EVERET WARE, born 26 October, 1857, died 13 November, 1861.

(3) EDWARD EVERET WARE 2d born 26 August, 1862, died 2 November, 1874.

(4) SARAH ELDREDGE WARE, born 19 October, 1865, married Samuel Mills Schellenger, and had: MARTHA SWAIN SCHELLENGER, born 23 June, 1887; MARIE MILLER SCHELLENGER, born 1888; RALPH WARE SCHELLENGER, born 2 August, 1890; SAMUEL MILLS SCHELLENGER, born 13 January, 1892, married Dorothy Decker.

(5) DR. JAMES W. WARE, born January, 1868, married Laura K. Davis, and had MAHALAH JANE WARE, born 28 September, 1904.

(6) THERESA ELDREDGE WARE, born 7 December, 1869, died 12 November, 1870.

(7) JEREMIAH STRATTON WARE, born 2 April, 1871, died 15 September, 1871.

(8) MARGARET NELSON WARE, born 10 July, 1872, died 11 December, 1916.

(9) JEREMIAH STRATTON WARE, born 10 June, 1876, married Edith May Baker.

SAMUEL FITHIAN WARE, M. D.

For ancestors leading back to the Mayflower see page 219.

SAMUEL FITHIAN WARE[9] (James Whilldin Ware[8], Deborah Whilldin[7], Jonathan Whilldin[6], James Whilldin[5], Joseph Whilldin[4], Hannah Gorham[3], Desire Howland[2], JOHN HOWLAND[1] THE PILGRIM), was born at Allowaystown, New Jersey, 23 July, 1848, married first at Cape May, 8 November, 1871, Louisa Eldredge Sawyer, born at Cape May, 9 September, 1852, died at Washington, D. C., 1 November, 1895.

Issue:—

(1) HARRIET ELDREDGE WARE, born 22 July, 1872, died 22 July, 1873.

(2) HARRIET SAWYER WARE, born 12 August, 1873, died 1 December, 1881.

(3) HARRY SAWYER WARE, born 1 February, 1876, died 25 December, 1881.

(4) EDITH WARE, born 25 December, 1877, died 4 August, 1878.

(5) SAMUEL FITHIAN WARE, born 20 August, 1879, died 22 December, 1881.

(6) LOUISE SAWYER WARE, born at Cape May, 14 November, 1883, married at Philadelphia, Pennsylvania, 29 August, 1901, Joseph K. Campbell, born at Philadelphia, Pennsylvania, 22 March, 1876, and had the following children:— CLARA LOUISE WARE CAMPBELL, born at Philadelphia, Pennsylvania, 6 July, 1903, and JOSEPH WARE CAMPBELL, died in infancy. Dr. Ware married second Helen Nora Crites.

MARY JANE WARE

For ancestors leading back to the Mayflower see page 237.

MARY JANE WARE[10], (Jeremiah Stratton Ware[9], James Whilldin Ware[8], Deborah Whilldin[7] Jonathan Whilldin[6], James Whilldin[5], Joseph Whilldin[4], Hannah Gorham[3], Desire Howland[2], JOHN HOWLAND[1] THE PILGRIM), on her father's side, and (MAHALAH JANE HALL[9], Jane Edmunds Whilldin[8], Isaac Whilldin[7], Matthew Whilldin[6], James Whilldin[5], Joseph Whilldin[4], Hannah Gorham[3], Desire Howland[2], JOHN HOWLAND[1] THE PILGRIM), and (MAHALAH JANE HALL[9], Jane Edmunds Whilldin[8], Mahalah Edmunds[7], Jane Whilldin[6], James Whilldin[5], Joseph Whilldin[4], Hannah Gorham[3], Desire Howland[2], JOHN HOWLAND[1] THE PILGRIM), on her mother's side, was born at West Cape May, New Jersey, 5 November, 1854, married at Cape May, 8 January, 1878, Lemuel Eldredge Miller, born at Green Creek, New Jersey, 1 August, 1854.

Issue:—

(1) EDWARD MARCY MILLER, born 19 January, 1880, married 1 September, 1917, Edith Sara Whann, born 18 March, 1884.

(2) FRANK WHITAKER MILLER, born 10 August, 1882.

(3) LEMUEL ELDREDGE MILLER, born 22 March, 1890, married 6 October, 1915, Ruth Walters, born 16 May, 1894, and had MARY JANE MILLER, born 20 November, 1916

HESTER ANN ELDRIDGE JOHNSON

For ancestors leading back to the Mayflower see page 224.

HESTER ANN ELDRIDGE JOHNSON[9], (Jane White Eldridge[8], Elizabeth Edmunds[7], Jane Whilldin[6], James Whilldin[5], Joseph Whilldin[4], Hannah Gorham[3], Desire Howland[2], JOHN HOWLAND[1] THE PILGRIM), was born at Philadelphia, Pennsylvania, 4 November, 1832, married 26 June, 1850, Richard Cresse Souder, born at Dennisville, New Jersey, 16 October, 1827, died 27 February, 1871.

Issue:—

(1) CHARLES B. SOUDER, born at Cape May, 10 September, 1851, died at Cape May, 3 September, 1902, married at Cape May, 15 October, 1876, Mary Church, and had, RICHARD CRESSE SOUDER and MARGARET SOUDER, who married Edmund Jones, and had MILDRED JONES.

(2) ADA SOUDER, born 12 August, 1853.

(3) JENNIE J. SOUDER, born at Atlantic City, New Jersey, 13 May, 1855, married at Cape May, 4 May, 1876, Edward M. Hughes.

(4) ELWOOD SOUDER, born 15 August, 1859, married Alice May Holt. (For descendants see page 247).

(5) LILLIE E. SOUDER, born at Atlantic City, 12 January, 1861, married Theodore Moore, and had ELSIE MOORE, CARROLL MOORE, ALICE MOORE, THEODORE MOORE, and FLORENCE MOORE.

(6) KATHARINE SOUDER, born at Cape May, 24 May, 1863.

(7) MAURICE B. SOUDER, born 6 October, 1865, married Anna Alberton, and had HESTER E. SOUDER, MARY J. SOUDER, FLORENCE M. SOUDER, and CHARLES B. SOUDER.

(8) DANIEL E. SOUDER, born 23 November, 1868, married Josephine Curriden, and had EARLE C. SOUDER.

(9) ELLA SOUDER.

(10) FANNIE SOUDER.

MAYFLOWER DESCENDANTS IN CAPE MAY COUNTY

JACOB ELDRIDGE JOHNSON

For ancestors leading back to the Mayflower see page 224.

JACOB ELDRIDGE JOHNSON[9], (Jane White Eldridge[8], Elizabeth Edmunds[7], Jane Whilldin[6], James Whilldin[5], Joseph Whilldin[4], Hannah Gorham[3], Desire Howland[2], JOHN HOWLAND[1] THE PILGRIM), was born at Philadelphia, Pennsylvania, 16 July, 1834, married Elizabeth Conover, born 1833.

Issue :—

(1) ALBINA JOHNSON, married first Edward Keating, married second Nathan Rand.

(2) MELVINA JOHNSON, born at Atlantic City, New Jersey, 5 July, 1858, married at Cape May, 4 April, 1882, Frederick Boerner, and had Dr. FREDERICK BOERNER, born 27 April, 1890, who married Esther Wilkie, and had ELEANOR BOERNER, DORIS BOERNER, FREDERICK BOERNER and ROBERT BOERNER.

(3) LILLIAN JOHNSON, married JUDSON BENNETT[10], (William Jackson Bennett[9], William Bennett[8], Mary Hughes[7], Jacob Hughes[6], Priscilla Leaming[5], Hannah Whilldin[4], Hannah Gorham[3], Desire Howland[2], JOHN HOWLAND[1] THE PILGRIM), (see page 164), and had ELLA BENNETT, J. HARVEY BENNETT and WALTER BENNETT, married MILDRED EDMUNDS. (See page 228).

J. HARVEY BENNETT married at Cape May, 19 October, 1910, REBECCA MECRAY CASSEDY, born at Cape May, 13 September, 1886, and had: WILLIAM F. CASSEDY BENNETT, born 26 July, 1911, died in infancy; and ROBERT STOCKTON BENNETT, born 24 September, 1913. (See page 283).

ELDRIDGE JOHNSON

For ancestors leading back to the Mayflower see page 224.

ELDRIDGE JOHNSON[9], (Jane White Eldridge[8], Elizabeth Edmunds[7], Jane Whilldin[6], James Whilldin[5], Joseph Whilldin[4], Hannah Gorham[3], Desire Howland[2], JOHN HOWLAND[1] THE PILGRIM), was born at Cape May, 1 January, 1839, married first at Cape May, 18 September, 1861, JANE SCHELLENGER HUGHES[9], (Albert Henry Hughes[8], Humphrey Hughes[7], Jane Whilldin[6], James Whilldin[5], Joseph Whilldin[4], Hannah Gorham[3], Desire Howland[2], JOHN HOWLAND[1] THE PILGRIM), who was born at Cape May, 5 August, 1841, died at Cape May, 21 March, 1888.

ELDRIDGE JOHNSON married second at Cape May, 1896, ABIGAIL COLLINS HUGHES[9], (Albert Henry Hughes[8], Humphrey Hughes[7], Jane Whilldin[6], James Whilldin[5], Joseph Whilldin[4], Hannah Gorham[3], Desire Howland[2], JOHN HOWLAND[1] THE PILGRIM), born at Cape May, 1 January, 1840.

Issue by first marriage:—

(1) EDWARD JOHNSON, born 2 October, 1862, died 10 January, 1863.

(2) ALBERT HUGHES JOHNSON, died 21 October, 1890.

(3) ANNIE LEAMING JOHNSON.

(4) FREDERIC LAYTON JOHNSON, M. D., died 10 December, 1899.

(5) HARRY HUGHES JOHNSON, married at Wooster, Ohio, 30 June, 1898, Katherine Stewart Lucas, and had, JAMES LUCAS JOHNSON, born 9 April, 1899, died 9 March, 1900, PHILIP LUCAS JOHNSON, born 26 July, 1912.

(6) FLORENCE HUGHES JOHNSON.

MATTHEW WHILLDIN HALL

For ancestors leading back to the Mayflower see page 226.

MATTHEW WHILLDIN HALL[9], (Jane Edmunds Whilldin[8], Mahala Edmunds[7], Jane Whilldin[6], James Whilldin[5], Joseph Whilldin[4], Hannah Gorham[3], Desire Howland[2], JOHN HOWLAND[1] THE PILGRIM), was born at Cape May Court House, New Jersey, 19 February, 1831, died at Cape May, 4 February, 1874, married at Cape May, June, 1855, ELEANOR LUDLAM EDMUNDS[9], (Lydia Hughes[8], Thomas Hurst Hughes[7], Ellis Hughes[6], Hannah Whilldin[5], Joseph Whilldin[4], Hannah Gorham[3], Desire Howland[2], JOHN HOWLAND[1] THE PILGRIM), born 20 September, 1833, died 24 May, 1911. (See page 263).

Issue:—

(1) EDMUNDS LUDLAM HALL, born at Cape May, 29 May, 1856, married at Philadelphia, 29 May, 1882, Lena Bryant, born 20 September, 1861, and had ISABEL CLAIR HALL, born 21 April, 1883, HELEN THOMPSON HALL, born, 17 February, 1887.

(2) FANNY LUDLAM HALL, born 1 November, 1858, died in infancy.

(3) JENNIE WHILLDIN HALL, born 25 December, 1859, married 21 May, 1888, Dr. Alexander Hubert Providence Leuf, and had: GRACE HALL LEUF, born 1 July, 1889, who married 1 October, 1912, Dr. Arthur Farrington Wilhelm, and had, DOROTHY JANE WILHELM, born 21 July, 1913; RALPH REA LEUF, born 27 July, 1892.

(4) JOSEPH HALL, twin brother of JENNIE WHILLDIN HALL, died in infancy.

(5) MATTHEW WHILLDIN HALL, born 22 April, 1871, died 18 February, 1920.

HARRIET ANN HALL

For ancestors leading back to the Mayflower see page 226.

HARRIET ANN HALL[9], (Jane Edmunds Whilldin[8], Mahalah Edmunds[7], Jane Whilldin[6], James Whilldin[5], Joseph Whilldin[4], Hannah, Gorham[3], Desire Howland[2], JOHN HOWLAND[1] THE PILGRIM), was born at Cape May, 3 February, 1837, died at Atlantic City, New Jersey, 8 June, 1911, married at Cape May, 27 March, 1855, Charles Alexander Shaw, born at Cape May, 9 November, 1835.

Issue :—

(1) JANE WHILLDIN SHAW, born at Cape May, 8 June, 1857, married at Cape May, 20 October, 1876, Jesse Hamilton Robinson, born at Allegheny, Pennsylvania, 10 September, 1843, and had CHARLES KILBURN ROBINSON, who married at Saint Louis, Missouri, 6 January, 1904, Mary A. Alexander, and had: HAMILTON ALEXANDER ROBINSON, born at Pittsburg, Pennsylvania, 16 September, 1904; ELIZABETH WEBB ROBINSON, born at Cape May, 22 October, 1882, married at Washington, D. C., 17 October, 1906, Harold Clinton Smith and had DOROTHY ELIZABETH SMITH, born at Washington, D. C., 13 May, 1909.

(2) ALEXANDER L. SHAW, born at Cape May, 19 August, 1859, married at Warren, Pennsylvania, 17 October, 1883, Alice Trueshall.

(3) WILLIAM FRANK SHAW, born at Cape May, 15 August, 1861, married at Camden, New Jersey, 1 January, 1890, Ida Almira Woolman, and had, ELIZABETH ROBINSON SHAW and HELLEN RIDGEWAY SHAW.

(4) ELIZABETH SHAW, born at Cape May, 29 August, 1863, died at Cape May, 12 March, 1867.

Harold Clinton Smith, husband of ELIZABETH WEBB ROBINSON, was born at Middlebury, Vermont, 19 March, 1882.

MARY BENNETT HALL

For ancestors leading back to the Mayflower see page 226.

MARY BENNETT HALL[9], (Jane Edmunds Whilldin[8], Mahalah Edmunds[7], Jane Whilldin[6], James Whilldin[5], Joseph Whilldin[4], Hannah Gorham[3], Desire Howland[2], JOHN HOWLAND[1] THE PILGRIM), was born at West Cape May, New Jersey, 21 December, 1843, married at Philadelphia, Pennsylvania, 15 October, 1863, John Church, born at Cold Spring, New Jersey, 19 March, 1842, died 1893.

Issue :—

(1) WILLIAM CHURCH, born at Cold Spring, New Jersey, 26 August, 1864, married Lorena Church and had: ANNA MAY CHURCH, married Cyrus Osler and had CHARLES WILLIAM CHURCH, died 28 January, 1920; HERMAN CHURCH; and WALTER CHURCH, who married EDNA YORK[11], (Martha Lavelle Bennett[10], Albert G. Reed Bennett[9], William Bennett[8], Mary Hughes[7], Jacob Hughes[6], Priscilla Leaming[5], Hannah Whilldin[4], Hannah Gorham[3], Desire Howland[2], JOHN HOWLAND[1] THE PILGRIM), and had EVELINA CHURCH and WALTER CHURCH, (see page 175).

(2) CHARLES SHAW CHURCH, born at West Cape May, New Jersey, 13 November, 1869, married at Wilmington, Delaware, 11 September, 1905, Lulu Belle Lloyd, born at Phillipsburg, Pennsylvania, 31 May, 1869.

(3) EVA CHURCH, born at West Cape May, New Jersey, 16 February, 1877, died 2 February, 1895.

(4) JOHN HOWARD CHURCH, born 1 May, 1879, married at Germantown, Pennsylvania, 6 August, 1902, Mary Elizabeth La Rose, born 21 April, 1878, and had: JOHN HOWARD CHURCH, born at Germantown, Pennsylvania, 9 April, 1904, and DOROTHY HALL CHURCH, born at Germantown, Pennsylvania, 4 June, 1907.

JAMES WARE ELDREDGE

For ancestors leading back to the Mayflower see page 234.

JAMES WARE ELDREDGE[10], (Daniel Crowell Eldredge[9], Deborah Whilldin Ware[8], Deborah Whilldin[7], Jonathan Whilldin[6], James Whilldin[5], Joseph Whilldin[4], Hannah Gorham[3], Desire Howland[2], JOHN HOWLAND[1] THE PILGRIM), was born at Cape May, 24 November, 1853, married at Cape May, 24 August, 1874, MARY CARLL FOSTER[9], (Ann Lawrence Hughes[8], James Rainy Hughes[7], Jacob Hughes[6], Priscilla Leaming[5], Hannah Whilldin[4], Hannah Gorham[3], Desire Howland[2], JOHN HOWLAND[1] THE PILGRIM), and (Ann Lawrence Hughes[9], Eliza Eldredge[8], Aaron Eldredge[7], Aaron Eldredge[6], Mercy Leaming[5], Hannah Whilldin[4], Hannah Gorham[3], Desire Howland[2], JOHN HOWLAND[1] THE PILGRIM), who was born at Cape May, 3 May, 1855. (See page 156).

Issue:—

(1) SAMUEL FOSTER ELDREDGE, born 11 April, 1875, married at Bellefonte, Pennsylvania, 17 October, 1901, Jessie Porter Laurie, born at Pen Yan, New York, 17 November, 1875, and had the following children, born at Cape May:— KATHRINE LAURIE ELDREDGE, born 28 January, 1902; SAMUEL FOSTER ELDREDGE, born 1 August, 1904; BERTHA ELIZABETH ELDREDGE, born 30 January, 1907; MARY ALICE ELDREDGE, born 24 February, 1913; ANN FOSTER ELDREDGE, born 21 February, 1918; JEAN MURDOCK ELDREDGE, born 21 February, 1918, died 13 May, 1918.

(2) DOWNS FOSTER ELDREDGE, born at Cape May, 1 August, 1876, died in infancy.

(3) GEORGE BOLTON ELDREDGE, born at Cape May, 26 April, 1878, died at Cape May, 24 August, 1915.

ELLWOOD SOUDER

For ancestors leading back to the Mayflower see page 240.

ELWOOD SOUDER[10], (Hester Ann Eldridge[9], Jane White Eldredge[8], Elizabeth Edmunds[7], Jane Whilldin[6], James Whilldin[5], Joseph Whilldin[4], Hannah Gorham[3], Desire Howland[2], JOHN HOWLAND[1] THE PILGRIM), was born 15 August, 1859, married 18 November, 1882, Alice May Holt, born 7 May, 1862.

Issue:—

(1) THOMAS ARGYLE SOUDER, born at Wilmington, Delaware, 29 March, 1884, married 1 September, 1909, Anna Smyth Feil, born 25 November, 1884.

(3) ELLWOOD SOUDER, born at Wilmington, Delaware, 22 September, 1887, married 10 November, 1909, DOROTHY MECRAY BOCKIUS[11], (Elizabeth Hughes Mecray[10], Elizabeth Schellenger Hughes[9], Albert Henry Hughes[8], Humphrey Hughes[7] Jane Whilldin[6], James Whilldin[5], Joseph Whilldin[4], Hannah Gorham[3], Desire Howland[2], JOHN HOWLAND[1] THE PILGRIM), born 13 August, 1889, and had, ELIZABETH MECRAY SOUDER, born 10 January, 1911. (See page 223).

(3) HAROLD CHARLES SOUDER, born at Wilmington, Delaware, 8 November, 1889, married 16 October, 1912, Esther Banks, born 14 April, 1889, and had, ALICE HOLT SOUDER, born 12 September, 1913.

(4) LILLIE MOORE SOUDER, born at Wilmington, Delaware, 28 February, 1892.

ZERUIAH HUGHES

For ancestors leading back to the Mayflower see page 204.

ZERUIAH HUGHES[7], (Memucan Hughes[6], Hannah Whilldin[5], Joseph Whilldin[4], Hannah Gorham[3], Desire Howland[2], JOHN HOWLAND[1] THE PILGRIM), was born at Cape May, 19 April, 1776, died at Cape May, 7 November, 1818, married 1 August, 1792, Robert Cummings Schenck, M. D., born near Freehold, New Jersey, 11 January, 1772, died at Cape May, 13 January, 1833. Dr. Schenck married second, 29 November, 1820, Mary Shaw.

Issue:—

(1) CATHARINE SCHENCK, born at Cape May, New Jersey, 19 July, 1793, married John Schellenger. (For descendants see page 253).

(2) WILLIAM SCHENCK, born 29 May, 1795, married Mary Steelman. He died August, 1854. (For descendants see page 254).

(3) ROBERT C. SCHENCK, born 4 August, 1796, lost at sea, March, 1831, married Arabel Aarons; no issue.

(4 and 5) NANCY and MARTHA SCHENCK, born 19 December, 1800; NANCY married Recompense Hand, 5 September, 1820. She died 23 May, 1854. (For descendants see page 255); MARTHA married Philip Hand; (for descendants see page 256).

(6) MARIA S. SCHENCK, born 12 July, 1806, married William Cassedy. (For descendants see page 257).

(7) MELINDA SCHENCK, born 14 February, 1809, married Joseph Ludlam and had one son, JOSEPH LUDLAM. She died in New York, 24 November, 1861.

ISRAEL HUGHES

For ancestors leading back to the Mayflower see page 204.

ISRAEL HUGHES[7], (Memucan Hughes[6], Hannah Whilldin[5], Joseph Whilldin[4], Hannah Gorham[3], Desire Howland[2], JOHN HOWLAND[1] THE PILGRIM), was born at Cape May, 9 May, 1778, died at Cape May, 7 February, 1833, (tombstone in Cold Spring Cemetery), married at Cape May, 3 August, 1896, Mary Eldredge, born at Cape May, 16 March, 1785, (25 February given as the date of birth in family bible—see page 33), died at Cape May, 16 June, 1863, (tombstone in Cold Spring Cemetery).

Issue:—

(1) ARTIS HUGHES, married Nancy Tomlinson, and had: LYDIA HUGHES, who married Isaac Connor, and had HARRY CONNOR and SOPHIE CONNOR; ELLEN HUGHES.

(2) MEMUCAN HUGHES, born at Cape May, 1810, married Mary P. Edmunds. (For descendants see page 329).

(3) SOPHIA HUGHES, born 14 October, 1812, married Aaron Bennett. (For descendants see page 258).

(4) ISABELLA HUGHES, died without issue.

(5) ISRAEL HUGHES, born 5 April, 1822, married Elizabeth H. Hoffman. (For descendants see page 259).

(6) MARY ANN HUGHES, married Evan Davis, and had, EDWIN LEWIS DAVIS, who married Cecelia Frances Roseman, and had: SARAH DAVIS, deceased; HARRY BARBOUR DAVIS, married Lois M. Whilldin, and had, HELENA FRANCES DAVIS, who married Thomas Garry, and EDWIN LEWIS DAVIS.

(7) MATILDA HUGHES, born 6 February, 1817, married Paul Barnes. (For descendants see page 260).

(8) MARTHA HUGHES, married ISAAC WHILLDIN, (see page 215).

(9) EVELINE HUGHES, died without issue.

(10) CHARLOTTE HUGHES, married Peter Bridenthal, no issue.

THOMAS HURST HUGHES

For ancestors leading back to the Mayflower see page 205.

THOMAS HURST HUGHES[7], (Ellis Hughes[6], Hannah Whilldin[5], Joseph Whilldin[4], Hannah Gorham[3], Desire Howland[2], JOHN HOWLAND[1] THE PILGRIM), was born at Cape May, 10 January, 1769, died at Cape May, 10 November, 1839, (tombstone in Cold Spring Cemetery, but the date of birth on the stone was determined by subtracting an assumed age from the date of death and is evidently not exact), married 3 December, 1788, Lydia Paige, born 13 May, 1767, died at Cape May, 3 May, 1828, (tombstone in Cold Spring Cemetery).

Issue :—

(1) THOMAS PAIGE HUGHES, born at Cape May, 19 January, 1790, married in Cumberland County, New Jersey, 25 September, 1810, Mary Boone, and had, BENJAMIN HUGHES, who married Mary Wales.

(2) ELLIS HUGHES, born at Cape May, 2 July, 1793, married first Sarah Higgins, married second Nancy Teal. (For descendants see page 261).

(3) LYDIA HUGHES, born at Cape May, 4 December, 1795, married Richard Edmunds. (For descendants see page 262).

(4) ELEANOR HUGHES, born at Cape May, 12 May, 1798, married Smith Ludlam, no issue.

(5) SARAH HUGHES, born at Cape May, 31 May, 1800, married Eli B. Wales. (For descendants see page 313).

(6) LOUISE HUGHES.

JOSEPH HUGHES

For ancestors leading back to the Mayflower see page 205.

JOSEPH HUGHES[7], (Ellis Hughes[6], Hannah Whilldin[5], Joseph Whilldin[4], Hannah Gorham[3], Desire Howland[2], JOHN HOWLAND[1] THE PILGRIM), was born at Cape May, 17 November, 1772, died at Cape May, 13 March, 1813, (tombstone in Cold Spring Cemetery), married Judith Bennett. (See also page 63).

Issue:—

(1) JUDITH HUGHES, married ISAAC WHILLDIN, who was born at Cape May, 15 February, 1784, died 13 May, 1867, ISAAC WHILLDIN married first MAHALA EDMUNDS. (See page 215).

(2) THOMAS BUCK HUGHES, born at Cape May, married Jane Kennedy Schellenger, and had one son, JOSEPH BOONE HUGHES, born 11 April, 1843, who married 1864, Sarah Townsend Stevens, born 30 August, 1843, died 23 February, 1916, and had the following:

Issue:—

GEORGE H. HUGHES, married Georgie Shaw.

MARY HUGHES, married Charles E. Markley, and had JOSEPH MARKLEY and FRANK MARKLEY.

SARAH HUGHES, married Winfield Scott Dilks.

JOSEPH B. HUGHES, born 29 March, 1875, married 10 November, 1902, Gertrude Entriken.

CAROLINE B. HUGHES, born at Cape May, 17 April, 1878, died 6 March, 1907, married 10 April, 1906, Henry Walker Hand.

HARRY TAYLOR HUGHES, born 23 July, 1880, married 23 October, 1907, LENA BLATTNER HUGHES[11], (Robert Chew Hughes[10], John Haney Hughes[9], Ellis Hughes[8], Thomas Hurst Hughes[7], Ellis Hughes[6], Hannah Whilldin[5], Joseph Whilldin[4], Hannah Gorham[3], Desire Howland[2], JOHN HOWLAND[1] THE PILGRIM), (see page 321).

THOMAS BUCK HUGHES, married first Clara Fenderson, married second Carrie Powell, and had, THOMAS POWELL HUGHES, born 20 December, 1917.

ELEANOR HUGHES

For ancestors leading back to the Mayflower see page 205.

ELEANOR HUGHES[7], (Ellis Hughes[6], Hannah Whilldin[5], Joseph Whilldin[4], Hannah Gorham[3], Desire Howland[2], JOHN HOWLAND[1] THE PILGRIM), was born at Cape May, 7 August, 1776, died at Cape May, 5 October, 1818, (tombstone in Cold Spring Cemtery), married at Cape May, 20 December, 1798, Silas Matthews, born at Fishing Creek, New Jersey, 17 September, 1777, died at Cape May, 8 September, 1830, (tombstone in Cold Spring Cemetery).

Issue:—

(1) WILLIAM MATTHEWS, born at Cape May, 9 March, 1800, married first Elizabeth Izard, married second Sarah Izard. (For descendants see pages 264, 265).

(2) THOMAS MATTHEWS, born at Cape May, 19 December, 1801, died early.

(3) ELEANOR MATTHEWS, born at Cape May, 26 June, 1804, married Mathias Lee.

(4) HANNAH MATTHEWS, born at Cape May, 24 September, 1806, married Thomas Page Crowell. (For descendants see page 266).

(5) THOMAS MATTHEWS, born at Cape May, 4 October, 1808, married Sarah ————.

(6) SILAS MATTHEWS, born at Cape May, 1 August, 1811, married CHARLOTTE LEAMING, and died without issue—see page 144.

(7) ISABELLA MATTHEWS, born at Cape May, 9 October, 1813, married Andrew H. Reeves. (For descendants see page 267).

(8) CHARLOTTE MATTHEWS, born at Cape May, 21 November, 1816, died 14 November, 1847, unmarried.

CATHARINE SCHENCK

For ancestors leading back to the Mayflower see page 248.

CATHARINE SCHENCK[8], (Zeruiah Hughes[7], Memucan Hughes[6], Hannah Whilldin[5], Joseph Whilldin[4], Hannah Gorham[3], Desire Howland[2], JOHN HOWLAND[1] THE PILGRIM), was born at Cape May, 19 July, 1793, married John Schellenger.

Issue:—

(1) JOHN SCHENCK SCHELLENGER, born 8 March, 1815, married Mary Davis, born 25 April, 1817. (For descendants see page 268).

(2) SARAH SCHELLENGER, married Washington Solomon, and had CATHARINE ELIZA SOLOMON.

(3) ZERUIAH SCHELLENGER, married Augustus Archambauld, and had EDWIN ARCHAMBAULD.

(4) and (5) ALICE and WILLIAM HENRY SCHELLENGER; WILLIAM HENRY died in infancy, ALICE SCHELLENGER, married ———— Young, and had ANNIE YOUNG, VIRGINIA YOUNG and ALONZO POTTER YOUNG.

(6) CATHARINE SCHELLENGER, married Andrew Jackson McKaraher, and had: CHARLES McKARAHER; who married Eleanor Tait, and had, CHARLES GETHEN McKARAHER, WILLIAM BROOKS McKARAHER, JOHN TAIT McKARAHER; JOHN GETHEN McKARAHER, son of Andrew J. and CATHARINE, married Ella L. Nicholson; WILLIAM BROOKS McKARAHER, and ANDREW J. McKARAHER, sons of Andrew J. and CATHARINE,, died in infancy.

(7) ARABELLA SCHELLENGER, married John Mayne, and had HARRY MAYNE, EUGENE MAYNE and MILDRED MAYNE.

(8) MELINDA SCHELLENGER, unmarried.

(9) EMMA SCHELLENGER, married George Wynkoop, and had JOSEPH WYNKOOP, CATHARINE WYNKOOP and GEORGE WYNKOOP.

(10) WILLIAM HENRY SCHELLENGER, married in the West.

WILLIAM SCHENCK

For ancestors leading back to the Mayflower see page 248.

WILLIAM SCHENCK[8], (Zeruiah Hughes[7], Memucan Hughes[6], Hannah Whilldin[5], Joseph Whilldin[4], Hannah Gorham[3], Desire Howland[2], JOHN HOWLAND[1] THE PILGRIM), was born at Cape May, 29 May, 1795, died August, 1855, married at Cape May, 4 March, 1820, Mary Steelman.

Issue:—

(1) PHILIP SCHENCK, born near May's Landing, New Jersey, 9 March, 1822, married first 6 December, 1841, Elizabeth Ann Taylor, born about 1825, died 1 May, 1853; married second, 6 December, 1866, Elizabeth Champion, born 17 January, 1847-8, and had by first wife:—PHILIP SCHENCK, born 1842, killed in Civil War; GEORGE SCHENCK, born 1844, killed in Civil War; SMITH SCHENCK, born 1846, died in Southern Hospital during same War; ANNA SCHENCK, born 1851; SEYMOUR SCHENCK, (by second wife) born 1868; REBECCA SCHENCK, born 23 September, 1870; SARAH SCHENCK, born 22, September, 1873.

(2) URIAH SCHENCK, born near May's Landing, New Jersey, about 1824, married Catharine Simpkins. (For descendants see page 270).

(3) JAMES W. SCHENCK, born 1826, near May's Landing, New Jersey, married Rose Ann Emmell. She was born 9 February, 1829. (For descendants see page 271).

(4) ROBERT SCHENCK, born 1828, near May's Landing, New Jersey, married Hannah Simpkins, and had ANN E. SCHENCK, born 1849, married 1868, Charles Pierce, born 26 March, 1851.

(5) RECOMPENSE SCHENCK, born near May's Landing, New Jersey, 1834, married Rachel Harris.

(6) REBECCA SCHENCK, born near May's Landing, 1837, married William Miskell.

NANCY SCHENCK

For ancestors leading back to the Mayflower see page 248.

NANCY SCHENCK[8], (Zeruiah Hughes[7], Memucan Hughes[6], Hannah Whilldin[5], Joseph Whilldin[4], Hannah Gorham[3], Desire Howland[2], JOHN HOWLAND[1] THE PILGRIM), was born 19 December, 1800, died at Cape May, 23 May, 1854, (tombstone in Cold Spring Cemetery), married 5 December, 1820, Recompence Hand, born at Rio Grande, New Jersey, 20 November, 1795, died at Cape May, 15 April, 1871, (tombstone in Cold Spring Cemetery).

Issue:—

(1) ROBERT S. HAND, born 1821, married JANE LEAMING. (For descendants see page 272).

(2) ISAAC M. HAND, born 13 October, 1823, died 14 March, 1899, married 21 May, 1848, Matilda S. Weeks, and had: CHARLES W. HAND, born 19 May, 1851, died 12 October, 1884, married 31 August, 1875, Katharine Smith, and had BESSIE HAND, born 1 October, 1878; WALTER T. HAND, born 25 December, 1853, died 27 February, 1876; MATILDA HAND, born 12 May, 1856; VIRGINIA HAND, born 14 October, 1860, married 2 June, 1890, Andrew T. Kay.

(3) HENRY HAND, born 31 January, 1826, married Eliza Doak. (For descendants see page 273).

(4) RECOMPENCE HAND, born 16 March, 1828, married Martha Thompson. (For descendants see page 275).

(5) WILLIAM F. HAND, married Ann M. Tomlin.

(6) ANNIE S. HAND, married Richard R. Thompson. (For descendants see page 276).

(7) HENRIETTA HAND, married WILLIAM J. BENNETT. (For descendants see page 164.)

(8) REBECCA HAND, married Nicholas Corson. No issue.

(9) ENOCH HAND, married Clara Green.

(10) JOSEPH HAND, married JOSEPHINE WARE. (For descendants see page 277).

(11) ELIZA HAND, married first SMITH HUGHES, married second Robert Chambers.

MARTHA SCHENCK

For ancestors leading back to the Mayflower see page 248.

MARTHA SCHENCK[8], (Zeruiah Hughes[7], Memucan Hughes[6], Hannah Whilldin[5], Joseph Whilldin[4], Hannah Gorham[3], Desire Howland[2], JOHN HOWLAND[1] THE PILGRIM), was born 19 December, 1800, died 11 October, 1836, married 3 December, 1821, Philip Hand, born 28 October, 1797, died 12 August, 1881, (tombstones in Cold Spring Cemetery).

Issue :—

(1) ACHSAH HAND, born 1 November, 1822, married first, 28 May, 1840, Walter Dyer Naves, born 2 May, 1820, married second John Wood. (For descendants see page 278).

(2) PHILIP HAND, born 6 June, 1824, married LYDIA PAIGE HUGHES. (For descendants see page 288).

(3) JOSIAH HAND, born 18 March, 1827, died in infancy.

(4) CALHOUN HAND, born 6 July, 1829, died in infancy.

(5) ALEXANDER McKINSEY HAND, born 30 November, 1830, died 9 December, 1855. No issue.

(6) MARTHA ANN HAND, born 4 December, 1832, married Alphonzo Durham Lee. (For descendants see page 279).

(7) RACHEL HAND, born 7 January, 1836, died in infancy.

MARIA STOCKTON SCHENCK

For ancestors leading back to the Mayflower see page 248.

MARIA STOCKTON SCHENCK[8], (Zeruiah Hughes[7], Memucan Hughes[6], Hannah Whilldin[5], Joseph Whilldin[4], Hannah Gorham[3], Desire Howland[2], JOHN HOWLAND[1] THE PILGRIM), was born at Cape May, 12 July, 1808, died at Cape May, 10 November, 1884, married at Cape May, 14 October, 1830, William Cassedy born 1807, died at Cape May, 11 August, 1854, (tombstones in Cold Spring Cemetery).

Issue:—

(1) ELLEN MARIA CASSEDY, born 15 November, 1834, married Benjamin Sparks. (For descendants see page 281).

(2) MARY ANN CASSEDY, born 27 April, 1836, married George Shaw. (For descendants see page 282).

(3) and (4) WILLIAM FRANCIS CASSEDY and LOUISE CASSEDY, born 26 January, 1843; WILLIAM married Emma Willets, (for descendants see page 283); LOUISE married Wilson Banks.

(5) SALLIE PENNOCK CASSEDY, born 29 August, 1845, married Enos Roger Williams. (For descendants see page 284).

(6) NANCY SCHENCK CASSEDY, born 10 March, 1847, died 15 June, 1885, married Harry J. White, and had the following children:—FLORENCE WHITE, married Harry Rudolph; ALBERT WHITE; GEORGIANNA WHITE, married William Smith; HARRY WHITE; WILLIAM WHITE; MARY ELLEN WHITE; SARAH WHITE; VIRGINIA WHITE; ANNIE WHITE, who married Edwin Mitchell, and had, ANNA LOUISE MITCHELL, born at Camden, New Jersey, 20 June, 1906.

SOPHIA HUGHES

For ancestors leading back to the Mayflower see page 249.

SOPHIA HUGHES[8], (Israel Hughes[7], Memucan Hughes[6], Hannah Whilldin[5], Joseph Whilldin[4], Hannah Gorham[3], Desire Howland[2], JOHN HOWLAND[1] THE PILGRIM), was born at Cape May, 14 October, 1812, died at Cape May, 22 January, 1847, (tombstone in Cold Spring Cemetery), married at Cape May, 30 October, 1830, Aaron Bennett, born at Cape May, 11 February, 1811, drowned in Delaware Bay, 8 November, 1850.

Issue :—

(1) JAMES C. BENNETT, deceased.

(2) ISABELLA BENNETT, born at Cape May, 29 March, 1835, died 8 August, 1904, married 24 January, 1855, Smith Gilbert, born 28 January, 1829, died 19 May, 1910, and had, MARY H. GILBERT, born 9 February, 1857, married 26 November, 1879, George Jonas, born 8 May, 1859, and had ANNA I. JONAS, born 17 August, 1881.

(3) SOPHIA H. BENNETT, born at Cape May, October, 1837, married John Ferguson.

(4) AARON BENNETT, deceased.

(5) HENRY BENNETT, deceased.

(6) OCIE BENNETT, born at Cape May, 20 August, 1846, married at Cape May, 9 June, 1869, JOSEPH COXE ELDREDGE[9], (Joseph Eldredge[8], Aaron Eldredge[7], Aaron Eldredge[6], Mercy Leaming[5], Hannah Whilldin[4], Hannah Gorham[3], Desire Howland[2], JOHN HOWLAND[1] THE PILGRIM). (For descendants see page 138).

MAYFLOWER DESCENDANTS IN CAPE MAY COUNTY

ISRAEL HUGHES

For ancestors leading back to the Mayflower see page 249.

ISRAEL HUGHES[8], (Israel Hughes[7], Memucan Hughes[6], Hannah Whilldin[5], Joseph Whilldin[4], Hannah Gorham[3], Desire Howland[2], JOHN HOWLAND[1] THE PILGRIM), was born at Cape May, 5 April, 1882, died at Cape May, 27 January, 1904, married at Cape May, 14 May, 1842, Elizabeth H. Hoffman, born 22 April, 1821, died 13 March, 1893.

Issue:—

(1) ELIZABETH H. HUGHES, born 9 April, 1843, died 16 January, 1872.

(2) JUDITH H. HUGHES, born 4 November, 1844, died 5 January, 1857.

(3) ISRAEL PUTNAM HUGHES, born 14 May, 1846, died 8 January, 1910, married Amanda Clark, and had: WARREN HUGHES, married Frances Atchison, and had GRACE HUGHES, JEAN HUGHES, BLANCHE HUGHES, WARRENA HUGHES, and EDITH HUGHES; BLANCHE HUGHES, married Joseph Stretch, and had BLANCHE STRETCH; FLOYD HUGHES, married Mary Shinn.

(4) JOSEPH WARREN HUGHES, born 5 September, 1850, died March, 1911, married Mary Ella Bass, and had: PERCY V. HUGHES, married Nellie Souder, and had MARY ELLA HUGHES and FRANCIS HUGHES; ELSIE P. HUGHES, married Charles Arnold, and had WARREN ARNOLD and CHARLES ARNOLD; ELIZABETH HUGHES married Andrew Kindberg, and had CARL KINDBERG and ELLA KINDBERG; EDWARD L. HUGHES, married Maude R. Corson, and had GWENDOLYN HUGHES, born 7 August, 1910.

(5) AZELIA HUGHES, born 3 May, 1852, died 1 December, 1912, married Enoch Hitchner, and had: RICHARD HITCHNER, ROYCE HITCHNER, and ELIZABETH HITCHNER, who married Leaming Hand, and had: KENNETH HAND, AZELIA HAND, and NATHALIE HAND. (Enoch J. Hitchner died 1 November, 1920).

(6) RICHARD HUGHES, born 30 May, 1854, died 9 September, 1889.

MATILDA HUGHES

For ancestors leading back to the Mayflower see page 249.

MATILDA HUGHES[8], (Israel Hughes[7], Memucan Hughes[6], Hannah Whilldin[5], Joseph Whilldin[4], Hannah Gorham[3], Desire Howland[2], JOHN HOWLAND[1] THE PILGRIM), was born at Cape May, 6 February, 1817, died at Philadelphia, Pennsylvania, 14 July, 1855, married 1 October, 1835, Paul Barnes, born 9 June, 1805, died at Philadelphia, 5 February, 1860.

Issue:—

(1) PAUL HENRY BARNES, born at Philadelphia, Pennsylvania, 26 May, 1841, died at Billingsport, New Jersey, 8 July, 1896, married at Philadelphia, 17 May, 1864, Mary Maull Maxwell, born at Philadelphia, 15 October, 1840, and had the following children:—MARY EMILY BARNES, born at Philadelphia, 22 October, 1865, deceased; IRENE MATILDA BARNES, born at Philadelphia, 8 August, 1867, deceased; PAUL HENRY BARNES, Jr., born at Philadelphia, 3 January, 1872; ANDREW MAXWELL BARNES, born at Philadelphia, 8 August, 1874, deceased; ELLERSLIE WALLACE BARNES, born at Philadelphia, 8 October, 1880; ALBERT MAULL BARNES, born at Philadelphia, 5 March, 1883.

(2) ISRAEL HUGHES BARNES, died in Civil War.

(3) MARY HUGHES BARNES, married George Stevenson, and had:—GEORGE BARNES STEVENSON, born at Philadelphia, 3 September, 1869; CLARA BRAINERD STEVENSON; HELEN HUGHES STEVENSON; MARY MATILDA STEVENSON.

(4) SARAH MATILDA BARNES, married Samuel Mason Graffen, and had:— CHARLES H. GRAFFEN, born at Philadelphia October, 1871; PAUL BARNES GRAFFEN, born at Philadelphia, 21 April, 1873; GEORGE STEVENSON GRAFFEN, born at Philadelphia, 20 August, 1876.

ELLIS HUGHES

For ancestors leading back to the Mayflower see page 250.

ELLIS HUGHES[8], (Thomas Hurst Hughes[7], Ellis Hughes[6], Hannah Whilldin[5], Joseph Whilldin[4], Hannah Gorham[3], Desire Howland[2], JOHN HOWLAND[1] THE PILGRIM), was born at Cape May, 2 June, 1793, died at Cape May, 1 June, 1863, (tombstone in Cold Spring Cemetery), married first at Cape May, 16 October, 1813, Sarah Higgins (see Session Book of Cold Spring Church in this volume page 46), who was born 1795, died 15 October, 1821; married second Nancy Teal, born 1802, died at Cape May, 7 February, 1869.

Issue:—

(1) ELLIS HUGHES, who married Hester Oram, and had: OLIVE HUGHES, married Samuel Wiley, and had, OLIVE WILEY and HELEN WILEY; EDWARD HUGHES, married Lavina Keeler, and had, PAUL S. HUGHES, who married Grace Childery, and had, MARION HUGHES, born 30 June, 1918, FRANK WILEY HUGHES, (son of EDWARD); SARAH HUGHES, married Lewis Corson, and had, GILBERT CORSON, who married Clara Somers; FRANK HUGHES, deceased; CLINTON HUGHES.

(2) SARAH HUGHES, born 7 January, 1816, married Randolph Marshall, M. D. (For descendants see page 285).

(3) THOMAS H. HUGHES (by second wife), born 27 June, 1827, married first Mary Teal, married second Hannah Grace Corson. (For descendants see page 286).

(4) JOHN HANEY HUGHES, born 9 April, 1834, married first Elizabeth Chew, married second Anna M. Brandriff. (For descendants see page 285).

(5) LYDIA PAIGE HUGHES, born 2 February, 1828, married Philip Hand. (For descendants see page 288).

(6) RICHARD HUGHES.

(7) SMITH HUGHES.

(8) ALBERT HUGHES.

(9) MARTHA HUGHES, died unmarried.

(10) ANNIE HUGHES, born 19 December, 1830, married Edward Hicks Phillips, M. D. (For descendants see page 287).

LYDIA HUGHES

For ancestors leading back to the Mayflower see page 250.

LYDIA HUGHES[8], (Thomas Hurst Hughes[7], Ellis Hughes[6], Hannah Whilldin[5], Joseph Whilldin[4], Hannah Gorham[3], Desire Howland[2], JOHN HOWLAND[1] THE PILGRIM), was born at Cape May, 4 December, 1795, died at Cold Spring 14 December, 1862 (tombstone in Cold Spring Cemetery), married at Cape May, 31 December, 1812, Richard Edmunds, born 22 December, 1785, died at Burlington, New Jersey, 28 October, 1846. (For record of marriage see page 46).

Issue :—

(1) FRANKLIN DAVENPORT EDMUNDS, born 3 June, 1814, married Ann Marshall Stanger. (For descendants see page 290).

(2) RICHARD DOWNS EDMUNDS, born 24 September, 1815, married Jane Stevens. (For descendants see page 291).

(3) THOMAS HUGHES EDMUNDS, born 16 August, 1818, married Mary D. Crane. (For descendants see page 292).

(4) EVAN EDMUNDS, died 16 March, 1885, married ————— Shute, and had son BENJAMIN EDMUNDS.

(5) PARSONS EDMUNDS, born 1 December, 1821, married Catharine Beck Rudiman. (For descendants see page 293).

(6) BENJAMIN EDMUNDS, born 20 May, 1824.

(7) ROBERT EDMUNDS, born 5 June, 1826, married Lydia Marshall. (For descendants see page 294).

(*Continued on Next Page*)

LYDIA HUGHES

(8)   PAGE EDMUNDS, born at Fishing Creek, New Jersey, 6 January, 1828, married Susan Elizabeth Cowart. (For descendants see page 295).

(9)   LYDIA PAGE EDMUNDS, born 18 December, 1829, died at Camden, New Jersey, 7 November, 1905, married first 8 May, 1846, Joseph Perkins, born in Burlington County, New Jersey, 28 February, 1822, died at Skippack, Pennsylvania, 1890.

Children of LYDIA PAGE EDMUNDS and Joseph Perkins her husband:—EMMA PERKINS, married first 30 August, 1866, Henry Augustus Carty, born at Philadelphia, 28 April, 1847, and had HENRY CARTY and CHARLES CARTY; married second Samuel Conway. ANNA C. PERKINS married first 15 September, 1869, Giovanni Patroni, and had ELEANOR PATRONI, married Henry Church Hullinger; EMMA PATRONI; LYDIA PATRONI; BERNARD PATRONI. ANNA C. PERKINS married second Washington Kugler.

LYDIA PAGE EDMUNDS married second John A. Wilson.

(10)   CHARLES CARROL EDMUNDS, born 11 December, 1831, died 18 May, 1897, married 20 February, 1855, Margaret Goeller, born 19 October, 1820, died 8 May, 1909, and had CHARLES CARROLL EDMUNDS, FREDRICA EDMUNDS, FRANCIS HENRY EDMUNDS, and BRISTOL HUBERT EDMUNDS. (See page 296).

(11)   ELEANOR LUDLAM EDMUNDS, born 20 September, 1833, died 24 May, 1911, married MATTHEW WHILLDIN HALL. (For descendants see page 243).

(12)   TRYPHENE CROWELL EDMUNDS, born 26 February, 1835, married first Benjamin Bellangy, married second John Weatherly. (For descendants see page 297).

WILLIAM MATTHEWS

For ancestors leading back to the Mayflower see page 252.

WILLIAM MATTHEWS[8], (Eleanor Hughes[7], Ellis Hughes[6], Hannah Whilldin[5], Joseph Whilldin[4], Hannah Gorham[3], Desire Howland[2], JOHN HOWLAND[1] THE PILGRIM), was born at Cape May, 9 March, 1800, died at Fishing Creek, New Jersey, 31 January, 1874, married first 12 September, 1821, Elizabeth Izard, born at Green Creek, New Jersey, 7 September, 1799, died at Fishing Creek, New Jersey, 25 November, 1827, (tombstones in Cold Spring Cemetery).

Issue:—

(1) RICHARD MATTHEWS, born 9 June, 1823, died 27 December, 1824.

(2) REV. ALBERT MATTHEWS, born at Fishing Creek, New Jersey, 5 January, 1825, died at Vineland, New Jersey, 6 December, 1906, married 19 March, 1847, EMILY LEAMING, and had the following children: WILLIAM L. MATTHEWS, LOTTIE L. MATTHEWS, MARY EMMA MATTHEWS, ALBERT H. MATTHEWS, KATE S. MATTHEWS. (For full record of family see page 300).

(3) RICHARD MATTHEWS 2nd, born at Dias Creek, New Jersey, 16 February, 1827, died at Cold Spring, 27 October, 1915, married first at Cape May, 14 December, 1854, Eliza Hand; married second at Cape May Court House, New Jersey, 18 December, 1864, Sarah Jones Bate, born at Camden, New Jersey, 21 September, 1836, died at Fishing Creek, New Jersey, 8 September, 1909, and had ALBERT J. MATTHEWS, born 25 December, 1865, married 31 October, 1897, Isabella Agnes Miller.

WILLIAM MATTHEWS

For ancestors leading back to the Mayflower see page 252.

WILLIAM MATTHEWS[8], (Eleanor Hughes[7], Ellis Hughes[6], Hannah Whilldin[5], Joseph Whilldin[4], Hannah Gorham[3], Desire Howland[2], JOHN HOWLAND[1] THE PILGRIM), was born at Cape May, 9 March, 1800, died at Fishing Creek, New Jersey, 31 January, 1874, married second at Cape May Court House, New Jersey, 19 October, 1828, Sarah Izard, sister of his first wife, born at Green Creek, New Jersey, 26 November, 1802, died at Fishing Creek, New Jersey, 26 May, 1879, (tombstone in Cold Spring Cemetery).

Issue:—

(1) ELIZABETH MATTHEWS, born at Fishing Creek, New Jersey, 7 July, 1830, married Clayton Sapp. (For descendants see page 301).

(2) WILLIAM HENRY MATTHEWS, born at Fishing Creek, 8 January, 1833, died 2 March, 1919, married Adeline Teal, and had AWILDA MATTHEWS.

(3) ISAAC PAGE MATTHEWS, born at Fishing Creek, 15 November, 1835, died 6 December, 1919, married Abigail Parsons Townsend.

(4) JONATHAN H. MATTHEWS, born at Fishing Creek, 20 July, 1838, married Martha Swain Price. (For descendants see page 302).

(5) SILAS MATTHEWS, born at Fishing Creek, 27 March, 1841, died 28 November, 1914, married JULIA HUGHES. (For descendants see page 146).

(6) CHARLES MATTHEWS, born at Fishing Creek, 7 June, 1844, married Tryphena Teal.

HANNAH MATTHEWS

For ancestors leading back to the Mayflower see page 252.

HANNAH MATTHEWS[8], (Eleanor Hughes[7], Ellis Hughes[6], Hannah Whilldin[5], Joseph Whilldin[4], Hannah Gorham[3], Desire Howland[2], JOHN HOWLAND[1] THE PILGRIM), was born at Fishing Creek, New Jersey, 24 September, 1806, died at Norfolk, Virginia, 11 February, 1875, married at Fishing Creek, 31 May, 1826, Capt. Thomas Page Crowell, born at Fishing Creek, 27 February, 1798, died at Cape May, 16 August, 1876.

Issue :—

(1) DeWITT CLINTON CROWELL, born at Philadelphia, Pennsylvania, 5 February, 1828, died at Norfolk, Virginia, 25 November, 1874, married at Cold Spring, New Jersey, 8 February, 1859, HANNAH A. ELDREDGE[9], (William Eldredge[8], Aaron Eldredge[7], Aaron Eldredge[6], Mercy Leaming[5], Hannah Whilldin[4], Hannah Gorham[3], Desire Howland[2], JOHN HOWLAND[1] THE PILGRIM). (For descendants see page 140).

(2) SARAH VIRGINIA CROWELL, born at Philadelphia, Pennsylvania, 8 November, 1829, died at Philadelphia, 10 June, 1831.

(3 THOMAS MONROE CROWELL, born at Philadelphia, 20 November, 1831, married 2 January, 1860, Hannah I. Shinn.

(4) VIRGINIA CAROLINE CROWELL, born at Philadelphia, 12 July, 1835, died at Philadelphia, 25 January, 1836.

(5) HARRIET CECELIA CROWELL, born at Philadelphia, 16 January, 1837, died 8 February, 1917, married George W. Munson, (no issue).

(6) LYDIA JANE CROWELL, born at Philadelphia, 10 March, 1842, died at Philadelphia, 2 February, 1905, married CAPTAIN ELI DOWNS EDMUNDS. (For descendants see page 303).

(7) EMMA LOUISA CROWELL, born at Philadelphia, 9 November, 1843, died at Houghton, Michigan, 3 April, 1874, married at Norfolk, Virginia, 26 October, 1869, Rev. James Henry Barnard.

ISABELLA MATTHEWS

For ancestors leading back to the Mayflower see page 252.

ISABELLA MATTHEWS[8], (Eleanor Hughes[7], Ellis Hughes[6], Hannah Whilldin[5], Joseph Whilldin[4], Hannah Gorham[3], Desire Howland[2], JOHN HOWLAND[1] THE PILGRIM), was born at Fishing Creek, New Jersey, 9 October, 1813, died at Cape May, 30 June, 1861, married 30 January, 1834, Andrew H. Reeves, born at Cape May, 10 April, 1805, died at Cape May, 6 February, 1875, (tombstone in Cold Spring Cemetery).

Issue :—

(1) CLEMENT B. REEVES, born at Cape May, 20 August, 1835, married HANNAH M. CRESSE. (See page 181).

(2) EMMA R. REEVES, born 22 November, 1837, died 12 May, 1838.

(3) SAMUEL W. REEVES, born 1 October, 1839, died at Philadelphia, Pennsylvania, 1 May, 1904, married TRYPHENA EDMUNDS. (For descendants see page 314).

(4) MARY ELIZABETH REEVES, born at Cape May, 15 July, 1841, married at Cape May, 31 August, 1862, ANTHONY CREESE. (See page 181).

(5) WILLIAM HENRY REEVES, born 17 January, 1843, married ELIZABETH B. EDMUNDS. (For descendants see page 311).

(6) CHARLES CLINTON REEVES, born 1 January, 1845, married Sarah S. Smith, and had ELIZABETH REEVES, JULIA REEVES and ANDREW REEVES.

(7) EMMA JULIA REEVES, born 30 May, 1848, married HENRY ELDREDGE. (For descendants see page 304).

(8) CHARLOTTE REEVES, born 15 October, 1850, married WALTER HAND. (See page 288).

JOHN SCHELLENGER

For ancestors leading back to the Mayflower see page 253.

JOHN SCHELLENGER[9], (Catharine Schenck[8], Zeruiah Hughes[7], Memucan Hughes[6], Hannah Whilldin[5], Joseph Whilldin[4], Hannah Gorham[3], Desire Howland[2], JOHN HOWLAND[1] THE PILGRIM), was born 8 March, 1815, married 25 October, 1835, Mary Davis.

Issue:—

(1) THOMAS BULL SCHELLENGER, born 22 August, 1837, married at Camden, New Jersey, 10 May, 1877, Mary Cloak, and had the following children: JOHN SCHENCK SCHELLENGER, born 7 February, 1880, married 24 June, 1907, Martha Butler; MARTHA SCHELLENGER, born 19 May, 1890, married 9 April, 1913, Harry Yoxal Smyth, and had, ANN YOXAL SMYTH, born 12 June, 1914, MARY EMILY SMYTH, born 17 August, 1916; ANN EMILIA SCHELLENGER, born 17 February, 1897.

(2) VIRGIL DAVIS SCHELLENGER, born 3 August, 1839, died 31 March, 1908, married 5 February, 1865, Emily Garrison, died 21 November, 1910, and had: LEVI SCHELLENGER, died in infancy; BERTHA SCHELLENGER, born 25 December, 1872, married WILLIAM HUDSON THOMPSON, (see page 276), and had, EMILY SCHELLENGER THOMPSON, born 25 July, 1891, who married 30 October, 1914, Gysbertus Rief, and had, VIRGIL SCHELLENGER RIEF, born 2 September, 1915.

(3) MARIA CROWELL SCHELLENGER, born 1842, died at the age of seven years.

(4) MARY ELIZABETH SCHELLENGER, born 24 February, 1847, married Thomas S. Stevens, and had the following children:—

(*Continued on Next Page*)

JOHN SCHELLENGER

Children of MARY ELIZABETH SCHELLENGER and Thomas S. Stevens, her husband:—MELINDA STEVENS, married DANIEL FITHIAN ELDREDGE[10], (Daniel Crowell Eldredge[9], Deborah Whilldin Ware[8], Deborah Whilldin[7], Jonathan Whilldin[6] James Whilldin[5], Joseph Whilldin[4], Hannah Gorham[3], Desire Howland[2], JOHN HOWLAND[1] THE PILGRIM), for children see page 234; CHARLES SMITH STEVENS, married SARAH GENEVIEVE SHEPPARD[10], (Abigail Hughes Leaming[9], Israel Leaming[8], Spicer Leaming[7], Christopher Leaming[6], Christopher Leaming[5], Hannah Whilldin[4], Hannah Gorham[3], Desire Howland[2], JOHN HOWLAND[1] THE PILGRIM), see page 182.

CAROLINE HALL STEVENS, married Franklin West Poynter, and had THOMAS POYNTER and FRANKLIN POYNTER.

(5) ZERUIAH SCHELLENGER, born 14 September, 1848, married Jonathan Crawford Stevens and had the following children:—THOMAS SCHELLENGER STEVENS, married Bessie Townsend, and had: RALPH STEVENS, who married Charlotte Kimball, and had DOROTHY KIMBALL STEVENS; ALFRED STEVENS; HELEN STEVENS and ELIZABETH STEVENS.

MARY STEVENS, married Edward Yeates.

REBECCA MECRAY STEVENS.

(6) MARIA SCHELLENGER, born 25 August, 1850, married Charles W. Corson.

(7) SARAH SCHELLENGER, born 25 January, 1852, married Charles White, and had: HARRIET WHITE, died at the age of seven years; FLORENCE WHITE, who married John Ashcroft, and had, JOHN ASHCROFT and FLORENCE ASHCROFT.

(8) MELINDA SCHELLENGER, born 1857, died in infancy.

(9) JOHN SCHELLENGER, died in infancy.

URIAH SCHENCK

For ancestors leading back to the Mayflower see page 254.

URIAH SCHENCK[9], (William Schenck[8], Zeruiah Hughes[7], Memucan Hughes[6], Hannah Whilldin[5], Joseph Whilldin[4], Hannah Gorham[3], Desire Howland[2], JOHN HOWLAND[1] THE PILGRIM), was born at "Oak Woods," near May's Landing, New Jersey, about 1824, died at Finches Hill, New Jersey, 1851, married Catharine Simpkins.

Issue:—

(1) JOHN SCHENCK, born near May's Landing, New Jersey, 1842, married 1864, Sarah E. Turpin, and had:— PRISCILLA SCHENCK, born 1864; URIAH SCHENCK, born 1866; BLANCHE SCHENCK, born 1868; SARAH SCHENCK, born 1873; KATE SCHENCK, born 1878.

(2) REV. WILLIAM S. SCHENCK, born near May's Landing, New Jersey, 1844, married 1866, Rachel Bounds, and had:—MARY ELLA SCHENCK, born 1867; WILLIAM S. SCHENCK, born 1873; JOHN S. SCHENCK, born 1878; RACHEL S. SCHENCK, born 1882. The REV. WILLIAM S. SCHENCK was pastor of the First Wesleyan Methodist Church at Vineland, New Jersey, in 1883.

(3) MARY SCHENCK, born at Finches Hill, New Jersey, 1846, married 1862, Jonathan Hand.

(4) ZECHERIA SCHENCK, born 1848, died in infancy.

(5) ABIGAIL SCHENCK, born at Finches Hill, New Jersey, 1851, married 1872, George Hunt.

JAMES W. SCHENCK

For ancestors leading back to the Mayflower see page 254.

JAMES W. SCHENCK[9], (William Schenck[8], Zeruiah Hughes[7], Memucan Hughes[6], Hannah Whilldin[5], Joseph Whilldin[4], Hannah Gorham[3], Desire Howland[2], JOHN HOWLAND[1] THE PILGRIM), was born at Oak Hill, near May's Landing, New Jersey, 1826, married 23 December, 1848, Rose Anna or Rosanna Emmell, born 9 February, 1829.

Issue:—

(1) AARON E. SCHENCK, born at Emelville, New Jersey, 30 April, 1849.

(2) ANNA MARIA SCHENCK, born at Emelville, New Jersey, 17 March, 1851, married 10 May, 1874, William Truitt.

(3) LEWIS E. SCHENCK, born at Emelville, New Jersey, 23 August, 1853.

(4) SARAH EMMA SCHENCK, born at Emelville, New Jersey, 8 September, 1855.

(5) WILLIAM W. SCHENCK, born at Emelville, New Jersey, 12 October, 1857.

(6) FRANCES S. SCHENCK, born at Emelville, New Jersey, 28 May, 1861.

(7) SYLVIN EMILY SCHENCK, born at Emelville, New Jersey, 24 August, 1863..

(8) WALTER SCHENCK, born at Emelville, New Jersey, 21 June, 1866.

(9) MARY L. SCHENCK, born at Emelville, New Jersey, 27 April, 1868.

(10) PHILIP SCHENCK, born at Emelville, New Jersey, 26 February, 1873.

For a full account of the Schenck family, see "The Rev. William Schenck—his Ancestry and his Descendants"; compiled by A. D. Schenck, U. S. Army, published at Washington, D. C., 1883.

ROBERT SCHENCK HAND

For ancestors leading back to the Mayflower see page 255.

ROBERT SCHENCK HAND[9], (Nancy Schenck[8], Zeruiah Hughes[7], Memucan Hughes[6], Hannah Whilldin[5], Joseph Whilldin[4], Hannah Gorham[3], Desire Howland[2], JOHN HOWLAND[1] THE PILGRIM), was born at Cape May, 1821, died at Cape May, 20 November, 1878, (tombstone in Cold Spring Cemetery), married at Cape May, 3 December, 1844, JANE LEAMING, (see page 180), who was born at Cape May, 1823, died at Cape May, 9 February, 1875, (tombstone in Cold Spring Cemetery).

Issue :—

(1) MARY JANE HAND, born at Cape May, 23 June, 1846, married James Hand, and had: DANIEL HAND, who married Emma Corson, and had, JAMES HAND and EDITH HAND; WALTER HAND, married Bertha Johnson, and had, LESLIE HAND and MELLA HAND, who married Russell Lyons, and had, JEAN LYONS; WILLIAM E. HAND.

(2) JULIA L. HAND, born at Cape May, 5 September, 1848, married John Kirby, and had: MATTIE KIRBY, who married Louis Washburn, and had, RICHARD WASHBURN; JENNIE KIRBY, and ELLA KIRBY, who married Edgar See.

(3) MELINDA LUDLAM HAND, born at Cape May, 1 September, 1850, married James Swain, and had, LINDA SWAIN.

(4) ELLA HAND, born 8 August, 1852, married Stillwell Eldredge, who died without issue 1 March, 1902, (tombstone in Cold Spring Cemetery).

(5) ROBERT SCHENCK HAND, born at Cape May, 19 March, 1854, married 2 January, 1881, Kate Stelzer Hebenthal, and had: ALICE BROWN HAND, born 21 April, 1882, died 24 May, 1889; Caroline Hebenthal Hand, born 19 September, 1885, married Karl L. Miller.

(6) MILTON HAND, born 11 December, 1856, married Annie Bishop ——he died 24 April, 1918.

(7) WILLIAM FREDERICK HAND, born 2 November, 1859, married Sallie Peterson, and had: SHERWOOD HAND, who married JULIA BLATTNER, and had, DOROTHY EDNA HAND; LINDA HAND.

HENRY HAND

For ancestors leading back to the Mayflower see page 255.

HENRY HAND[9], (Nancy Schenck[8], Zeruiah Hughes[7], Memucan Hughes[6], Hannah Whilldin[5], Joseph Whilldin[4], Hannah Gorham[3], Desire Howland[2] JOHN HOWLAND[1] THE PILGRIM), was born at Cape May, 31 January, 1826, died at Cape May, 7 October, 1897, married at Cape May, 28 September, 1852, Eliza Doak, born at Philadelphia, Pennsylvania, 1 May, 1830.

Issue :—

(1) JOHN M. HAND, born at Cape May, 18 June, 1853, married first, 17 October, 1883, Lillian Eleanor Arnold, who died 14 April, 1912, and had RECOMPENSE ARNOLD HAND, born at Warren, Pennsylvania, 13 April, 1887, married 31 August, 1914, Rose Irene Smart, and had BARBARA HELEN HAND, born at Warren, Pennsylvania, 7 October, 1915; LILLIAN ELEANOR HAND, born at Warren, Pennsylvania, August, 1918. JOHN M. HAND married second Mrs. Hattie Newton.

(2) WILLIAM C. HAND, born at Cape May, 12 December, 1854, died in infancy.

(3) ANNIE T. HAND, born at Cape May, 24 March, 1856, died at Philadelphia, Pennsylvania, 20 September, 1916, married at Cape May, 1 March, 1876, Arthur M. Sidney, and had FLORENCE CUSTIS SIDNEY, at Cape May, 25 October, 1880, died 29 July, 1888.

(*Continued on next page*)

HENRY HAND

(4) LENA D. HAND, born in Minnesota, 9 January, 1859, married at Cape May, 8 September, 1878, George M. Jones, at Camden, New Jersey, and had the following children:

HENRY HAND JONES, born 3 May, 1879, married 3 April, 1905, Florence Woltemate, and had ROBERT HENRY JONES, born 14 February, 1906, died 3 January, 1920, MARION W. JONES, born 12 October, 1910, STEPHEN SCHENCK JONES and ELIZABETH HAND JONES, born 18 January, 1914.

GEORGE HARVEY JONES, born 6 February, 1881.

HELEN CUSTIS JONES, born 1 March, 1883, married 5 December, 1906, Albert W. Woltemate, and had ALBERT W. WOLTEMATE, born at Mt. Airy, Pennsylvania, 17 November, 1908; EDWARD WOLTEMATE, born at Mt. Airy, 14 March, 1912; GEORGE MILLARD WOLTEMATE, born at Mt. Airy, 20 April, 1914; RICHARD CUSTIS WOLTEMATE, born at Mt. Airy, 24 July, 1916.

MILLARD BOEHM JONES, born 17 November, 1890.

(5) GEORGE M. HAND, born at Cape May, 20 August, 1862.

(6) HENRY F. HAND, born at Cape May, 26 October, 1869, died 9 February, 1918, married Emma Bennett, and had one child, died in infancy.

(7) JESSE RAYMOND HAND, born at Cape May, 9 July, 1872, married 25 August, 1906, Clara Florence Sylvus, and had ANNIE SIDNEY HAND, born at New York, 26 May, 1907; FLORENCE SYLVUS HAND, born at Philadelphia, 4 May, 1910.

RECOMPENCE HAND

For ancestors leading back to the Mayflower see page 255.

RECOMPENCE HAND[9], (Nancy Schenck[8], Zeruiah Hughes[7], Memucan Hughes[6], Hannah Whilldin[5], Joseph Whilldin[4], Hannah Gorham[3], Desire Howland[2], JOHN HOWLAND[1] THE PILGRIM), was born at Cape May, 16 March, 1828, married Martha Thompson, born 7 May, 1830.

Issue:—

(1) HARRY B. HAND, born at Cape May, 3 September, 1851, married first at Philadelphia, Pennsylvania, 17 September, 1874, Mary Ella Perkinpine, who died 5 February, 1885, (tombstone in Cold Spring Cemetery); married second 26 June, 1888, Alwilda Fisher. (For descendants see page 305).

(2) ALFRED A. HAND, born at Cape May, 12 December, 1845, married Ada Bennett, and had: ALFRED A. HAND, born at Cape May, 17 November, 1883, married Marie Clemonson, and had, CLEMENS HAND, born 26 July, 1915; CHARLES WAITE HAND, born at Cape May, 24 March, 1890; LENORA HAND, born at Cape May, 3 December, 1892; ROBERT BETTY HAND, born at Cape May, 8 June, 1894; ISABELLE HAND, born at Cape May, 8 March, 1897, married Mellross Denny.

(3) MARY HOWARD HAND, born 27 March, 1862, married Albert H. Perkinpine. (For descendants see page 306).

(4) BELLA HAND, born 5 February, 1864, married 20 May, 1885, George C. Crawford, and had: GEORGE LESLIE CRAWFORD, who married Della Weaver, and had GEORGE LESLIE CRAWFORD; ALBERT PERKINPINE CRAWFORD, born 28 June, 1893.

(5) RICHARD HAND, born at Cape May, 9 February, 1866, married at Cape May, Lillian Robinson, and had: RICHARD HAND, born at Cape May, 13 February, 1890, who married at Cape May, Miranda Stillwell, and had, REBECCA DOAK HAND, born at Cape May, 1 September, 1910; HARRY HAND, born at Cape May, 13 October, 1894, married at Cape May, 23 December, 1917, Jennie Sutton, and had, LIDA DOAK HAND, born at Cape May, 12 December, 1918.

HARRY B. HAND married third, 8 February, 1917, Eliza Stilwell Doak.

ANNIE SCHENCK HAND

For ancestors leading back to the Mayflower see page 255.

ANNIE SCHENCK HAND[9], (Nancy Schenck[8], Zeruiah Hughes[7], Memucan Hughes[6], Hannah Whilldin[5], Joseph Whilldin[4], Hannah Gorham[3], Desire Howland[2], JOHN HOWLAND[1] THE PILGRIM), was born at Cape May, 1832, died at Cape May, 28 April, 1882, (burial in Cold Spring Cemetery), married 19 January, 1851, Richard Ryland Thompson, born 1823, died 19 January, 1878, (burial in Cold Spring Cemetery).

Issue:—

(1) HENRY CLEAVELAND THOMPSON, born 31 October, 1851, married April, 1871, Linda May Kennedy, and had: ANNIE SCHENCK THOMPSON; CHARLOTTE KENNEDY THOMPSON; ELEANOR HUGHES THOMPSON; RICHARD RYLAND THOMPSON; MADGE CLIFFORD THOMPSON, died 2 July, 1887, (burial in Cold Spring Cemetery).

(2) RICHARD H. THOMPSON, born 11 October, 1853, married Sadie Martin, and had, GEORGE THOMPSON and RICHARD THOMPSON.

(3) JOURDAN M. THOMPSON, born 17 October, 1855, married May Clements.

(4) JOHN WEST THOMPSON, born 17 June, 1857, married March 1882, Mary Schellenger, and had:—LOUISE THOMPSON, born 31 April, 1884, who married Walter Fenderson, Jr., and had, ROBERT CARROLL FENDERSON, born 11 February, 1916; FRANCES THOMPSON, born 10 June, 1890; MARIE THOMPSON, born 9 April, 1894.

(5) SAMUEL B. THOMPSON, born 9 April, 1859, deceased.

(6) ANNIE HAND THOMPSON, born 24 November, 1863, died 9 February, 1865.

(7) WILLIAM HUDSON THOMPSON, born 8 January, 1867, married BERTHA SCHELLENGER. (For descendants see page 268).

(8) JOSEPH LUDLAM THOMPSON, born 16 September, 1869.

JOSEPH HAND

For ancestors leading back to the Mayflower see page 255.

JOSEPH HAND[9], (Nancy Schenck[8], Zeruiah Hughes[7], Memucan Hughes[6], Hannah Whilldin[5], Joseph Whilldin[4], Hannah Gorham[3], Desire Howland[2], JOHN HOWLAND[1] THE PILGRIM), was born at Cape May, 21 November, 1841, married 27 January, 1863, JOSEPHINE WARE[9], (Joseph Ware[8], Harriet Whilldin[7], Jonathan Whilldin[6], James Whilldin[5], Joseph Whilldin[4], Hannah Gorham[3], Desire Howland[2], JOHN HOWLAND[1] THE PILGRIM), born at Cape May, 15 October, 1844, died at Cape May, 4 February, 1900, (tombstone in Cold Spring Cemetery). See page 220).

Issue:—

   (1) ALBERT HAND, died in infancy.

   (2) FLORENCE HAND.

   (3) HARRIET HAND, married Richard Ware, and had: FLORENCE FILMORE WARE, who married JESSE OLIVER RUTHERFORD, (see page 328), and CLIFTON WARE. Richard Ware died 7 December, 1919.

   (4) RODNEY PARKER HAND, married Emma Weaver, and had, ALLEN WESTLEY HAND.

   (5) MARION CLEVELAND HAND, married William Hickey.

   (6) HAROLD HAND, married JENNIE CROWELL, and had, HAROLD HAND and RALSTON HAND.

   (7) ARTHUR GARFIELD HAND, died at the age of five years.

   (8) JOSEPH HAND, married Sarah Krause, and had: JOSEPHINE ELIZABETH HAND, born 10 May, 1914; RODNEY PARKER HAND, born 25 May, 1915, his twin sister died at birth); DOROTHY KRAUSE HAND, born 12 August, 1917.

   (9) MILDRED FULLER HAND

For Pilgrim Ancestry of JENNIE CROWELL, see descendants of JANE CRESSE on page 186.

MAYFLOWER DESCENDANTS IN CAPE MAY COUNTY

ACHSAH HAND

For ancestors leading back to the Mayflower see page 256.

ACHSAH HAND[9], (Martha Schenck[8]), Zeruiah Hughes[7], Memucan Hughes[6], Hannah Whilldin[5], Joseph Whilldin[4], Hannah Gorham[3], Desire Howland[2], JOHN HOWLAND[1] THE PILGRIM), was born at Cape May, 1 November, 1823, died 11 September, 1913, married first 28 May, 1840, Walter Dyer Naves, born 2 May, 1820, died at San Francisco, California, 17 November, 1849; married second John W. Wood.

Issue:—

(1) BENJAMIN WALTER NAVES, born 17 February, 1841, died 29 January, 1876, married November 7, 1870, Margaret Agnes Robb, and had the following children:—

MARTHA ACHSAH NAVES, born at Philadelphia, Pennsylvania, 28 September, 1871, married at Philadelphia, Pennsylvania, 23 August, 1894, William Sharpless, and had: MARGARET AGNES SHARPLESS, born at Philadelphia, Pennsylvania, 7 January, 1897; RUTHANNA SHARPLESS, born at Philadelphia, Pennsylvania, 2 May, 1900; MARTHA ACHSAH SHARPLESS, born at Philadelphia, Pennsylvania, 20 October, 1906.

ELIZA R. NAVES, born at Philadelphia, Pennsylvania, 15 March, 1873.

BENJAMIN WALTER NAVES, born at Philadelphia, Pennsylvania, 10 August, 1874, married at Philadelphia, Pennsylvania, 26 September, 1900, Mary Frances Woodhull, and had, CORA GERALDINE NAVES, born at Philadelphia, Pennsylvania, 15 September, 1902; MARTHA FRANCES NAVES, born at Philadelphia, Pennsylvania, 2 September, 1910.

JAMES A. NAVES, born at Philadelphia, Pennsylvania, 29 March, 1876, married at Philadelphia, Pennsylvania, 28 November, 1905, Marie Shur.

(2 and 3) PHILIP NAVES and MARTHA ANN NAVES, born 11 September, 1843.

PHILIP NAVES, died 25 February, 1845; MARTHA ANN NAVES died 22 May, 1870, married ALBERT G. REED BENNETT. (See page 165).

MARTHA ANN HAND

For ancestors leading back to the Mayflower see page 256.

MARTHA ANN HAND[9], (Martha H. Schenck[8], Zeruiah Hughes[7], Memucan Hughes[6], Hannah Whilldin[5], Joseph Whilldin[4], Hannah Gorham[3], Desire Howland[2], JOHN HOWLAND[1] THE PILGRIM), was born at Cape May, 4 December, 1832, died at Cape May, 26 August, 1907, married at Cape May, 10 September, 1852, Alphonzo D. Lee, born at Dennisville, New Jersey, 15 January, 1827.

Issue:—

(1) JULIA ETTA LEE, born at Cape May, 10 March, 1854, married at Cape May, 25 November, 1878, John Henry Ginder, born at Trenton, New Jersey, 1853, died at Chester, Pennsylvania, 5 November, 1917, and had, CHARLES RICHARDSON GINDER, born at Philadelphia, Pennsylvania, 7 September, 1879, who married at Cape May, 23 March, 1903, Arnulda Van Kessel Douglass, born 21 December, 1884, died at West Cape May, New Jersey, 29 August, 1918, and had WILBERT WILLIAM GINDER, born at Cape May, 7 December, 1904, and EARL DOUGLASS GINDER, born at Cape May, 1 April, 1906.

(2) and (3) SARAH LEE and ELIZABETH LEE, born at Cape May, 1 March, 1856, died in infancy.

Arnulda Van Kessel Douglass, wife of CHARLES RICHARDSON GINDER, was the daughter of Freeman and Josephine Schellenger Douglass.

(*Continued on next page*)

(Issue of MARTHA ANN HAND and ALPHONZO D. LEE continued).

(4) LIZZIE HORTENSE LEE, born at Cape May, 1 September, 1858, married at Cape May, 25 November, 1878, Charles Wilbert Richardson, born at Rio Grande, New Jersey, 1853, (deceased), and had MABEL GOBEL RICHARDSON, born 8 October, 1892, married John Thompson Hewitt. (See page 144).

(5) ALEXANDER LEE, born at Cape May, 28 February, 1860, died 5 March, 1860.

(6) and (7) MADELINE NAVES LEE and ANETTA LEE, born at Cape May, 1 March, 1862.

ANETTA LEE died in infancy; MADELINE NAVES LEE married at Cold Spring, New Jersey, William Soph Barnett, born at Cold Spring, New Jersey, 13 May, 1866, and had, OSCAR BARNETT, born at Cold Spring, New Jersey, 11 September, 1891, who married at Jacksonville, Florida, 11 December, 1917, Estelle Whitehead, born at Athens, Georgia, and had MADELENE BARNETT, born at Jacksonville, Florida.

William Soph Barnett, husband of MADELENE NAVES LEE, was the son of Furman and Sarah Hollingsworth Barnett; she (MADELENE NAVES LEE) died 25 February, 1911.

ELLEN MARIA CASSEDY

For ancestors leading back to the Mayflower see page 257.

ELLEN MARIA CASSEDY[9], (Maria Stockton Schenck[8], Zeruiah Hughes[7], Memucan Hughes[6], Hannah Whilldin[5], Joseph Whilldin[4], Hannah Gorham[3], Desire Howland[2], JOHN HOWLAND[1] THE PILGRIM), was born at Cape May, 15 November, 1834, married at Cape May, 12 May, 1853, John Benjamin Sparks, born at Philadelphia, Pennsylvania, 11 February, 1828.

Issue:—

(1) EDWARD SPARKS, born at Cape May, 5 June, 1854, married at Philadelphia, Pennsylvania, 30 May, 1878, Laura Lonsdale West, born at Philadelphia, Pennsylvania, 19 April, 1856, and had: EARL LONSDALE SPARKS, born at Philadelphia, Pennsylvania, 29 November, 1880; STANLEY VAUGH SPARKS, born at Philadelphia, Pennsylvania, 14 November, 1883.

EDWARD SPARKS died at Philadelphia, Pennsylvania, 26 May, 1888.

(2) FRANK A. SPARKS, born at Philadelphia, Pennsylvania, 20 September, 1859, married at Millville, New Jersey, 15 February, 1896, Elizabeth Maylin Newell, born at Millville, New Jersey, 5 May, 1860, and had:—

MARGARET MAYLIN SPARKS, born at Woodbury, New Jersey, 12 January, 1897.

WILLIAM NEWELL SPARKS, born at Leamington, England, 20 December, 1899.

MAYFLOWER DESCENDANTS IN CAPE MAY COUNTY

MARY ANN CASSEDY

For ancestors leading back to the Mayflower see page 257.

MARY ANN CASSEDY[9], (Maria Stockton Schenck[8], Zeruiah Hughes[7], Memucan Hughes[6], Hannah Whilldin[5], Joseph Whilldin[4], Hannah Gorham[3], Desire Howland[2], JOHN HOWLAND[1] THE PILGRIM), was born at Cape May, 27 April, 1836, married at Millville, New Jersey, 20 April, 1858, George Shaw, born at Cumberland, New Jersey, 13 February, 1828.

Issue:—

(1) ALICE R. SHAW, born at Millville, New Jersey, 2 November, 1859, died in infancy.

(2) HARRIET W. SHAW, born at Millville, New Jersey, 27 February, 1861, married at Millville, New Jersey, William C. Loper, died 26 July, 1896, and had WILLIAM STULTZ LOPER, born 26 November, 1890, died in infancy.

(3) GEORGIANNA SHAW, born at Millville, New Jersey, 21 May, 1866, married George H. Hughes, and had the following children:—

EUGENE B. HUGHES, born 6 December, 1888, married Minnie Steffin, and had, DOROTHY J. HUGHES and EUGENE HUGHES.

HARRIET S. HUGHES, born 22 May, 1890, married Charles J. Kauffman, and had CHARLES KAUFFMAN.

HARVEY H. HUGHES, born 22 January, 1892, died young.

WILLIAM C. HUGHES, born 5 August, 1893, married Helen Garrison, and had GEORGE F. HUGHES.

MABEL I. HUGHES, born 31 October, 1894, married Alex McGee.

WILLIAM FRANCIS CASSEDY

For ancestors leading back to the Mayflower see page 257.

WILLIAM FRANCIS CASSEDY[9], (Maria Stockton Schenck[8], Zeruiah Hughes[7], Memucan Hughes[6], Hannah Whilldin[5], Joseph Whilldin[4], Hannah Gorham[3], Desire Howland[2], JOHN HOWLAND[1] THE PILGRIM), was born at Cape May, 26 January, 1843, died at Cape May, 26 July, 1914, married at Cold Spring, New Jersey, 13 March, 1878, Emma L. Willets, born at Green Creek, New Jersey, 12 May, 1852.

Issue:—

(1) FRANK WILLETTS CASSEDY, born at Cape May, 13 July, 1879, married 8 March, 1911, Helen Wales Landis, and had FLORENCE LANDIS CASSEDY, born 5 March, 1912; FRANK W. CASSEDY, born 13 November, 1913.

(2) WILLIAM MORRIS CASSEDY, born at Cape May, 2 August, 1881, married at Gloucester, New Jersey, 24 April, 1916, MARTHA TOMLIN WALES[11], (Westley Rogers Wales[10], Thomas Roger Wales[9], Sarah Hughes[8], Thomas Hurst Hughes[7], Ellis Hughes[6], Hannah Whilldin[5], Joseph Whilldin[4], Hannah Gorham[3], Desire Howland[2], JOHN HOWLAND[1] THE PILGRIM). (See page 317).

(3 REBECCA MECRAY CASSEDY, born at Cape May, 13 September, 1886, married 19 October, 1910, J. HARVEY BENNETT, (see page 241), and had, WILLIAM F. CASSEDY BENNETT, born 26 July, 1911, died in infancy; ROBERT STOCKTON BENNETT, born 24 September, 1913.

SALLIE PENNOCK CASSEDY

For ancestors leading back to the Mayflower see page 257.

SALLIE PENNOCK CASSEDY[9], (Maria Stockton Schenck[8], Zeruiah Hughes[7], Memucan Hughes[6], Hannah Whilldin[5], Joseph Whilldin[4], Hannah Gorham[3], Desire Howland[2], JOHN HOWLAND[1] THE PILGRIM), was born at Cape May, 29 August, 1845, married at Cape May, 13 November, 1867, Enos Roger Williams, born at Wallingford, Pennsylvania, 27 February, 1842, died at Cape May, 14 April, 1895.

Issue :—

(1) LIZZIE WILLIAMS, born 26 August, 1868, died in infancy.

(2) ANNIE CASSEDY WILLIAMS, born 5 September, 1869, married 13 October, 1889, Winfield Scott Boody, and had WINIFRED ROGER BOODY, born 1 April, 1897.

(3) WILLIAM FRANCIS WILLIAMS, born 28 March, 1872, married 4 December, 1901, Sara Irene Melvin, and had FREDERICK MELVIN WILLIAMS, born 7 February, 1904.

(4) HELEN BROWN WILLIAMS, born 10 January, 1881, married 6 November, 1901, Virgil Maro Dow Marcy, M. D., and had, VIRGIL MARO DOW MARCY, born 11 June, 1906.

(5) CHARLES B. WILLIAMS, born 3 December, 1882, died in infancy.

SARAH HUGHES

For ancestors leading back to the Mayflower see page 261.

SARAH HUGHES[9], (Ellis Hughes[8], Thomas Hurst Hughes[7], Ellis Hughes[6], Hannah Whilldin[5], Joseph Whilldin[4], Hannah Gorham[3], Desire Howland[2], JOHN HOWLAND[1] THE PILGRIM), was born at Cape May, 7 January, 1816, married 21 May, 1835, Randolph Marshall, M. D., born at Port Elizabeth, New Jersey, 9 January, 1811, died at Marshallville, New Jersey, 19 February, 1879.

Issue:—

(1) ELLEN MARSHALL, born 6 April, 1836, married Belford Smith.

(2) SARAH MARSHALL, born 7 September, 1838, married Henry S. Steelman, and had, ELLA STEELMAN, DANIEL STEELMAN and JENNIE STEELMAN.

(3) BENJAMIN H. MARSHALL, born 25 September, 1840, married Eliza Ogden, and had HARRIET O. MARSHALL and SARAH H. MARSHALL.

(4) JAMES L. MARSHALL, born 20 January, 1844, married Emma Smith, and had BURROUGHS MARSHALL and EMMA MARSHALL.

(5) ELLIS H. MARSHALL, born 19 September, 1845, married first Hattie Shoemaker and had SARAH H. MARSHALL; married second Lydia Gandy, and had THOMAS MARSHALL.

(6) JOSEPH C. MARSHALL, M. D., born 3 July, 1848.

(7) RANDOLPH MARSHALL, M. D., born 11 June, 1854, married Rae Steelman.

THOMAS H. HUGHES

For ancestors leading back to the Mayflower see page 261.

THOMAS H. HUGHES[9], (Ellis Hughes[8], Thomas Hurst Hughes[7], Ellis Hughes[6], Hannah Whilldin[5], Joseph Whilldin[4], Hannah Gorham[3], Desire Howland[2], John HOWLAND[1] THE PILGRIM), was born at Cape May, 27 June, 1827, died at West Cape May, New Jersey, 13 February, 1913, married first at Cold Spring, New Jersey, 4 July, 1852, Mary Teal; married second at Cold Spring, New Jersey, 8 August, 1870, Hannah Grace Corson.

Issue :—

(1) and (2)   ELI HUGHES and ANNA HUGHES, born 24 September, 1854, died in infancy.

(3)   ALEXANDER HUGHES, born 19 September, 1856, died 10 May, 1879.

(4)   PAULINE HUGHES, born 20 January, 1859, died 3 February, 1862.

(5)   MARY HUGHES, born 5 November, 1871, married 2 October, 1894, Theodore W. Reeves, and had ORION HUGHES REEVES, who married 11 May, 1918, IRENE B. MATTHEWS, and had, DOROTHY BEATRICE REEVES, born 12 August, 1920.   (See page 302).

(6)   GILBERT C. HUGHES, born 29 April, 1874, married 19 October, 1897, HARRIET WHILLDIN STITES[10], (Harriet Whilldin Ware[9], Wilmon W. Ware,[8] Harriet Whilldin[7], Jonathan Whilldin[6], James Whilldin[5], Joseph Whilldin[4], Hannah Gorham[3], Desire Howland[2], JOHN HOWLAND[1] THE PILGRIM). For children see under descendants of HARRIET WHILLDIN WARE, page 221.

(7)   THOMAS HOWARD HUGHES, born 29 May, 1877, died 16 October, 1902, married 19 April, 1901, Juliet Cherry, and had LESLIE C. HUGHES.

(8)   CAROLINE HUGHES, born 29 September, 1880, married 5 October, 1905, Walter R. Smith, and had WALTER RAYMOND SMITH, born 2 July, 1908.

JOHN HANEY HUGHES

For ancestors leading back to the Mayflower see page 261.

JOHN HANEY HUGHES[9], (Ellis Hughes[8], Thomas Hurst Hughes[7], Ellis Hughes[6], Hannah Whilldin[5], Joseph Whilldin[4], Hannah Gorham[3], Desire Howland[2], JOHN HOWLAND[1] THE PILGRIM), was born at Cape May, 9 April, 1834, died at Cape May, (tombstone in Cold Spring Cemetery), married first at Cape May, 24 September, 1853, Elizabeth Chew, married second, 1 November, 1871, Anna Maria Brandriff, born 1832.

Issue:—

(1) ROBERT CHEW HUGHES, born at Iona, New Jersey, 17 May, 1856, married at Trenton, New Jersey, 4 May, 1881, Sarah Cresse. (For descendants see page 321).

(2) LUCRISSA HUGHES, born at The Lake, New Jersey, 1858, married at Cape May, 2 March, 1882, Stephen Reeves, born at Port Elizabeth, New Jersey, 12 March, 1856, and had: THOMAS M. REEVES, born at Port Elizabeth, New Jersey, 31 January, 1883, married at Cape May, Mary McIntyre, and had ELIZABETH L. REEVES; FRANK B. F. REEVES, born at Cape May, 27 February, 1888.

(3) LENA HUGHES, born at The Lake, New Jersey, 17 May, 1861, married at Cape May, 2 November, 1880, William G. Blattner, born at Philadelphia, Pennsylvania, 27 November, 1857, and had:—ELIZABETH BLATTNER, married Dr. Reu Hand; ETHEL BLATTNER; JULIA BLATTNER, married SHERWOOD H. HAND, and had, DOROTHY EDNA HAND; ROBERT BLATTNER. (For Pilgrim Ancestry of SHERWOOD H. HAND, see page 272).

LYDIA PAIGE HUGHES

For ancestors leading back to the Mayflower see page 261.

LYDIA PAIGE HUGHES[9], (Ellis Hughes[8], Thomas Hurst Hughes[7], Ellis Hughes[6], Hannah Whilldin[5], Joseph Whilldin[4], Hannah Gorham[3], Desire Howland[2], JOHN HOWLAND[1] THE PILGRIM), was born at Cape May, 2 February, 1828, died at West Cape May, New Jersey, 28 September, 1895, married PHILIP HAND[9], (Martha H. Schenck[8], Zeruiah Hughes[7], Memucan Hughes[6], Hannah Whilldin[5], Joseph Whilldin[4], Hannah Gorham[3], Desire Howland[2], JOHN HOWLAND[1] THE PILGRIM), born at Cape May, 6 June, 1824, died at West Cape May, New Jersey, 7 December, 1888, (tombstone in Cold Spring Cemetery). (See page 256).

Issue:—

(1) WALTER NAVES HAND, born at West Cape May, 1848, died 23 May, 1918, married CHARLOTTE M. REEVES, (see page 267), who died 14 February, 1913.

(2) IDA HAND, born at West Cape May, 8 July, 1852, died at West Cape May, 20 January, 1912, married at West Cape May, 14 December, 1879, Benjamin Jevon Savage, born at Staffordshire, England, 26 March, 1850, and had:—WALTER HAND SAVAGE, born at West Cape May, 19 January, 1881, married at West Cape May, 5 October, 1909, Sara Ann Land, born at Cape May, 9 July, 1882, and had, WALTER BENJAMIN SAVAGE, born 2 August, 1912, IDA ELIZABETH SAVAGE, born 21 March, 1914; ANNA PHILLIP SAVAGE, born 25 December, 1884, died in infancy.

(3) NELLIE LUDLAM HAND, born at West Cape MAY, 24 November, 1855.

ANNIE HUGHES

For ancestors leading back to the Mayflower see page 261.

ANNIE HUGHES[9], (Ellis Hughes[8], Thomas Hurst Hughes[7], Ellis Hughes[6], Hannah Whilldin[5], Joseph Whilldin[4], Hannah Gorham[3], Desire Howland[2], JOHN HOWLAND[1] THE PILGRIM), was born at Cape May, 19 December, 1839, married at West Cape May, New Jersey, 24 September, 1868, Edward Hicks Phillips, M. D., born at Middletown township, Neshaminy Falls, Bucks County, Pennsylvania, 7 April, 1832, died at Cape May, 20 September, 1908, (tombstone in Cold Spring Cemetery).

Issue:—

(1)   WALTER HAND PHILLIPS, M. D., born at Cape May, 17 October, 1869, married 7 October, 1909, May Hackett, born at Scranton, Pennsylvania, 6 October, 1882.

(2)   EDWARD DOUGLASS PHILLIPS, born at Cape May, 14 March, 1871, married 10 January, 1891, Ella Ewing. (For descendants see page 307).

(3)   ALBERT HUGHES PHILLIPS, born at Patterson, New Jersey, 24 February, 1873, married 22 November, 1898, Cora B. Garretson, born at Cape May Court House, 13 December, 1876.

(4)   WILLIAM BAMBER PHILLIPS, born at Cape May, 10 October, 1880, married November, 1909, Elizabeth Cochran.

FRANKLIN DAVENPORT EDMUNDS

For ancestors leading back to the Mayflower see page 262.

FRANKLIN DAVENPORT EDMUNDS[9], (Lydia Hughes[8], Thomas Hurst Hughes[7], Ellis Hughes[6], Hannah Whilldin[5], Joseph Whilldin[4], Hannah Gorham[3], Desire Howland[2], JOHN HOWLAND[1] THE PILGRIM), was born at Fishing Creek, New Jersey, 3 June, 1814, died at Philadelphia, Pennsylvania, 4 February, 1859, married at Port Elizabeth, New Jersey, 24 November, 1836, Ann Marshall Stanger, born at Marshallville, New Jersey, 11 February, 1815, died at Philadelphia, Pennsylvania, 18 March, 1897.

Issue:—

(1) HANNAH STANGER EDMUNDS, born at Philadelphia, 12 August, 1838, died at Westville, New Jersey, 6 January, 1903, married Philip Goeller.

(2) HENRY REEVES EDMUNDS, born at Philadelphia, 17 January, 1840, married Anna Hunter Welsh. (For descendants see page 308).

(3) MARY JANE EDMUNDS, born 19 April, 1843, married Joel Cook. (For descendants see page 309).

(4) FREDERICK STANGER EDMUNDS, born at Tuckahoe, New Jersey, 7 May, 1845, died at Plymouth Township, Montgomery County, Pennsylvania, 11 November, 1907, married at Philadelphia, Pennsylvania, 27 March, 1873, Mary Ann Okill, born at Philadelphia, Pennsylvania, 1 November, 1850, and had:—ALICE MAY EDMUNDS, born 17 April, 1874, married 27 October, 1897, Clarence Arlington Weaver, M. D., born 19 January, 1871.

(5) RICHARD EDMUNDS, born 21 March, 1847, married Mary Elizabeth Irwin. (For descendants see page 326).

(6) ALEXANDER FRANKLIN EDMUNDS, born 14 September, 1850, died in infancy.

RICHARD DOWNS EDMUNDS

For ancestors leading back to the Mayflower see page 262.

RICHARD DOWNS EDMUNDS[9], (Lydia Hughes[8], Thomas Hurst Hughes[7], Ellis Hughes[6], Hannah Whilldin[5], Joseph Whilldin[4], Hannah Gorham[3], Desire Howland[2], JOHN HOWLAND[1] THE PILGRIM), was born 24 September, 1815, died at Cape May, 8 October, 1879, (tombstone in Cold Spring Cemetery), married Jane Stevens, born at Cape May, 27 September, 1814, died at Cape May, 21 April, 1883, (tombstone in Cold Spring Cemetery).

Issue:—

(1) SARAH JANE EDMUNDS, born at Philadelphia, Pennsylvania, 13 December, 1837, died at Philadelphia, Pennsylvania, 20 March, 1901, married at Cold Spring, New Jersey, 2 January, 1859, Daniel Furman Crowell, born 31 March, 1832, and had JAMES FRANK CROWELL; JULIA HUNT CROWELL; MARIA SMITH CROWELL; ALBERT EDMUNDS CROWELL. (For descendants see page 298).

(2) RICHARD HENRY EDMUNDS, born 17 April, 1839, died in infancy.

(3) ALBERT STEVENS EDMUNDS, born 7 May, 1840, died at Battle of Fredricksburg, 13 December, 1862.

(4) MIRANDA SEYBERT EDMUNDS, born at Cold Spring, New Jersey, 21 January, 1842, married Courtland Van Ransalaer Reeves. (For descendants see page 310).

(5) VIRGINIA D. EDMUNDS, born 1 May, 1844, died in infancy.

(6) RICHARD EZEKIEL EDMUNDS, born 3 September, 1945, died in infancy.

(7) JAMES HENRY EDMUNDS, born 7 August, 1847, married Georgeanna Cummings, and had LOUISA S. EDMUNDS.

(8) ELIZABETH BATEMAN EDMUNDS, born 28 March, 1849, married first William Henry Reeves, married second John Woolson Reeves. (For descendants see page 311).

THOMAS HUGHES EDMUNDS

For ancestors leading back to the Mayflower see page 262.

THOMAS HUGHES EDMUNDS[9], (Lydia Hughes[8], Thomas Hurst Hughes[7], Ellis Hughes[6], Hannah Whilldin[5], Joseph Whilldin[4], Hannah Gorham[3], Desire Howland[2], JOHN HOWLAND[1] THE PILGRIM), was born 16 August, 1818, died 13 January, 1857, married Mary Dorsett Crane, born at Richmond, Virginia, 29 May, 1814, died at Baltimore, Maryland, 24 December, 1864.

Issue:—

(1) MARY LYDIA EDMUNDS, born at Baltimore, Maryland, 5 February, 1841, married first at Baltimore, Maryland, 11 May, 1863, Moreau Forrest Frush, born in Maryland, 3 August, 1841, died at Hamstead, Maryland, 6 April, 1864, and had MOREAU FORREST FRUSH; married second at Baltimore, Maryland, 18 September, 1874, Charles Merwyn Young, born at York, Pennsylvania, 20 February, 1850, died at Baltimore, Maryland, 12 December, 1889, and had CHARLES MERWYN YOUNG.

(2) WILLIAM THOMAS EDMUNDS, born 27 September, 1842, died 6 December, 1863, (supposed to have been drowned).

(3) JOSEPHINE ISABEL EDMUNDS, born 5 September, 1844, died in infancy.

(4) JAMES RICHARD EDMUNDS, born 22 April, 1846, married Anna Keyser. (For descendants see page 312).

(5) JOSEPHINE MANSELL EDMUNDS, born at Richmond, Virginia, 2 September, 1852.

(6) CHARLES HUGHES EDMUNDS, born 24 October, 1853, died in infancy.

(7) HARRIET CRANE EDMUNDS, born 10 July, 1854, married William Seal Reins, and had WILLIAM EDMUNDS REINS, born 1 March, 1899.

PARSONS EDMUNDS

For ancestors leading back to the Mayflower see page 262.

PARSONS EDMUNDS[9], (Lydia Hughes[8], Thomas Hurst Hughes[7] Ellis Hughes[6], Hannah Whilldin[5], Joseph Whilldin[4], Hannah Gorham[3], Desire Howland[2], JOHN HOWLAND[1] THE PILGRIM), was born at Fishing Creek, New Jersey, 1 December, 1821, married at Philadelphia, Pennsylvania, 7 March, 1847, Catharine Beck Ruddiman, who died at Philadelphia, Pennsylvania, 20 June 1898.

Issue :—

(1) HELEN RUDDIMAN EDMUNDS, born at Philadelphia, Pennsylvania, 23 October, 1847.

(2) MARY RUDDIMAN EDMUNDS, born at Philadelphia, 12 June, 1849, married first 14 August, 1872, George Washington Collins, married second 3 July, 1890, Charles Walter Stanton, born at Philadelphia, Pennsylvania, 18 March, 1860.

(3) LYDIA HUGHES EDMUNDS, born at Philadelphia, Pennsylvania, 16 June, 1851, married at Philadelphia, Pennsylvania, 16 May, 1872, Thomas Joseph Ogden, born at Philadelphia, Pennsylvania, 29 May, 1850, and had, ELLA MAY OGDEN, born 21 April, 1873; PARSONS EDMUNDS OGDEN, born 15 August, 1875; WILLIAM HENRY RUDDIMAN OGDEN, born 23 May, 1877; WALTER TAYLOR OGDEN, born 6 September, 1879; CLARE M. OGDEN, born 2 January, 1882; KATHARINE EDMUNDS OGDEN, born 9 January, 1884; THOMAS JOSEPH OGDEN, born 13 March, 1894. (For descendants see page 299).

(4) JOHN DUNLEAVY EDMUNDS, born 24 October, 1854, died in infancy.

Catharine Beck Ruddiman, wife of Parsons Edmunds, was the daughter of William Henry and Mary Dunleavy Ruddiman.

MAYFLOWER DESCENDANTS IN CAPE MAY COUNTY

ROBERT EDMUNDS

For ancestors leading back to the Mayflower see page 262.

ROBERT EDMUNDS[9], (Lydia Hughes[8], Thomas Hurst Hughes[7], Ellis Hughes[6], Hannah Whilldin[5], Joseph Whilldin[4], Hannah Gorham[3], Desire Howland[2], JOHN HOWLAND[1] THE PILGRIM), was born at Fishing Creek, New Jersey, 6 June, 1826, died at Norristown, Pennsylvania, 31 July, 1905, married at Tuckahoe, New Jersey, 17 September, 1845, Lydia Marshall, born at Absecon, New Jersey, 20 March, 1826.

Issue:—

(1) MARY GANDY EDMUNDS, born at Tuckahoe, New Jersey, 24 November, 1846.

(2) HANNAH CORSON EDMUNDS, born 30 June, 1849, married at Norristown, Pennsylvania, 15 August, 1879, Elwood Conrad, born 27 August, 1844, and had: FRANK EDMUNDS CONRAD, born 15 February, 1880, married 10 August, 1911, Evelyn Woodman; JENNIE NEWCOMB CONRAD, born 2 December, 1882; LYDIA EDMUNDS CONRAD, born 20 May, 1885; MARY EDMUNDS CONRAD, born 15 June, 1887; ALICE GILBERT CONRAD, born 3 March, 1892, died 18 March, 1894.

(3 SARAH HUGHES EDMUNDS, born 11 March, 1853, married at Norristown, 18 May, 1881, Frederick Gilbert, born 18 June, 1852, and had ALICE EDMUNDS GILBERT, who married Joseph Earle, and MARGUERITE GILBERT.

(4) MELVINA WILLITS EDMUNDS, born 3 January, 1855, died 22 July, 1859.

(5) JOHN CORSON EDMUNDS, born at Tuckahoe, New Jersey, 18 November, 1856, married at Aura, Gloucester County, New Jersey, 5 January, 1878, Hannah Iredell, born at Hardingville, New Jersey, 22 May, 1853.

(6) THOMAS MARSHALL EDMUNDS, born at Marshallville, New Jersey, 11 December, 1858, married 13 May, 1887, Ruth Pierson Casper, and had: LINDA M. EDMUNDS, who married Warren L. Edwards; HELEN M. EDMUNDS, JULIA W. EDMUNDS,

(7) ROBERT EDMUNDS, born 20 February, 1862, married Anna K. Snyder, and had MABEL CHRISTINE EDMUNDS.

294

PAGE EDMUNDS

For ancestors leading back to the Mayflower see page 263.

PAGE EDMUNDS[9], (Lydia Hughes[8], Thomas Hurst Hughes[7], Ellis Hughes[6], Hannah Whilldin[5], Joseph Whilldin[4], Hannah Gorham[3], Desire Howland[2], JOHN HOWLAND[1] THE PILGRIM), was born at Fishing Creek, New Jersey, 6 January, 1828, died at Baltimore, Maryland, 2 December, 1893, married at Northumberland County, Virginia, 1853, Susan Elizabeth Cowart, born at Baltimore, Maryland, 9 September, 1833.

Issue:—

(1) LYDIA LETITIA EDMUNDS, born 19 November, 1854, married 1 May, 1877, John Traverse Kirwan, and had:— WALTER CLIFTON KIRWAN, born 19 February, 1879; LAVINIA L. KIRWAN, born 6 November, 1881; ROBERT EDMUNDS KIRWAN, born 4 May, 1882; MARY COWART KIRWAN, born 20 May, 1884; SUSAN ELIZABETH KIRWAN, born 30 June, 1887.

(2) LEILA VIRGINIA EDMUNDS, born at Northumberland County, Virginia, 26 April, 1858, married at Baltimore, Maryland, 16 June, 1892, John David Galloway, and had JENNIE EDMUNDS GALLOWAY, born at Baltimore, Maryland, 14 August, 1893.

(3) WILLIAM COWART EDMUNDS, born at Northumberland County, Virginia, 24 August, 1860, married at Baltimore, Maryland, 12 January, 1887, Mildred Russ Lewis, and had COWART ROLAND EDMUNDS, born at Baltimore, 12 December, 1888, and MILDRED LEWIS EDMUNDS, born at Baltimore, November, 1899.

(4) SUSAN MAY EDMUNDS, born at Northumberland County, Maryland, 7 May, 1865, married at Baltimore, Maryland, 26 June, 1900, Daniel Boone Chambers, and had BENJAMIN CHAMBERS, born at Baltimore, 1 October, 1901.

(5) PAGE EDMUNDS, born 9 April, 1872, married at Cumberland, Maryland, 30 May, 1907, Millicent Geare, born in England, 23 October, 1883.

CHARLES CARROLL EDMUNDS

For ancestors leading back to the Mayflower see page 263.

CHARLES CARROLL EDMUNDS[9], (Lydia Hughes[8], Thomas Hurst Hughes[7], Ellis Hughes[6], Hannah Whilldin[5], Joseph Whilldin[4], Hannah Gorham[3], Desire Howland[2], JOHN HOWLAND[1] THE PILGRIM), was born 11 December, 1831, died 18 May, 1897, married 20 February, 1855, Margaret Goeller, born 19 October, 1829, died 8 May, 1909.

Issue :—

(1) REV. CHARLES CARROLL EDMUNDS, born at Green Bay, Wisconsin, 18 June, 1858, married at Johnstown, New York, 2 June, 1881, Mary Dudley, born at Johnstown, New York, 19 December, 1859, and had the following children: MARGARET MARIA EDMUNDS, born at Fort Edward, New York, 19 August, 1883, married at Newark, New Jersey, 8 January, 1907, William Young Webbe, born at Newark, New Jersey, 18 June, 1882, and had, CHARLES EDMUND WEBBE and GALE DUDLEY WEBBE; KATHARINE EDMUNDS, born 24 May, 1887; MARY DUDLEY EDMUNDS, born 30 May, 1889; FRANCIS DUDLEY EDMUNDS, born 7 May, 1891; EDGAR BERNARD EDMUNDS, born 11 December, 1892; ANNA FREDERICA EDMUNDS, born 26 December, 1894.

(2) FREDERICA EDMUNDS, born 28 June, 1860.

(3) FRANCIS HENRY EDMUNDS, born 3 April, 1865, married 1 October, 1890, Olive May, and had ROBERTA MAY EDMUNDS, born 23 July, 1891, and CHARLES CARROLL EDMUNDS, born 8 November, 1893.

(4) BRISTOL HUBERT EDMUNDS, died in infancy.

TRYPHENE CROWELL EDMUNDS

For ancestors leading back to the Mayflower see page 263.

TRYPHENE CROWELL EDMUNDS[9], (Lydia Hughes[8], Thomas Hughes[7], Ellis Hughes[6], Hannah Whilldin[5], Joseph Whilldin[4], Hannah Gorham[3], Desire Howland[2], JOHN HOWLAND[1] THE PILGRIM), was born at Philadelphia, 26 February, 1835, died at Camden, New Jersey, 1 August, 1883, married first Benjamin Bellangy, born at Wilmington, Delaware, 26 April, 1832, died at Wilmington.

Issue :—

(1) CHARLES BELLANGY, born at Cape May, 3 March, 1857, married first at Cape May, 10 September, 1876, Ellen Montague, and had: HENRY EDMUNDS BELLANGY, born at Cape May, 7 March, 1878, married ETTA MAY BENNETT, (see page 166); SARAH A. BELLANGY, born at Cape May, 28 October, 1880, married Samuel A. Connelly, and had CHARLOTTE RUTH CONNELLY and PAUL BELLANGY CONNELLY; ELLA BELLANGY, married Galen Green; MARY ADELAIDE BELLANGY; CHARLES BELLANGY, married second at Cape May, 23 November, 1898, Lucy Norton.

(2) KATHERINE BELLANGY, born at Cape May, 14 April, 1853, married John Getty.

(3) JOHN BELLANGY, married Susan Smith.

TRYPHENE CROWELL EDMUNDS married second John Weatherly.

Issue by second marriage :—

(1) ANN WEATHERLY.
(2) MARY WEATHERLY, born at Atlantic City, New Jersey, 26 July, 1875.

MAYFLOWER DESCENDANTS IN CAPE MAY COUNTY

SARAH JANE EDMUNDS

For ancestors leading back to the Mayflower see page 291.

SARAH JANE EDMUNDS[10], (Richard Downs Edmunds[9], Lydia Hughes[8], Thomas Hurst Hughes[7], Ellis Hughes[6], Hannah Whilldin[5], Joseph Whilldin[4], Hannah Gorham[3], Desire Howland[2], JOHN HOWLAND[1] THE PILGRIM), was born at Philadelphia, Pennsylvania, 13 December, 1837, died at Philadelphia, Pennsylvania, 20 March, 1901, married at Cold Spring, New Jersey, 2 January, 1859, Daniel Furman Crowell, born 31 March, 1832.

Issue:—

(1) JAMES FRANK CROWELL, born 10 January, 1860, married 15 October, 1884, Sarah J. Simpson, and had: THOMAS MILLET CROWELL, born 9 August, 1886; GEORGEANNA EDMUNDS CROWELL, born 4 August, 1887, married G. Collins Stratton, and had, GEORGE COLLINS STRATTON, JAMES CROWELL STRATTON, DOROTHY STRATTON.

(2) JULIA HUNT CROWELL, born at Cape May, 27 January, 1867, died at Cape May, 8 September, 1868.

(3) MARIA SMITH CROWELL, born at Cape May, 11 January, 1869, married at Cape May, 3 January, 1894, John Wheriot Cox, who was born at Washington, North Carolina, 28 May, 1869, (son of Ross and Sarah Louisa Keech Cox), and had: LOUISA EDMUNDS COX, born 19 July, 1898; ELEANOR CROWELL COX, born at Cape May, 16 August, 1903.

(4) ALBERT EDMUNDS CROWELL, born at Cape May, 28 November, 1871, married at Vineland, New Jersey, 27 June, 1900, Marie Pearl Cooper, born at Riverhead, Long Island, 19 January, 1875, (daughter of William Bramwell and Emilia Hobart Cooper), and had, MARION HOBART CROWELL, born at Laurel Springs, New Jersey, 21 February, 1905.

MAYFLOWER DESCENDANTS IN CAPE MAY COUNTY

LYDIA HUGHES EDMUNDS

For ancestors leading back to the Mayflower see page 293.

LYDIA HUGHES EDMUNDS[10], (Parsons Edmunds[9], Lydia Hughes[8], Thomas Hurst Hughes[7], Ellis Hughes[6], Hannah Whilldin[5], Joseph Whilldin[4], Hannah Gorham[3], Desire Howland[2], JOHN HOWLAND[1] THE PILGRIM), was born at Philadelphia, 16 June, 1851, married at Philadelphia, Pennsylvania, 16 May, 1872, Thomas Joseph Ogden, born at Philadelphia, Pennsylvania, 29 May, 1850.

Issue:—
(1) ELLA MAY OGDEN, born at Philadelphia, Pennsylvania, 21 April, 1873, married at Philadelphia, Pennsylvania, 8 April, 1895, Robert Patton, born 9 September, 1873, (son of John and Agnes Stickler Patton), and had, ROBERT WALTER PATTON, born at Philadelphia, Pennsylvania, 21 November, 1897.
(2) PARSONS EDMUNDS OGDEN, born at Philadelphia, Pennsylvania, 15 August, 1875, died at Philadelphia, Pennsylvania, 2 July, 1876.
(3) WILLIAM HENRY RUDDIMAN OGDEN, born at Philadelphia, Pennsylvania, 23 May, 1877, married 26 September, 1903, Estella Davis, born at Magnolia, New Jersey, 18 November, 1877, (daughter of John and Anna Ogg Davis), and had: KATHARINE EDMUNDS OGDEN, born at Lindenwold, New Jersey, 24 October, 1904; ELLA MARY OGDEN, born 1907.
(4) WALTER TAYLOR OGDEN, born at Philadelphia, Pennsylvania, 6 September, 1879.
(5) CLARA MAULL OGDEN, born at Philadelphia, Pennsylvania, 2 January, 1882, married at Haddonfield, New Jersey, 30 May, 1904, Henry Moore,.
(6) KATHARINE EDMUNDS OGDEN, born at Philadelphia, Pennsylvania, 9 January, 1884, married at Lindenwold, New Jersey, 31 October, 1906, William Pratt Braddock, born at Lindenwold, New Jersey, 1 March, 1886, (son of Isaiah Norcross and Hannah Edwards Pratt Braddock), and had: WALTER ISAIAH BRADDOCK, born 8 October, 1907, died 7 December, 1908.
(7) THOMAS JOSEPH OGDEN, born at Philadelphia, Pennsylvania, 13 March, 1894, died 3 July, 1911.

REV. ALBERT MATTHEWS

For ancestors leading back to the Mayflower see page 264.

REV. ALBERT MATTHEWS[9], (William Matthews[8], Eleanor Hughes[7], Ellis Hughes[6], Hannah Whilldin[5], Joseph Whilldin[4], Hannah Gorham[3], Desire Howland[2], JOHN HOWLAND[1] THE PILGRIM), was born at Fishing Creek, New Jersey, 5 January, 1825, died at Vineland, New Jersey, 5 December, 1906, married 19 March, 1847, EMILY LEAMING, born 5 February, 1822, died 13 January, 1908. (See page 144 for the Pilgrim Ancestry of EMILY LEAMING).

Issue:—

(1) WILLIAM L. MATTHEWS, born 5 June, 1849, died 10 July, 1910, married November, 1876, Kate Allard, who died 14 July, 1911, and had ETHEL L. MATTHEWS, born October, 1892, died December, 1895.

(2) LOTTIE L. MATTHEWS, born 5 July, 1852, died 28 May, 1908.

(3) MARY EMMA MATTHEWS, born 4 September, 1854, married 21 December, 1881, L. S. Parvin, and had' EDNA L. PARVIN, born 36 December, 1882; GUSSIE H. PARVIN, born 4 July, 1885; ALBERT M. PARVIN, born 21 May, 1895.

(4) ALBERT H. MATTHEWS, born 30 May, 1857,, married October, 1895, May Sutton, and had EVA H. MATTHEWS, born May, 1896.

(5) KATE S. MATTHEWS, born 15 March, 1862, died 24 August, 1862.

ELIZABETH MATTHEWS

For ancestors leading back to the Mayflower see page 265.

ELIZABETH MATTHEWS[9], (William Matthews[8], Eleanor Hughes[7], Ellis Hughes[6], Hannah Whilldin[5], Joseph Whilldin[4], Hannah Gorham[3], Desire Howland[2], JOHN HOWLAND[1] THE PILGRIM), was born at Fishing Creek, New Jersey, 7 July, 1830, married in Cape May County, 8 November, 1853, Clayton G. Sapp, born in Cape May County, 24 March, 1831. Issue:—

(1) SARAH E. SAPP, born at Fishing Creek, New Jersey, 4 January, 1856, married at Fishing Creek, New Jersey, 6 November, 1876, Martin F. Harris, and had GERTRUDE JOHNSON HARRIS, born 29 May, 1880, married 10 August, 1899, J. Chester McWilliams; PEARLA M. HARRIS, born 12 June, 1895.

(2) ROXANNA S. SAPP, born at Fishing Creek, New Jersey, 10 May, 1858, married at Cold Spring, New Jersey, 25 December, 1877, Alva Eldredge, and had: CLAYTON S. ELDREDGE, born 15 May, 1887, married October, 1914, Nellie Peterson; ELLA T. ELDREDGE, born at Fishing Creek, New Jersey, 9 September, 1881, married June, 1900, Edward Taylor.

(3) ELMIRA T. SAPP, born at Green Creek, New Jersey, 1 June, 1861, married 26 November, 1884, Wilbert Davis, and had: MAUD E. DAVIS, born 20 February, 1886, married 26 November, 1914, Charles Wood; LINWOOD DAVIS, born 13 September, 1890, married 14 February, 1908, Carrie Fisher.

JONATHAN H. MATTHEWS

For ancestors leading back to the Mayflower see page 265.

JONATHAN H. MATTHEWS[9], (William Matthews[8], Eleanor Hughes[7], Ellis Hughes[6], Hannah Whilldin[5], Joseph Whilldin[4], Hannah Gorham[3], Desire Howland[2], JOHN HOWLAND[1] THE PILGRIM), was born at Fishing Creek, New Jersey, 20 July, 1838, married 16 June, 1860, Martha Swain Price, daughter of Rev. John Price, of Cold Spring, New Jersey.

Issue:—

(1) MARY ELIZABETH MATTHEWS, born at Cape May, 6 September, 1861, died at Cape May, 18 February, 1886, married at Cape May, 1 January, 1882, Larder Furman Smith, born at Port Republic, Atlantic County, New Jersey, 8 October, 1854, and had: MARY ELIZABETH SMITH, who married at Cape May, 16 April, 1916, Augustus Stiefel.

(2) FRANKLIN H. MATTHEWS, born 29 July, 1864, died 20 February, 1902, married Mary C. Rosebaum, and had: ANNA MATTHEWS, born 7 July, 1887, who married Evert Mattox, of Camden, New Jersey.

(3) WILLIAM PRICE MATTHEWS, born 29 December, 1871, married CLARA HUGHES, of West Cape May, and had, IRENE B. MATTHEWS, born 9 December, 1895, who married 11 May, 1918, ORION HUGHES REEVES[11], (Mary Hughes[10], Thomas H. Hughes[9], Ellis Hughes[8], Thomas Hurst Hughes[7], Ellis Hughes[6], Hannah Whilldin[5], Joseph Whilldin[4], Hannah Gorham[3], Desire Howland[2], JOHN HOWLAND[1] THE PILGRIM). (See page 286, and also 167).

(4) JENNIE E. MATTHEWS, born 6 June, 1875, married at Cape May, 20 November, 1897, Charles S. Craig, and had: FREDERICK C. CRAIG, born 10 December, 1899; ASHTON MATTHEWS CRAIG, born 15 March, 1912.

(5) JONATHAN H. MATTHEWS, born 8 August, 1878, married Florence Tuttle, (deceased) and had, THELMA MATTHEWS, born 27 May, 1900; he married second Anna Sheppard.

(6) WALTER SCOTT MATTHEWS, born 9 January, 1883, died in infancy.

LYDIA JANE CROWELL

For ancestors leading back to the Mayflower see page 266.

LYDIA JANE CROWELL[9], (Hannah Matthews[8], Eleanor Hughes[7], Ellis Hughes[6], Hannah Whilldin[5], Joseph Whilldin[4], Hannah Gorham[3], Desire Howland[2], JOHN HOWLAND[1] THE PILGRIM), was born at Philadelphia, Pennsylvania, 10 March, 1842, died at Philadelphia, 2 February, 1905, married at Philadelphia, 14 April, 1866, CAPTAIN ELI DOWNS EDMUNDS, born 6 February, 1841. (See page 314 for Pilgrim Ancestry).

Issue:—

(1) LYDIA JANE CROWELL EDMUNDS, born at Norfolk, Virginia, 3 October, 1871, married 7 November, 1905, Isaac Killian Bower Hansell, and had:—LYDIA EDMUNDS HANSELL, born at Ambler, Pennsylvania, 19 July, 1907; JOHN LEWIS HANSELL, born at Ambler, Pennsylvania, 26 November, 1908; RACHEL HANSELL, born at Ambler, Pennsylvania, 14 August, 1911.

(2) EMMA LOUISA EDMUNDS, born at Norfolk, Virginia, 7 April, 1874, died at Philadelphia, 10 November, 1883.

(3) HARRIET CECILIA EDMUNDS, born at Philadelphia, Pennsylvania, 14 May, 1877, married at Philadelphia, 9 October, 1907, Ellsworth Lovell Posey, and had:—ELIZABETH EDMUNDS POSEY, born at Ambler, Pennsylvania, 19 October, 1911, died at Ambler, 31 June, 1913; ELI EDMUNDS POSEY, born at Ambler, Pennsylvania, 23 April, 1915.

(4) SARAH WALES EDMUNDS, born at Philadelphia, 3 March, 1879, died at Philadelphia, 3 April, 1883.

EMMA JULIA REEVES

For ancestors leading back to the Mayflower see page 267.

EMMA JULIA REEVES[9], (Isabella Matthews[8], Eleanor Hughes[7], Ellis Hughes[6], Hannah Whilldin[5], Joseph Whilldin[4], Hannah Gorham[3], Desire Howland[2], JOHN HOWLAND[1] THE PILGRIM), was born at Cape May, New Jersey, 30 May, 1848, married at Cape May, New Jersey, 13 November, 1867, Henry Hand Eldredge, born at Cape May, New Jersey, 11 August, 1844.

Issue:—

(1) CLARENCE SELBY ELDREDGE, M. D., born at West Cape May, New Jersey, 25 January, 1869, married first at Philadelphia, Pennsylvania, 16 June, 1896, Eleanor Elizabeth Packer, born 24 November, 1869, died 25 February, 1907; married second at Philadelphia, Pennsylvania, 5 April, 1909, Kathryn Pease, born at Crown Point, New York, 16 January, 1870.

(2) HENRY HAND ELDREDGE, born at West Cape May, New Jersey, 23 November, 1881, married at West Pittston, Pennsylvania, 25 October, 1910, Charlotte L. W. Lindsay, born at Pittston, Pennsylvania, 21 December, 1885, and had the following children:—

JANET LINDSAY ELDREDGE, born at West Cape May, New Jersey, 2 June, 1912.

CHARLOTTE REEVES ELDREDGE, born at West Cape May, New Jersey, 18 February, 1914.

HENRY HAND ELDREDGE, born at West Cape May, New Jersey, 17 November, 1918.

HARRY B. HAND

For ancestors leading back to the Mayflower see page 275.

HARRY B. HAND[10], (Recompence Hand[9], Nancy Schenck[8], Zeruiah Hughes[7], Memucan Hughes[6], Hannah Whilldin[5], Joseph Whilldin[4] Hannah Gorham[3], Desire Howland[2], JOHN HOWLAND[1] THE PILGRIM), was born at Cape May, 3 September, 1851, married first at Philadelphia, Pennsylvania, 17 September, 1874, Mary Ella Perkinpine, who died 5 February, 1885, (tombstone in Cold Spring Cemetery); married second 26 June, 1888, Alwilda Fisher; married third, 8 February, 1917, Eliza Stilwell Doak.

Issue:—

(1) ETHEL LYNN HAND, born at Cape May, 21 July, 1876, married at Cape May, 22 April, 1903, Harry M. Jackson.

(2) LORENE HAND, died 1880.

(3) ELVA HAND, born at Cape May, 20 March, 1881, married at Riverside, New Jersey, Willis Benckert, and had, FRANCES BENCKERT, born at Bridgeton, New Jersey, 2 May, 1912, WILLIS BENCKERT, born at Bridgeton, New Jersey, 21 October, 1913.

(4) JOHN PERKINPINE HAND, born at Cape May, 26 November, 1883, married 30 April, 1910, Frances Doane, and had, FRANCES CLAIRE HAND, born 8 April, 1916, and JOHN PERKINPINE HAND, born 28 December, 1918.

(5) ARTHUR FISHER HAND, born at Cape May, 8 September, 1890.

(6) MILLICENT GRACE HAND, born at Cape May, 29 March, 1893, married at Princeton, New Jersey, 8 December, 1918, Robert Penrose Hewitt.

(7) GEORGE CRAWFORD HAND, born at Cape May, 16 October, 1894, married at Pensacola, Florida, 24 May, 1918, Marian Atchison Rainey, and had, GEORGE CRAWFORD HAND, born at Philadelphia, Pennsylvania, 12 August, 1919.

MARY HOWARD HAND

For ancestors leading back to the Mayflower see page 275.

MARY HOWARD HAND[10], (Recompence Hand[9], Nancy Schenck[8], Zeruiah Hughes[7], Memucan Hughes[6], Hannah Whilldin[5], Joseph Whilldin[4], Hannah Gorham[3], Desire Howland[2], JOHN HOWLAND[1] THE PILGRIM), was born at Cape May, 27 March, 1862, married at Cape May, 21 October, 1888, Albert Higgins Perkinpine, born at Philadelphia, Pa., on 4 January, 1864, (son of John Merkins Perkinpine and Elizabeth Duffy Perkinpine.

Issue:—

(1) ELLA HAND PERKINPINE, born at Philadelphia, Pennsylvania, 23 August, 1889, married at Philadelphia, Pennsylvania, 30 June, 1917, Frederick Wintersteen, born at Philadelphia, Pennsylvania, 15 November, 1889, (son of John Philip Wintersteen and Katherine Wintersteen) and had MILDRED ELAINE WINTERSTEEN, born at Philadelphia, Pennsylvania, 13 January, 1920.

(2) ELVA LYNN PERKINPINE, born at Philadelphia, Pennsylvania, 13 November, 1890, married at Philadelphia, Pennsylvania, 28 June, 1911, Adam Hall, born at Camden, N. J., 22 January, 1886 (son of Wesley Hall and Elizabeth Hall), and had ELVA LYNN HALL, born at Philadelphia, Pennsylvania, 30 April, 1913; HELEN ELLA HALL, born at Philadelphia, Pennsylvania, 10 February, 1916; ETHEL LORENE HALL, born at Philadelphia, Pennsylvania, 26 February, 1917.

(3) FANNY MARY PERKINPINE, born at Philadelphia, Pennsylvania, 11 December, 1893.

(4) ELIZABETH MARTHA PERKINPINE, born at Philadelphia, Pennsylvania, 16 September, 1896, married at Baltimore, Maryland, 5 July, 1917, William Earl Cahall, born at Philadelphia, Pennsylvania, 9 February, 1892, and had ELLA FRANCES CAHALL, born at Philadelphia, Pennsylvania, 16 April, 1918. William Earl Cahall is the son of William Archibald Cahall and Mary Elizabeth Cahall.

EDWARD DOUGLASS PHILLIPS

For ancestors leading back to the Mayflower see page 289.

EDWARD DOUGLASS PHILLIPS[10], (Annie Hughes[9], Ellis Hughes[8], Thomas Hurst Hughes[7], Ellis Hughes[6], Hannah Whilldin[5], Joseph Whilldin[4], Hannah Gorham[3], Desire Howland[2], JOHN HOWLAND[1] THE PILGRIM), was born at Cape May, 14 March, 1871, married 10 January, 1891, Ella Ewing, born 5 March, 1872.

Issue:—

(1) CLAUD B. PHILLIPS, born at Cold Spring, New Jersey, 19 September, 1891.

(2) ROBERT SAUTER PHILLIPS, born at West Cape May, New Jersey, 12 February, 1893.

(3) EDWARD DOUGLASS PHILLIPS, born at West Cape May, New Jersey, 18 March, 1896, married 11 February, 1917, Louise Corson Wheaton, born at West Cape May, New Jersey, 2 December, 1898.

Issue of EDWARD DOUGLASS PHILLIPS and his wife Louise Corson Wheaton:—

RONALD BACON PHILLIPS, born at Wildwood, New Jersey, 25 May, 1919.

Ella Ewing, (daughter of James Ewing, who was born at Cold Spring, 2 November, 1842, and his wife Emma Bennett Stratton).

Louise C. Wheaton, (daughter of Joseph Morgan Wheaton, born 17 August, 1858, and his wife Artie Bacon).

HENRY REEVES EDMUNDS

For ancestors leading back to the Mayflower see page 290.

HENRY REEVES EDMUNDS[10], (Franklin Davenport Edmunds[9], Lydia Hughes[8], Thomas Hurst Hughes[7], Ellis Hughes[6], Hannah Whilldin[5], Joseph Whilldin[4], Hannah Gorham[3], Desire Howland[2], JOHN HOWLAND[1] THE PILGRIM), was born at Philadelphia, Pennsylvania, 17 January, 1840, married at Southwark, Philadelphia, Pennsylvania, 27 April, 1871, Anna Hunter Welsh, born at Philadelphia, Pennsylvania, 28 May, 1845, daughter of Charles and Adeline Hufty Welsh.

Issue :—

(1) CHARLES WELSH EDMUNDS, born at Philadelphia, Pennsylvania, 24 April, 1872, died at Philadelphia, Pennsylvania, 26 April, 1918.

(2) FRANKLIN DAVENPORT EDMUNDS, born at Philadelphia, Pennsylvania, 10 October, 1874, married at Philadelphia, Pennsylvania, 26 June, 1909, Sue Price Paxton, born at Philadelphia, Pennsylvania, 28 September, 1878, daughter of John Barton and Anne Jones Price Paxton and had, ANNE PAXTON EDMUNDS, born 20 August, 1911; ADELINE WELSH EDMUNDS, born 18 March, 1915; HENRY REEVES EDMUNDS, born 18 December, 1918.

(3) ADELINE WELSH EDMUNDS, born at Philadelphia, Pennsylvania, 6 April, 1877, married at Philadelphia, Pennsylvania, 5 February, 1919, Frederick Justinus Froriep.

(4) ANNA GRACE EDMUNDS, born at Philadelphia, Pennsylvania, 8 May, 1887.

MAYFLOWER DESCENDANTS IN CAPE MAY COUNTY

MARY JANE EDMUNDS

For ancestors leading back to the Mayflower see page 290.

MARY JANE EDMUNDS[10], (Franklin Davenport Edmunds[9] Lydia Hughes[8], Thomas Hurst Hughes[7], Ellis Hughes[6], Hannah Whilldin[5], Joseph Whilldin[4], Hannah Gorham[3], Desire Howland[2], JOHN HOWLAND[1] THE PILGRIM), was born at Philadelphia, Pennsylvania, 19 April, 1843, died at Plymouth Township, Montgomery County, Pennsylvania, 27 June, 1916, married at Philadelphia, Pennsylvania, 19 September, 1865, Joel Cook, born at Philadelphia, Pennsylvania, 20 March, 1842, died at Philadelphia, 15 December, 1910.

Issue:—

(1) ANNIE EDMUNDS COOK, born at Philadelphia, Pennsylvania, 5 October, 1866, died in infancy.

(2) GEORGE WILLIAMS CHILDS COOK, born at Philadelphia, Pennsylvania, 21 April, 1868, married first at Philadelphia, Pennsylvania, 19 November, 1902, Mary Robinson, born at Philadelphia, Pennsylvania, 6 July, 1871, died 14 January, 1914, (daughter of Joseph and Eleanor Anderson Robinson), and had MARY COOK, born at Norwood, Pennsylvania, 26 January, 1905, died in infancy, married second 2 April, 1917, Lillian Buckman, born 13 January, 1869.

(3) MARY PAUL COOK, born at Philadelphia, Pennsylvania, 6 February, 1872, married at Philadelphia, Pennsylvania, 18 October, 1892, Edmund Harris Kase, born at Carbondale, Pennsylvania, (son of John and Martha Elizabeth Siebold Kase), and had:—MABEL COOK KASE, born at Philadelphia, Pennsylvania, 18 November, 1897; EDMUND HARRIS KASE, born at Mt. Airy, Philadelphia, 2 December, 1905.

MIRANDA SEYBERT EDMUNDS

For ancestors leading back to the Mayflower see page 291.

MIRANDA SEYBERT EDMUNDS[10], (Richard Downs Edmunds[9], Lydia Hughes[8], Thomas Hurst Hughes[7], Ellis Hughes[6], Hannah Whilldin[5], Joseph Whilldin[4], Hannah Gorham[3], Desire Howland[2], JOHN HOWLAND[1] THE PILGRIM), was born at Cold Spring, New Jersey, 21 January, 1842, married at Cold Spring, New Jersey, 11 March, 1868, Courtland Van Renselaer Reeves, born at Cape May, 27 October, 1837.

Issue:—

(1) MARTHA SWAIN REEVES, born at Cape May, 11 May, 1870, died in infancy.

(2) JENNIE EDMUNDS REEVES, born at Cape May, 10 June, 1872, married at Cape May, 27 October, 1891, Charles L. Leaming, born at Cape May, 27 May, 1867.

(3) RICHARD DOWNS EDMUNDS REEVES, born at Cape May, 1 September, 1877, married at Cold Spring, New Jersey, 3 April, 1901, Elsie G. Oliver, born at Fishing Creek, New Jersey, 26 September, 1882, and had ELEANOR EDMUNDS REEVES.

(4) ABIJAH DAVIS REEVES, born at West Cape May, New Jersey, 23 August, 1880, married at Cold Spring, New Jersey, 23 November, 1903, Mabel Search, born at Philadelphia, Pennsylvania, 22 October, 1882, and had REBECCA REEVES, born 20 February, 1905, JANE REEVES, born 4 May, 1914, CHARLES DAVIS REEVES, born 10 February, 1920.

ELIZABETH BATEMAN EDMUNDS

For ancestors leading back to the Mayflower see page 291.

ELIZABETH BATEMAN EDMUNDS[10], (Richard Downs Edmunds[9], Lydia Hughes[8], Thomas Hurst Hughes[7], Ellis Hughes[6], Hannah Whilldin[5], Joseph Whilldin[4], Hannah Gorham[3], Desire Howland[2], JOHN HOWLAND[1] THE PILGRIM), was born 28 March, 1849, married first 1 May, 1868, WILLIAM HENRY REEVES, born 1844, died 4 September, 1901. (See page 267).

Issue :—

(1)   JENNIE REEVES, born 7 July, 1870, died in infancy.

(2)   ETHEL REEVES, born 10 February, 1873, died 27 February, 1898, married 30 August, 1892, Marcus Scull, born 15 April, 1875, and had: ETHEL REEVES SCULL, born 12 March, 1893, married 30 October, 1918, George W. Ottinger, and had, LAURA ELIZABETH OTTINGER, born 6 February, 1920; JENNIE HIGBEE SCULL, born 2 April, 1894, married 26 March, 1918, Dr. John C. Rodriguez.

(3)   MARTHA REEVES, born 19 November, 1873, died in infancy.

(4)   EMMA REEVES, born 24 May, 1881, married 24 May, 1899, Marcus Scull, who first married her sister, ETHEL REEVES.

(5)   WILLIAM HENRY REEVES, born 18 October, 1882, died in infancy.

(6)   JAMES HENRY REEVES, born 25 May, 1885, died 21 February, 1920, married at Millville, New Jersey, 31 March, 1907, Etta Taylor, born at Millville, New Jersey, 31 December, 1885, and had RICHARD CAMPION REEVES and WILLIAM HENRY REEVES.

(7)   ESMONDE H. REEVES, born 12 April, 1888, died in infancy.

ELIZABETH BATEMAN EDMUNDS, married second John Woolson Reeves.

JAMES RICHARDS EDMUNDS

For ancestors leading back to the Mayflower see page 292.

JAMES RICHARD EDMUNDS[10], (Thomas Hughes Edmunds[9], Lydia Hughes[8], Thomas Hurst Hughes[7], Ellis Hughes[6], Hannah Whilldin[5], Joseph Whilldin[4], Hannah Gorham[3], Desire Howland[2], JOHN HOWLAND[1] THE PILGRIM), was born 22 April, 1846, mar ᴝd 29 October, 1873, Anna S. Keyser.

Issue:—

(1) MARY EDMUNDS, born at Baltimore, Maryland, 18 October, 1874, married at Baltimore, Maryland, 11 June, 1903, Henry Farnham Perkins, born at Burlington, Virginia, 10 May, 1877, and had ANNA KEYSER PERKINS.

(2) CHARLES KEYSER EDMUNDS, born 21 September, 1876, married at Baltimore County, Maryland, 30 June, 1909, Sarah Katharine Poorbaugh.

(3) ANNA EDMUNDS, born 9 January, 1878, married at Canton, China, 5 March, 1907, Carl Clyde Rutledge.

(4) GRACE GILMORE EDMUNDS, born 3 September, 1879, married at Baltimore, Maryland, 15 June, 1904, John Branham Deming, and had JOHN BRANHAM DEMING.

(5) HELEN EDMUNDS, born at Baltimore, Maryland, 14 October, 1882, married at Baltimore, Maryland, 3 June, 1902, Arthur Weeks Robinson, born at Louisville, Kentucky, 1 September, 1880, and had, HELEN EDMUNDS ROBINSON; ANNA KETURA ROBINSON and ARTHUR WEEKS ROBINSON.

(6) JAMES RICHARD EDMUNDS, born 1 April, 1890.

SARAH HUGHES

For ancestors leading back to the Mayflower see page 250.

SARAH HUGHES[8], (Thomas Hurst Hughes[7], Ellis Hughes[6], Hannah Whilldin[5], Joseph Whilldin[4], Hannah Gorham[3], Desire Howland[2], JOHN HOWLAND[1] THE PILGRIM), was born at Cape May, 31 May, 1800, died 27 January, 1839, married 22 January, 1818, Eli B. Wales, born at Gettysburg, Pennsylvania, 10 July, 1798, died at Cold Spring, New Jersey, 24 September, 1883.

Issue:—

(1) SARAH HUGHES WALES, was born at Cape May, 3 February, 1819, died at Cape May, 21 July, 1849, married Downs Edmunds, born at Fishing Creek, New Jersey, 10 October, 1813, died at West Cape May, New Jersey, 1 April, 1890. (For descendants see page 314).

(2) HARRIET BENTLEY WALES, born at Cold Spring, New Jersey, 29 August, 1825, married Joseph Young. (For descendants see page 315).

(3) ELEANOR WALES, married Downs Edmunds.

(4) THOMAS ROGER WALES, born 3 February, 1830, died at Cape May, 16 January, 1908, married 10 June, 1854, Martha Cresse Tomlin. (For descendants see page 316).

(5) LYDIA HUGHES WALES, born at Cold Spring, New Jersey, 28 October, 1832, died at Cape May, 4 January, 1862, married at Cape May, December, 1854, Alvin Parker Hildreth, born at Cold Spring, New Jersey, 11 June, 1831, died at Cape May, 3 August, 1897. (For descendants see page 318).

(6) MARY HUGHES WALES, born at Cold Spring, New Jersey, 25 November, 1836, married at Cold Spring, New Jersey, 8 December, 1862, Walter Almer Barrows. (For descendants see page 319).

(7) ELI BENTLEY WALES.

SARAH HUGHES WALES

For ancestors leading back to the Mayflower see page 313.

SARAH HUGHES WALES⁹, (Sarah Hughes⁸, Thomas Hurst Hughes⁷, Ellis Hughes⁶, Hannah Whilldin⁵, Joseph Whilldin⁴, Hannah Gorham³, Desire Howland², JOHN HOWLAND¹ THE PILGRIM), was born at Cape May, 3 February, 1819, died at Cape May, 21 July, 1849, (tombstone in Cold Spring Cemetery), married Downs Edmunds, born at Fishing Creek, New Jersey, 10 October, 1813, died at West Cape May, New Jersey, 1 April, 1890.

Issue :—

(1) SARAH ELIZABETH EDMUNDS, born 21 December, 1837, married 14 October, 1867, EDGAR PAGE STITES, (see page 214), born at Cape May, 22 March, 1836, and had, EDGAR PAGE STITES, who married Mary Holmes, and had EDGAR PAGE STITES; FLETCHER WILBUR STITES, who married Edith Gillespie Austin, and had RICHARD AUSTIN STITES, born 14 March, 1912.

(2) ELI DOWNS EDMUNDS, born 6 February, 1841, married LYDIA JANE CROWELL. (For descendants see page 303).

(3) TRYPHENA BELINDA EDMUNDS, born 19 April, 1843, died at Cape May, 28 September, 1900, married SAMUEL WINCHESTER REEVES, (see page 267), and had: LOTTIE BELLE REEVES, born 12 June, 1873, married first, 3 December, 1895, Robert H. Barr; married second, 30 April, 1904, William Edgar Bell, born at Philadelphia, 17 June, 1884; JENNIE M. REEVES, born 23 November, 1875, died in infancy; HARRY McCOOK REEVES, born 21 November, 1878, died in infancy; NELLIE WATT REEVES, born at Philadelphia, 23 January, 1880, married 27 October, 1903, Charles Wilson Guest, born at Honeybrook, Pennsylvania, 23 April, 1880, and had SAMUEL WINCHESTER REEVES GUEST.

HARRIET BENTLEY WALES

For ancestors leading back to the Mayflower see page 313.

HARRIET BENTLEY WALES[9], (Sarah Hughes[8], Thomas Hurst Hughes[7], Ellis Hughes[6], Hannah Whilldin[5], Joseph Whilldin[4], Hannah Gorham[3], Desire Howland[2], JOHN HOWLAND[1] THE PILGRIM), was born at Cold Spring, New Jersey, 29 August, 1825, died at Petersburg, New Jersey, 27 October, 1889, married at Philadelphia, Pennsylvania, 30 January, 1884, Joseph Young, born at Petersburg, New Jersey, 1 December, 1807, died at Petersburg, 10 June, 1889.

Issue:—

(1) SARAH BELINDA YOUNG.

(2) EDMUND LEVI BULL WALES YOUNG, born at Petersburg, New Jersey, 16 August, 1847, died at Philadelphia, Pennsylvania, 29 August, 1898, married first at Philadelphia, February, 1873, Mary W. Smith, married second at Philadelphia, August, 1891, Elizabeth Rohn. Children by first wife:— MARIA S. YOUNG, MARY S. YOUNG, FLORENCE B. YOUNG; by second wife, EDMUND YOUNG.

(3) BENTLEY WALES YOUNG, born at Petersburg, New Jersey, 13 May, 1853, married at Seaville, New Jersey, August, 1874, Judith Morris, and had:—FLOYD WHITTLEMORE YOUNG, married Lina Thomas; BENTLEY WALES YOUNG, born 6 March, 1876, married 10 March, 1912, Mabel Mathis; EDMUND B. YOUNG.

(4) JOSEPHINE YOUNG.

(5) MARY H. YOUNG.

(6) HOWARD W. YOUNG.

THOMAS ROGER WALES

For ancestors leading back to the Mayflower see page 313.

THOMAS ROGER WALES[9], (Sarah Hughes[8], Thomas Hurst Hughes[7], Ellis Hughes[6], Hannah Whilldin[5], Joseph Whilldin[4], Hannah Gorham[3], Desire Howland[2], JOHN HOWLAND[1] THE PILGRIM), was born at Cold Spring, New Jersey, 3 February, 1830, died at Cape May, 16 January, 1908, (interment at Cold Spring Cemetery), married at Cape May Court House, New Jersey, 10 June, 1854, Martha Cresse Tomlin, born at Goshen, New Jersey, 10 June, 1835, died at Cape May, 18 June, 1893, (tombstone in Cold Spring Cemetery).

Issue:—

(1) SARAH HUGHES WALES, born at Cold Spring, New Jersey, 3 January, 1856, married 5 February, 1880, Warren Cameron Van Gilder.

(2) EDMUND BENTLEY WALES, born at Cold Spring, New Jersey, 16 October, 1858, married at Cape May, 2 August, 1882, Sarah Leaming of Fishing Creek. She died at West Philadelphia, Pennsylvania, 8 April, 1892.

(3) LYDIA HILDRETH WALES, born at Cape May, 4 January, 1862, died in infancy.

(4) JANE SCHELLENGER WALES, born at Cold Spring, New Jersey, 12 July, 1863.

(Continued on next page)

THOMAS ROGER WALES

(5)   WESTLEY ROGERS WALES, M. D., born at Cape May, 21 October, 1869, died at Atlantic City, New Jersey, 11 August, 1914, (tombstone in Cold Spring Cemetery), married 24 April, 1892, ORILLA AYERS EDMUNDS, (see page 228), and had the following children:—

THOMAS ROGER WALES, died in infancy; MARTHA TOMLIN WALES, born at May's Landing, New Jersey, 3 October, 1896, married at Gloucester, New Jersey, 24 April, 1916, WILLIAM MORRIS CASSEDY[10], (William Francis Cessedy[9], Maria Stockton Schenck[8], Zeruiah Hughes[7], Memucan Hughes[6], Hannah Whilldin[5], Joseph Whilldin[4], Hannah Gorham[3], Desire Howland[2], JOHN HOWLAND[1] THE PILGRIM), (see page 283), and had MARTHA WALES CASSEDY, born at Gloucester, New Jersey, 22 September, 1917, and WILLIAM MORRIS CASSEDY, born at Cape May, 23 November, 1919.

(6)   JOHN ALLEN WALES, born at Cape May, 22 June, 1873, married at York, Pennsylvania, 12 April, 1904, CORA LEAMING WARE, (see page 220), and had EDITH HELENE WALES, born at Cape May, 5 March, 1906.

LYDIA HUGHES WALES

For ancestors leading back to the Mayflower see page 313.

LYDIA HUGHES WALES[9], (Sarah Hughes[8], Thomas Hurst Hughes[7], Ellis Hughes[6], Hannah Whilldin[5], Joseph Whilldin[4], Hannah Gorham[3], Desire Howland[2], JOHN HOWLAND[1] THE PILGRIM), was born at Cold Spring, New Jersey, 28 October, 1832, died at Cape May, 4 January, 1862, (tombstone in Cold Spring Cemetery), married at Cape May, December, 1854, Alvin Parker Hildreth, born at Cold Spring, New Jersey, 11 June, 1831, died at Cape May, 3 August, 1897, (tombstone in Cold Spring Cemetery).

Issue:—

(1) HOWARD WALES HILDRETH, born 1856, died 5 June, 1857, (tombstone in Cold Spring Cemetery).

(2) FRANK HARDING HILDRETH, born 12 March, 1857.

(3) JAMES MONROE EDMUNDS HILDRETH, born at Cape May, 9 December, 1858, married 12 November, 1884, Martha Orr Mecray, and had, MARY MECRAY HILDRETH, born 24 October, 1885, who married 5 April, 1906, John D. Johnson, and had KATHRYN HILDRETH JOHNSON, born 18 May, 1907, and MARY ELIZABETH JOHNSON, born 28 October, 1911.

(4) ALVIN PARKER HILDRETH, born 1861, died 2 May, 1867, (tombstone in Cold Spring Cemetery).

MARY HUGHES WALES

For ancestors leading back to the Mayflower see page 313.

MARY HUGHES WALES[9], (Sarah Hughes[8], Thomas Hurst Hughes[7], Ellis Hughes[6], Hannah Whilldin[5], Joseph Whilldin[4], Hannah Gorham[3], Desire Howland[2], JOHN HOWLAND[1] THE PILGRIM), was born at Cold Spring, New Jersey, 25 November, 1836, married at Cold Spring, New Jersey, 8 December, 1862, Walter Almer Barrows.

Issue:—

(1) FERDINAND BARROWS, died in infancy.

(2) WALTER ALMER BARROWS, born at Cold Spring, New Jersey, 31 December, 1865, married at Cleveland, Ohio, 26 September, 1888, Sarah Byers and had: WALTER ALMER BARROWS, born at Sharpsville, Pennsylvania, 22 July, 1890; DONALD BARROWS, born at Youngstown, Ohio, 16 February, 1898.

(3) HELEN WORK BARROWS, born at Frankford, Philadelphia, 14 November, 1867, married at Mt. Holly, New Jersey, 29 October, 1891, Charles K. Chambers, and had: MARY WALES CHAMBERS, born 29 August, 1892; FRANCES WOODWARD CHAMBERS, born 16 August, 1896.

(4) FREDERICK VOORHEES BARROWS, died in infancy.

(5) CHARLES MURRAY SLOAN BARROWS, died in infancy.

(6) MARY McMULLEN BARROWS, born at Mt. Holly, New Jersey, 8 March, 1876, married at Mt. Holly, 10 June, 1904, James H. Dunham, and had, BARROWS DUNHAM, born 10 October, 1905.

WALTER ALMER BARROWS 3rd, son of WALTER and Sarah Byers BARROWS, married at Cleveland, Ohio, 3 June, 1916, Dorothy L. Bulkeley, and had: MARGARET BULKELEY BARROWS, born 22 September, 1917; WALTER ALMER BARROWS 4th born 18 August, 1919.

MARY WALES CHAMBERS, daughter of Charles K. and HELEN WORK BARROWS CHAMBERS, married at Philadelphia, 16 June, 1917, John W. Faucett, of Oil City, Pennsylvania.

FRANCES WOODWARD CHAMBERS married 16 August, 1917, William Richard Littleton, and had, HELEN ANN LITTLETON, born 25 April, 1919.

DESIRE GORHAM

For ancestors leading back to the Mayflower see page 97.

DESIRE GORHAM³, sister of the HANNAH GOR-
HAM³ who with her husband Joseph Whilldin moved to Cape
May, (Desire Howland², JOHN HOWLAND¹ THE PILGRIM),
was born at Plymouth, 20 May, 1664, married John Haws (see
"Wast Book" on page 8), and had, EXPERIENCE HAWS,
who married EBENEZER SPROAT³, (Elizabeth Sampson²,
HENRY SAMPSON¹ THE PILGRIM).

Their daughter THANKFUL SPROAT, married JOSEPH
BENNETT⁴, (Priscilla Howland³, Isaac Howland², JOHN
HOWLAND¹ THE PILGRIM), and had ELIZABETH BEN-
NETT, who married JOHN MORTON⁵, (Ebenezer Morton⁴,
Mary Ring³, Deborah Hopkins², STEPHEN HOPKINS¹ THE
PILGRIM).

Their daughter, LUCY MORTON, married JABEZ
SOULE⁶, (Zachariah Soule⁵, Zachariah Soule⁴, Benjamin
Soule³, John Soule², GEORGE SOULE¹ THE PILGRIM), Zach-
ariah Soule⁵, Mary Eaton⁴, Benjamin Eaton³, Benjamin Eaton²,
FRANCIS EATON¹ THE PILGRIM), (Zachariah Soule⁵,
Zachariah Soule⁴, Sarah Standish³, Alexander Standish², MYL-
ES STANDISH¹ THE PILGRIM), (Zachariah Soule⁵, Zach-
ariah Soule⁴, Sarah Standish³, Sarah Alden², JOHN ALDEN¹
THE PILGRIM), (Zachariah Soule⁶, Zachariah Soule⁵, Sarah
Standish⁴, Sarah Alden³, PRISCILLA MULLINS², WILLIAM
MULLINS¹ THE PILGRIM).

Their daughter, SARAH SOULE, married DEPEND-
ENCE STURTEVANT⁶, (Hannah Church⁵, Richard Church⁴,
Nathaniel Church³, Elizabeth Warren², RICHARD WARREN¹
THE PILGRIM), and had: MARY SOULE STURTEVANT,
born in PLYMOUTH COUNTY, who married Rev. Elbridge
Gerry Howe, and had, REV. PAUL STURTEVANT HOWE,
who moved to Cape May.

ROBERT CHEW HUGHES

For ancestors leading back to the Mayflower see page 287.

ROBERT CHEW HUGHES[10], (John Haney Hughes[9], Ellis Hughes[8], Thomas Hurst Hughes[7], Ellis Hughes[6], Hannah Whilldin[5], Joseph Whilldin[4], Hannah Gorham[3], Desire Howland[2], JOHN HOWLAND[1] THE PILGRIM), was born at Iona, New Jersey, 17 May, 1856, married at Trenton, New Jersey, 4 May, 1881, Sarah Ann Cresse, born at Burleigh, Cape May County, New Jersey, 5 September, 1855.

Issue :—

(1) LUCRISSA REEVES HUGHES, born at Cape May, 7 November, 1883, married at Cape May, 30 June, 1916, Thomas William Millet, born at Cape May, 25 January, 1882, and had, THOMAS WILLIAM MILLET, 3rd, born at Philadelphia, Pennsylvania, 10 December, 1918.

(2) LENA BLATTNER HUGHES, born at Cape May, 6 March, 1886, married at Cape May, 23 October, 1907, HARRY TAYLOR HUGHES[10], (Joseph B. Hughes[9], Thomas B. Hughes[8], Joseph Hughes[7], Ellis Hughes[6], Hannah Whilldin[5], Joseph Whilldin[4], Hannah Gorham[3], Desire Howland[2], JOHN HOWLAND[1] THE PILGRIM), who was born 23 July, 1880, and had, SARAH ELIZABETH HUGHES, born at Cape May, 8 June, 1914. For family and Pilgrim ancestry of HARRY TAYLOR HUGHES, see family and descendants of JOSEPH HUGHES and his wife Judith Bennett on page 251

JAMES ROBB MERRITT

For ancestors leading back to the Mayflower see page 153.

JAMES ROBB MERRITT[10], (John Bennett, Merritt[9], Louisa Stevens Merritt[8], Mary Hughes[7], Jacob Hughes[6], Priscilla Leaming[5], Hannah Whilldin[4], Hannah Gorham[3], Desire Howland[2], JOHN HOWLAND[1] THE PILGRIM), was born at Philadelphia, Pennsylvania, 30 December, 1860, died 15 May, 1907, married 5 April, 1882, Maxamelia Douglas Taylor, born at Philadelphia, Pennsylvania, 13 May, 1861.

Issue:—

(1) FRANCES MERRITT, born at Philadelphia, Pennsylvania, 20 March, 1883, married first at Philadelphia, Pennsylvania, 6 September, 1909, Harry Evans Fox, born at Philadelphia, Pennsylvania, 23 August, 1880, died 28 March, 1918; married second 10 October, 1920, Irvin Clark, born at Philadelphia, Pennsylvania, 15 January, 1878.

(2) JOHN HENRY MERRITT, born at Philadelphia, Pennsylvania, 24 November, 1885, died 15 February, 1887.

(3) ANNA MARIE MERRITT, born at Philadelphia, Pennsylvania, 24 June, 1887, married 4 August, 1909, Harold Alwine, born at Aldan, Pennsylvania, 23 December, 1888.

(4) JAMES ROBB MERRITT, born at Philadelphia, Pennsylvania, 10 June, 1889, married 27 June, 1917, Josephine Evelyn Smith, born at Glen Mills, Pennsylvania, 18 August, 1894.

(5) EDNA MAY MERRITT, born 8 April, 1891, died 11 March, 1892.

(6) JOHN BENNETT MERRITT, born 20 December, 1892, died 24 June, 1893.

(7) HELEN MAR MERRITT, born at Aldan, Pennsylvania, 16 April, 1894, married 21 October, 1913, William Ainsworth Zook, born at Downingtown, Pennsylvania, 10 February, 1890.

(8) EDWIN MERRITT, born at Clifton Heights, Pennsylvania, 7 August, 1895, married 7 May, 1919, Anna Louisa Rownds, born at Salisbury, Maryland, 28 November, 1895.

JAMES GORHAM

For ancestors leading back to the Mayflower see page 11.

JAMES GORHAM[3], brother of the HANNAH GORHAM[3], (Desire Howland[2], JOHN HOWLAND[1] THE PILGRIM), who married Joseph Whilldin and with her husband removed to Cape May, was born at Marshfield, Plymouth Colony, 28 April, 1650, died 1707, married Hannah Huckins, and had, EXPERIENCE GORHAM, born 23 July, 1678, who married Thomas Lothrop. Their daughter MEHITABLE LOTHROP, baptized 27 June, 1725, married Daniel Davis, and had MARY DAVIS, born 29 April, 1740, who married George Lewis.

Their son REV. DANIEL DAVIS LEWIS, born at Barnstable, Massachusetts, 22 July, 1777, died at New Brunswick, New Jersey, September, 1849, married Mary Dyer, who died 17 August, 1876, in her 96th year, and had ALMIRA BUTTERFIELD DAVIS, who married Charles B. Quinn, of Philadelphia, son of William Quinn, of Norristown, Pennsylvania.

Their son WILLIAM HENRY QUINN, born 22 September, 1839, died 8 January, 1915, married 27 December, 1864, Dorothy Packer Hewett, of Paulsboro, New Jersey, and had MARY LEWIS QUINN, born 25 January, 1874, and MARTHA HEWETT QUINN, born 28 August, 1878.

MARY LEWIS QUINN, daughter of WILLIAM HENRY, married 3 July, 1894, Louis B. Moffett, born 22 March, 1874, at Swedesboro, New Jersey, and had LOUIS B. MOFFETT, Jr., born 24 June, 1895.

See "Wast Book" of Col. John Gorham on page 8, for parentage of JAMES GORHAM, and page 11 for date of birth.

ALBERT NORTON WOOD

GEORGE SOULE of the Mayflower, born circa 1602, died 1680, married Mary Beckett and had GEORGE SOULE, who married Deborah ————. Their daughter MARY SOULE married Joseph Davol and had MARY DAVOL, born at Dartmouth, Massachusetts, 14 July, 1705, married at Little Compton, 23 November, 1726, Nathaniel Potter, born at Dartmouth, 7 January, 1709, died at Dartmouth, 1782, and had STOKES POTTER, born at Dartmouth, 10 December, 1731, married at Little Compton, 11 May, 1750, Rebecca Shaw.

Their daughter PHEBE POTTER, born 1755, died at Morrisville, New York, 27 August, 1833, married at Little Compton, 31 May, 1778, Abner Wood, born at Little Compton, 16 June, 1758, died at Morrisville, New York, September, 1838, and had THURSTON WOOD, born at Little Compton, 23 January, 1792, died at McConnell, Georgia, 24 March, 1878, married at Madison Center, New York, 25 March, 1819, Hannah Hitchcock, born at Hamilton, New York, 4 September, 1801, died at Dayton, Ohio, 3 December, 1878.

Their son CHARLES WOOD, born at Madison County, New York, 18 May, 1824, died at Madison, Indiana, 24 February, 1881, married at Madison, Indiana, 31 October, 1848, Cynica Carpenter, born at Lexington, Indiana, 9 August, 1828, died at Chicago, Illinois, 27 October, 1900, and had ALBERT NORTON WOOD, born at Madison, Indiana, 19 March, 1857, married at Navy Yard, New York, 24 June, 1893, Edith Elmer, born at Portsmouth, New Hampshire, 24 September, 1871, and had the following children:—

HORACE ELMER WOOD, born at Washington, 22 October, 1894, died at Yokohama, Japan, 18 July, 1898; THURSTON ELMER WOOD, born at Cape May Court House, 14 September, 1896, killed in battle in France, near Vierzy, Aisne, 21 July, 1918; HORACE ELMER WOOD, born at Portland, Oregon, 6 February, 1901; ALBERT ELMER WOOD, born at Cape May Court House, 22 September, 1910.

EDWARD KENT ARMSTRONG, M. D.

WILLIAM BRADFORD of the Mayflower, second governor of Plymouth Colony, was born at Austerfield, England, 29 March, 1590, New Style, died at Plymouth, 19 May, 1657, married Alice Carpenter, widow of Edward Southworth, and had WILLIAM BRADFORD, born at Plymouth, 17 June, 1624, died at Plymouth, 1 March, 1704, New Style, who married Alice Richards.

Their daughter ALICE BRADFORD married Rev. William Adams, and had ELIZABETH ADAMS, who married Rev. Samuel Whiting.

Their son SAMUEL WHITING married Elizabeth Judson, and had ELIZABETH WHITING, who married Judson Lewis.

Their son ISAAC LEWIS married Lydia Gates, and had HELEN LEWIS, who married Luther Kent.

Their daughter MINNIE KENT, married Harold B. Armstrong, and had EDWARD KENT ARMSTRONG, M. D., born at Englewood, Illinois, 1 July, 1881, died in Red Cross Service, at Beirut, Syria, 31 May, 1919, married at Cape May, 11 August, 1914, Carrie Holmes Focer, born at Cape May, 29 April, 1892, and had, BARBARA ARMSTRONG, born at Chicago, Illinois, 25 March, 1917, residing at Cape May.

For an account of Governor Bradford's manuscript "The History of Plymouth Plantation," improperly called the "Log of the Mayflower"—the loss of the famous manuscript and its recovery, see page 73. See also note on Governor Bradford's long term of office on page 85.

RICHARD EDMUNDS

For ancestors leading back to the Mayflower see page 290.

RICHARD EDMUNDS[10], (Franklin Davenport Edmunds[9], Lydia Hughes[8], Thomas Hurst Hughes[7], Ellis Hughes[6], Hannah Whilldin[5], Joseph Whilldin[4], Hannah Gorham[3], Desire Howland[2], JOHN HOWLAND[1] THE PILGRIM), was born at Tuckahoe, New Jersey, 21 March, 1847, married at Germantown, Philadelphia, Pennsylvania, 1 November, 1867, Mary Elizabeth Irwin, daughter of Thomas Rutherford and Louisa (Wythe) Irwin.

Issue:—

(1) ANNIE LOUISA EDMUNDS, born at Philadelphia, Pennsylvania, 26 October, 1868, married at Merchantville, New Jersey, 24 May, 1890, William Potts Brooks, born at Roxborough, Philadelphia, 24 September, 1869, and had:—ANNIE MARSHALL BROOKS, born at Philadelphia, 19 March, 1891; FLORENCE ELIZABETH BROOKS, born at Roxborough, Philadelphia, 14 August, 1898.

(2) VIRGINIA MARY EDMUNDS, born at Philadelphia, Pennsylvania, 13 January, 1872, married at Roxborough, Philadelphia, 26 October, 1893, Walter Brooks Smith, born 26 March, 1870, died at Roxborough, Philadelphia, 2 June, 1905, and had:—RICHARD EDMUNDS SMITH, born at Philadelphia, 16 September, 1896.

(3) HANNAH GOELLER EDMUNDS, born at Harding Township, Gloucester County, New Jersey, 29 October, 1877, married at Roxborough, Philadelphia, 3 September, 1902, John Pierce Churchill, born at Three Oaks, Michigan, 15 May, 1875, son of Owen and Flora Eulalia (Little) Churchill.

DANIEL HUGHES RUSSELL

For ancestors leading back to the Mayflower see page 145.

DANIEL HUGHES RUSSELL[11], (Ellen Hughes[10], Priscilla Leaming[9], Hannah Stites[8], Priscilla Leaming[7], Margaret Stites[6], Priscilla Leaming[5], Hannah Whilldin[4], Hannah Gorham[3], Desire Howland[2], JOHN HOWLAND[1] THE PILGRIM), was born at Cold Spring, New Jersey, 3 October, 1875, married at Cape May, 23 September, 1894, Mabel Foster, born at Cape May, 1 June, 1880.

Issue:—

(1) MAUDE HUGHES RUSSELL, born at Cape May, died in infancy.

(2) HELEN MAUDE RUSSELL, born at Cape May, 4 July, 1897, married at Tuckahoe, New Jersey, 20 September, 1914, Harry Kehr, born at Philadelphia, Pennsylvania, 21 August, 1893, and had, ALLAN HARRY KEHR, born at Cape May, 19 November, 1915, and DONALD CLAYTON KEHR, born at Cape May, 29 May, 1920.

(3) LOUISA LEAMING RUSSELL, born at Cape May, 8 February, 1901, married at Cape May, 12 February, 1915, Raymond Whilldin, born at Heislerville, New Jersey, 13 April, 1894, and had, NORMA RAY WHILLDIN, born at Cape May, 3 February, 1920.

(3) DONALD HUGHES RUSSELL, born at Cape May, 23 January, 1908.

LOUISA SAINT BENNETT

For ancestors leading back to the Mayflower see page 215.

LOUISA SAINT BENNETT[9], (Mary Whilldin[8], Isaac Whilldin[7], Matthew Whilldin[6], James Whilldin[5], Joseph Whilldin[4], Hannah Gorham[3], Desire Howland[2], JOHN HOWLAND[1] THE PILGRIM), was born at Cape May, 4 May, 1850, married at Cape May, 18 December, 1869, Charles Henry Rutherford, born at Cape May, 11 July, 1847.

Issue:—

(1) OCIE IRWIN RUTHERFORD, born at Cape May, 1 January, 1871, married at Cape May, 15 June, 1896, John Patrick Coyle.

(2) ELIZA CLARK BENNETT RUTHERFORD, born at Cape May, 5 July, 1873, married at Cape May, 22 June, 1898, Thomas Ledlum Van Winkle.

(3) LUETTE BENNETT RUTHERFORD, born at Cape May, 4 March, 1875, married at Cape May, 1 November, 1892, Lafayette Howard Miller, and had: JAMES LAFAYETTE MILLER, born at Cape May, 27 February, 1895, married 4 June, 1917, Helen R. Brumbach.

(4) CORA LEE RUTHERFORD, born at Cape May, 26 May, 1877, married at Cape May, 4 October, 1900, Edwin Cummings Miller, and had, KENNETH LEE MILLER, born at Cape May, 25 April, 1907, MARY LOUISA BENNETT MILLER, born at Cape May, 3 December, 1914.

(5) EDYTH RUTHERFORD.

(6) LINDA HUDSON RUTHERFORD, born at Cape May, 4 September, 1888, married at Cape May, 20 December, 1913, Walter Bossard Hatfield, and had, WALTER RUTHERFORD HATFIELD, born 22 August, 1916.

(7) and (8) ALBERT COTTON RUTHERFORD and JESSE OLIVER RUTHERFORD, born at Cape May, 29 July, 1891. JESSE OLIVER married at Cape May, 5 June, 1918, FLORENCE FILMORE WARE, (see page 277).

MEMUCAN HUGHES

For ancestors leading back to the Mayflower see page 249.

MEMUCAN HUGHES[8], (Israel Hughes[7], Memucan Hughes[6], Hannah Whilldin[5], Joseph Whilldin[4], Hannah Gorham[3], Desire Howland[2], JOHN HOWLAND[1] THE PILGRIM), was born at Cape May, 1810, (see page 58 for baptism), died at Cape May, 17 August, 1857, (tombstone in Cold Spring Cemetery), married Mary P. Edmunds, born at Cape May, 1821, died at Cape May, 27 November, 1856, (tombstone in Cold Spring Cemetery).

(1) ROBERT EDMUNDS HUGHES, born at Cape May, 24 June, 1846, married Harriet Schellenger, born at Cape May, 30 March, 1853, and had:—MILLICENT SCHELLENGER HUGHES, born at Cape May, 25 January, 1876, married at Cape May, 18 April, 1900, Frank Bacon Mecray, born at Cape May, 23 April, 1877, and had, HARRIET HUGHES MECRAY, born at Cape May, 4 January, 1905; CHARLOTTE BRIDEN-THAL HUGHES, born at Cape May, 2 January, 1878, married at Cape May, 11 November, 1904, Percy Rothell, born at Cape May, 29 February, 1872.

(2) MARY EDMUNDS HUGHES, born at Cape May, 24 March, 1851, married at Cape May, 25 February, 1879, Joseph Paul Hughes, born at Philadelphia, Pennsylvania, 13 January, 1852, and had, JOSEPH BOONE HUGHES, born at Chicago, Illinois, 24 November, 1879, ROBERT EDMUNDS HUGHES, born at Chicago, Illinois, 3 December, 1882, PAUL EDMUNDS HUGHES, born at Chicago, Illinois, 19 March, 1888.

(3) MEMUCAN HUGHES, married first Jennie Champion, and had: EARLE C. HUGHES, born at Cape May, 24 April, 1879, who married Louisa Bush, born at Cape May, 6 January, 1879, and had, EARLE M. HUGHES, born at Cape May, 14 July, 1907, EDWIN R. HUGHES, born at Dewey, Oklahoma, 10 April, 1909, MARY JANE HUGHES, born at Buffalo, New York, 27 June, 1912, LOUISA HUGHES, born at Santa Maria, California, 2 September, 1915; MARY HUGHES; LAURA HUGHES.

Memucan Hughes 3rd married second Mrs. Martha Schellenger Stites.

LEAMING M. RICE

For ancestors leading back to the Mayflower see page 179.

LEAMING M. RICE[9], (Edward Rice[8], Hannah Leaming[7], Christopher Leaming[6], Christopher Leaming[5], Hannah Whilldin[4], Hannah Gorham[3], Desire Howland[2], JOHN HOWLAND[1] THE PILGRIM), was born 25 March, 1828, died 14 October, 1902, married 21 February, 1853, Maria Swain Ludlam, born 20 May, 1828, died 12 December, 1882.

Issue:—

(1) JAMES D. RICE, born 23 November, 1853, died 4 March, 1883, without issue.

(2) MARY B. RICE, born 1 February, 1855, married Uriah Gandy, and had:—ROXANA S. GANDY; JANE R. GANDY, died in childhood; MARTHA GANDY, deceased, who married Claude Town, and had, MARTHA G. TOWN; LEAMING R. GANDY; MARY L. GANDY, who married Lewis Everingham.

(3) HANNAH LEAMING RICE, born 13 November, 1856, married Lewis B. Lloyd, and had: EDWARD R. LLOYD, who married Rebecca Gandy; RACHEL LLOYD, who married Jay E. Mecray, and had, JAMES MECRAY and REBECCA MECRAY; EUGENE W. LLOYD, who married Mabel Wentzel, and had, STANLEY LLOYD; MARIA LLOYD, died in childhood; IMOGENE LLOYD; LEAMING R. LLOYD.

(4) JANE S. RICE, born 21 January, 1859, married Vincent O. Miller, and had, MARCIA MILLER, who married Charles Vernon Smith, and had, CHARLES VERNON SMITH and JANE R. SMITH; MARIA R. MILLER; VINCENT MILLER.

(5) EDWARD L. RICE, born 25 January, 1864, married 11 February, 1891, Phoebe T. Steelman, and had:—DOROTHY RICE, born 13 March, 1892; EDWARD RICE, born 23 October, 1893, married 11 October, 1919, Eleanor Wister Garrett; MARTHA SMITH RICE, born 6 January, 1896, married July, 1918, Raymond Errickson, and had, DOROTHY RICE ERRICKSON, born 22 May, 1919.

(6) LEAMING M. RICE, born 4 August, 1866, married Sarah E. Goff, and had, WILLIAM LEAMING RICE, BEATRICE RICE, JAMES D. RICE, SARAH ELIZABETH RICE and LEAMING M. RICE.

JUDITH WHILLDIN ELDREDGE

For ancestors leading back to the Mayflower see page 218.

JUDITH WHILLDIN ELDREDGE[9], (Deborah Whilldin Ware[8], Deborah Whilldin[7], Jonathan Whilldin[6], James Whilldin[5], Joseph Whilldin[4], Hannah Gorham[3], Desire Howland[2], JOHN HOWLAND[1] THE PILGRIM), was born at Cape May, 15 August, 1839, died at Philadelphia, 25 March, 1908, (tombstone in Cold Spring Cemetery), married at Cape May, 1 July, 1858, William Hoffman, born at Cape May, 18 May, 1825, died at Cape May, 19 August, 1880, (tombstone in Cold Spring Cemetery).

Issue:—

(1) LIZZIE WHILLDIN HOFFMAN, born at Cape May, 24 March, 1859, married at Cape May, 1 December, 1878, Robert E. Hand, born at Cape May, 28 June, 1854, died at Cape May, 12 March, 1917, (tombstone in Cold Spring Cemetery).

(2) WILLMIRA HOFFMAN, born at Cape May, 2 September, 1861.

(3) DEBORAH ELDREDGE HOFFMAN, born at Cape May, 24 August, 1863, married at Cape May, 25 December, 1898, Alexander Carlton Hildreth.

(4) MELISSA HOFFMAN, born at Cape May, 14 August, 1865, married at Cape May, 15 October, 1888, Horace Richardson, born at Cape May, 22 February, 1867, and had:—ETHEL RICHARDSON, born at Cape May, 2 September, 1889, married at Cape May, 30 June, 1909, William John Bethell, born June, 1888, and had, JOHN HORACE BETHELL, born at Cape May, 31 March, 1913; LIZZIE RICHARDSON, born 22 February, 1894, died 31 August, 1900.

(5) ANNA LOUISA HOFFMAN, born at Cape May, 15 September, 1867, married at Cape May, 5 January, 1890, William Reeves Cresse, born at Cape May, 24 February, 1867, and had, WALTER WORTH CRESSE, born at Cape May, 13 May, 1891, married at Camden, New Jersey, 27 December, 1915, Marion Mixner; ALFRED SHARP CRESSE, born at Cape May, 13 January, 1896; ROBERT HAND CRESSE, born at Cape May, 6 November, 1897; LEWIS HOFFMAN CRESSE, born at Cape May, 8 October, 1901; ARTHUR BENJAMIN CRESSE, born at Cape May, 8 September, 1904.

(6) GEORGE SWAIN HOFFMAN, born at Cape May, 5 July, 1869, died at Cape May, 18 May, 1894, without issue.

(7) LEWIS STILLWELL HOFFMAN, born at Cape May, 15 March, 1875, married at Cape May, 17 December, 1910, Ocie May McNeill, born at Cold Spring, 7 April, 1888.

DEBORAH WHILLDIN ELDREDGE

For ancestors leading back to the Mayflower see page 218.

DEBORAH WHILLDIN ELDREDGE[8], (Deborah Whilldin Ware[8], Deborah Whilldin[7], Jonathan Whilldin[6], James Whilldin[5], Joseph Whilldin[4], Hannah Gorham[3], Desire Howland[2], JOHN HOWLAND[1] THE PILGRIM), was born at Cape May, 29 January, 1841, died at West Cape May, New Jersey, 1 February, 1872, (tombstone in Cold Spring Cemetery), married at Cape May, Reuben Hoffman, born at Cape May, 14 August, 1830.

Issue:—

(1) JUDITH ELDREDGE HOFFMAN, born at West Cape May, New Jersey, 27 November, 1865, died at West Cape May, New Jersey, 14 October, 1904, married at West Cape May, New Jersey, 27 November, 1885, LIVINGSTON ELDREDGE[10], (William Tomlin Eldredge[9], Jeremnah Leaming Eldredge[8], Aaron Eldredge[7], Aaron Eldredge[6], Mercy Leaming[5], Hannah Whilldin[4], Hannah Gorham[3], Desire Howland[2], JOHN HOWLAND[1] THE PILGRIM), who was born at Cape May, 27 April, 1862, died at Cape May, 6 June, 1906, and had:—

FLORENCE ELDREDGE, born at West Cape May, New Jersey, 10 December, 1888, married at Camden, New Jersey, 8 May, 1908, Thomas Stillwell Sayre, born at Cape May, 28 September, 1881.

REUBEN ELDREDGE, born at West Cape May, 24 September, 1895, married at Wildwood, New Jersey, Florence Brown, born at Philadelphia, and had, EMMA ELDREDGE, born at West Cape May, New Jersey, 10, May, 1917; EDNA ELDREDGE, born at Wildwood, New Jersey, 21 May, 1918.

STILLWELL ELDREDGE, born at West Cape May, 26 October, 1901, married 1 January, 1921, Emma Willis.

(2) LILBURN TOWNSEND HOFFMAN, born at Cape May, married Minnie Vanaman, daughter of David Vanaman, and had, VIDA HOFFMAN and ANNA HOFFMAN.

(3) ENOS HOFFMAN, died in infancy.

For Pilgrim ancestry of LIVINGSTON ELDREDGE see under family of WILLIAM TOMLIN ELDREDGE, page 132.

Genealogical
Notes

Genealogical Notes

The old families of Pilgrim posterity of Cape May County are descendants of three Mayflower passengers:—John Howland, his wife Elizabeth Tilley and her father John Tilley. The last died the first year, and although of a generation preceding John Howland, is not given in this volume or in the requirements of the Society of Mayflower Descendants as the first Pilgrim ancestor, out of deference to the long service to the Pilgrim Colony of his son in law, John Howland. Bridget, the wife of John Tilley who accompanied him in the passage to the New World, has not been proved the mother of his daughter Elizabeth, and cannot be claimed as a Mayflower ancestor. She died as did her husband the first year. There are now living in the County of Cape May descendants of fifteen passengers of the Mayflower—John Howland, John Tilley, Elizabeth Tilley, William Bradford, Myles Standish, John Alden, Priscilla Mullins, William Mullins, Alice Mullins, George Soule, Richard Warren, Francis Eaton, Stephen Hopkins, Elizabeth Hopkins, Henry Sampson.

The genealogical tables preceding by no means include all the families of Pilgrim descent of the County—many records are incomplete through failure of families to respond to requests for information, and intermarriages in the early years of the Pilgrim stock with the Crowell, Crawford and Schellenger families have not been touched upon and require long investigation of wills, deeds and tombstone records, in the absence of vital records of any kind. 'In another effort the author will attempt to include all the Mayflower families of the County and of those who have gone out from us. It is regrettable that initial letters instead of full names are universally used among us, and further that sometimes fanciful names are given children in prefernce to the good old Pilgrim names we have a right to use.

The Rev. Daniel Lawrence, father of Ann Lawrence, wife of Jacob Hughes and great grandfather of the Rev. Daniel Lawrence Hughes, D. D., was born on Long Island in 1718, died at Cape May, 13 September, 1766, (tombstone in Cold Spring Cemetery). His wife Sarah is buried beside him, the inscrption on the tombstone reading: "Mrs. Sarah Lawrence, died 20 January, 1768, aged 45 years." Their two children were, Ann Lawrence, whose marriage to Jacob Hughes is recorded on page 103, and Daniel, of whom we have no record, except that his son bore the name of his grandfather, was a Presbyterian clergyman, and was born in Philadelphia, 28 December, 1795, died at Lewistown, Pennsylvania, 30 August, 1875. (The Rev. Dr. D. L. Hughes also mentions two sisters, Deborah and Catherine).

337

name, married at Philadelphia, 3 January, 1825, Sarah Dare Fithian, and had eleven children—the list is given in "The Divine Covenant Fulfilled," by Rev. Dr. D. L. Hughes, pages 17, 18. Whether this Lawrence family is related to the New England family of the same name is a problem for future investigation. The appearance of the ancestor on Long Island seems to point to that conclusion.

————————

The several branches of the Hand family of Cape May County are descended from John Hand, who was at Lynn in Massachusetts Bay Colony as early as 1636, and removed to the whaling settlement at Southampton, Long Island, before 7 March, 1644. He married Alice Gransden, and had nine children, (Nash's Fifty Puritan Ancestors), as follows:—John, born about 1633; Stephen, born about 1635; Joseph, born 1638; Mary, married before 1657, Charles Barnes; Shamgar, moved to Cape May, and died there about 1727; Benjamin, born about 1644, died in Cape May County; James, born in Easthampton, died there 13 March, 1733; Thomas, one of the Cape May whaleman, born 1646, drowned off Cape May, 2 October, 1814, a daughter, probably Alice. The following line of descent continues this ancient Cape May family through ten generations to the present time:—

JOHN HAND, an arrival in Massachusetts Bay before 1636, married Alice Gransden, and had THOMAS HAND, born 1646, died 1714, married Katherine, and had JOHN HAND, born at East Hampton, about 1666, died at Cape May before 27 April, 1736, married Mercy, who died at Cape May before 19 April, 1746, and had SILAS HAND, born at Cape May about 1722, died at Cape May, May, 1770, married at Cape May, 1751, Sarah Crowell, and had ELISHA HAND, born at Cape May, January 1752, died at Cape May, 18 November, 1814, married at Cape May, 25 March, 1783, Esther Teal, born 10 November, 1762, died at Cape May, 4 June, 1802, and had AARON B. HAND, born at Cape May, 5 May, 1791, died at Cape May, 23 December, 1861, married at Cape May, 18 February, 1818, Jane Hand Bancroft, born at Cape May, 20 August, 1793, died at Cape May, January 14, 1864, and had NOAH HAND, born at Cape May, 26 July, 1829, died at Cape May, 28 July, 1907, married at Philadelphia, 9 November, 1851, Jane Hannah, born at County Derry, Ireland, 1818, died at Cape May, 31 December, 1905, and had AARON W. HAND, born at Camden, New Jersey, 10 February, 1857, married 6 March, 1877, Letitia Byers Reeves, born at Cape May, 16 January, 1857, and had the following children:—

338

(1)   ALBERT REEVES HAND, born at Cape May, 24 March, 1878, married at Cape May, 30 October, 1901, Sara Elizabeth Millet, and had THOMAS MILLET HAND, born at Cape May, 7 July, 1903.

(2)   BERNARD HAND, born at Cape May, 18 January, 1880, married at Philadelphia, 1904, Martha Brown, born at Green Creek, New Jersey, 26 September, 1884, and had MILDRED HAND, AARON W. HAND and BERNICE HAND.

(3)   DR. REU ABIJAH HAND, born at Cape May, 7 April, 1882, married at Cape May, 11 May, 1909, Elizabeth Blattner, born at Cape May, 11 May, 1882.

(4)   ELLWOOD STOKES HAND, born at Cape May, 9 August, 1884, died at Colon, Panama, 11 July, 1914.

(5) and (6)   JEANNE REEVES HAND and ANITA REEVES HAND, born at Cape May, 17 June, 1890.

For Mayflower ancestry of Elizabeth Blattner, wife of Dr. Reu Abijah Hand, see page 287.

William Price, the ancestor of the Prices of southern New Jersey, was born in England near the Welsh border about 1705-10. He came to America when a young man, and settled in Burlington County, New Jersey, where he married in 1736 Rebecca Church, and had two sons; William, born about 1738, died 1819; and John, born about 1742. The latter, a major in the revolution, married Polly Potter, and had one child, Anne, who married a John Smith and moved west. William, the other son, was a captain in the revolution. In 1789 he purchased the old Price Farm where the original Cape Town was located on the bay shore. Captain Price married Rebecca Jobs (who died 1814) and had six children:—

1.   Edward, born 26 July, 1767, died 21 January, 1825; married 1792, Sarah Cozens (born 26 August, 1772, died 19 October, 1819) and had John, Sarah, William, Rebecca, Deborah, Edward and Joseph.

2.   William, died a young man without issue.

3.   Mary, who married first Joseph Sweatman, and had James and Mary; secondly, George Matthews, and had James and Artemisia.

4.   Rebecca, who married Isaac Wynn and had William, Benjamin and Rebecca.

5.   Deborah, who married Joel Stratton, and had a daughter.

6.   Joseph, living 1846, who married first Kitty Bassett and secondly Sarah Clark, and had Sarah, Edward, Mary, Anne, Catharine, Joseph, William, Sarah 2d, Harriet and Clark.

The grand parents on her father's side of Elmira Williams Hughes, wife of Rev. Dr. Daniel Lawrence Hughes, (see page 157), were Humphrey Hughes and Jane Whilldin, daughter of James and sister of Elder Matthew Whilldin, (see page 202); on her mother's side her grand parents were William Williams of Loudon County, Virginia, and Hetty Zanes Collins, of Gloucester County, N. J. (See Divine Covenant fulfilled in Pious Households" by Rev. D. L. Hughes, D. D., page 109).

An account of the ancestor of the Leamings of Cape May has been given on page 25 in a quotation from the Diary of Aaron Leaming second, and in a quotation from the Anecdotes of Thomas, son of the first Christopher, on page 14, which notes were incorporated in the Diary of his nephew, the above named Aaron Leaming second.

———

The account of James Whilldin and Richard Crawford, executors of the last Will and Testament of Joseph Whilldin second, (see pages 27, 100), exhibited before the Prerogative Office at Burlington, 19 May, 1749, prays allowance for the payment of the following legacies:

	Pounds		
By moneys paid Abigail Whildin in full of her legacy	50	0	0
By money paid David Whildin in part of his Legacy__	50	0	0
By moneys paid Mathew Whildin in full of his Legacy	56	0	5
By moneys paid Loes Whildin in full of her Legacy____	60	7	5
By moneys pd Ellis Hughes in full of his wifes Legacy	24	1	11
By money pd David Whildin in full of his legacy_____	24	1	11
By moneys to Richard Crawford in full of his wifes Legacy _____	24	1	11
By moneys paid Richard Crawford, Ellis Hughes and Matthew Crowell in part for the negro girl_____	15		
By moneys to be paid to Uriah Hughes 2 Children____	5	0	0
By moneys to James Whildin in part for the negro girl _____	5	0	0

Ellis Hughes was son-in-law of Joseph Whilldin second, and his will (see page 29), gives the name of his wife Hannah and his son Memucan. The grandson "Memukin" Hughes to whom Joseph Whilldin second gives "one ten year old hefer or stear" was the son of Ellis and Hannah Whilldin, and could be the son of no other daughter of Joseph Whilldin, Rachel's legacy being paid to her husband Richard Crawford and Loes receiving hers, at least in part, in her own name—and further the two children of the deceased daughter Mary (Mercy) are named in both the will and accounting of the executors. Memucan, as the comparison of his will and tombstone shows, was born 12 April, 1739, died 8 January, 1812. Ellis, his full brother, born 16 August, 1745, named in the will of Ellis senior, was also the son of Hannah who survived her husband, and after his death in 1752 married an Eldredge.

A legacy of 2 pounds 10 Shillings each is given by Joseph Whilldin second to "my Daughter Marey (Mercy) Deceased Children Ellis and Judith" and the executors account for "5 Pounds to be paid to Uriah Hughes 2 Children." The author feels great diffidence in calling in question the conclusions of Mr. S. Gordon Smyth, whose unfailing assistance and patience have contributed a large share in determining the descent of the Pilgrim strain through the Whilldin-Hughes line, but it seems evident that the assumption that Ellis Hughes senior first married Mary and had Ellis and Judith is not borne out by the record of the will and accounting.

A further erroneous conclusion (and here Mr. S. Gordon Smyth is in full accord with the author) is that Ellis Hughes, son of Uriah and Mary Whilldin was the Ellis Hughes, junior, ancestor of the late Major Charles Welsh Edmunds of Philadelphia. Mr. George E. Bowman of Boston has shown that the conclusions of State historians of the Society of Mayflower Descendants are not always reliable, and the author ventures to say that the arbitrary choice of Ellis, son of Uriah, as the Ellis junior of testamentary and tombstone records, with no connecting link, is entirely without support. Ellis junior was not the junior of an uncle, or of his cousin; he was the junior of his father, and his mother was Hannah Whilldin, and the connecting link which is entirely lacking in the arbitrary assumption of Uriah as his father is found in the memorandum of Thomas Hurst Hughes in the family Bible of Franklin Davenport Edmunds, (see page 37). While the memorandum is not first authority and must give way to certain documentary evidence, it confirms the record, and it is incredible that Congressman Thomas Hurst Hughes, whose father, Ellis junior, was living when he was 48 years of age, was mistaken as to the names of both paternal grand parents.

---o---

The following list of tombstones collected by Mr. William Evans Price from Tabernacle Cemetery, Cape May County, is of great value in confirming the record of the foregoing genealogical tables and is of general interest to the many descendants who have migrated to distant parts of the country.

Memucan Hughes, Sr., born 12 April, 1739, died 8 January, 1812, (see pages 197 and 204).

Parsons Edmunds, died 9 January, 1851, in his 70th year; Ruth Edmunds, wife of Parsons, died 20 January, 1846, aged 47 years, 9 months, 17 days.

Philip Cresse, died 25 March, 1853, in his 74th year; Margaret, wife of Philip, died 30 April, 1864, in her 78th year.

Aaron Hand, died 28 December, 1851, in his 51st year.

William Price, born 16 January, 1898, died 18 September, 1858; wife, Mary C., died 11 November, 1875, aged 67 years, 3 months, 20 days.

Rev. John Price, born 10 October, 1793, died 21 May, 1863; wife, Kezia, born 18 August, 1798, died 7 August, 1886.

Edward Price, died 21 January, 1825, aged 57 years, 5 months, 26 days; wife, Sarah, died 19 October, 1819, aged 47 years, 1 month, 23 days.

Deborah Price, wife of Aaron Schellenger, born 26 February, 1830, died 20 October, 1917.

Madeline T. Reeves, born 1866, died 1905.

Albert E. Reeves, born 1863, died 1894.

Lambert W. Hughes, born 16 December, 1850, died 22 November, 1885.

Israel Hughes, died 27 January, 1904, aged 81 years, 9 months, (see pages 249, 259); wife, Elizabeth H., born 22 April, 1821, died 13 March, 1893, (see pages 249, 259). Daughters, Elizabeth and Judith, son Richard.

Jacob Corson, born 1815, died 1896; wife, Margaret M., born 1814, died 1896. Daughters Mary E., Albertina, Theodocia, son Solon.

Charles S. Corson, born 11 May, 1849, died 7 February, 1909.

Smith Stites, born 25 August, 1808, died 10 August, 1872.

Mary A. Stites, born 18 August, 1811, died 2 August, 1872.

Philip C. Stites, died 7 December, 1898, in his 44th year.

Cornelius Leaming, died 4 June, 1897, aged 65 years.

Rev. Israel Townsend, born 12 May, 1782, died 3 November, 1862; wife, Abigail, born 24 April, 1786, died 5 December, 1868.

Aaron Hughes, died 17 October, 1842, aged 63 years, 11 months, 17 days.

Meribah Hughes, died 16 April, 1825, aged 33 years, 5 months.

Daniel B. Hughes, born 20 July, 1816, died 1 June, 1888, (see pages 144, 146); wife, Priscilla Leaming, born 8 January, 1820, died 29 June, 1915.

Lemuel Leaming, born 2 October, 1809, died 3 May, 1879, (see page 177).

Aaron Leaming, born 15 May, 1784, died 7 January, 1836, (see pages 108, 144); wife, Hannah, died 12 April, 1862, aged 73 years, 6 months, (see pages 143, 144). Daughter, Charlotte Matthews, born 28 May, 1810, died 30 July, 1854; daughter, Mary L. Compton, died 31 July, 1862, aged 33 years, 5 months, 15 days.

Rev. Parsons Townsend, born 18 October, 1807, died 7 October, 1886; wife, Abigail, born 7 December, 1811, died 2 March, 1906. Son, Samuel, born 7 September, 1838, died 25 October, 1918.

Israel Townsend, died 11 July, 1841, in 28th year.

Rev. Socrates Townsend, born 4 February, 1816, died 13 September, 1899; wife, Sarah Garretson, born 8 June, 1823, died 11 February, 1858.

Elijah Miller, died 22 February, 1855, aged 74 years, 7 months, 24 days; wife, Catharine M., born 30 June, 1783, died 27 July, 1877.

Silas M. Hand, died 22 January, 1879, aged 73 years; wife, Mary B., died 4 August, 1893, aged 77 years, 5 months, 1 day.

Ezekiel Eldredge, of New England Township, Cape May County, made his will 6 June, 1710, proved 2 February, 1711-12, naming his wife Sarah—five sons and three daughters not named. The names of the children, in the absence of vital records, are collected from the Eldredge wills of the next generation. Elisha Eldredge made his will 1 December, 1732, naming his brothers Ezekiel, Samuel, William (see page 99), and Jacob, sisters, Lydia Eldredge, Bethia Parsons and Sarah Stiles (Stites?). Ezekiel Eldredge died intestate before 30 October, 1739, administration granted to widow, Elizabeth, and son Ezekiel. For will of Samuel Eldredge see page 29.

Tombstones in Cold Spring Cemetery

Dates Collected From the Older Stones

COLD SPRING CEMETERY

The Burial Place of Many Pilgrim Descendants, Cold Spring, New Jersey

AMBROSE—Isaac, born 22 October, 1882; died 28 December, 1882, aged 2 months, 6 days.

BAILEY—Harriet, born 26 May, 1883; died 18 June, 1883, aged 17 days.
Martha, born 26 May, 1883; died 8 June, 1883, aged 12 days.

BANCROFT—Albert.
Anna.
Ephraim.
James.
James.
Julia.

BARCLIFF—Albert.

BARNARD—Emma L., born 1844; died 3 April, 1874, aged 30 years.

BARNES—Edward, born 20 March, 1774; died 20 June, 1829, aged 55 years, 3 months.

BARROWS—Ferdie, died 31 December, 1863.
Freddie, died 8 August, 1869.
Charlie, born 8 January, 1871; died 4 February, 1871, aged 26 days.

BARNETT—E.
L.

BARNEY—Deborah, born 27 October, 1753; died 27 January, 1826, aged 72 years, 3 months.

BARTON—Clarence M., born 12 October, 1870; died 12 November, 1871, aged 8 years, 1 month.
Edwin D., born 2 December, 1866; died 5 March, 1867, aged 3 months, 3 days.

BATE—Anna Gaddie, born 1855; died 1 March, 1868, aged 13 years.
Elizabeth C., born 1838; died 29 August, 1841, aged 3 years.
William J., born 17 October, 1808; died 16 November, 1866, aged 78 years, 9 days.

BATEMAN—Elizabeth, born 1826; died 29 July, 1848, aged 22 years.

BATTERSALL—CARL W., born 18 August, 1884; died 18 November, 1886, aged 2 years, 3 months.

THOMAS, born 30 September, 1837; died 30 May, 1873, aged 35 years, 8 months.

BENEZET—WILLIAM H., born 1841; died 10 August, 1886, aged 46 years.

BENNETT—CAPT. AARON, born 10 September, 1764, died 8 August, 1840, aged 75 years, 10 months, 28 days.

ABRAHAM, born 1795; died 18 January, 1852, aged 57 years.

ALBERT G., born 28 March, 1855; died 19 July, 1861, aged 6 years, 3 months, 21 days.

ELIZA C., born 1855; died 24 January, 1872, aged 17 years.

EMMA, aged 2 years, 2 months.

GEORGE, born 1805; died 18 August, 1869, aged 64 years.

LOUISA, born 1741; died 19 March, 1814, aged 73 years.

MARTHA S., born 1844; died 22 May, 1870, aged 26 years.

MARY, born 23 December, 1769; died 27 January, 1820, aged 50 years, 1 month, 4 days.

MARY, born 1820; died 9 August, 1888, aged 68 years.

SARAH C., born 9 August, 1840; died 21 September, 1842, aged 2 years, 1 month, 12 days.

SOPHIA, born 14 October, 1812; died 22 January, 1847, aged 34 years, 3 months, 8 days.

SOPHIA H., born 5 January, 1853; died 14 July, 1861, aged 8 years, 6 months, 9 days.

SPICER, born 1805; died 1832, aged 29 years.

STEPHEN D., born 1844; died 27 May, 1862, aged 18 years.

STEPHEN, born 1815; died 5 July, 1871, aged 55 years.

WILLIAM.

MRS. W.

BISHOP—RACHEL, born 1769; died 30 November, 1839, aged 70 years.

BLAKE—CARRIE, born 1867; died 21 August, 1888, aged 21 years.

GEORGE, born 22 February, 1826; died 2 November, 1888, aged 62 years(8 months, 10 days.

SYLVIA, born 3 July, 1875; died 7 January, 1887, aged 11 years, 6 months, 4 days.

BLATTNER—Eugene J., born 20 June, 1813; died 12 February, 1886, aged 72 years, 7 months, 22 days.

BOCKIUS—Bessie, born 7 September, 1886; died 13 June, 1888, aged 1 year, 9 months, 6 days.

BOHM—Amelius, born 17 April, 1822; died 4 July, 1877, aged 55 years, 2 months, 17 days.

BORTON—Edward, died 22 February, 1889.

BOWEN—Eliza, born 1806; died 15 February, 1882, aged 76 years.
Silvanus, born 1747; died 6 November, 1761, aged 14 years.
Smith, born 1814; died 30 December, 1888, aged 74 years.

BREWTON—Emma C., born 26 December, 1880; died 23 January, 1882, aged 1 year, 27 days.
Lizzie S., born 16 September, 1870; died 16 March, 1873, aged 2 years, 6 months.
Sarah G., born 9 January, 1879; died 4 September, 1879, aged 7 months, 25 days.

BUCK—Aaron, born 12 April, 1773; died 12 February, 1790, aged 16 years, 10 days.
Frederick, born 1760; died 2 September, 1828, aged 68 years.
Tabitha, born 1768; died 21 May, 1836, aged 68 years.
Thomas, born 1744, died 24 February, 1790, aged 46 years.

BULL—Lydia, born 1761; died 19 July, 1842, aged 81 years.

BUSH—Francine, born 1 August, 1886; died 4 April, 1889, aged 2 years, 9 months, 4 days.
Samuel, aged 4 days.

CAKE—Lawrence, born 20 September, 1861; died 20 March, 1867, aged 5 years, 6 months.

CASSEDY—Albert Judson, born 1839; died 27 June, 1863, aged 24 years.
Maria S., born 10 July, 1806; died 10 November, 1884, aged 78 years, 4 months.
William, born 1807; died 11 August, 1854, aged 47 years.
Willie, born 1838; died 2 March, 1842, aged 4 years.

CHRISTMAN—ELIZABETH S., born 23 August, 1811; died 22 October, 1874, aged 63 years, 2 months, 4 days.

CHURCH—ELIZA P., born 26 January, 1839; died 15 July, 1839, aged 5 months, 19 days.
HARRY R., born 7 July, 1879; died 25 April, 1881, aged 1 year, 9 months, 18 days.
JOHN R., born 1818; died 30 July, 1859, aged 41 years.
MARY, born 1817; died 6 June, 1864, aged 47 years.
NATHAN, born 3 July, 1913; died 25 November, 1862, aged 49 years, 4 months, 22 days.
SMITH, born 5 August, 1807; died 2 February, 1885, aged 77 years, 5 months, 27 days.
WILLIAM H., born 15 May, 1838; died 4 November, 1852, aged 14 years, 5 months, 19 days.

CLARKE—JAMES, born 7 June, 1798; died 10 December, 1859, aged 61 years, 6 months, 8 days.
REV. THOMAS D., born 1809; died 11 February, 1870, aged 61 years.

CLIVER—JONATHAN R., born 1841; died 25 July, 1885, aged 44 years.

CLOPPER—EDWARD N., born 1775; died 22 July, 1822, aged 47 years.

CORGIE—JUDITH, born 1801; died 16 September, 1843, aged 42 years.
LYDIA, born 1758; died 23 December, 1817, aged 59 years.
ROBERT, born 1742; died 25 April, 1807, aged 65 years.
WILLIAM, born 1793; died 23 November, 1856, aged 63 years.

CORSON—ELIZABETH, born 1794; died 19 March, 1853.
REBECCA D., born 5 April, 1837; died 2 October, 1861, aged 24 years, 5 months, 27 days.

CRAWFORD—ELIZA, born 1811; died 3 February, 1889, aged 78 years.
HANNAH, born 1790; died 15 March, 1862, aged 72 years.
JONATHAN, born 1787; died 23 Apirl, 1866, aged 79 years.
JOSEPHENE, born 1836; died 21 May, 1888, aged 52 years.
RICHARD, born 1766; died 9 November, 1811, aged 45 years.
WILLIAM, born 15 May, 1811; died 28 June, 1874, aged 63 years, 1 month, 13 days.

CRESSE—ANTHONY, born 4 January, 1773; died 23 January, 1834, aged 61 years, 19 days.

ANTHONY, born 1811; died 20 March, 1857, aged 46 years.

DAVID, born 1800; died 18 October, 1849, aged 49 years.

DAVID, Jr., born 1841; died 4 February, 1862, aged 21 years .

GERTIE, born 10 February, 1873; died 25 February, 1878, aged 5 years, 15 days.

GEORGE, born 25 December, 1781; died 14 June, 1868, aged 86 years, 5 months 19 days.

JUDITH, born 21 March, 1773; died 25 January, 1843, aged 69 years, 10 months, 4 days.

JUDITH, born 1 June, 1781; died 17 December, 1870, aged 89 years, 6 months, 16 days.

JULIA, born 1848; died 11 March, 1852, aged 4 years.

MARIA TOMLIN, born 1806; died 28 February, 1875, aged 69 years.

MARY S., born 25 October, 1805; died 7 September, 1831, aged 25 years, 11 months, 11 days.

URIAH H., born 1832; died 23 August, 1833, aged 1 year.

URIAH H., born 1806; died 3 March, 1870, aged 64 years.

CROWELL—AARON, born 20 October, 1771; died 15 January, 1860, aged 89 years, 2 months, 26 days.

ABIGAIL, born 28 July, 1810; died 12 May, 1842, aged 31 years, 9 months, 14 days.

BARNABAS, born 1766; died 5 March, 1819, aged 53 years.

DANIEL, born 1751; died 16 November, 1815, aged 64 years.

DEWITT C., born 5 February, 1828; died 25 November, 1874, aged 46 years, 9 months, 20 days.

ELIZABETH, born 1768; died 13 January, 1836, aged 68 years.

ELIZA F., born 1798; died July, 1821, aged 23 years.

EMMA, born 23 March, 1874; died 27 May, 1874, aged 12 months, 4 days.

ESTHER, born 9 March, 1799; died 22 September, 1882, aged 83 years, 6 months, 13 days.

FURMAN, born 1792; died 14 February, 1853, aged 61 years.

1875, aged 68 years, 4 months, 17 days.

HANNAH M., born 24 September, 1806; died 11 February, 1875, aged 68 years, 4 months, 17 days.

JULIA, born 8 February, 1867; died 8 September, 1868, aged 1 year, 7 months.

MARIA, born 1798; died 20 May, 1885, aged 87 years.

CAPT. PAGE, born 6 June, 1806; died 23 August, 1886, aged 80 years, 2 months, 17 days.

SARAH, born 8 July, 1777; died 6 June, 1857, aged 79 years, 10 months, 28 days.

SARAH, born 1810; died 8 October, 1881, aged 71 years.

THOMAS P., born 27 February, 1798; died 16 August, 1876, aged 78 years, 5 months, 19 days.

THOMAS S.; died 28 June, 1858.

TRYPHENE, born 20 February, 1809; died 29 November, 1834 aged 25 years, 9 months, 9 days.

CUMMINGS—EMMA E., born 1874; died 14 September, 1887, aged 13 years.

HARRY E., born 3 June, 1870; died 3 March, 1875, aged 4 years, 5 months.

JONATHAN, born 2 August, 1769; died 5 May, 1825, aged 55 years, 9 months, 5 days.

LEONARD, born 4 June, 1810; died 18 November, 1886, aged 76 years, 5 months, 14 days.

LOUISA, born 10 January, 1815; died 20 September, 1837, aged 21 years, 8 months, 20 days.

MARY ELLA, born 1856; died 8 January, 1861, aged 5 years.

RACHEL, born 1786; died 22 May, 1864, aged 78 years.

SAMUEL S., born 1 September, 1842; died 12 October, 1887, aged 45 years, 1 month, 11 days.

DAVIS—ABIGAIL, born 10 February, 1759; died 24 February, 1847, aged 88 years, 14 days.

ELIZABETH, born 1788; died 3 June, 1829, aged 41 years.

VIRGIL M.

DENIZOT—ALBERT, born 25 July, 1885; died 22 January, 1886, aged 5 months, 27 days.

JULIA, born 20 November, 1883; died 15 July, 1884, aged 7 months, 25 days.

DOUGLASS—ANNA FRANCIS, born 19 January, 1841; died 29 June, 1841, aged 5 months, 10 days.

DOWNS—BERTHA, born 30 June, 1870; died 23 October, 1885, aged 15 years, 3 months, 23 days.

EDMUND, aged 2 months.

GEORGE W., born 3 January, 1824; died 25 November, 1870, aged 46 years, 10 months, 22 days.

MARGARET L., born 9 January, 1833; died 31 March, 1883, aged 50 years, 2 months, 22 days.

MAURICE C.

EDMONDS—AARON, born 14 September, 1766; died 23 June, 1844, aged 79 years, 9 months, 9 days.

LYDIA, born 1770; died 30 January, 1795, aged 25 years.

EDMUNDS—AARON, born 22 June, 1793; died 25 November, 1856, aged 63 years, 5 months, 2 days.

ABIGAIL, born 3 June, 1858; died 24 November, 1879, aged 21 years, 5 months, 21 days.

ADA H., born 22 February, 1870; died 22 July, 1870, aged 5 months.

ALBERT S., born 1839; died 13 December, 1862, aged 23 years.

ALFRED A.; 37 years, 8 months.

ANN, born 1783; died 27 November, 1847, aged 64 years.

ANNA, born 1792; died January, 1870, aged 78 years.

CARDWELL, born 7 July, 1839; died 17 July, 1839, aged 10 days.

CHARLIE, born 1 April, 1854; died 2 November, 1861, aged 7 years, 7 months, 1 day.

DOWNS, born 1782; died 7 December, 1861, aged 79 years.

DOWNIE F., born 1 September, 1876; died 1 August, 1878, aged 1 year, 11 months.

ELIZA S., born 1780; died 11 March, 1867, aged 87 years.

ELLEN B., born 16 December, 1827; died 29 August, 1851, aged 23 years, 8 months, 13 days.

ELLEN W.; died 9 February, 1877.

EMMA, born 31 July, 1840; died 24 March, 1845, aged 5 years, 8 months.

ENOCH, born 1829; died 1 May, 1855, aged 26 years.

ENOCH, born 1799; died 30 March, 1867, aged 68 years.

ENOS S., born 9 June, 1847; died 9 August, 1848, aged 1 year, 2 months.

EVAN, born 1781; died 18 November, 1844, aged 63 years.

EDMUNDS—Evan, born 8 September, 1818; died 9 March, 1855, aged 66 years, 7 months, 1 day.

Evin B., born 1850; died 23 May, 1881, aged 31 years.

Harriet J., born 29 June, 1845; died 25 December, 1845, aged 5 months, 26 days.

James, born 9 September, 1800; died 27 September, 1833, aged 33 years, 18 days.

Jane, born 1814; died 21 April, 1883, aged 69 years.

Jeremiah, born 1815; died 11 April, 1884, aged 70 years.

John, born 29 July, 1794; died 11 August, 1794, aged 12 days.

Judith, born 1791; died 12 August, 1794, aged 3 years.

Louisa W., born 1805; died 21 August, 1860, aged 55

Luther C., born 27 January, 1851; died 22 August, 1851, aged 6 months, 25 days.

Lutie S., born 9 March, 1872; died 3 April, 1874, aged 2 years, 24 days.

Lydia H., born 4 December, 1795; died 14 December, 1862, aged 67 years 10 days.

Mary, born 12 January, 1820; died 11 May, 1868, aged 48 years, 3 months, 29 days.

Mary E., born 1848; died 5 October, 1886, aged 38 years.

Mary Miller, born 15 May, 1804; died 3 July, 1883, aged 79 years, 1 month, 18 days.

Miller, born 11 June, 1796; died 30 June, 1796, aged 19 days.

Richard, born 22 December, 1785; died 28 October, 1846, aged 60 years, 10 months, 6 days.

Richard D., born 1814; died 8 October, 1879, aged 65 years.

Richard H.; aged 1 month.

Richard E.; aged 3 months.

Robert, born 1761; died 17 February, 1822, aged 61 years.

Robert, Jr., born 1797; died 15 January, 1826, aged 29 years.

Sarah, born 20 February, 1767; died 20 January, 1846, aged 78 years, 11 months.

Sarah H., born 3 February, 1819; died 21 July, 1849, aged 30 years, 5 months, 18 days.

EDMUNDS—THANKFUL, born 29 June, 1755; died 19 March, 1798, aged 42 years, 9 months, 20 days.

TRYPHENIA, born 1761; died 13 September, 1824, aged 63 years.

VIRGINIA D.; aged 3 months.

EDWARDS—REV. DAVID, born 1776; died 30 December, 1815, aged 39 years.

GEORGE A., born 6 February, 1812; died 15 February, 1812, aged 9 days.

JANE, born 13 November, 1799; died 13 December, 1813, aged 34 years, 1 month.

ELDREDGE—AARON, born 13 June, 1771; died 21 August, 1819, aged 48 years, 2 months, 8 days.

AARON, Jr., born 6 June, 1795; died 10 August, 1832, aged 37 years, 2 months, 4 days.

AARON, born 1 March, 1839; died 1 December, 1784, aged 5 years, 9 months.

ABIGAIL, born 1820; died 26 March, 1874, aged 54 years.

ANN M., born 18 May, 1800; died 20 July, 1880, aged 80 years, 2 months, 2 days.

CHARLES, born 6 June, 1826; died 6 May, 1831, aged 4 years, 11 months.

CHRISTOPHER, born 30 October, 1830; died 17 September, 1861, aged 30 years, 10 months, 18 days.

DANIEL W., born 3 February, 1815; died 23 October, 1894.

DEBORAH, born 1804; died 29 January, 1866, aged 62 years.

DOWNIE F., born 1 September, 1876; died 1 August, 1878, aged 1 year, 11 months.

ELIZA H., born 22 July, 1825; died 10 March, 1878, aged 52 years, 7 months, 14 days.

ELIZABETH, born 4 December, 1780; died 11 January, 1868, aged 87 years, 1 month, 7 days.

ELIZABETH, born 1776; died 1852, aged 75 years.

ELIZABETH, born 4 February, 1786; died 16 January, 1811, aged 24 years, 11 months, 12 days.

ELLA, born 26 February, 1858; died 10 September, 1858, aged 6 months, 14 days.

ELLIS C., born 15 December, 1847; died 10 September, 1849, aged 1 year, 8 months, 25 days.

ELDREDGE—ENOCH, born 27 July, 1819; died 30 July, 1819, aged 3 days.

EMMA H., born 4 May, 1858; died 8 August, 1858, aged 3 months, 7 days.

ENOCH, born 26 May, 1822; died 30 June, 1868, aged 46 years, 1 month, 4 days.

ENOCH, born 9 October, 1870; died 3 March, 1873, aged 2 years, 4 months, 24 days.

ENOS, born 21 March, 1779; died 21 July, 1839, aged 60 years, 4 months.

EPHRAIM, born 30 March, 1787; died 30 August, 1812, aged 25 years, 5 months.

ESTHER REEVES, born 12 August, 1867; died 27 June, 1881, aged 13 years, 10 months, 15 days.

ESTER A., born 8 July, 1811; died 11 October, 1897.

GEORGIE B., born 25 March, 1870; died 14 July, 1874, aged 4 years, 3 months, 19 days.

HANNAH, born 14 June, 1800; died 21 April, 1831, aged 30 years, 10 months, 7 days.

HANNAH, born 21 December, 1774; died 6 June, 1836, aged 61 years, 5 months, 15 days.

HARRIET, born 3 December, 1805; died 23 October, 1863, aged 57 years, 10 months, 30 days.

JACOB, born 1775; died 1850, aged 75 years.

JEREMIAH, born 5 September, 1822; died 10 August, 1838, aged 15 years, 11 months, 5 days.

JEREMIAH, born 14 July, 1793; died 10 July, 1849, aged 55 years, 11 months, 26 days.

JEHEMIAH, born 5 August, 1745; died 28 April, 1795, aged 49 years, 8 months, 23 days.

JOSEPH, born 9 August, 1798; died 21 March, 1879, aged 80 years, 7 months, 12 days.

JUDITH, born 8 August, 1759; died 26 August, 1831, aged 72 years, 18 months.

JUDITH, born 6 September, 1793; died 14 August, 1832, aged 38 years, 11 months, 8 days.

MARIETTA, born 8 August, 1856; died 30 August, 1875, aged 19 years, 19 days.

MARY, born 30 August, 1779; died 26 September, 1838, aged 59 years, 26 days.

MARY C., born 10 March, 1855; died 5 February, 1885, aged 29 years, 10 months, 22 days.

ELDREDGE—MAHLON R., born 1852; died 16 September, 1885, aged 33 years.

MARY E., born 1863; died 19 August, 1881, aged 18 years.

MARY ELIZABETH, born 14 February, 1839; died 14 August, 1850, aged 11 years, 6 months.

MARY MCNEVAN, born 4 October, 1881; died 21 March, 1882, aged 5 months, 17 days.

NANCY LEAMING, born 5 February, 1833; died 3 May, 1837, aged 4 years, 2 months.

NELSON, born 13 October, 1833; died 16 June, 1886, aged 52 years, 8 months, 3 days.

SARAH, born 1747; died 12 February, 1804, aged 57 years.

THOMAS, born 21 January, 1798; died 29 January, 1849, aged 51 years, 8 days.

WILLIAM, born 24 December, 1791; died 7 August, 1832; aged 40 years, 7 months, 13 days.

WILLIAM; died 1809.

WILLIAM A., born 1852; died 24 February, 1879, aged 27 years.

WILLIAM T., born 1821; died 4 December, 1888, aged 68 years.

ELDRIDGE—LEMUEL, born 1780; died 14 January, 1821, aged 41 years.

LETITIA, born 1841; died 21 July, 1869, aged 28 years.

LEVI, born 17 October, 1776; died 23 November, 1822, aged 46 years, 1 month, 6 days.

WILLIAM, born 30 April, 1804, died 29 June, 1886.

ENTRIKEN—FARRAN P.; aged 3 months.

HARRY, born 20 November, 1885; died 13 October, 1886, aged 10 months, 23 days.

EPLER—MARY, born 18 April, 1844; died 5 July, 1844, aged 2 months, 17 days.

EWING—DAVID, born 1804; died 3 February, 1888, aged 84 years.

LEAMING, born 1791; died 20 April, 1867, aged 76 years.

LIZZIE D., born 15 August, 1870; died 21 June, 1873, aged 2 years, 10 months, 6 days.

SAMUEL F., born 22 September, 1771; died 22 October, 1772, aged 1 year, 1 month.

FARROW—J. HARRY, born 12 April, 1832; died 29 January, 1884, aged 51 years, 9 months, 17 days.

FISHER—JOSEPH, born 13 August, 1791; died 20 May, 1795, aged 3 years, 9 months, 7 days.

FITHIAN—WILLIAM J., born 12 May, 1856; died 22 July, 1883, aged 27 years, 2 months, 10 days.

FRANKS—JENNIE, born 30 April, 1875; died 30 February, 1880, aged 4 years, 9 months, 3 days.

FOREST—THOMAS, born 7 October, 1774; died 5 June, 1819, aged 44 years, 7 months, 28 days.
RHODA, born 1770; died 10 February, 1826, aged 56 years.

FOSTER—ANN L., born 16 November, 1817; died 16 February, 1865, aged 47 years, 3 months.
DOWNS E., born 1807; died 20 October, 1886, aged 79 years.
ELIZA E., born 16 July, 1850; died 4 June, 1851, aged 10 months, 18 days.
ELIZABETH, born 1812; died 16 December, 1864, aged 52 years.
GEORGE, born 1800; died 1871, aged 71 years.
GILBERT, born 30 October, 1877; died 30 June, 1878, aged 8 months.
HANNAH; aged 72.
JACOB, born 1774; died 8 November, 1845, aged 71 years.
JANE, born 1782; died 13 September, 1829, aged 47 years.
JANE C., born 11 November, 1808; died 22 November, 1832, aged 24 years, 11 days.
JOANNA E., born 18 May, 1812; died 29 September, 1882, aged 70 years, 5 months, 11 days.
JOSEPH H., born 8 January, 1857; died 10 June, 1862, aged 5 years, 5 months, 2 days.
MARCY, born 1775; died 15 September, 1819, aged 44 years.
MATTHIAS, Sr., born 1776; died 11 October, 1866, aged 90 years.
NANCY, born 4 April, 1810; died 8 July, 1811, aged 1 year, 3 months, 4 days.
NANCY E., born 1781; died 6 August, 1855, aged 74 years.

FOSTER—Lydia E., born 22 May, 1805; died 24 December, 1837, aged 32 years, 7 months, 21 days.

Rachel, born 1784; died 29 July, 1878, aged 94 years.

Reuben, born 14 September, 1780, died 24 June, 1870, aged 89 years, 9 months, 10 days.

Reuben, born 31 March, 1810, died 8 July, 1811.

Roanna, born 1764; died 20 February, 1845, aged 81 years.

FOWLER—Lydia E., born 22 May, 1805; died 24 December, 1837, aged 32 years, 7 months, 24 days.

Reuben, born 14 September, 1780; died 24 June, 1870, aged 89 years.

Reuben, born 31 March, 1810; died 8 July, 1811, aged 1 year, 3 months, 8 days.

Sallie, born 27 April, 1862; died 2 September, 1863, aged 1 year, 4 months, 5 days.

GASS—James, born 1818; died 5 December, 1882, aged 64 years.

GERMON—Ralph, born 4 June, 1886; died 14 June, 1889, aged 3 years, 10 days.

GORDON—Oceola, born 1 July, 1877; died 11 November, 1878, aged 1 year, 4 months.

Robert H., born 8 February, 1875; died 18 November, 1878, aged 3 years, 9 months, 10 days.

Ross, born 31 December, 1867; died 9 November, 1878, aged 10 years, 10 months, 9 days.

GREGORY—Elizabeth A., born 29 July, 1804; died 25 July, 1884, aged

Mary Jane, born 9 April, 1845; died 21 November, 1861.

William C., born 17 June, 1803; died 24 April, 1883.

HALEY—Samuel, born 3 January, 1846; died 9 June, 1886, aged 40 years, 5 months, 6 days.

HALL—Fannie L., born 20 October, 1857; died 13 January, 1858, aged 2 months, 23 days.

Isaac H., born 1839; died 15 October, 1866, aged 27 years.

Jane E., born 24 December, 1809; died 21 March, 1887, aged 77 years, 2 months, 27 days.

Joseph, Sr., born 18 February, 1807; died 21 June, 1897, in 91st year.

HALL—LAFAYETTE M., born 19 June, 1843, died 23 April,
1907, aged 57 years.
MATTHEW W., born 9 September, 1831, died 4 February,
1874, aged 42 years, 7 months, 25 days.

HAND—AARON, born 1790; died 31 December, 1861, aged 71
years.
AARON, born 5 May, 1791; died 23 December, 1861, aged
70 years, 8 months, 18 days.
ALBERT G., born 16 August, 1864; died 9 April, 1867,
aged 2 years, 7 months, 23 days.
ALEXANDER M., born 1829; died 9 December, 1855, aged
26 years.
ANNA E., born 5 March, 1862; died 29 November, 1862,
aged 8 months, 24 days.
ARCHIBALD, born 1832; died 15 August, 1855, aged 23
years.
ARTHUR G., born 4 June, 1880; died 27 October, 1885,
aged 5 years, 4 months, 23 days.
CABEL, born 1760; died 20 December, 1772, aged 12
years.
CHARLOTTE, born 9 February, 1811; died 9 September,
1852, aged 41 years, 7 months.
CORNELIA, born 29 August, 1785; died 27 December,
1866, aged 81 years, 3 months, 28 days.
DAVID E., born 23 May, 1803; died 22 February, 1860,
aged 56 years, 9 months.
DAVID E., born 1841; died 26 January, 1863.
E. B.; died 1822.
EDMUND H., born 21 August, 1878; died 15 August,
1879, aged 11 months, 24 days.
ELI DOWNS, born 11 June, 1857; died 11 May, 1862, aged
4 years, 11 months.
ELIAS, born 15 January, 1797; died 14 August, 1798,
aged 1 year, 6 months, 29 days.
ELISHA, born 17 January, 1752; died 18 November, 1814,
aged 62 years, 10 months, 1 day.
ELIZABETH, born 31 April, 1740; died 31 December, 1788,
aged 48 years, 8 months.
ELIZABETH S., born 21 May, 1792; died 2 July, 1880,
aged 88 years, 1 month, 12 days.
ESTHER, born 10 November, 1766; died 4 June, 1802,
aged 35 years, 6 months, 24 days.

HAND—GEORGE, born 1758; died 1822, aged 64 years.

HENRY, born 1728; died 26 September, 1787, aged 59 years.

HENRY, born 5 November, 1793; died 30 January, 1820, aged 26 years, 2 months, 25 days.

HETTIE, born 21 April, 1817; died 25 October, 1833, aged 16 years, 6 months, 4 days.

ISAIAH, born 1723; died 28 February, 1765, aged 42 years.

CAPT. JAMES, born 4 October, 1781; died 12 March, 1829, aged 47 years, 5 months, 8 days.

JAMES A., born 5 February, 1859; died 21 August, 1863, aged 4 years, 6 months, 16 days.

JANE B., born 25 January, 1819; died 4 January, 1821, aged 2 years, 11 months, 9 days.

JANE B., born 20 August, 1793; died 14 January, 1864, aged 70 years, 4 months, 24 days.

JANE B., born 1823; died 9 February, 1875, aged 52 years.

JENNIE, born 31 March, 1871; died 31 August, 1871, aged 5 months.

JOSEPH A., born 1829; died 17 September, 1862, aged 33 years.

JOSEPH, born 1861; died 17 August, 1866, aged 5 years.

JOSEPH; died 1832.

JUDITH, born 1808; died 18 July, 1837, aged 29 years.

LORINE S., born 10 January, 1879; died 10 March, 1880, aged 1 year, 2 months.

MARTHA ANN, wife of Alphonzo D. Lee, born 4 December, 1832; died 26 August, 1907.

MARTHA, born 19 December, 1800; died 11 October, 1836, aged 35 years, 9 months, 22 days.

MARTHA, born 1829; died 9 July, 1888, aged 59 years.

MARTHA, born 24 February, 1780; died 22 December, 1845, aged 65 years, 9 months, 28 days.

MARY ELLA, born 6 August, 1852; died 6 February, 1884, aged 31 years, 6 months.

MATTHEW W., born 9 September, 1831; died 4 February, 1874, aged 42 years, 7 months, 25 days.

MERCY, born 1727; died 31 January, 1775, aged 48 years.

NANCY, born 19 December, 1800; died 26 May, 1854, aged 53 years, 5 months, 7 days.

NOAH, born 24 March, 1789; died 12 June, 1825, aged 36 years, 2 months, 18 days.

HAND—PARSONS, born 14 September, 1803; died 11 April, 1876, aged 72 years, 6 months, 27 days.

PATIANS, born 14 February, 1726; died 20 November, 1746, aged 20 years, 9 months, 6 days.

PHILIP, born 27 October, 1797; died 12 August, 1881, aged 83 years, 9 months, 15 days.

PHILIP, born 7 June, 1824; died 7 December, 1888, aged 64 years, 6 months.

RECOMPENSE, born 20 November, 1795; died 15 April, 1871; aged 75 years, 4 months, 25 days.

RECOMPENSE, born 1827; died 9 June, 1886, aged 59 years.

RHODA, born 1763; died 27 June, 1820, aged 57 years.

RICHFIELD, born 1848; died 23 April, 1886, aged 38 years.

ROBERT S., born 1821; died 20 November, 1878, aged 57 years.

SARAH, born 1 September, 1807; died 2 July, 1844, aged 36 years, 10 months, 1 day.

SETH M., born 8 May, 1838; died 8 February, 1842, aged 3 years, 9 months.

SOUTHARD, born 29 February, 1839; died 29 September, 1874, aged 35 years, 7 months.

SPICER L., born 1867; died 23 November, 1883, aged 16 years.

SYNTHA, born 1841; died 1863, aged 22 years.

THERESA H., born 13 December, 1839; died 12 April, 1883, aged 43 years, 3 months, 29 days.

THOMAS, born 1705; died 2 April, 1785, aged 80 years.

THOMAS, born 1791; died 5 July, 1809, aged 18 years.

THOMAS P., born 7 August, 1836; died 29 May, 1869, aged 32 years, 9 months, 22 days.

URIAH, born 25 November, 1777; died 16 December, 1829, aged 52 years, 21 days.

WALTER, born 8 November, 1868; died 3 July, 1869, aged 7 months, 25 days.

WILLIAM F., born 1830; died 18 May, 1877, aged 47 years.

WILLIAM M., born 1833; died 25 April, 1879, aged 46 years.

WILLIE, born 12 November, 1858.

HANEY—ELIZABETH, born 15 January, 1794; died 28 April, 1870, aged 76 years, 3 months, 13 days.
JOHN, born 1796; died 30 December, 1873, aged 77 years.

HARPER—JAMES A., born 15 June, 1859; died 2 June, 1889, aged 29 years, 11 months, 17 days.

HAYS—GARVIL, born 29 September, 1781; died 29 May, 1835, aged 53 years, 8 months.

HEWITT—JAMES S., born 29 December, 1859; died 15 January, 1866, aged 6 years, 16 days.
MARY B., born 13 February, 1798; died 14 July, 1857, aged 59 years, 5 months, 1 day.

HIGBEE—GEORGE H., born 29 April, 1799; died 29 July, 1824, aged 25 years, 3 months.
JOSEPH S., born 9 October, 1796; died 4 February, 1872, aged 75 years, 3 months, 25 days.
MARY, born 31 July, 1801; died 15 August, 1863, aged 62 years, 15 days.

HIGGINS—LOAS, born 21 August, 1757; died 5 September, 1811, aged 54 years, 14 days.

HILDRETH—ALVIN P., born 11 June, 1831; died 3 August, 1897.
DANIEL, born 1791; died 22 May, 1862, aged 71 years.
HOWARD W., born 5 January, 1856; died 5 June, 1857, aged 1 year, 5 months.
LYDIA H., born 28 October, 1832; died 4 January, 1862, aged 29 years, 2 months, 6 days.
SARAH, born 1829, died 3 September, 1880, aged 51 years.

HOFFMAN—BEULAH S., born 5 March, 1873; died 21 March, 1873, aged 16 days.
DEBORAH, born 1842; died 1 February, 1872, aged 30 years.
ENOS W., born 18 June, 1867; died 24 October, 1868, aged 1 year, 4 months, 5 days.
FRANK B., born 1854; died 23 August, 1877, aged 23 years.
HARRY F., born 24 May, 1853; died 24 April, 1874, aged 20 years, 11 months.
HELEN, born 31 December, 1879; died 15 February, 1887, aged 7 years, 1 month, 14 days.

HOFFMAN—HOLLIS P., born 14 August, 1849; died 16 March, 1850, aged 7 months, 2 days.

JAMES, born 3 April, 1788; died 29 March, 1831.

JUDITH, born 17 May, 1793; died 2 September, 1848, aged 55 years, 3 months, 15 days.

MARY ELIZA, born 9 April, 1851; died 9 August, 1852, aged 1 year, 5 months.

REUBEN, Jr., born 14 January, 1872; died 5 February, 1872, aged 21 days.

SARAH E., born 18 September, 1855; died 18 June, 1872, aged 16 years, 9 months.

WILLIAM S., born 18 May, 1825; died 19 August, 1880, aged 55 years, 3 months, 1 day.

HUGHES—ABIGAIL, born 5 June, 1816; died 26 August, 1832, aged 16 years, 2 months, 21 days.

ALBERT, born 1835; died 5 November, 1873, aged 38 years.

BENJAMIN B., Sr., born 29 October, 1810; died 26 November, 1872, aged 62 years, 27 days.

BERTHA M., born 16 January, 1884; died 4 January, 1887, aged 2 years, 11 months, 18 days.

CHARLES, born 7 July, 1818; died 7 February, 1819, aged 7 months.

CHARLOTTE C., born 1814; died 17 November, 1819, aged 5 years.

DR. DANIEL, born 1779; died 3 July, 1815, aged 36 years.

DANIEL L.; died 5 August, 1846.

DAVID, born 9 October, 1749; died 23 November, 1815, aged 66 years, 1 month, 4 days.

ELENOR, born 5 March, 1747; died 11 April, 1786, aged 39 years, 1 month.

ELIJAH, born 1708; died 19 February, 1762, aged 54 years.

ELIJAH, born 15 February, 1744; died 26 November, 1797, aged 53 years, 9 months, 11 days.

ELIZA, born 7 February, 1803; died 1 September, 1904, aged 1 year, 6 months, 24 days.

ELLIS, born 16 August, 1745; died 16 April, 1817, aged 71 years, 8 months.

ELLIS; died 1 June, 1863.

ELLIS, born 2 February, 1816; died 8 April, 1889, aged 73 years, 2 months, 6 days.

HUGHES—ELIZA E., born 1797; died 6 January, 1876, aged 79 years.

ELIZABETH, born 7 May, 1817; died 14 April, 1844, aged 26 years, 11 months, 7 days.

EVELINE, born 30 September, 1819; died 29 September, 1880, aged 60 years, 11 months, 29 days.

EXPERIENCE, born 1824; died 28 January, 1886, aged 62 years.

GEORGE W., born 7 October, 1804; died 11 October, 1854, aged 50 years, 4 months.

HANNAH; died 25 November, aged 50.

HAROLD, born 5 December, 1883; died 5 March, 1886, aged 2 years, 3 months.

HETTY W., born 14 December, 1781; died 4 February, 1870, aged 88 years, 1 month, 20 days.

HUMPHREYS, born 1734; died 20 February, 1754, aged 20 years.

CAPT. HUMPHREY, born 1775; died 21 August, 1858, aged 83 years.

ISAAC COLLINS, born 15 April, 1814; died 8 June, 1815, aged 1 year, 1 month, 23 days.

ISABELLA, born 9 January, 1815; died 9 September, 1825, aged 10 months, 9 days.

ISRAEL, born 9 May, 1778; died 7 February, 1833, aged 54 years, 8 months, 28 days.

JACOB, born 9 August, 1746; died 22 March, 1796, aged 49 years, 7 months, 13 days.

JACOB, born 1711; died 28 September, 1772, aged 61 years.

JAMES R., born 6 July, 1791; died 13 March, 1865, aged 73 years, 8 months, 7 days.

JEREMIAH, born 1783; died 23 February, 1815, aged 32 years.

LYDIA, born 13 May, 1767; died 3 May, 1828, aged 60 years, 11 months, 20 days.

MARTHA, born 1837; died 19 August, 1887.

MARY, born 16 March, 1785; died 16 June, 1863, aged 78 years, 3 months.

MARY, born 1752; died 24 April, 1773, aged 21 years.

MARY, born 22 August, 1776; died 22 September, 1779, aged 3 years, 1 month.

MARY, born 1803; died 8 February, 1866, aged 63 years.

MARY A. DAVIS, born 1808; died 11 July, 1857, aged 49 years.

HUGHES—MARY B., born 18 January, 1788; died 3 April, 1865, aged 77 years, 2 months, 15 days.

MARY B., born 23 July, 1812, died 3 September, 1835, aged 23 years, 1 month, 10 days.

MARY E. L., born 16 November, 1848; died 16 January, 1850, aged 14 months.

MARY P., born 1821; died 27 November, 1856, aged 35 years.

MEMUCAN, born 1810; died 17 August, 1857, aged 47 years.

JESSIE, born 1770; died 14 January, 1845, aged 75 years.

JOSEPH, MAJOR, born 17 November, 1772, died 13 March, 1813 aged 40 years, 3 months, 26 days.

JOSEPH B., born 28 March, 1799; died 7 March, 1842, aged 42 years, 11 months, 9 days.

JUDITH, born 17 September, 1754; died 7 August, 1795, aged 40 years, 10 months, 20 days.

JUDITH, born 10 July, 1795; died 18 August, 1798, aged 3 years, 1 month, 8 days.

JUDITH, born 1760; died 8 November, 1789, aged 29 years.

JUDITH, born 1 May, 1790; died 3 January, 1855, aged 64 years, 8 months, 2 days.

JUDITH; aged 69 years.

LEMUEL, born 14 January, 1798; died 13 March, 1841, aged 43 years, 1 month, 29 days.

LEMUEL, Jr., born 11 March, 1823; died 20 March, 1828, aged 5 years, 9 days.

LEVI, born 1800; died 22 October, 1814, aged 14 years.

LOUISA, born 2 December, 1814; died 12 December, 1814, aged 10 days.

SARAH, born 29 June, 1799; died 2 May, 1852, aged 52 years, 10 months, 3 days.

SARAH, born 12 August, 1781; died 12 January, 1786, aged 4 years, 5 months.

SMITH, born 1832; died 17 December, 1886, aged 54 years.

SPICER, born 1777; died 1849, aged 72 years.

THOMAS H., born 10 January, 1769; died 10 November, 1839, aged 70 years, 10 months.

THOMAS P., born 19 January, 1790; died 9 September, 1863, aged 73 years, 7 months, 20 days.

WILLIAM G., born 13 April, 1823; died 28 September, 1824, aged 1 year, 5 months, 15 days.

HUGHES—William S., born 5 August, 1843; died 5 May, 1845, aged 1 year, 9 months.

Prudence, born 26 August, 1776; died 7 August, 1841, aged 65 years, 11 months, 12 days.

Rachel, born 29 October, 1756; died 13 December, 1818, aged 62 years, 1 month, 14 days.

Richard, born 2 February, 1788; died 5 February, 1819, aged 31 years, 2 months, 3 days.

Robert E., born 29 August, 1873; died 8 April, 1875, aged 1 year, 7 months, 9 days.

INGELLS—Mary; 35 years.

IRELAND—Mary, born 1800; died March, 1875, aged 75 years.

IRVING—Emmaline, born 5 August, 1836; died 2 August, 1882, aged 45 years, 11 months, 27 days.

ISARD—Deborah, born 10 August, 1777; died 16 November, 1836, aged 59 years, 3 months, 6 days.

Henry, born 28 December, 1765; died 9 March, 1845, aged 79 years, 2 months, 11 days.

JACKSON—Nellie V., born 10 October, 1875; died 10 April, 1879, aged 3 years, 6 months.

JOHNS—Mary; aged 85 years.

JOHNSON—Edmund, born 5 March, 1862; died 22 April, 1887, aged 25 years, 1 month, 17 days.

Hannah V., born 3 February, 1830; died 25 March, 1886, aged 56 years, 1 month, 22 days.

Jane S., born 1841; died 21 March, 1888, aged 47 years.

Jane W., born 10 May, 1810; died 26 November, 1881, aged 71 years, 6 months, 16 days.

Lydia B., born 29 December, 1826; died 16 September, 1885, aged 58 years, 8 months, 17 days.

Sarah S., born 1776; died 7 September, 1839, aged 63 years.

KEELER—William A., born 27 July, 1813; died 18 May, 1882, aged 68 years, 10 months, 21 days.

KENNEDY—ALEXANDER W., born 6 October, 1848; died 2 April, 1851, aged 2 years, 5 months, 26 days.

JAMES F., born 1855; died 16 July, 1871, aged 16 years.

JAMES S. M. D., born 16 January, 1807; died 20 June, 1876, aged 69 years, 5 months, 4 days.

MARIA S., born 30 April, 1858; died 10 May, 1858, aged 11 days.

MILTON S., born 21 September, 1846; died 9 January, 1847, aged 3 months, 18 days.

MONTRAVILLE, born 11 November, 1850; died 16 August, 1851, aged 9 months, 5 days.

KENT—EPHRAIM, born 1795; died February, 1828, aged 33 years.

EPHRAIM, born 25 February, 1765; died 1 April, 1821, aged 56 years, 1 month, 6 days.

JEREMIAH, born 12 May, 1800; died 1 May, 1854, aged 53 years, 11 months, 19 days.

RACHEL, born 5 February, 1758; died 20 September, 1822, aged 64 years, 6 months, 15 days.

KIRK—SUSAN, born 12 June, 1755; died 15 August, 1844, aged 79 years, 2 months, 3 days.

KITCHEN—HENRY N., born 1797; died 10 September, 1833, aged 36 years.

JOSEPHINE, born 7 April, 1833; died 16 July, 1833, aged 3 months, 9 days.

LANG—MARY W., born 16 October, 1807; died 20 May, 1888, aged 80 years, 7 months, 4 days.

LANGSHAW—WILLIE, born 17 October, 1873; died 24 July, 1874, aged 9 months, 7 days.

LAWRENCE—BENJAMIN, born 1724; died 17 October, 1854, aged 30 years.

DANIEL, born 1718; died 13 April, 1766, aged 48 years.

ELIZABETH, born 1722; died 1 December, 1754, aged 32 years.

SARAH, born 1723; died 20 January, 1768, aged 45 years.

LEAMING—ALLIE, born 4 September, 1851; died October, 1862, aged 11 years, 1 month, 11 days.

CHARLOTTE, born 15 August, 1800; died 10 February, 1802, aged 1 year, 5 months.

CHRISTOPHER, born 19 June, 1799; died 3 November, 1865, aged 66 years, 4 months, 14 days.

EVA, born 26 August, 1868; died 24 August, 1876, aged 7 years, 11 months, 28 days.

HANNAH, born 3 March, 1767; died 11 September, 1857, aged 90 years, 6 months 8 days.

HARRIET A., born 17 June, 1831; died 24 September, 1915.

HARRY, born 21 September, 1864; died 18 April, 1867, aged 2 years, 6 months, 27 days.

HENRY L., born 9 August, 1847; died 9 February, 1852, aged 4 years, 6 months, 7 days.

ISRAEL, born 14 February, 1808; died 11 October, 1878, aged 70 years, 7 months, 27 days.

JACOB, born 16 January, 1812; died 6 January, 1888, aged 75 years, 11 months, 20 days.

JAMES, born 6 June, 1857; died 28 October, 1904.

JAMES, born 1788; died 12 August, 1870, aged 82 years.

JUDITH E., born 28 September, 1818; died 28 July, 1860, aged 41 years, 10 months.

LYDIA, born 19 January, 1790; died 13 February, 1856, aged 66 years, 24 days.

MARY B., born 4 March, 1875; died 15 February, 1852, aged 6 years, 11 months, 11 days.

PERSONS, born 1756; died 9 March, 1807, aged 51 years.

PERSONS, born 12 October, 1790; died 2 November, 1820, aged 30 years, 1 month.

SPICER, born 14 April, 1762; died 1 October, 1838, aged 76 years, 5 months, 17 days.

SPICER, born 20 March, 1792; died 18 October, 1814, aged 22 years, 6 months, 28 days.

LEE—LETITIA R., born 13 August, 1849; died 13 September, 1850, aged 1 year, 1 month.

MIRANDA R., born 9 August, 1871; died 9 December, 1877, aged 6 years, 4 months.

THOMAS C., Jr.; aged 11 months.

THOMAS C., Jr.; aged 7 months.

LEMON—George T., born 23 May, 1811; died 27 July, 1886, aged 75 years, 2 months, 4 days.

LINDHEIMER—Frederick, born 9 January, 1817; died 17 October, 1883, aged 66 years, 9 months, 8 days.
Frank; died June, 1888.

LITTLE—Sarah B., born 25 August, 1807; died 17 April, 1872, aged 64 years, 7 months, 22 days.

LUDLAM—Eleanor, born 1798; died 30 June, 1862, aged 64 years.
George, born 1816; died 7 July, 1863, aged 47 years.
T. Reed, born 15 March, 1880; died 29 November, 1880, aged 8 months, 14 days.

MACE—Walter Roy, born 20 July, 1888; died 30 April, 1889, aged 9 months, 10 days.

MANLOVE—Frances, born November, 1828; died October, 1867, aged 38 years, 11 months.

MARCY—Frederick A., born 13 October, 1854; died 17 November, 1861, aged 7 years, 1 month, 14 days.
Hannah, born 22 December, 1788; died 19 December, 1878, aged 89 years, 11 months, 27 days.
Hannah A., born 29 September, 1837; died 14 January, 1888, aged 50 years, 3 months, 15 days.
John Walter, born 29 April, 1880; died 8 January, 1881, aged 8 months, 9 days.
Matthew, born 1801; died 10 October, 1874, aged 73 years.
Samuel S., M. D., born 1793; died 13 February, 1882, aged 89 years.
Thankful B., born 1800; died 30 June, 1880, aged 80 years.

MARRYOTTE—Carl, born 27 November, 1888; died 28 July, 1889, aged 8 months, 1 day.
Charles, born 10 May, 1876; died 29 March, 1878, aged 1 year, 10 months, 19 days.
George Robert, born 26 August, 1880; died 22 August, 1881, aged 11 months, 26 days.
Mary W., born 25 May, 1882; died 4 December, 1885, aged 3 years, 6 months, 6 days.

MARRYOTTE—ROBURTHA, born 28 August, 1886; died 25 August, 1887, aged 11 months, 27 days.

McCOLLUM—IRENE, born 26 May, 1875; died 8 October, 1875, aged 4 months, 12 days.

MATTHEWS—JOANNA, born 24 February, 1788; died 11 July, 1847, aged 59 years.

ANNA, born 1 August, 1858; died 8 November, 1861, aged 3 years, 3 months, 7 days.

ANNA E., born 11 February, 1823; died 26 November, 1843, aged 20 years, 9 months, 15 days.

CHARLOTTE, born 3 December, 1816; died 14 November, 1847, aged 30 years, 11 months, 11 days.

ELEANOR, born 7 August, 1808; died 5 October, 1818, aged 10 years, 1 month.

ELIZA T., born 19 October, 1828; died 26 February, 1862, aged 33 years, 4 months, 7 days.

ELIZABETH, born 6 September, 1799; died 26 November, 1827, aged 28 years, 2 months, 20 days.

RICHARD, born 29 April, 1821; died 15 November, 1822,

SILAS, born 7 September, 1795; died 8 September, 1830, aged 1 year 6 months, 6 days.

SILAS, born 7 September, 1795; died 8 September, 1830, aged 35 years.

SILAS, born 1812; died 28 August, 1834, aged 22 years.

SILAS, born 29 November, 1833; died 13 August, 1852, aged 18 years, 8 months, 16 days.

THOMAS, born 4 October, 1808; died 21 November, 1848, aged 40 years, 1 month, 17 days.

WILLIAM, born 1800; died 31 January, 1874, aged 74 years.

MAY—HARRIET, born 1806; died 9 September, 1840, aged 34 years.

MECRAY—CHARLIE, born 18 September, 1847; died 18 March, 1851, aged 3 years, 6 months.

FRANK, born 27 June, 1853; died 27 July, 1857, aged 4 years, 1 month.

GABRIEL, born 16 April, 1845; died 16 March, 1851, aged 5 years, 11 months.

HANNAH, born 1788; died 14 March, 1866, aged 78 years.

HULDAH, born 18 December, 1869; died 4 February, 1870, aged 1 month, 16 days.

MECRAY—John, born 12 March, 1783; died 20 October, 1811, aged 28 years, 7 months, 8 days.

John, born 1839; died 5 May, 1862, aged 23 years.
Mary Ann, born 25 December, 1814; died 6 May, 1861, aged 46 years, 4 months, 11 days.
Mellie, born 10 January, 1851; died 5 June, 1875, aged 24 years, 4 months, 25 days.
Rachel S., born 1829; died 24 December, 1870, aged 41 years.
Willie, born 20 March, 1856; died 2 November, 1863, aged 7 years, 7 months, 12 days.

MERRITT—Alexis G., born 1815; died 29 October, 1831, aged 16 years.
Ella O., born 1851; died 1 February, 1868, aged 17 years.
Isaac P., Jr., born 21 February, 1843; died 11 August, 1843, aged 5 months, 21 days.

METCALFE—Samuel L., born 1800; died 17 July, 1856, aged 56 years.

McINNES—Duncan, born 1760; died 25 June, 1807, aged 47 years.

McKEAN—Alexander, born 30 November, 1826; died 31 January, 1870, aged 43 years, 2 days.
Alexander, born 1770; died 5 March, 1841, aged 71 years.
Alexander, born 1834; died 7 July, 1838, aged 4 years.
Anna Roseman, born 16 July, 1881; died 16 September, 1883, aged 2 years, 2 months.
James, born 1797; died 20 September, 1864, aged 67 years.
James, born 1824; died 3 October, 1825, aged 1 year.
James, born 21 September, 1855; died 31 July, 1857, aged 1 year, 10 months, 10 days.
Jane S., born 1 April, 1826; died 1 November, 1861, aged 35 years, 7 months.
Judith, born 1797; died 11 March, 1872, aged 75 years.
Mary Ella, born 19 October, 1850; died 19 August, 1852, aged 1 year, 10 months.
Sarah, born 23 November, 1829; died 23 April, 1831, aged 1 year, 5 months.

McKNIGHT—JEREMIAH, born 31 March, 1802; died 18 August, 1863, aged 61 years, 4 months, 17 days.

MARTHA, born 18 November, 1815; died 14 December, 1844, aged 28 years, 27 days.

MILLER—AARON, born 9 January, 1774; died 17 October, 1814, aged 40 years, 8 months, 9 days.

AARON, born 1823; died 7 June, 1870, aged 47 years.

ANETTE M., born 22 March, 1864; died 22 September, 1882, aged 18 years, 6 months.

CONSTANT, born 1801; died 2 April, 1826, aged 24 years.

ELIZABETH, born 1769; died 18 October, 1841, aged 72 years.

JAMES, born 1764; died 6 January, 1841, aged 77 years.

LAFIE, born 1856; died 1 April, 1859, aged 3 years.

LEMUEL, born 16 January, 1795; died 16 September, 1846, aged 51 years.

LOUISA H., born 1824; died 13 January, 1857, aged 33 years.

LYDIA EWING, born 1807; died 19 April, 1884, aged 77 years.

M. DE LAFAYETTE, born 1821; died 3 September, 1847, aged 26 years.

MARY, born 1770; died 18 March, 1849, aged 79 years.

OBED, born 23 March, 1835; died 7 January, 1852, aged 16 years.

SARAH JANE, born 17 November, 1847; died 17 August, 1849, aged 1 year, 9 months.

SETH, born 23 November, 1798; died 28 December, 1853, aged 55 years, 5 months, 1 day.

WATERS B., born 8 May, 1825; died 6 September, 1892.

MILLS—EPHRAIM, born 5 August, 1796; died 25 August, 1796, aged 20 days.

LOIS, born 1730; died 20 March, 1756, aged 26 years.

RUTH, born 1791; died 2 August, 1794, aged 3 years.

W. H., born 18 July, 1800; died 28 April, 1802, aged 1 year 9 months, 10 days.

MULFORD—SARAH, born 1775; died 1840, aged 65 years.

NEAL—C.; died 1830.

    C.; died 1842.

    E.; died 1837.

    M.; died 1837.

    S. N.; died 1837.

    T.; died 1826.

    T.; died 1837.

NERLINGER—ANNA K.; died 23 August, 1884.

NEWMAN—JOHN, born 14 October, 1776; died 21 July, 1802, aged 25 years, 9 months, 7 days.

NEWTON—ISAAC, Jr., born 1741; died 30 January, 1777, aged 29 years.

    TRYPHOSE, born 1751; died 15 April, 1770, aged 19 years.

NOTT—JOHN M., born 1847; died 26 August, 1888, aged 41 years.

    MARY L., born 1850; died 28 February, 1887, aged 37 years.

ORR—GABRIEL, born 1792; died 4 July, 1828, aged 36 years.

    MARY, born 17 January, 1798; died 27 October, 1829, aged 31 years, 9 months, 10 days.

OWENS—GEORGE, born 10 March, 1800; died 30 June, 1883, aged 83 years, 3 months, 20 days.

    HANNAH, born 16 May, 1800; died 18 May, 1872, aged 72 years, 2 days.

    IDA V., born 11 September, 1865; died 11 February, 1869, aged 3 years, 5 months.

PARMEINTER—ISABELLE M., born 1845; died 25 May, 1882, aged 37 years.

PARSONS—ELIZABETH, born 1791; died 15 February, 1847, aged 56 years.

    ROBERT, born 1785; died 7 August, 1860, aged 75 years.

    SARAH, born 8 March, 1835; died 22 October, 1837, aged 2 years, 7 months, 14 days.

PIERSON—AMANDA F., born 1846; died 8 March, 1872, aged 26 years.

ALBERT B., born 13 January, 1833; died 20 October, 1907.

CHARLES, born 16 September, 1864; died 16 November, 1865, aged 1 year, 2 months.

ELIZA, born 1782; died 28 July, 1868, aged 86 years.

ELIZABETH, born 9 October, 1780; died 10 October, 1814, aged 32 years, 1 day.

ELIZABETH, born 1791; died 15 February, 1847, aged 56 years.

FANNIE, born 4 January, 1869; died 4 July, 1869, aged 7 months.

HANNAH, born 1822; died 30 May, 1860, aged 38 years.

HATTIE M., born 1854; died 23 March, 1882, aged 28 years.

JOSEPH R., born 1851; died 21 September, 1874, aged 23 years.

SARAH A., born 6 May, 1858; died 25 January, 1862, aged 3 years, 8 months, 19 days.

SARAH H., born 24 July, 1835; died 19 December, 1917.

STEPHEN, born 1777; died 30 May, 1851, aged 74 years.

STEPHEN, born 1844; died 18 November, 1862, aged 18 years.

RANDOLPH—ZEPTHA F., born 1803; died 5 July, 1885, aged 82 years.

REEVES—ABIJAH.

ABRAHAM, born 22 October, 1802; died 5 May, 1884, aged 81 years, 6 months, 13 days.

ANDREW, born 1805; died 5 February, 1875, aged 70 years.

CHARLES S., born 1870; died 22 October, 1889, aged 19 years.

C. W.; died 1844.

C. W., born 20 April, 1861; died 22 June, 1861, aged 2 months, 6 days.

COURTLAND, V., aged 5 years, 6 months.

DAVID, born 1804; died 3 October, 1876, aged 72 years.

EMIL V., born 2 January, 1842; died 9 March, 1866, aged 24 years, 2 months, 7 days.

REEVES—EMMA T., born 12 January, 1868; died 12 September, 1868, aged 8 months.

ESMONDE HARPER, born 12 April, 1888; died 2 August, 1888, aged 3 months, 21 days.

GEORGE B., born 1 March, 1879; died 8 November, 1879, aged 8 months, 7 days.

HARRIET H., aged 2 years, 11 months.

HARRY M'C., born 21 November, 1878; died 25 April, 1879, aged 5 months, 4 days.

ISABELLA, born 1838; died 23 June, 1861.

JANE EDMUNDS, born 7 July, 1870; died 19 August, 1870, aged 1 month, 12 days.

JENNIE M., born 22 November, 1876; died 11 January, 1877, aged 1 month, 19 days.

JOHN, born 4 July, 1785; died 2 December, 1852, aged 67 years, 4 months, 25 days.

JOSHUA H., born 22 July, 1808; died 26 November, 1855, aged 47 years, 4 months, 4 days.

LETITIA D., born 1802; died 1842, aged 40 years.

LOUIS T., born 1 June, 1873; died 1 April, 1874, aged 10 months.

LYDIA T., born 18 July, 1872; died 15 August, 1872, aged 27 days.

MARIA, born 20 June, 1798; died 9 January, 1865, aged 67 years, 6 months, 29 days.

MARTHA SWAIN, born 19 November, 1873; died 17 April, 1874, aged 4 months, 28 days.

MASSIE.

TRYPHENA, born 1806; died 12 October, 1868, aged 62 years.

WALTER D., born 24 May, 1875; died 24 August, 1875, aged 3 months.

WILLIAM HENRY, born 18 October, 1882; died 29 November, 1882, aged 1 month, 11 days.

RICHARDSON—CHARLOTTE N., born 13 April, 1842; died 13 September, 1849, aged 7 years, 5 months, 1 day.

ELIZABETH, born 21 May, 1794; died 21 March, 1816, aged 21 years, 10 months.

ELLEN, born 30 November, 1795; died 17 September, 1846, aged 50 years, 9 months, 17 days.

RICHARDSON—JACOB, born 29 March, 1817; died 24 November, 1851, aged 34 years, 7 months, 25 days.

JOHN, born 28 July, 1791; died 15 October, 1858, aged 68 years, 2 months, 17 days.

JONATHAN, born 23 March, 1826; died 13 August, 1827, aged 1 year, 4 months, 20 days.

SAMUEL, born 1784; died 27 May, 1850, aged 66 years.

SAMUEL H., born 5 January, 1832; died 24 July, 1834, aged 2 years, 6 months, 19 days.

SARAH, born 4 June, 1794; died 4 January, 1870, aged 75

ROBERTSON—CAPT. ROBERT, born 21 March, 1766; died 8 August, 1806, aged 40 years, 4 months, 7 days.

RODAN—HELEN G.; died 1889, aged 4 months, 26 days.

ROGERS—HARRIET A., born 1808; died 27 November, 1881, aged 73 years.

CAPT. WESLEY, born 1807; died 20 June, 1875, aged 68 years.

ROSEMAN—CADDIE, born 1861; died 3 May, 1876, aged 15 years.

GEORGE, born 12 August, 1796; died 15 March, 1879, aged 83 years, 1 month, 3 days.

MARY E., born 1834; died 28 February, 1875, aged 41 years.

SARAH, born 8 October, 1799; died 29 August, 1866, aged 66 years, 10 months, 21 days.

THOMAS, born 19 April, 1824; died 22 April, 1886, aged 62 years, 3 days.

ROSS—JOHN, born 18 November, 1781; died 9 October, 1850, aged 68 years, 10 months, 21 days.

JULIA B., born 12 February, 1845; died 21 September, 1855, aged 10 years, 7 days.

LOUISA B., born 1 October, 1855; died 4 June, 1878, aged 22 years, 3 months, 8 days.

RACHEL, born 20 June, 1771; died 16 March, 1824, aged 52 years, 8 months, 26 days.

SARAH M., born 27 March, 1805; died 17 September, 1879, aged 74 years, 5 months, 20 days.

RUSSELL—ALBERT H., born 20 July, 1863; died 20 March, 1886, aged 22 years, 8 months.

CAPT. DAVID, born 15 December, 1813; died 21 February,

ELLEN, born 12 November, 1844; died 27 November, 1881, aged 37 years, 15 days.

1875, aged 61 years, 2 months, 6 days.

SARAH, born 9 September, 1786; died 22 March, 1856, aged 69 years, 6 months, 13 days.

RUTHERFORD—ANN, born 26 June, 1825; died 17 August, 1826, aged 1 year, 1 month, 21 days.

ANN ELIZA, wife of John Rutherford, died 12 October, 1829; died 21 October, 1905.

HARRY, born 7 June, 1876; died 20 March, 1879, aged 2 years, 9 months, 13 days.

IDA, born 7 July, 1875; died 13 July, 1875, aged 6 days.

JAMES, born 16 November, 1803; died 8 September, 1883, aged 79 years, 9 months, 22 days.

JOHN, born 2 September, 1826; died 25 March, 1891.

JOHN, born 31 December, 1795; died 19 April, 1871, aged 75 years, 3 months, 18 days.

JOSEPH, born 2 September, 1829; died 7 September, 1829, aged 5 days.

KEZIA, born — February, 1886; died 15 December, 1888, aged 2 years, 10 months.

MARY, born 6 May, 1792; died 21 April, 1841, aged 48 years, 11 months, 15 days.

SAMUEL, born 5 July, 1851; died 31 August, 1882, aged 31 years, 1 month, 26 days.

WILLIAM C., born 1823; died 1 July, 1870, aged 47 years.

SAWYER—HARRIET W., born 9 September, 1829; died 23 May, 1889, aged 59 years, 8 months, 14 days.

THOMAS E., born 28 March, 1855; died 28 September, 1864, aged 9 years, 6 months.

THOMAS E., born 31 October, 1851; died 23 November, 1853, aged 2 years, 23 days.

SHAW—AARON, born 26 October, 1795; died 8 March, 1856, aged 60 years, 4 months, 12 days.

ELIDA H., born 29 August, 1863; died 9 March, 1866, aged 3 years, 6 months, 11 days.

EXPERIENCE, born 13 March, 1775; died 8 October, 1834, aged 59 years, 6 months, 25 days.

SHAW—JOHN A., died 13 September, 1807.

LEMUEL, died 25 September, 1811.

OVID, born 1777; died 14 December, 1871, aged 94 years.

STILLWELL, born 19 September, 1767; died 15 August, 1825, aged 57 years, 10 months, 26 days.

SCHELLENGER—AARON, born 1784; died 17 November, 1872, aged 88 years.

ABIGAIL, born 1777; died 19 June, 1834, aged 57 years.

ALICE C., born 23 August, 1871; died 27 April, 1873, aged 1 year, 8 months, 4 days.

ANNE M., born 1809; died 5 March, 1866, aged 57 years.

CATHERINE, born 1793; died 23 December, 1868, aged 75 year.s

CHARLES, born 24 September, 1792; died 9 July, 1823, aged 30 years, 9 months, 15 days.

CHARLOTTE, born 11 September, 1788; died 1 July, 1846, aged 57 years, 9 months, 20 days.

ELIZA M., born 1792; died 4 February, 1860, aged 68 years.

ELIZA M., born 1823; died 23 September, 1846, aged 23 years.

ELIZABETH H., born 20 May, 1848; died 14 February, 1849, aged 8 months, 24 days.

ELLA M., born 1869; died 30 June, 1869, aged 5 months, 1 day.

EMELIA, born 3 January, 1842; died 2 July, 1876, aged 34 years, 5 months, 28 days.

EMMA L., born June, 1850; died 15 May, 1852, aged 1 year, 11 months, 14 days.

ENOS, born 1752; died 16 January, 1809, aged 57 years.

ENOS, born 1787; died 1 September, 1832, aged 45 years.

ENOS; aged 13 years.

FANNIE; aged 75 years.

JAMES, born 1751; died 25 June, 1846, aged 95 years.

JANE E., born 22 November, 1852; died 21 January, 1855, aged 3 years, 1 month, 29 days.

JEREMIAH, born 13 September, 1781; died 3 August, 1831, aged 49 years, 10 months, 20 days.

JOHN, born 1788; died 18 January, 1860, aged 72 years.

JOHN K. F., born 1 September, 1854; died 2 March, 1856, aged 1 year, 6 months, 1 day.

SCHELLENGER—Joseph, born 1829; died 15 November, 1877, aged 48 years.

Levi, born 4 August, 1867; died 21 March, 1868, aged 7 months, 17 days.

Louisa B., born 1845; died 17 November, 1871, aged 26 years.

Lynda G., born 1 April, 1858; died 21 October, 1863, aged 5 years, 6 months, 20 days.

Maria C., born 18 January, 1842; died 15 August, 1848, aged 6 years, 6 months, 27 days.

Martha S., born 1829; died 7 March, 1883, aged 54 years.

Mary P., born 1820; died 8 November, 1845, aged 25 years.

Philomelia, born 1752; died 8 February, 1793, aged 41 years.

Rebecca, born 4 June, 1742; died 21 July, 1828, aged 86 years, 1 month, 17 days.

Sallie R., born 26 November, 1867; died 8 December, 1875, aged 8 years, 12 days.

Samuel; aged 4 years.

Sophia B., born 1791; died 31 October, 1876, aged 85 years.

Washington, born 17 October, 1845; died 3 September, 1876, aged 30 years, 10 months, 16 days.

William, born 1746; died 15 June, 1827, aged 81 years.

SCHENK—Dr. and Wife.

SCHILLINKS—Lydia, born 1726; died 14 January, 1748, aged 22 years.

SHEPPARD—Abigail H,, born 1840; died 14 April, 1889, aged 49 years.

W. R., M. D., born 1831; died 12 March, 1879, aged 48 years.

SHERIDAN—Abraham, born 26 August, 1755; died 12 July, 1821, aged 65 years, 10 months, 16 days.

SHIELDS—Addie Davis, born 8 July, 1871; died 25 March, 1872, aged 8 months, 17 days.

Lillie C.; born 21 November, 1863.

SMITH—ANNIE E., born 23 July, 1831; died 19 July, 1878, aged 46 years, 11 months, 23 days.

AUGUSTUS B., born 1864; died 23 November, 1877, aged 13 years.

CAPT. CHARLES, born 1830; died 22 April, 1874, aged 44 years.

HANNAH W., born 30 June, 1805; died 3 May, 1889, aged 83 years, 10 months 3 days.

ISAAC, born 1771; died 1 July, 1822, aged 51 years.

ISAAC, born 28 February, 1805; died 17 October, 1881, aged 76 years, 7 months, 7 days.

SMITH—JANE, born 10 November, 1829; died 31 January, 1859, aged 29 years, 2 months, 21 days.

JEANNIE H., born 1862; died 21 March, 1885, aged 23 years.

JEREMIAH P., born 1832; died 4 October, 1873, aged 41 years.

LOUISA, born 9 November, 1756; died 4 Novmeber, 1821, aged 64 years.

LOUISA W., born 30 October, 1842; died 27 December, 1846, aged 4 years, 1 month, 7 days.

MARY E., born 6 September, 1861; died 17 February, 1886, aged 24 years, 5 months, 11 days.

MARY JANE, born 9 February, 1840; died 18 August, 1863, aged 23 years, 6 months, 9 days.

PHILOMELIA, born 2 December, 1839; died 2 November, 1883, aged 43 years, 11 months.

SARAH, born 1775; died 25 September, 1811, aged 36 years.

SNYDER—JOHN, born 28 May, 1813; died 3 September, 1887, aged 74 years, 3 months, 6 days.

LIZZIE, born 30 December, 1874; died 30 June, 1879, aged 5 years, 6 months.

LOIS U., born 1806; died 8 June, 1868, aged 62 years.

THOMAS F., born 20 September, 1839; died 20 October, 1860, aged 21 years, 2 days.

WILLIAM, born 23 January, 1784; died 30 May, 1866, aged 82 years, 4 months, 7 days.

SPEER—ALEXANDER, born 1791; died 19 July, 1825, aged 34 years.

SPENCER—Sarah, born 1802; died 19 August, 1844, aged 42 years.

SPICER—SARAH, born 1677; died 25 July, 1742, aged 65 years.

STEEL—JOHN, born 1780; died 9 September, 1805, aged 25 years.

STEPHENS—JOHNATHAN C., born 7 August, 1843; died 18 August, 1879, aged 36 years.

STEVENS—ALLY, born 1858; died 7 September, 1861, aged 3 years.

    A. HIGGINS, born 20 November, 1817; died 3 January, 1887, aged 69 years, 1 month, 13 days.

    ALBERT G., born 11 January, 1819; died 16 August, 1860, aged 41 years, 7 months, 5 days.

    ARCHIBALD M., born 10 May, 1841; died 1 December, 1843, aged 2 years, 7 months, 21 days.

    BELL T., born 6 March, 1856; died 5 November, 1871, aged 15 years, 7 months, 29 days.

    DANIEL, born 17 July, 1771; died 17 January, 1828, aged 56 years, 6 months.

    ELLEN W., born 28 April, 1845; died 23 December, 1871, aged 26 years, 7 months, 23 days.

    EZEKIEL, born 19 March, 1787; died 1 July, 1861, aged 74 years, 3 months, 12 days.

    GEORGE H. H., born 28 April, 1825; died 5 August, 1826, aged 1 year, 3 months, 7 days.

    GEORGE H. H., born 1826; died 13 December, 1866, aged 40 years.

    HETTY T., born 10 February, 1843; died 11 February, 1843, aged 1 day.

    HORACE A., born 25 May, 1875; died 17 August, 1875, aged 2 months, 22 days.

    JOHN L. G., born 6 August, 1845; died 17 March, 1857, aged 11 years, 7 months, 11 days.

    LEONORA M., born 27 February, 1847; died 22 May, 1871, aged 24 years, 2 months, 25 days.

    LOIS, born 19 February, 1792; died 28 March, 1853, aged 61 years, 1 month, 9 days.

    MARY ELLA, born 17 January, 1855; died 29 July, 1872, aged 17 years, 6 months, 12 days.

STEVENS—PHILOMELIA, born 1773; died 5 February, 1833, aged 60 years.

REBECCA, born 1818; died 23 January, 1879, aged 61 years.

SARAH H., born 16 January, 1825; died 28 July, 1882, aged 57 years, 6 months, 12 days.

STEWARD—JOHN, Jr., born 28 February, 1823; died 13 April, 1831, aged 8 years, 1 month, 15 days.

STEWART—HARRIET, born 1789; died 13 February, 1826, aged 37 years.

HARRIET, born 14 January, 1813; died 18 January, 1866, aged 53 years, 4 days.

JOHN, born 15 August, 1788; died 18 February, 1871, aged 82 years, 6 months, 3 days.

STILLWELL—THOMAS, born 24 September, 1732; died 24 January, 1820, aged 87 years, 4 months.

THOMAS, born 14 October, 1821; died 14 December, 1822, aged 1 year, 2 months.

STIMSON—CHARLES P., born 26 April, 1813; died 27 December, 1879, aged 66 years, 8 months, 1 day.

ELIZABETH, born 1820; died 22 November, 1861, aged 41 years.

MARY G., born 1812; died 23 April, 1863, aged 51 years.

PHEBE, born 1781; died 10 October, 1874, aged 93 years.

PHEBE JANE, born 1854; died 14 October, 1871, aged 17 years.

ROBERT C., born 1811; died 30 July, 1864, aged 53 years.

SOPHIA, born 1784; died 10 March, 1810, aged 26 years.

STEPHEN, born 1769; died 12 October, 1848, aged 79 years.

STEPHEN D., born 1845; died 28 November, 1864, aged 19 years.

STINEFORD—SARAH H., born 1768; died 3 September, 1824, aged 56 years.

STITES—ABIGAIL, born 1764; died 30 March, 1839, aged 75 years.

    CHARLOTTE, born 5 July, 1776; died 2 January, 1826, aged 49 years, 5 months, 27 days.

    ELIZA, born 2 September, 1800; died 12 March, 1873, aged 72 years, 6 months, 10 days.

    ELIZA E., born 1820; died 29 March, 1849, aged 29 years.

    ELIZABETH, born 1816; died 24 January, 1871, aged 55 years.

    JANE, born 1752; died 3 August, 1817, aged 65 years.

    JANE, born 1780; died 10 November, 1847, aged 67 years.

    JANE E., born 1829; died 28 June, 1864, aged 35 years, 4 days.

    JOHN, born 1756; died 12 December, 1840, aged 84 years.

    JOHN K. F., born 10 January, 1821; died 25 February, 1883, aged 62 years, 1 month, 15 days.

    MARIA L., born 1834; died 20 May, 1866, aged 32 years.

    MARY H., born 1830, died 21 March, 1837, aged 7 years.

    NATHAN, born 6 February, 1769; died 15 August, 1823, aged 54 years, 6 months, 9 days.

    PAGE, born 1 January, 1791; died 2 May, 1867, aged 76 years, 6 months, 1 day.

    SARAH E., born 21 December, 1837; died 18 April, 1909.

    SAMUEL S. M., born 25 February, 1835; died 25 August, 1844, aged 9 years, 6 months.

    WILLIAM, born 1838; died 16 February, 1857, aged 19 years.

STODDARD—CARRIE, born 1852; died 11 January, 1872, aged 20 years.

STRATTON—ABIGAIL, born 1813; died 28 February, 1885, aged 72 years.

    BERNARD C. M., born 1842; died 19 December, 1863, aged 21 years.

    ISADORA H., born 1847; died 23 December, 1863, aged 16 years.

    SALLIE T., born 1851; died 25 December, 1863, aged 12 years.

STUBBELBINE—LOUISA, born 1840; died 22 September, 1872, aged 32 years.

SUTHARD—Reuben, born 19 September, 1791; died 15 August, 1815, aged 23 years, 10 months, 26 days.

SWAIN—Abigail, born 24 March, 1793; died 29 December, 1872, aged 79 years, 9 months, 5 days.
Daniel, born 4 April, 1762; died 4 June, 1834, aged 72 years, 2 days.
Elizabeth, born 13 August, 1768; died 26 August, 1849, aged 81 years, 13 days.
James S., born 2 September, 1851; died 15 September, 1861, aged 10 years, 13 days.
Kitty, born 28 April, 1786; died 10 October, 1786, aged 5 months, 12 days.
Lemuel, born 29 June, 1794; died 26 October, 1873, aged 79 years, 3 months, 27 days.
Lemuel, Jr., born 29 April, 1823; died 28 March, 1887, aged 63 years, 10 months, 29 days.
Lydia L., born 1 September, 1850; died 3 October, 1877, aged 27 years, 1 month, 2 days.
Nezer, born 1756; died 18 June, 1796, aged 40 years.

TALLANT—Mary Emma, born 29 September, 1823; died August, 1824, aged 11 months.

TAYLOR—Harry A., born 7 December, 1859; died 18 August, 1878, aged 18 years, 8 months, 11 days.

TEAL—Elizabeth, born 7 October, 1795; died 29 November, 1827, aged 32 years, 1 month, 22 days.
Heatty, born 1799; died 13 November, 1878, aged 79 years.
Lydia C., born 14 April, 1812; died 7 March, 1833, aged 20 years, 10 months, 23 days.
Seth, born 1793; died 10 April, 1837, aged 44 years.

THOMAS—John R., born 1794; died — August, 1822, aged 28 years.

THOMPSON—Anna S., born 1832; died 28 April, 1882, aged 50 years.
Charlotte, born 24 April, 1765; died 3 December, 1812, aged 47 years, 7 months, 9 days.
Hannah, born 21 March, 1818; died 21 October, 1832, aged 14 years, 7 months.

THOMPSON—MADGE C., born 10 November, 1886; died 2 July, 1887, aged 7 months, 22 days.

RALPH, born 27 May, 1889; died 27 August, 1889, aged 3 months.

RICHARD, born 1823; died 19 January, 1878, aged 55 years.

TOWN—ELIZABETH, born 1770; died 6 December, 1862, aged 92 years.

TOWNSEND—BESSIE C., born 1 May, 1876; died 6 April, 1880, aged 3 years, 11 months, 5 days.

FLORENCE L., born 11 November, 1883; died 2 September, 1884, aged 9 months, 21 days.

MARY F., born 1821; died 5 February, 1884, aged 63 years.

UPSON—CHARLES, born 1705; died 2 April, 1785, aged 80 years.

VAN MANNERICK—LYDIA, born 22 August, 1751; died 16 July, 1798, aged 46 years, 10 months, 24 days.

VILLARET—PAUL, born 1844; died 14 July, 1881, aged 37 years.

WALES—BELINDA, born 14 December, 1821; died 11 March, 1826, aged 4 years, 2 months, 27 days.

DR. E. L. B., born 5 March, 1805; died 11 August, 1882, aged 77 years, 5 months, 4 days.

EDMOND, born 15 July, 1831; died 11 August, 1835, aged 4 years, 26 days.

EDMOND B., born 25 December, 1834; died 30 December, 1844, aged 10 years, 5 days.

ELI B., born 10 July, 1798; died 24 September, 1883, aged 85 years, 1 month, 14 days.

GEORGE H., born 1842; died 3 March, 1870, aged 28 years.

HARRIET, born 1 November, 1773; died 18 December, 1822, aged 49 years, 1 month, 17 days.

HARRIET H., born 1800; died 12 September, 1844, aged 44 years.

JANE S., born 1791; died 19 July, 1878, aged 87 years.

WALES—MARY, born 3 December, 1810; died 3 September, 1831, aged 21 years, 9 months.

DR. ROGER, born 1768; died 30 September, 1835, aged 67 years.

SARAH H., born 1800; died 27 January, 1839, aged 39 years.

WARD—HENRY L., born 1797; died 17 December, 1862, aged 65 years.

WARE—ADELIA, born 1848; died 4 September, 1866, aged 18 years.

DAVID, born 1725; died 17 March, 1762, aged 37 years.

DEBORAH, born 24 March, 1806; died 30 March, 1864, aged 58 years, 6 days.

EDITH H., born 25 December, 1877; died 4 August, 1878, aged 7 months, 9 days.

EDWARD E., born 26 October, 1857; died 13 November, 1861, aged 4 years, 17 days.

EDWARD E., born 25 August, 1862; died 2 November, 1874, aged 12 years, 2 months, 7 days.

ELIZA L., born 1856; died 31 December, 1859, aged 6

ELIZA S.; aged 11 months, 17 days.

ESTHER, born 17 February, 1801; died 3 September, 1866, aged 67 years, 6 months, 16 days.

FRANK H., born 15 June, 1859; died 11 September, 1888, aged 29 years, 2 months, 26 days.

HARRIET F., born 1848; died 26 November, 1859, aged 11 years.

HARRIET W., born 1785; died 3 August, 1851, aged 66 years.

HATTIE, born 12 August, 1873; died 21 December, 1881, aged 8 years, 4 months, 9 days.

JOSEPH, born 1771; died 13 February, 1827, aged 56 years.

JOSEPH, born 1861; died 22 July, 1863, aged 2 years.

LAMBERT W., born 1850; died 1 March, 1886, aged 36 years.

LEAH, born 1822; died 1 June, 1864, aged 42 years.

LYDIA L., born 1817; died 23 October, 1886, aged 69 years.

LYDIA R., born 5 January, 1823; died 12 May, 1884, aged 61 years, 4 months, 7 days.

WARE—MARCY C., born 1848; died 19 December, 1867, aged 19 years.

Mary B., born 2 September, 1823; died 8 September, 1845, aged 22 years, 6 days.

Mary W., born 28 December, 1838; died 24 August, 1869, aged 30 years, 7 months, 26 days.

Pauline, born 1852; died 2 June, 1855, aged 3 years.

Ruth, born 1777; died 7 March, 1791, aged 14 years.

J. Stratton, born 2 April, 1871; died 15 September, 1871, aged 5 months, 13 days.

Samuel F., born 16 October, 1800; died 10 May, 1877, aged 76 years, 6 months, 24 days.

Samuel F., born 20 August, 1879; died 22 December, 1881, aged 2 years, 4 months, 2 days.

Sarah E., born 22 August, 1833; died 11 October, 1856, aged 23 years, 1 month, 19 days.

Theresa E., born 7 December, 1869; died 12 November, 1870, aged 11 months, 5 days.

Wilmon, born 1739; died 20 February, 1766, aged 27 years.

Wilmon, born 27 April, 1846; died 22 January, 1852, aged 5 years, 8 months, 25 days.

WATSON—Rebecca, born 1 May, 1765; died 27 February, 1797, aged 31 years, 9 months, 6 days.

WATTS—Hannah, born 7 December, 1756; died 7 April, 1787, aged 30 years, 4 months.

Rev. James, born 1743; died 19 November, 1789, aged 46 years.

Rachel, born 29 March, 1748; died 29 November, 1782. aged 34 years, 8 months.

Rachel, born 12 December, 1784; died 12 April, 1785, aged 4 months.

WEEKS—Charles H., born 21 July, 1838; died 16 May, 1865, aged 26 years, 9 months, 25 days.

William, born 1797; died 16 March, 1871, aged 74 years.

WHEATON—Clara P., born 28 June, 1860; died 31 October, 1888, aged 28 years, 4 months, 3 days.

Milletts, born 17 July, 1881; died 11 October, 1881, aged 2 months, 24 days.

WHILLDIN—DAVID, born 1792; died 10 December, 1813, aged 21 years.

CAPT. DANIEL, son of James and Rhoda, lost at sea, 23 December, 1811, aged 36 years. — on same stone with record of his daughter Rhoda.

DAVID, died 17 March, 1762, aged 37 years.

EVELINE H., born 14 October, 1850; died 8 April, 1852, aged 1 year, 5 months, 24 days.

EVELINE H., born 1852; died 25 April, 1870, aged 18 years.

GRACIAN, born 1817; died 7 October, 1851, aged 34 years.

ISAAC, born 15 February, 1784; died 13 May, 1867, aged 83 years, 2 months, 28 days.

ISAAC, born 1824; died 8 September, 1876, aged 52 years.

JAMES, born 1714; died 5 November, 1780, aged 66 years.

JAMES G., born 23 September, 1850; died 22 April, 1852, aged 1 year, 6 months, 29 days.

JANE, born 1719; died 8 November, 1760, aged 41 years.

JOSEPH, born 1690; died 18 March, 1748, aged 58 years.

MAHALA, born 1782; died 12 November, 1840, aged 58 years.

MARTHA H., born 26 November, 1851; died 1 April, 1852, aged 4 months, 5 days.

MARY, born 1689; died 8 April, 1743, aged 54 years.

MARY JANE, born 1840; died 12 May, 1843, aged 3 years.

MATTHEW, born 1749; died 16 July, 1828, aged 79 years.

MATTHEW, born 1816; died 15 March, 1875, aged 59 years.

MATTHEW, born 8 July, 1853; died 8 August, 1854, aged 1 year, 1 month, 1 day.

OLIVE, born 1819; died 20 July, 1868, aged 49 years.

PHEBE, born 1753; died 14 June, 1798, aged 45 years.

RHODA, born 1755; died 9 September, 1801, aged 46 years.

RHODA, born 16 February, 1803; died 4 June, 1805, aged 2 years, 3 months, 19 days.

WILLIE W., born 1868; died 26 April, 1870, aged 2 years.

WILMON, died 20 February, 1766, aged 27 years.

RUTH, daughter of J. and R., died 7 March, 1791, in fourth year.

WILLITS—HANNAH, born 1778; died 26 February, 1829, aged 51 years.

WILLITTS—ANNA M., born 1828; died 28 February, 1873, aged 45 years.
CHARLES, aged 9 years, 9 months, 28 days.
FRANK B., born 1855; died 22 April, 1874, aged 19 years.
CAPT. SILVANUS, born 16 September, 1828; died 5 October 1868, aged 40 years, 19 days.

WILLIAMS—CHARLES, aged 1 month, 12 days.
LIZZIE, aged 2 months.

WILLIAMSON—LYDIA, born 3 January, 1798; died 3 September, 1862, aged 64 years, 8 months.
EMILY, wife of Rev. Moses Williamson, born 19 November, 1817; died 18 December, 1888.
REV. MOSES, born 7 May, 1802; died 30 October, 1880, aged 78 years, 5 months, 23 days.
THOMAS H., born 1852; died 7 October, 1886, aged 34 years.

WOOLSON—CAPT. AARON, born 1778; died 11 October, 1824, aged 46 years.
RICHARD S., born 8 May, 1821; died 28 January, 1879, aged 57 years, 8 months, 20 days.
SARAH, born 6 April, 1780; died 20 November, 1850, aged 70 years, 7 months, 14 days.

WORRALL—LEWIS, born 1787; died 24 March, 1860, aged 73 years.
MILLICENT, born 1790; died 2 November, 1865, aged 75 years.

General Index of Names, Subjects and Places.

General Index of Names, Subjects and Places.

(Not including the alphabetically arranged list of tombstones in Cold Spring Cemetery)

The name of the parent—father or mother—through whom the Pilgrim Ancestry descends, and the names of husbands or wives of Mayflower descendants are given.

ABBEYVILLE, Louisiana, 112, 130.
ABBOTT, Ellen Falkenburg, daughter of Susan Falkenburg Leaming, family, 115.
Abbott, Gertrude, daughter of Susan Falkenburg Leaming, 115.
Abbott, Redman, husband of Susan Falkenburg Leaming, 115.
Abbott, William Louis, M. D., son of Susan Falkenburg Leaming, 115.
ABIGAIL ————, wife named in will of Joseph Whilldin 2nd, 100.
ABINGTON, Pennsylvania, 191.
ABSECON, New Jersey, 294.
ADAMS, Beatrice, wife of John Laughlin Williamson, 213.
Adams, Elizabeth, daughter of Alice Bradford, 325.
Adams, Rev. William, husband of Alice Bradford, 325.
ADDAMS, Mattie, wife of Luther Hudson Edmunds, 231.
AISNE, France, 324.
ALBERTSON, Anna, wife of Maurice B. Souder, 240.
ALDAN, Pennsylvania, 322.
ALDEN, John the Pilgrim, husband of Priscilla Mullins, 81, imprisonment at Boston, 90, descendant in Cape May County, 320.
ALLARD, Kate, wife of William Matthews, 300.
ALLEN, Rhoda, second wife of Memucan Hughes, 204.
ALLERTON, Mary, the Pilgrim, wife of Elder Thomas Cushman, last survivor of the passengers of the Mayflower, 25, 93.
ALLISON, Daisy, wife of Marion Eldredge, 130.
ALTOONA, Pennsylvania, 161.
ALWINE, Harold, husband of Anna Marie Merritt, 322.
AMBLER, Pennsylvania, 303.
AMENIA Union, New York, 147.
AMES, John, admitted to church membership, 51.
Ames, Sarah, admitted to church membership, 48.
ANDREW, Catherine Hughes, baptized, 53.
Andrew, Daniel, admitted to church membership, 51.
Andrew, Hannah, admitted to church membership, 51.
ANDREWS, Jesse Hughes, baptized, 53.
Andrews, Lois, baptized, 53.
ANN, ship, arrived at Plymouth 1623, 66.
ANNAPOLIS ROYAL, 7.
ANTOINE, Fannie, wife of John Bennett Merritt, 153.
ARCHAMBAULD, Edwin, son of Zeruiah Schellenger, family, 253.
ARDMORE, Pennsylvania, 194.
ARMSTRONG, Barbara, daughter of Edward Kent Armstrong, M. D., 325.
Armstrong, Edward Kent, M. D., son of Minnie Kent, family, 325.
Armstrong, Harold, husband of Minnie Kent, 325.
ARNOLD, Charles, husband of Elsie P. Hughes, 259.
Arnold, Charles, son of Elsie P. Hughes, 259.
Arnold, Lillian Eleanor, wife of John M. Hand, 273.
Arnold, Warren, son of Elsie P. Hughes, 259.
ASCARATE, Mercedes Ysabel, wife of Richard Thompson Miller, 210.
ASHCROFT, Florence, daughter of Florence White, 269.
Ashcroft, John, husband of Florence White, 269.
Ashcroft, John, son of Florence White, 269.
ATCHISON, Frances, wife of Warren Hughes, 259.
ATHENS, Georgia, 280.
ATHERTON, John H., husband of Elinor Curwen Austin, 117.

393

396

Crowell, Lydia Jane, daughter Hannah Matthews, 266, family and descendants, 303, 314.
Crowell, Marie Leaming, daughter of Jane Cresse, family, 186.
Crowell, Maria Smith, daughter of Sarah Jane Edmunds, family, 298.
Crowell, Mary Cecelia, daughter of DeWitt Clinton Crowell, 140.
Crowell, Marion Hobart, child of Albert Edmunds Crowell, 298.
Crowell, Mary E., wife of Douglass Foster, 155.
Crowell, Mason, baptized, 59.
Crowell, Sarah, admitted to church membership, 51.
Crowell, Sarah E., daughter of Jane Ann Foster, family, 170.
Crowell, Sarah Virginia, daughter of Hannah Matthews, (infant), 266.
Crowell, Thomas Millet, son of James Frank Crowell, 298.
Crowell, Theodore Whilden, son of Edward M. Crowell, 170.
Crowell, Thomas Monroe, son of Hannah Matthews, 266.
Crowell, Thomas Page, husband of Hannah Matthews, 252, 266.
Crowell, Thomas S., son of Jane Ann Foster, family, 170.
Crowell, Tryphene P., daughter of Jane Ann Foster, family, 170.
Crowell, Virginia Caroline, daughter of Hannah Matthews, (infant), 266.
Crowell, Willie H., son of Thomas S. Crowell, 170.
CUMBERLAND COUNTY, New Jersey, 124, 208, 209, 282.
CUMMINGS, Dorothy Wheaton, daughter of Ralph Lee Cummings, 172.
Cummings, Edwin J., husband of Harriet N. Hughes, 146.
Cummings, Edwin Jones, son of George Ogden and Beulah Estella Bate, 172.
Cummings, Emma Eldredge, daughter of Rhoda Forest Foster, 172.
Cummings, Florence H., daughter of Harriet N. Hughes, 146.
Cummings, George Herbert, son of George Ogden and Beulah Estella Bate, 172.
Cummings, George Ogden, son of Rhoda Forest Foster, family, 146, 172.
Cummings, Georgeanna, wife of James Henry Edmunds, 291.
Cummings, Harry Edmunds, son of Rhoda Forest Foster, 172.
Cummings, Leonard, father of William Leonard Cummings, 156.
Cummings, Lydia, mother of William Leonard Cummings, 156.
Cummings, Ralph Lee, son of Rhoda Forest Foster, family, 172.
Cummings, William Leonard, husband of Rhoda Forest Foster, 156, 172.
CURRIDEN, Josephine, wife of Daniel E. Souder, 240.
CURTIS, Thomas J., marriage, 46.
CURWEN, Mary, wife of Furman Leaming, 113, 116.
CUSHMAN, Mrs. Mary Allerton, last survivor of the Pilgrim passengers, 25, 26.
Cushman, Robert, Agent of the Pilgrims, 68, (where name is wrongly printed "Thomas"), defection of, 69, 87.
Cushman, Thomas, Elder of Pilgrim Church, 26.
DAILY, Edna R., second wife of Jacob Spicer Leaming, 183.
DALE, Susanna, first wife of Alexis Grasson Merritt, 153, 176.
DARES, Bert, son of Harriet Eldredge Parson, 120.
Dares, Bert Elmer, husband of Harriet Eldredge Parsons, 120.
DARBY, Pennsylvania, 138.
DARTMOUTH, Massachusetts, 324.
DATESMAN, Helen, wife of Charles Elmer Townsend, 183.
DAVENPORT, Harry, husband of Mae Richardson Paul, 221.
DAVIS, Anna Ogg, mother of Estella Davis, 299.
Davis, Charles Henry, son of Elizabeth Cresse Eldredge, 185.
Davis, Chester, husband of Elizabeth Cresse Eldredge, 185.
Davis, Daniel, husband of Mehitable Lothrop, 323.
Davis, Dorothy Lorena, daughter of Elizabeth Cresse Eldredge, 181.
Davis, Emma V., wife of Francis Springer Eldredge, 136.
Davis, Estella, wife of William Henry Ruddiman Ogden, 299.
Davis, John, father of Estella Davis, 299.
Davis, Laura K., wife of Dr. James W. Ware, 237.
Davis, Linwood, son of Elmira T. Sapp, 301.
Davis, Mary, daughter of Mehitable Lothrop, 323.
Davis, Mary, wife of John Schellenger, 253, 268.
Davis, Maud E., daughter of Elmira T. Sapp, 301.
Davis, Virgil, marriage, 46.
Davis, Wilbert, husband of Elmira T. Sapp, 301.
DAYTON, Ohio, 324.
DAVOL, Joseph, husband of Mary Soule, 324.
Davol, Mary, daughter of Mary Soule, 324.
DEATHS, recorded in Session Book of Cold Spring Presbyterian Church, 1810-1813, pages 58-64.

405

EDMONDS, Aaron, son of Lydia Eldredge, 110, family and descenda·
121.
Edmonds, Aaron, son of Aaron Edmonds, 1221.
Edmonds, Aaron H., son of Joseph S. Edmonds, 123.
Edmonds, Amelia C., daughter of Joseph S. Edmonds, family, 123.
Edmonds, Anna B., daughter of Joseph S. Edmonds, family, 123.
Edmonds, Arte, son of Samuel C. Edmonds, 121.
Edmonds, Arthur G., son of Frank C. Edmonds, 123.
Edmonds, Frank C., son of Joseph S. Edmonds, family, 123.
Edmonds, Evin, marriage, 45.
Edmonds, Joseph, son of Samuel C. Edmonds, 121.
Edmonds, Joseph P., son of Joseph S. Edmonds, 123.
Edmonds, Joseph, S., son of Aaron Edmonds, 121, family and descenc
123.
Edmonds, Laura, daughter of Samuel C., 121.
Edmonds, Matthew W., M. D., son of Aaron Edmonds, family, 121.
Edmonds, Mary, daughter of Aaron Edmonds, 121.
Edmonds, Mary, daughter of Samuel C. Edmonds, 121.
Edmonds, Mary M., daughter Matthew W. Edmonds, 121.
Edmonds, Minnie, daughter Samuel C. Edmonds, 121.
Edmonds, Samuel C., son of Aaron Edmonds, family and descendants, 121.
EDMUNDS, Aaron, husband (1) of Lydia Eldredge, (2) of Sarah Eldredge,
107, 109, 110.
Edmunds, Abigail Stites, baptized, 60.
Edmunds, Ada Mills, daughter of Levi Eldredge Edmunds, 230.
Edmunds, Adeline Welsh, daughter of Henry Reeves Edmunds, 308.
Edmunds, Adeline Welsh, daughter of Franklin Davenport Edmunds, 308.
Edmunds, Albert, son of Evan B. Edmunds, 230.
Edmunds, Albert Augustus, son of Robert Edmunds, family, 231.
Edmunds, Albert Ellis, son of Levi Eldredge Edmunds, 230.
Edmunds, Albert Lawrence, son of Albert Augustus Edmunds, 231.
Edmunds, Albert Stevens, son of Richard Downs Edmunds, 291.
Edmunds, Alberta, daughter of Evan B. Edmunds, 230.
Edmunds, Alfred, son of Jeremiah Edmunds, family, 228.
Edmunds, Alfred, son of Watters Borrows Miller Edmunds, family, 239.
Edmunds, Alexander Franklin, son of Franklin Davenport Edmunds,
(infant), 290.
Edmunds, Alice Annie, daughter of Levi Eldredge Edmunds, 230.
Edmunds, Alice May, daughter of Frederick Stanger Edmunds, 290.
Edmunds, Andrew Jackson, son of Jeremiah Edmunds, family, 216.
Edmunds, Anna, daughter of James Richard Edmunds, 312.
Edmunds, Anna Grace, daughter of Henry Reeves Edmunds, 308.
Edmunds, Anna Frederica, dau. of Rev. Charles Carroll Edmunds, 296.
Edmunds, Anne Paxton, daughter of Franklin Davenport Edmunds, 308.
Edmunds, Annie Louisa, daughter of Richard Edmunds, family, 326.
Edmunds, Annie Loruhamah, daughter of Robert Edmunds, family, 231.
Edmunds, Benjamin, son of Evan, 262.
Edmunds, Benjamin, son of Lydia Hughes, 262.
Edmunds, Bessie Dorothy, daughter of Levi Eldredge Edmunds, 230.
Edmunds, Blanche, daughter of Evan B. Edmunds, 230.
Edmunds, Blanche Daniella, daughter of Levi Eldredge Edmunds, (in-
fant), 230.
Edmunds, Bristol Hubert, son of Charles Carroll Edmunds, (infant), 296,
Edmunds, Carswell, son of Jeremiah Edmunds, (infant), 228.
Edmunds, Charles Carroll, son of Lydia Hughes, 263, family and de-
scendants, 296.
Edmunds, Charles Carroll, son of Francis Henry Edmunds, 296.
Edmunds, Rev. Charles Carroll, son of Charles Carroll Edmunds, family,
296.
Edmunds, Charles Hughes, son of Thomas Hughes Edmunds, (infant),
292.
Edmunds, Charles Keyser, son of James Richard Edmunds, 312.
Edmunds, Charles Welsh, son of Henry Reeves Edmunds, 308.
Edmunds, Cowart Roland, son of William Cowart Edmunds, 295.
Edmunds, Daniella Mahalah Whilldin, daughter of Robert Edmunds, 230.
Edmunds, Dora, daughter of Samuel Shields Edmunds, 216.
Edmunds, Downs, marriage, 44.
Edmunds, Downs, husband of Eleanor Wales, 313.
Edmunds, Downs, husband of Sarah Hughes Wales, 313, 314.
Edmunds, Edgar Bernard, son of Rev. Charles Carroll Edmunds, 296.

Edmunds, Eleanor Ludlam, daughter of Lydia Hughes, 263, family and descendants, 243.

Edmunds, Electra H., wife of Joseph Schellinger, 153.

Edmunds, Eli Downs, son of Sarah Hughes Wales, family and descendants, 266, 303, 314.

Edmunds, Elizabeth, admitted to church membership, 47.

Edmunds, Elizabeth, daughter of Lydia Eldredge, family and descendants, 110.

Edmunds, Elizabeth, daughter of Jane Whilldin, 203, family and descendants, 214.

Edmunds, Elizabeth, daughter of Hugh H. Edmunds, 216.

Edmunds, Elizabeth Bateman, daughter of Richard Downs Edmunds, family and descendants, 291, 311.

Edmunds, Elizabeth S., daughter of Louisa Williams Hughes, 211.

Edmunds, Emily J., daughter of Rev. James Edmunds, 109.

Edmunds, Emma Louisa, daughter of Eli Downs Edmunds and Lydia Jane Crowell, 303.

Edmunds, Emma, daughter of Jeremiah Edmunds, 228.

Edmunds, Emma, daughter of Luther Hudson Edmunds, 231.

Edmunds, Enoch, husband of Louisa William Hughes, 202, 210.

Edmunds, Enoch, son of Louisa Williams Hughes, 211.

Edmunds, Enos Schellenger, son of Jeremiah Edmunds, (infant), 229.

Edmunds, Enos Schellenger, son of Jeremiah Edmunds, family, 229.

Edmunds, Ephraim Eldredge, son of Sarah Eldredge, 109.

Edmunds, Evan B., son of Robert Edmunds, family, 230.

Edmunds, Evan, son of Lydia Hughes, family, 262.

Edmunds, Ester, admitted to church membership, 51.

Edmunds, Ethel May, daughter of Samuel Shields Edmunds, 216.

Edmunds, Florence Anna, dau. of Albert Augustus Edmunds, (infant), 231

Edmunds, Francis Dudley, son of Rev. Charles Carroll Edmunds, 296.

Edmunds, Franklin Davenport, son of Lydia Hughes, 262, family and descendants, 290.

Edmunds, Franklin D., family Bible, 37.

Edmunds, Franklin Davenport, son of Henry Reeves Edmunds, family 303.

Edmunds, Frederica, daughter of Charles Carroll Edmunds, 296.

Edmunds, Frederick Stanger, son of Franklin Davenport Edmunds, family, 290.

Edmunds, George Crawford, son of Enos Schellenger Edmunds, family, 229.

Edmunds, Grace Gilmour, dau. of James Richard Edmunds, family, 312.

Edmunds, Hannah Corson, daughter of Robert Edmunds, family, 294.

Edmunds, Hannah Goeller, daughter of Richard Edmunds, 326.

Edmunds, Hannah Stanger, daughter of Franklin D., 290.

Edmunds, Harriet Cecelia, daughter of Eli Downs Edmunds and Lydia Jane Crowell, family, 303.

Edmunds, Helen, daughter of James Richard Edmunds, family, 312.

Edmunds, Helen Ruddiman, daughter of Parsons Edmunds, 293.

Edmunds, Helen M., daughter of Thomas Marshall Edmunds, 294.

Edmunds, Harriet Crane, dau. of Thomas Hughes Edmunds, family, 292.

Edmunds, Harry, son of Evan B. Edmunds, 230.

Edmunds, Henry Reeves, son of Franklin D. Edmunds, 290, family and descendants, 308.

Edmunds, Henry Reeves, son of Franklin D. Edmunds, 303.

Edmunds, Hugh H., son of Jeremiah Edmunds, family, 216.

Edmunds, Ida May, daughter of Jesse Edmunds, 228.

Edmunds, James Henry, son of Richard Downs Edmunds, family, 291.

Edmunds, Rev. James, son of Sarah Eldredge, family and descendants, 109.

Edmunds, James Richard, son of Thomas H. Edmunds, 292, family and descendants, 312.

Edmunds, James Richard, son of James Richard Edmunds, 312.

Edmunds, James Watts, son of Robert Edmunds, 231.

Edmunds, Jeremiah, son of Jane Whilldin, 203, family and descendants, 216.

Edmunds, Jeremiah, son of Jeremiah, 216, family and descendants, 228, 229.

Edmunds, Jesse, son of Alfred Edmunds, family, 228.

Edmunds, John Corson, son of Robert Edmunds, 294.

Edmunds, John D., son of Parsons, 293.

Edmunds, Josephine, daughter of Thomas Hurst Edmunds, 292.

Edmunds, Sarah Hughes, daughter of Robert Edmunds, family, 294.
Edmunds, Sarah Jane, daughter of Richard D. Edmunds, 291, family and descendants, 298.
Edmunds, Sarah Wales, daughter of Eli Downs Edmunds and Lydia Jane Crowell, 303.
Edmunds, Silvia, daughter of Jeremiah Edmunds, 216.
Edmunds, Stephen A. Douglass, son of Robert Edmunds, 231.
Edmunds, Susan May, daughter of Page Edmunds, family, 295.
Edmunds, Theodore Crawford, son of George Crawford Edmunds, 229.
Edmunds, Thomas Hughes, son of Lydia Hughes, 262, family and descendants, 292.
Edmunds, Thomas Marshall, son of Robert Edmunds, family, 294.
Edmunds, Tryphene, admitted to church membership, 48.
Edmunds, Tryphene, daughter of Lydia Hughes, 263, family and descendants, 297.
Edmunds, Tryphena Belinda, daughter of Sarah Hughes Wales, family and descendants, 267, 314.
Edmunds, Virginia D., dau. of Richard Downs Edmunds, (infant), 291.
Edmunds, Virginia Mary, daughter of Richard Edmunds, family, 326.
Edmunds, Washington B., son of Jeremiah Edmunds, 216.
Edmunds, Watters Borrows Miller, son of Jeremiah Edmunds, family, 229.
Edmunds, William Alfred, son of Alfred Edmunds, 229.
Edmunds, William Cowart, son of Page Edmunds, family, 295.
Edmunds, William Thomas, son of Thomas Hughes Edmunds, 292.
Edmunds, William W., son of Rev. James Edmunds, family, 109.
EDWARDS, Alexander, baptized, 49.
Edwards, Anna M., wife of Frank Leaming, 115.
Edwards, Anna Robertson, baptized, 60.
Edwards, Rev. David, pastor of Cold Spring Presbyterian Church, records of, 1804-1815, pages 41-64.
Edwards, David, son of Rev. David Edwards, baptized, 52.
Edwards, Jane, wife of Rev. David Edwards, death, 64.
Edwards, Jane, admitted to church membership, 51.
Edwards, John, baptized, 49.
Edwards, Lydia, first wife of Edward D. Springer, 199.
Edwards, Warren L., husband of Linda M. Edmunds, 294.
EGNER, Charles, husband of Mabel Isabella Edmunds, 231.
EICHELBURGER, Bessie, 2nd wife of Henry Leaming, 113.
ELDERS OF THE COLD SPRING PRESBYTERIAN CHURCH, 1808-1815, see Session Book, 41, 47, 65.
ELDORA, New Jersey, 137, 168.
ELDREDGE, family, ancestry of, 3, 30.
Eldredge, family Bible, 31.
Eldredge, ————, second husband of Hannah Whilldin, 197.
Eldredge, Aaron, son of Mercy Leaming, 101, family and descendants, 107. 107.
Eldredge, Aaron, son of Aaron Eldredge, 107, family and descendants, 111, 112.
Eldredge, Aaron, son of Aaron Eldredge, 53, 111, family and descendants, 126.
Eldredge, Abbie P., daughter of Charles Eldredge, family and descendants, 134.
Eldredge, Abraham B., son of Eli H. Eldredge, 126.
Eldredge, Ada, daughter of Rev. William Henry Eldredge, 131.
Eldredge, Allen Bennett, son of Irvin Howard Eldredge, 138.
Eldredge, Alonzo, son of Jeremiah L. Eldredge, 125.
Eldredge, Alva, husband of Roxanna S. Sapp, 301.
Eldredge, Anna M., daughter of Eli H. Eldredge, 126.
Eldredge, Anna Linerd, daughter of James Henry Eldredge, 129.
Eldredge, Annie Lucile, daughter of Marion Langdon Eldredge, 130.
Eldredge, Anna Maria, daughter of Daniel Crowell Eldredge, family, 234.
Eldredge, Augustus, son of James S. Eldredge, 125.
Eldredge, Barrington Sanford, son of Ephraim Eldredge, family, 131.
Eldredge, Beatrice Alberta, daughter of Loring Brewster Eldridge, 136.
Eldredge, Bessie, daughter of Daniel Fithian Eldredge, 234.
Eldredge, Blanche L., daughter of Francis Springer Eldredge, 136.
Eldredge, Charles, son of Jeremiah Leaming Eldredge, 124, family and descendants, 134.
Eldredge, Charles H., son of Charles Stillwell Eldredge, 129.
Eldredge, Charles Hoover, son of Stillwell Eldredge, famiy and descendants, 129.

Eldredge, Charles P., husband of Julia Mecray Cresse, 185.
Eldredge, Charles S., son of James S. Eldredge, 125.
Eldredge, Charles Stevens, son of Daniel Fithian Eldredge, 234.
Eldredge, Charles Stillwell, son of Charles Hoover Eldredge, family, 129.
Eldredge, Charlotta, daughter of Aaron Eldredge, 107, family and descendants, 108.
Eldredge, Charlotte Reeves, daughter of Henry Hand Eldredge, 304.
Eldredge, Clara, daughter of James E. Eldredge, 125.
Eldredge, Clara Hanson, daughter of Rev. William Henry Eldredge, 131.
Eldredge, Clayton S., son of Roxanna S. Sapp, 301.
Eldridge, Clarence Selby, M. D., son of Emma Julia Reeves, 304.
Eldredge, Claude, husband of Medora Woolson, 119.
Eldredge, Clementine Farr, daughter of Daniel Crowell Eldredge, 234.
Eldredge, Daniel Crowell, son of Deborah Whilldin Ware, 218, family and descendants, 234.
Eldredge, Daniel Fithian, son of Daniel Crowell Eldredge, family, 234.
Eldredge, Deborah Whilldin, daughter of Deborah Whilldin Ware, family and descendants, 332.
Eldredge, DeWitt C., son of John S. Eldredge, family, 128.
Eldredge, Edna, daughter of Reuben Eldredge, 132.
Eldredge, Edna, daughter of Daniel Fithian Eldredge, 234.
Eldredge, Edward L., son of Eli H. Eldredge, 126.
Eldredge, Eleanore Andrew, daughter of Irvin Howard Eldredge, 138.
Eldredge, Eli H., son of Aaron Eldredge, family, 126.
Eldredge, Eli H., son of Eli H. Eldredge, 126.
Eldredge, Elida Kimber, daughter of Thomas Eldredge, 182, 236.
Eldredge, Elijah, admitted to church membership, death, 63.
Eldredge, Eliza, daughter Jeremiah Leaming Eldredge, 124, family and descendants, 133.
Eldredge, Eliza, daughter of Aaron Eldredge, 53, 104, 111, family and descendants, 150.
Eldredge, Eliza L., daughter of William Eldredge, 128.
Eldredge, Eliza T., daughter of Joseph Eldredge, 127.
Eldredge, Eliza Hand, daughter of Nelson Tomlin Eldredge, 135.
Eldredge, Elizabeth, birth, 33.
Eldredge, Elizabeth, daughter of William Tomlin, family, 132.
Eldredge, Elizabeth B., daughter of Eli H. Eldredge, 126.
Eldredge, Eliazbeth Cresse, daughter of Julia Mecray Cresse, family, 185.
Eldredge, Elizabeth Smallwood, dau. of Jacob Smallwood Eldredge, 135.
Eldredge, Elsie Dinsmore, daughter of Ellis Corson Eldredge, 132.
Eldredge, Ella, daughter of Nelson Tomlin Eldredge, (infant), 135.
Eldredge, Ella T., daughter of Roxanna S. Sapp, 301.
Eldredge, Ella V., daughter of Eli H. Eldredge, 126.
Eldredge, Ellis Corson, son of William Tomlin Eldredge, family, 132.
Eldredge, Emiline V., daughter of William Eldredge, 128.
Eldredge, Emma, daughter of Reuben Eldredge, 132.
Eldredge, Emma L., daughter of Stillwell Eldredge, 129.
Eldredge, Emma Lorraine Elizabeth, daughter of Löring Brewster Eldredge, 136.
Eldredge, Emma T., daughter of Thomas Eldredge, family, 236.
Eldredge, Emma S., daughter of Eli H. Eldredge, 126.
Eldredge, Enoch, birth, 33.
Eldredge, Enoch, marriage, 43.
Eldredge, Ephraim, son of Aaron Eldredge, 112, family and descendants, 131.
Eldredge, Ester, baptized, 50.
Eldredge, Esther Forbes, daughter of Irvin Howard Eldredge, 138.
Eldredge, Eva, daughter of William Brooks Eldredge, 218.
Eldredge, Ezekiel, of New England Township, Cape May County, 343.
Eldredge, Flora Keeler, daughter of Ellis Corson Eldredge, 132.
Eldredge, Florence, daughter of Livingston Eldredge, 132.
Eldredge, Florence Beatrice, daughter of Barrington Sanford, 131.
Eldredge, Frances, daughter of Jacob Smallwood Eldredge, (infant), 135.
Eldredge, Francis Goodell, son of Francis Springer Eldredge, family, 136.
Eldredge, Francis Springer, son of Jeremiah Leaming Eldredge, 124, family and descendants, 136.
Eldredge, Francis Springer, son of Joseph Johnson Eldredge, family, 136.
Eldredge, Francis Springer, son of Francis Springer Eldredge, 136.
Eldredge, Frank H., son of Jeremiah Leaming Eldredge, 125.
Eldredge, Frederick D., son of Mahlon Eldredge, family, 128.
Eldredge, George, baptized, 58.

410

411

Matthews, Albert J., son of Richard Matthews, 264.
Matthews, Albert H., son of Rev. Albert Matthews, family, 300.
Matthews, Alfred, husband of Florence Hughes, 167.
Matthews, Alice V., daughter of Silas Matthews, 146.
Matthews, Anna, daughter of Franklin H. Matthews, 302.
Matthews, Awilda, daughter of William Henry Matthews, 265.
Matthews, Charles Alfred, son of Florence Hughes, 167.
Matthews, Charles, son of William Matthews, 265.
Matthews, Clarence H., son of Silas Matthews, 146.
Matthews, Eleanore, baptized, 57.
Matthews, Elizabeth, daughter of William Matthews, 265, family and descendants, 301.
Matthews, Ethel L., daughter of William L. Matthews, 300.
Matthews, Eva H., daughter of Albert H. Matthews, 300.
Matthews, F. S., husband of Mary Beesley, 179.
Matthews, Francis, son of Mary Tuft Beesley, 179.
Matthews, Franklin H., son of Jonathan H. Matthews, family, 302.
Matthews, Hannah, daughter of Eleanor Hughes, 252, family and descendants, 266.
Matthews, Hannah, baptized, 57.
Matthews, Isaac Page, son of William Matthews, 265.
Matthews, Irene, daughter of William Price Matthews, 167, 302.
Matthews, Irene B., daughter of William Price Matthews, 286, 302.
Matthews, Isabella, daughter of Eleanor Hughes, 252, family and descendants, 267.
Matthews, Jennie E., daughter of Jonathan H. Matthews, family, 302.
Matthews, Jonathan H., son of William Matthews, 265, family and descendants, 302.
Matthews, Jonathan H., son of Jonathan H. Matthews, 302.
Matthews, Kate S., daughter of Rev. Albert Matthews, (infant), 300.
Matthews, Lottie L., daughter of Rev. Albert Matthews, 300.
Matthews, Mary, wife of Montgomery C. Meigs, family, 113.
Matthews, Mary Elizabeth, daughter of Mary Tuft Beesley, 179.
Matthews, Mary Elizabeth, daughter of Jonathan H. Matthews, family, 302.
Matthews, Mary Emma, daughter of Rev. Albert Matthews, family, 300.
Matthews, Richard, son of William Matthews, (infant), 264.
Matthews, Richard, son of William Matthews, family, 264.
Matthews, Silas, husband of Eleanor Hughes, 205, 252.
Matthews, Silas, son of William Matthews, family, 146, 265.
Matthews, Silas, baptized, 64.
Matthews, Thelma, daughter of Jonathan H. Matthews, 302.
Matthews, Thomas, baptized, 57.
Matthews, Thomas, son of Eleanor Hughes, 252.
Matthews, Walter Scott, son of Jonathan H. Matthews, 302.
Matthews, William, baptized, 57.
Matthews, William, son of Eleanor Hughes, 252, family and descendants, 264, 265.
Matthews William Henry, son of William Matthews, family, 265.
Matthews, William L., son of Rev. Albert Matthews, family, 300.
Matthews, William Price, son of Jonathan H. Matthews, family, 167, 302.
Matthias (Matthews?) Silas, admitted to church membership, 55.
MAXWELL, Mary Maull, wife of Paul Henry Barnes, 260.
MAY, OLIVE, wife of Francis Henry Edmunds, 296.
MAYFLOWER, ship, 66, 68, passengers, 71, 72, return of 85, "Log" of 325.
MAYNE, John, husband of Arabella Schellenger, family, 253.
MAY'S LANDING, New Jersey, 270, 271, 317.
MAYS, C. C., husband of Marion Tuthill, 198.
MEARS, Howard Foster, son of Marion Upham Foster, 171.
Mears, James Albert, husband of Marion Upham Foster, 171.
Mears, James Albert, son of Marion Upham Foster, 171.
Mears, John Carr, son of Marion Upham Foster, (infant), 171.
Mears, Samuel, son of Marion Upham Foster, 171.
MECRAY, Ann, wife of Christopher Leaming, 105.
Mecray, Elizabeth Hughes, daughter of Elizabeth Schellenger Hughes, family, 223.
Mecray, Frank Bacon, husband of Millicant Schellenger Hughes, 329.
Mecray, Harriet Hughes, daughter of Millicent Schellenger Hughes, 329.
Mecray, Helen Boyer, daughter of Paul Mulford Mecray, M. D., 223.

Reed, Frederick Foster, son of Lillian Foster, 171.
Reed, Maud, wife of Herbert Ware, 222.
REEVES, Abijah Davis, son of Miranda Seybert Edmunds, family, 310.
Reeves, Andrew, son of Charles Clinton Reeves, 267.
Reeves, Andrew H., husband of Isabella Matthews, 252, 267.
Reeves, Charles Clinton, son of Isabella Matthews, family, 267.
Reeves, Charles Davis, son of Abijah Davis Reeves, 310.
Reeves, Charlotte, daughter of Isabella Matthews, 267, 288.
Reeves, Clement B., son of Isabella Matthews, 181, 267.
Reeves, Courtland Van Renselaer, husband of Miranda Seybert Edmunds, 291, 310.
Reeves, Dorothy Beatrice, daughter of Orion Hughes Reeves and Irene B. Matthews, 286.
Reeves, Eleanor Edmunds, daughter of Richard Downs Edmunds Reeves, 310.
Reeves, Elizabeth, daughter of Charles Clinton Reeves, 267.
Reeves, Elizabeth L., daughter of Thomas M. Reeves, 287.
Reeves, Elmer Willets, husband of Dora Edmunds, 216.
Reeves, Emma, daughter of William Henry Reeves, 311.
Reeves, Emma Julia, daughter of Isabella Matthews, 267, family and descendants, 304.
Reeves, Emma R., daughter of Isabella Matthews, (infant), 267.
Reeves, Ethel, daughter of William Henry Reeves, family, 311.
Reeves, Ethel May, daughter of Dora Edmunds, 216.
Reeves, Frank B. F., son of Lucrissa Hughes, 287.
Reeves, Harry McCook, son of Samuel Winchester Reeves, (infant), 314.
Reeves, Helen, wife of Joseph Brooks, 209.
Reeves, James Henry, son of William Henry Reeves, family, 311.
Reeves, Jane, daughter of Abijah Davis Reeves, 310.
Reeves, Jennie, daughter of William Henry Reeves, (infant), 311.
Reeves, Jennie Edmunds, daughter of Miranda Seybert Edmunds, 310.
Reeves, Jennie M., daughter of Samuel Winchester Reeves, (infant), 314.
Reeves, John, 14.
Reeves, John Woolson, second husband of Elizabeth Bateman Edmunds, 291, 311.
Reeves, Julia, daughter of Charles Clinton Reeves, 267.
Reeves, Lottie Belle, daughter of Samuel Winchester Reeves, 314.
Reeves, Martha, daughter of William Henry Reeves, (infant), 311.
Reeves, Martha Swain, daughter of Miranda Seybert Edmunds, (infant), 310.
Reeves, Mary Elizabeth(daughter of Isabella Matthews, 181, 267.
Reeves, Nellie Watt, daughter of Samuel Winchester Reeves, family, 314.
Reeves, Orion Hughes, son of Mary Hughes, 167, 286, 302.
Reeves, Rebecca, daughter of Abijah Davis Reeves, 310.
Reeves, Richard Campion, son of James Henry Reeves, 311.
Reeves, Richard Downs, son of Miranda Seybert Edmunds, family, 310.
Reeves, Samuel Winchester, son of Isabella Matthews, family and descendants, 267, 314.
Reeves, Stephen, husband of Lucrissa Hughes, 287.
Reeves, Theodore W., husband of Mary Hughes, 286.
Reeves, Thomas M., son of Lucrissa Hughes, family, 287.
Reeves, William Henry, son of Isabella Matthews, 267, family and descendants, 311.
Reeves, William Henry, son of William Henry Reeves, (infant), 311.
Reeves, William Henry, son of James Henry Reeves, 311.
REINS, William Edmunds, son of Harrit Crane Edmunds, 292.
Reins, William Seal, husband of Harriet Crane Edmunds, 292.
RICHMAN, Whilldin Lippincott, son of Louisa Whilldin Harris, (infant), 227.
Richman, William, husband of Louisa Whilldin Harris, 227.
RIEF, Gysbertus, husband of Emily Schellenger Thompson, 268.
Rief, Virgil Schellenger, son of Emily Schellenger Thompson, 268.
REYNOLDS, Joseph, husband of Josephine Whilldin, 215.
REYONS, D., marriage, 44.
RHEUM, (coloured), admitted to church membership, 55.
RICE, Beatrice, daughter of Leaming M. Rice, 330.
Rice, Deborah, daughter of Edward Rice, (infant), 179.
Rice, Dorothy, daughter of Edward L. Rice, 330.
Rice, Edward, first husband of Hannah Leaming, 105, 179.
Rice, Edward, son of Hannah Leaming, 179.

Shaw, Walter Y., husband of Elsie May Hand, 187.
Shaw, William, baptized, 57.
SHAWANO, Wisconsin, 151.
SHEETS, Mary Helen, wife of Francis Hoffman, 145.
SHEPPARD, Abbie, daughter of Abigail Hughes Leaming, family, 182.
Sheppard, Anna, second wife of Jonathan H. Matthews, 302.
Sheppard, Dorothy Mecray, daughter of Israel Leaming Sheppard, family, 182.
Sheppard, Frank Spicer, son of Abigail Hughes Leaming, family, 182.
Sheppard, Genevieve, daughter of Abigail Hughes Leaming, 182, 269.
Sheppard, Judith Florence, daughter of Abigail Hughes Leaming, family, 182.
Sheppard, Israel Leaming, son of Abigail Hughes Leaming, family, 182.
Sheppard, Mary Esther, daughter of Israel Leaming Sheppard, 182.
Sheppard, Samuel Bailey, son of Frank Spicer Sheppard, 182.
Sheppard, Sarah Genevieve, daughter of Abigail Hughes Leaming, 182, 269.
Sheppard, William Rose, M. D., husband of Abigail Hughes Leaming, 177, 182.
Sheppard, William Rose, son of Abigail Hughes Leaming, 182, 236.
SHIELDS, Charles, husband of Helen York, 175.
Shields, Lizzie, wife of David Cresse Crowell, 186.
Shields, Margaret J., wife of Robert S. Oakley, 158.
SHILOH, New Jersey, 134.
SHIMADA, Francis K., husband of Harriet Louise Duke, 235.
SHINN, Mary, wife of Floyd Hughes, 259.
SHIRLEY, Governor, 5, 7, 8.
SHOEMAKER, Hattie, first wife of Ellis H. Marshall, 285.
SHUR, Marie, wife of James A. Naves, 278.
SHUTE, ————, wife of Evan Edmunds, 262.
SIDNEY, Arthur M., husband of Annie T. Hand, 273.
Sidney, Florence Custis, daughter of Annie T. Hand, 273.
SIMKINS, Gertrude, wife of Louis James Sayre, 186.
SIMISON, Cora, wife of William Inskeep, 116.
Simison, Frank M., husband of Mary Leaming Austin, 117.
SIMMINGTON, Charles C., husband of Emma T. Eldredge, 236.
Simmington, Harriet Eldredge, daughter of Emma T. Eldredge, 23(
Simmington, Mary T., daughter of Emma T. Eldredge, 236.
Simpkins, Catharine, wife of Uriah Schenck, 254, 270.
Simpson, Sarah J., wife of James Frank Crowell, 298.
SINKING VALLEY, Blair County, Pennsylvania, 129.
SINCLAIR, John, husband of Charlotte Bennett, 148.
SKALLENGER, Jacobus, 15.
SKELLINKS, Cornelius, 13.
SKIPPACK, Pennsylvania, 263.
SMALLWOOD, Elizabeth, second wife of Albert G. Reed Bennett, 152, 165.
SMART, Rose Irene, wife of Recompence Arnold Hand, 273.
SMITH, Alfred, son of Henry Hollingsworth Smith, M. D., 190.
Smith, Alice Grant, daughter of Thomas L. Smith, 190.
Smith, Anna Elizabeth, daughter of Mary Springer Keeler, 206.
Smith, Belford, husband of Ellen Marshall, 285.
Smith, Belfora, wife of Joseph Schellenger Stites, 221.
Smith, Charles, husband of Martha H. Whilldin, 215.
Smith, Charles Alfred, husband of Helen Burnshouse, 141.
Smith, Charles Alfred, son of Helen Burnshouse, 141.
Smith, Charles Vernon, husband of Marcia Miller, 330.
Smith, Charles Vernon, son of Marcia Miller, 330.
Smith, Clarissa Gay, mother of Charles Alfred Smith, 141.
Smith, Cooper, son of James Somers Smith, 191.
Smith, Edith, wife of Edward M. Germon, 170.
Smith, Elizabeth Shute, daughter of Lydia Leaming, 188.
Smith, Elizabeth Washington, daughter of William Horner Smith, family, 194.
Smith, Ellen Hollingshead, daughter of James Rundle Smith, family, 195.
Smith, Eloise Crowell, daughter of Eva Jane Crowell, 140.
Smith, Emma, wife of James L. Marshall, 285.
Smith, Emma V., wife of Henry Clay Hand, 207.
Smith, Eugenia Horner, daughter of Henry Hollingsworth Smith, M. D., 190.
Smith, Eva Virginia, daughter of Eva Jane Crowell, 140.
Smith, Everett L., husband of Mary Springer Keeler, 206.
Smith, Fisher Coleman, son of Lydia Leaming, 188.

451

Somers, Experience, wife of Joseph Eldredge Hughes, 150.
SOMERS POINT, New Jeresy, 128, 129, 151.
SOUDER, Ada, daughter of Hester Ann Eldridge Johnson, 240.
Souder, Alice Holt, daughter of Harold Charles, 247.
Souder, Charles B., son of Hester Ann Eldridge Johnson, family, 240.
Souder, Charles B., son of Maurice B. Souder, 240.
Souder, Daniel E., son of Hester Ann Eldridge Johnson, family, 240.
Souder, Earle C., son of Daniel E. Souder, 240.
Souder, Elizabeth Mecray, daughter of Ellwood and Dorothy Mecray Bock-
     ius Souder, 223, 247.
Souder, Ella, daughter of Hester Ann Eldridge Johnson, 240.
Souder, Ellwood, son of Hester Ann Eldridge Johnson, 240, family and
     descendants, 247.
Souder, Ellwood, son of Ellwood Souder, 247, family, 223.
Souder, Fannie, daughter of Hester Ann Eldridge Johnson, 240.
Souder, Florence M., daughter of Maurice B. Souder, 240.
Souder, Harold Charles, son of Ellwood, family, 247.
Souder, Hester E., daughter of Maurice B. Souder, 240.
Souder, Jennie J., daughter of Hester Ann Eldridge Johnson, 240.
Souder, Katharine, daughter of Hester Ann Eldridge Johnson, 240.
Souder, Lillie E., daughter of Hester Ann Eldridge Johnson, family, 240.
Souder, Lillie Moore, daughter of Ellwood, 247.
Souder, Margaret, daughter of Charles B. Souder, family, 240.
Souder, Maurie Annie, wife of Rev. William Henry Eldredge, 131.
Souder, Maurice B., son of Hester Ann Eldridge Johnson, family, 240.
Souder, Mary J., daughter of Maurice B. Souder, 240.
Souder, Nellie, wife of Percy V. Hughes, 259.
Souder, Priscilla, wife of Henry S. Rutherford, 232.
Souder, Richard Cresse, husband of Hester Ann Eldridge Johnson, 240.
Souder, Richard Cresse, son of Charles B. Souder, 240.
Souder, Thomas Argyle, son of Ellwood, 247.
SOULE, George the Pilgrim, descendants in Cape May County, 320, 324.
Soule, George, son of George, 324.
Soule, Jabez, son of Zachuriah Soule, 320.
Soule, Mary, daughter of George Soule, 324.
Soule, Sarah, daughter of Jabez Soule, 320.
SPARKS, Earl Lonsdale, son of Edward Sparks, 281.
Sparks, Edward, son of Ellen Maria Cassedy, family, 281.
Sparks, Frank A., son of Ellen Maria Cassedy, family, 281.
Sparks, John Benjamin, husband of Ellen Maria Cassedy, 257, 281.
Sparks, Margaret Maylin, daughter of Frank A. Sparks, 281.
Sparks, Matilda, wife of John Johnson, 225.
Sparks, Sophronia, wife of Jeremiah Eldredge Hughes, 150.
Sparks, Stanley Vaughn, son of Edward Sparks, 281.
Sparks, William Newell, son of Frank A. Sparks, 281.
SPEEDWELL, Ship, 68.
SPENCE, Robert, husband of Judith T. Eldredge, 134.
SPENCER, Sarah, wife of Levi Eldridge Johnson, 224.
SPICER, Jacob, 24.
Spicer, Sarah, wife of Christopher Leaming, 105.
SPRINGER, Alexander W., son of Amelia Stillwell Whilldin, 199, family
     and descendants, 206.
Springer, Alice, daughter of Samuel Springer, 198.
Springer, Alice Hoffman, daughter of Joseph Springer, 234.
Springer, Amelia, daughter of Amelia Stillwell Whilldin, 199.
Springer, Amelia, daughter of Alexander W. Springer, family, 206.
Springer, Amelia Fifield, daughter of Joseph Springer, (infant), 234.
Springer, Anna, daughter of Alexander W. Springer, family, 206.
Springer, Annie E., daughter of Edward D. Springer, 199.
Springer, Charles, son of Alexander W. Springer, 206.
Springer, Clara, daughter of Samuel Springer, 198.
Springer, Danielia, daughter of Amelia Stillwell Whilldin, 199.
Springer, Edna, daughter of Edward D. Springer, 199.
Springer, Edward Whilldin, son of Alexander W. Springer, 206.
Springer, Edward D., son of Amelia Stillwell Whilldin, family, 199.
Springer, Eliza C., daughter of Whilldin Springer, family, 198.
Springer, Ella, daughter of Alexander W. Springer 206.
Springer, Elsie Gates, daughter of Joseph Springer, family, 234.
Springer, Eva W., daughter of Edward D. Springer, 199.
Springer, Emma H., daughter of Edward D. Springer, 199.

Stevens, Thomas S., husband of Mary Elizabeth Schellenger, 268.
Stevens, Thomas Schellenger, son of Zeruiah Schellenger, family, 269.
Stevens, William, baptized, 52.
STEVENSON, Charles Simmington, son of Ida Eldredge Stevens, 236.
Stevenson, Clara Brainard, daughter of Mary Hughes Barnes, 260.
Stevenson, Daniel, son of Ida Eldredge Stevens, 326.
Stevenson, Frank Wallace, husband of Ida Eldredge Stevens, 236.
Stevenson, Frank Wallace, son of Ida Eldredge Stevens, 236
Stevenson, George, husband of Mary Hughes Barnes, 260.
Stevenson, George Barnes, son of Mary Hughes Barnes, 260.
Stevenson, Helen Hughes, daughter of Mary Hughes Barnes, 260.
Stevenson, Mary, Matilda, daughter of Mary Hughes Barnes, 260.
STIMPSON, Latitia, wife of James S. Eldredge, 125.
STILLWELL, Miranda, wife of Richard Hand, 275.
Stillwell, Sophia, wife of Jacob Hughes, 103.
Stillwell, Elder Richard, 30.
Stillwell, Thomas, received into church, baptized, 48, 49.
STEWARD, John, marriage, 45.
STEWART, Alice, wife of George Curwen Leaming, family, 117.
Stewart, Mary, wife of William A. Eldredge, 128.
STIDWORTHY, John William, husband of Ella Shaw Hoffman, 145.
Stidworthy, William McNaughton, son of Ella Shaw Hoffman, 145.
STIEFEL, Augustus, husband of Mary Elizabeth Smith, 302.
Stillwell, (Leamings of Cape May), 5.
Stillwell, Elizabeth, wife of Aaron Eldredge, 101, 107.
Stillwell, Jane, wife of Daniel Whilldin, 198.
STIMPSON, Phebe, baptized, admitted into church membership, 63.
Stimpson, Robert Corgee, baptized, 60.
Stimpson, Rhoda Corgee, baptized, 60.
Stimpson, Stephen, baptized, 48.
Stimpson, Stevens, marriage, 45.
Stimpson, Stephen, admitted to church, 48.
STOVER, Irene, wife of Jere Lilburn Cresse, 143.
STITES, Abigail, baptized, admitted into church membership, 48.
Stites, Annie Tindall, daughter of Harriet Whilldin Ware, (infant), 221.
Stites, Charles Linford, son of Harriet Whilldin Ware, 221.
Stites, Charlotte, admitted to church membership, 48.
Stites, Charlotte, baptized, 54.
Stites, Charolette, baptized, 60.
Stites, Edgar Page, son of Eliza Eldridge, 214, family, 314.
Stites, Edgar Page, son of Edgar Page Stites, and Sarah Eldredge Edmunds, 314.
Stites, Elias Ellis, husband of Danielia Mahalah Whilldin Edmunds, 230.
Stites, Eliza, daughter of Priscilla Leaming, family and descendants, 143.
Stites, Ella Merret, daughter of Harriet Whilldin Ware, family, 221.
Stites, Fletcher Wilbur, son of Edgar Page Stites and Sarah Elizabeth Edmunds, 314.
Stites, Hannah, daughter of Priscilla Leaming, 143, family and descendants, 144.
Stites, Hannah, baptized, 50.
S tites, Harriet Whilldin, daughter of Harriet Whilldin Ware, family, 221, 286.
Stites, Harriet Whilldin, daughter of Harriet Whilldin Ware, family, 221, 286.
Stites, Humphrey, husband of Priscilla Leaming, 35, 102, 143.
Stites, Humphrey, son of Priscilla Leaming, 143.
Stites, John, married, 35.
Stites, John, Elder, Session Book, 41.
Stites, John, first husband of Priscilla Leaming, 36, 102, 156.
Stites, Joseph Schellenger, son of Harriet Whilldin Ware, 221.
Stites, Laura S., daughter of Harriet Whilldin Ware, 135, 221.
Stites, Lois, baptized, 50.
Stites, Margaret, daughter of Priscilla Leaming, 35, 102.
Stites, Margaret, daughter of Priscilla Leaming second, family, 143.
Stites, Martha, admitted into church membership 51, death, 62.
Stites, Mrs. Martha Schellenger, second wife of Memucan Hughes, 329.
Stites, Mary, wife of Humphrey Leaming, 105, 178.
Stites, Mary, daughter of Priscilla Leaming, family, 143.
Stites, Mary, wife of Samuel Fithian Ware, Jr., 217.
Stites, Mary, baptized, 54.

457

www.ingramcontent.com/pod-product-compliance
Lightning Source LLC
Chambersburg PA
CBHW050551270326
41926CB00012B/2003